IDENTITIES AT WORK

UNESCO-UNEVOC Book Series
Technical and Vocational Education and Training:
Issues, Concerns and Prospects

Volume 5

Identities at Work

Edited by

ALAN BROWN
University of Warwick, UK

SIMONE KIRPAL
University of Bremen, Germany

and

FELIX RAUNER
University of Bremen, Germany

A C.I.P. Catalogue record for this book is available from the Library of Congress.

ISBN-10 1-4020-4988-9 (HB)
ISBN-13 978-1-4020-4988-0 (HB)
ISBN-10 1-4020-4989-7 (e-book)
ISBN-13 978-1-4020-4989-7 (e-book)

Published by Springer,
P.O. Box 17, 3300 AA Dordrecht, The Netherlands.

www.springer.com

Printed on acid-free paper

BOOK SERIES SCOPE

The purpose of this Book Series is to meet the needs of those interested in an in-depth analysis of current developments concerning various aspects of education for the world of work with particular reference to technical and vocational education and training. The Series examines areas that are at the 'cutting edge' of the field and are innovative in nature. It presents best and innovative practices, explores controversial topics and uses case studies as examples.

The audience for the Book Series includes policy-makers, practitioners, administrators, planners, researchers, teachers, teacher-educators, students and colleagues in other fields interested in learning about TVET, in both developed and developing countries, countries in transition and countries in a post-conflict situation.

The Series complements the **International Handbook of Technical and Vocational Education and Training**, with the elaboration of specific topics, themes and case studies in greater breadth and depth than is possible in the Handbook. The Book Series also augments the various other publications in the **International Library of Technical and Vocational Education and Training**.

Topics to be covered in the Series include: training for the informal economy in developing countries; education of adolescents and youth for academic and vocational work; financing education for work; lifelong learning in the workplace; women and girls in technical and vocational education and training; effectively harnessing ICT's in support of TVET; planning of education systems to promote education for the world of work; recognition, evaluation and assessment; education and training of demobilized soldiers in post-conflict situations; TVET research; and school-to-work transition.

The Book Series **Technical and Vocational Education and Training: Issues, Concerns and Prospects**, and other publications in the **International Library of Technical and Vocational Education and Training**, are publications of the UNESCO-UNEVOC International Centre for Technical and Vocational Education and Training (UNESCO-UNEVOC) in Bonn, Germany.

Those interested in obtaining more information about the Book Series, or who wish to explore the possibility of contributing a manuscript, should (in the first instance) contact the publishers.

Books published to date in the series:

1. Vocationalisation of Secondary Education Revisited
   Edited by Jon Lauglo and Rupert Maclean
2. Meeting Basic Learning Needs in the Informal Sector:
   Integrating Education and Training for Decent Work, Empowerment and Citizenship
   Edited by Madhu Singh
3. Training for Work in the Informal Micro-Enterprise Sector:
   Fresh Evidence from Sub-Sahara Africa
   Hans Christiaan Haan
4. The Transformation of Vocational Education and Training (VET) in the Baltic States—
   Survey of Reforms and Developments
   Edited by Frank Bünning
5. Identities at Work
   Edited by Alan Brown, Simone Kirpal and Felix Rauner

INTRODUCTION BY THE SERIES EDITORS

Work is a central feature in the life of most people. Not only does it provide them with the means of survival in terms of food, shelter and clothing, but for most the type of work undertaken gives purpose and meaning to their life, and, if they are fortunate enough to be undertaking work that they truly like, it is a major source of pleasure and satisfaction in their life. Because of such matters, most of those who are unemployed suffer from feelings of alienation, and a loss of self esteem, work-related identify and status.

It is also no coincidence that when we meet someone for the first time we are often keen to find out 'what they do for a living'. This is because to know a person's occupation gives the inquisitive observer a great deal of information about the person in question, such as their likely level of income, educational attainment, standard of living, and the types of people they associate with in both work and leisure time. This information is also likely to provide an indication of their likely attitudes and values regarding a wide range of social, political and economic issues. In other words, a person's work has a significant influence on their *identify*, both as individuals and as members of social groups.

The relationship between an individual and their work is an interactive one, in that while work helps define an individual's identity, so an individual's identify impacts on and helps shape their work, and their relationships with their employer, fellow employees, and the occupational group with which they work.

For many in the workplace, due to a shift from the *Industrial Age* to the *Information Age*, and related matters such as globalisation, and the greater mobility of employees across national and international borders, individuals are increasingly working in rapidly changing environments where they need to take on new areas of responsibility and master increasingly complex work situations. The extent to which individuals and groups of employees are able to cope with, and adjust to, such major change does not only rely on their commitment to, interest and training for the job in question, but also upon their level of commitment and identification with their employment. That is, it affects their *Identities at Work*, which is the subject of this book.

In this age of increasing mobility of workers across national borders, an individual's ties and commitment to a particular employer or company tends to become weakened, as does the commitment of employers to those they employ. The impact of *globalisation*, particularly the *outsourcing* of jobs, also affects these ties and commitment.

This volume examines the interdependence between employees' identification with work and their work commitment. As such, it relates to such important matters as an individuals' commitment to their work organisation and employer in terms of loyalty and motivation, which in turn impacts on workforce stability and improved performance. It also addresses *how* work identities are formed, learned and obtained.

A feature of this book, which contributes to its importance in the field, is that it adopts a truly multi-disciplinary approach and international perspective, drawing as it does on research insights offered by the disciplines sociology and psychology, and on the literature relating to organisational management and to vocational education and training.

Rupert Maclean,
Director of the UNESCO-UNEVOC International Centre,
Bonn, Germany

and

David N. Wilson,
Professor Emeritus at OISE,
University of Toronto, Canada

TABLE OF CONTENTS

Part One   Vocational Identity in Theory and Empirical Research

Part Two   Work and Personal Identity

LIST OF FIGURES AND TABLES

Figures

Tables

CONTRIBUTORS

Yehuda Baruch is Professor of Management at UEA Norwich, UK and formerly a visiting Research Fellow at London Business School and Visiting Professor at the University of Texas at Arlington, USA. His research interests are careers, strategic and global human resource management and technology impact on management. He has published numerous papers in refereed journals and has recently published a book on 'Managing Career: Theory and Practice'. He is also the editor of the academic journal *Career Development International* and past chair for the Careers Division of the Academy of Management.

Stephen Billett has worked as a vocational educator, educational administrator, teacher educator, professional development practitioner and policy developer within the Australian vocational education system and more recently as a teacher and researcher at Griffith University, Nathan, Australia. His research interests include the social and cultural construction of vocational knowledge and learning in and through working life. In addition, he has a broad interest in policy and practice within adult and vocational education.

Alan Brown is a Professorial Fellow at the Institute for Employment Research at the University of Warwick, UK. He is also Associate Director of the UK's Teaching and Learning Research Programme (TLRP) with responsibility for workplace learning, professional learning and links with other international and national programmes with a focus on knowledge and learning. He has been centrally involved in a number of national and European research and development projects, concerned with the use of ICT to enhance learning, work-based learning, career development and skill formation.

Aaron Cohen is Associate Professor at the Department of Political Science, University of Haifa, Israel. He received his Ph.D. in

Management at the Technion-Israel Institute of Technology and taught three years at the University of Lethbridge, Alberta, Canada. His current research interests include commitment in the workplace, organisational citizenship behaviour (OCB) and cross-cultural research. His most recent work has been published in journals of management, vocational and organisational behaviour, human resource management and human relations.

M'Hamed Dif is an Associate Senior Researcher at BETA/Céreq Alsace (University Louis Pasteur of Strasbourg, France) working on various multidisciplinary (regional, national and European) research programmes as an expert in vocational education and training and human resource management. He is a member of VETNET Board and reviewer for the European Conference on Educational Research (ECER/EERA) and has been involved in various European research projects on learning, skill formation and career development. He also worked outside of France and Europe for 12 years as an Associate Professor, Consultant and Project Manager.

David Finegold is Professor of Strategy and Organisation at the Keck Graduate Institute (KGI) of Applied Life Sciences in Claremont, California, and is leading the development of KGI's strategy, management and ethics curriculum. He is the author of numerous journal articles and book chapters and has recently written a book on 'BioIndustry Ethics' (Academic Press, 2005). He consults and provides executive education and coaching to public and private sector organisations on issues about designing effective organisations. His current research includes: models of ethical decision-making in bioscience firms, business models of Asian bioscience companies, international comparisons of successful life science businesses and elements of effective corporate governance.

Gudela Grote is Professor of Work and Organizational Psychology at the ETH Zurich, Switzerland. In her research she focuses on psychologically-based concepts and methods for integrative job and organisational design under conditions of changing technological, economic and societal demands and opportunities with a special interest in the increasing flexibility and virtuality of work and the consequences for the individual and organisational management of uncertainty. Application fields of her research are the design of high-risk work systems, intra- and inter-organisational planning, support for individual employability and learning and cooperation in distributed teams.

Bernd Haasler is Assistant Professor at the Institute Technology and Education (ITB), University of Bremen, Germany in the Department of Work Processes and Vocational Training. His areas of teaching and research centre around vocational education and training research with a focus on vocational competence development, qualification research and domain-specific expertise in technical work areas, predominantly in metal work and engineering.

Akihiro Ishikawa is Professor of Sociology at Chuo University, Tokyo, Japan. He has done extensive research on social change, labour relations and working life in an international comparative perspective. His more recent studies concentrate on transforming processes at the intermediate level of society in ex-socialist countries in particular.

Karen Jensen is Professor at the Institute for Educational Research, University of Oslo, Norway. She has published widely on issues of professional learning and moral motivation, especially related to health care professions. She is currently scientific leader for the research project 'Professional Learning in a Changing Society' financed by the Research Council of Norway, a comparative study of four professional groups that aims to develop theories of professional learning and identity formation in a direction that is sensitive to the shifts in knowledge and culture characteristic of today's society.

Simone Kirpal is a Junior Research Fellow at the Institute for Empirical and Applied Sociology (EMPAS) and a researcher and lecturer at the Institute Technology and Education (ITB), University of Bremen, Germany. She has been involved in several European research projects dealing with skills formation and assessment, careers, work orientations and employee commitment in an international comparative perspective. Before joining the University of Bremen she worked as Education Specialist for the Human Development Network of the World Bank in Washington, DC.

Robert Matousek studied Science and Innovation Management and Computer Science at the University of Utrecht in the Netherlands. His main interests are innovations in the biosciences and informatics. He was a visiting scholar at the Keck Graduate Institute of Applied Life Sciences in Claremont, California, where he studied the integration of computers and biology using cross-functional teams under the supervision of David Finegold.

Monika Nerland is a Postdoctoral Research Fellow at the Institute for Educational Research, University of Oslo, Norway. Her research interests relate to institutional practices in professional education and work as well as in the field of music education. Her doctoral dissertation (2003) is a study of cultural practices in the education of professional musicians. She is currently working on the research project 'Professional Learning in a Changing Society' financed by the Research Council of Norway, which aims to develop theories on professional learning and identity formation.

Nikitas Patiniotis is Professor of Sociology at the Panteion University of Athens, Greece. His areas of research include education and its relation to employment, skills formation and qualification, educational policy and quality assessment of education and lifelong learning. He has published several books and journal articles in Greek and foreign academic journals. He has also officially represented Greece at numerous working groups of the European Commission and other international bodies and has often served as head or member of the Board of Directors of several Greek research institutions.

Gwendolyn Paul worked as a researcher at the Center for Research in General and Vocational Education, Technical University of Darmstadt, Germany in the pilot project JAMBA that supported the participation of young single mothers in vocational training programmes. Currently, she is a member of academic staff at a State Government Office ('Landesstelle') dealing with the vocational socialisation and integration of women and further vocational training in a European perspective.

Gerasimos Prodromitis is Assistant Professor of Experimental Social Psychology at the Department of Psychology of Panteion University, Athens, Greece. His current research interests focus on social influence processes and the mechanisms of formation, diffusion, and transformation of social representations.

Sabine Raeder is a Senior Researcher in the Organisation, Work and Technology Group at the ETH Zurich, Switzerland. Her current research activities focus on the consequences of increasing work flexibility for individuals and their employment relationships, particularly in relation to psychological contracts and vocational identity. Her wider research interests in organisational sciences encompass alternative and critical approaches towards the organisation and organisational culture.

Felix Rauner is Professor for Technical Vocational Education and Training at the University of Bremen and founder of the Institute Technology and Education (ITB), Germany's largest independent research institute in the field of vocational education. His domains of expertise cover vocational qualification research, analysis and development of vocational training systems, human resource development and comparative perspectives on industrial cultures. He is member of several expert committees for the German government and at European level. He holds visiting professor status at the Tongji-University, Shanghai, the Institute of Education in London and the University of California.

Morten Smistrup is Assistant Professor at the Department of Educational Studies, Roskilde University, Denmark. While his earlier studies focused on the interdependence between the vocational identity and qualification demands among Danish bankers, his current research interests are within the area of work-life learning and vocational education and training. He is currently working on a research project dealing with the transition from vocational training into gainful employment.

Uta Zybell is a researcher at the Center for Research in General and Vocational Education, Technical University of Darmstadt, Germany focusing on vocational education and gender studies. Based on her involvement in the scientific monitoring of the pilot project JAMBA (1998–2003), her doctoral dissertation (2003) is a study of the conflicting demands that young mothers experience who undergo a vocational training programme and raise children at the same time. Currently, she is providing scientific support to a project on career paths support ('BerufsWegeBegleitung') that deals with the integration of young people who have difficulties entering the job market.

Introduction and Overview

**Alan Brown*, Simone Kirpal[†] and
Felix Rauner[†]**
*University of Warwick, UK;
[†]University of Bremen, Germany

This edited volume on *Identities at Work* brings together international theory and empirical research that deals with continuity and change in identity formation processes at work in the context of changes in working processes and labour market requirements, one outcome of which may lead to new forms of mobility and flexibility for both employers and employees. By emphasising perspectives from sociology, psychology, organisational management and vocational education and training the different contributions connect the debates of human resources development, skills formation and career development with those relating to individual's work commitment and vocational orientations. In this sense this volume presents a new research area embedded in a wholly interdisciplinary and international perspective.

Some modern work settings that make use of decentralised organisational structures based on flat hierarchies and team working also require that employees at all skills levels are able to assume much broader responsibilities, master complex work processes, work independently, take initiative and organise their own, partly self-directed, work-related learning. Modern work processes in manufacturing and service organisations increasingly rely upon responsible and competent employees who are willing and able to engage both with the tasks that their job requires and in learning and developing their skills. The degree to which employees are successful in taking on new forms of responsibility and mastering complex work situations is, however, not only dependent upon employees' skills composition and how well they have been trained, it also relates to the extent to which employees identify with what they do and their

1

A. Brown, S. Kirpal and F. Rauner (eds.), Identities at Work, 1–10.
© 2007 *Springer.*

commitment to their work and performance of their tasks. Employee responses to changing work processes are therefore not just a matter of skill development, they essentially involve development in the forms of identification, identity building and commitment that employees experience while engaging with changing work processes and contexts.

Studies of management and behavioural sciences have long since confirmed the interdependence between employees' identification with work and their work commitment. Organisational commitment in particular has received considerable attention, as it is believed (and has been tested) that individuals' commitment towards their employing organisation correlates with outcomes such as loyalty and motivation of employees, workforce stability and improved performance. While these (predominantly quantitative) approaches tend to emphasise the organisational or management perspective on enhancing workforce effectiveness, recent studies stress that organisational commitment is essentially a dual trust-based relationship that also requires commitment from the organisation towards its employees. Under conditions of increased international competition and pressures of rationalisation and economic constraints organisations tend to undermine commitment to their employees resulting in the psychological contract undergoing change and in some cases both parties investing less in establishing forms of commitment and building trust-based relationships.

Perspectives focused more on the employee have emphasised that individuals are challenged to develop and exhibit forms of commitment and identification with work that do not just relate to the organisation. The concept of multiple commitments shifts the focus beyond the organisation to include other sources or dimensions of commitment and identification such as work group, occupational specialisation, task performance or the union, for example. This approach analytically differentiates between organisational commitment, occupational commitment, job involvement, work involvement and group commitment, or in more broader terms, between workplace commitment relating to the direct work environment such as the employing organisation, professional roles, colleagues and the work team, and those commitments external to the immediate workplace such as to the union, occupation, professional association or future career prospects (for more on this see Baruch and Cohen in this volume). Such research suggests that work outcomes can be better understood and explained as a function of several forms of commitment in combination rather than by just exploring one kind of commitment alone, and this has meant that occupational commitment and job involvement in particular are gaining renewed importance as foci for analysis.

Studies on work identities connect occupational commitment, job involvement and levels of tasks performance (work outcomes) to employees' vocational socialisation and skills development. From this perspective, vocational socialisation and becoming skilled are the basis for individuals identifying with their work and vocational roles and developing work commitment and a professional ethic, which can constitute the basis for effective and productive performance. In countries where the tradition of vocational training and apprenticeship programmes is strong, becoming a member of a 'community of practice' is closely linked to developing a vocational identity. Furthermore, developing an occupational commitment and high levels of identification with work are believed to foster the integration of young people into society, particularly of those who perform relatively poorly at school. Hence developing an occupational identity is regarded as an important tool to foster labour market integration and stabilise school-to-work transitions, both at the first threshold (making the transition from general education to vocational training) and the second threshold (making the transition from training into gainful employment). That those processes are intrinsically linked and interdependent with the development of a person's overall identity is the focus of another strand of research in this area that is strongly represented in this volume.

The latter approaches tend to underline a subjective-oriented perspective (hence, at least in this volume, qualitative methods predominate), which develops in the complex interplay between structure and individual agency. Against the interdependence between developing forms of identity at work and a personal identity these approaches acknowledge that individuals' patterns of identification and commitment at work may vary in the intensity with which they are held and in the significance individuals ascribe to them, and that if and how employees identify with their work is dependent upon a variety of factors and conditions. As a pioneering work, this volume aims at investigating in more detail some of those factors and conditions. At the same time it seeks to provide a framework for presenting the factors that influence the development of work identities in their full complexity and to encourage and stimulate the creation of fruitful linkages as a basis for further research.

Changes in work contexts, employment conditions and patterns of work organisation affect individuals' career orientations and in many contexts patterns of commitment and identification with work are themselves undergoing significant change. At the same time the occupation continues to remain a key factor in supporting work-related identity

development and work socialisation as well as often constituting a significant element of a person's more general social identity. Some commentators express concerns that the increasing flexibility of skills, work
and employment may negatively affect employees' work motivation,
learning aptitude and commitment and even carry the danger of having
disruptive effects on the development of an individual's overall personality. By investigating the role and meaning of identity formation
processes in different work contexts and under conditions of increasing
flexibility of work and employment, the contributions in this volume
provide theoretically and empirically grounded insights that provide
a significant contribution towards addressing this topic of wider social,
political and academic interest.

Changes in work contexts and patterns of employment may mean that
some employers and employees are more open to building in more flexibility and independence in the organisation of work, but in other contexts there are dangers that these changes will lead to lower levels of
identification with the company, lack of work commitment and instabilities for both the employer and the employees. In practice, the loosening
of the employer-employee contract may mean that risk management and
responsibility for individual development at work are largely transferred
from the company to the individual, requiring from the employees
a much higher level of self-initiative and individual agency in making
sure their skills and competences are valued in the labour market. While
empowered employees may benefit from this trend and may even assert
their flexibility and independence by taking their intelligence and know-
how with them upon leaving the company to enhance their career
chances, disempowered and less qualified employees on the periphery of
organisations will more likely tend to be over-challenged when dealing
with and adjusting to expectations of self-initiated learning and career
planning. The latter group bears a higher risk of long-term labour market
exclusion. At the same time some companies increasingly invest in
aligning and integrating corporate and individual goals and values for
those they consider their key employees, who in return are expected to
commit to and identify with the organisation.

Fostering the development of forms of identification with work can
help employees to overcome uncertainties in employment conditions and
instabilities at work. On the other hand, under the conditions of flexible
labour markets and organisational restructuring, strong work identities
and the persistence of previous forms of organisational commitment
may be a barrier to enhancing the mobility of the workforce and the
flexibility of economic processes. Thus in certain work contexts some

employers and employees may consider strong work identities and occupational attachments produce strong inter-firm demarcations and confine employees to particular job positions in ways that may restrict the competitiveness of companies. In such circumstances there may be tensions between an employer's desire for more flexibility and a wish that employees had more adaptable forms of attachments and those employees who wish to retain former attachments and values.

Certainly, we can identify conflicting interests and a number of unanswered questions. Although the different book chapters do not address all of the questions and issues raised, we hope that with this compilation of results from theoretical and empirical research some of those issues can be addressed and clarified. Most of all, however, we hope to have contributed to a reinvigoration of the debate about the nature and development of work-related identities and that discussions of these issues will continue.

The volume is structured into four parts. The first part presents ideas and concepts about work-related identities from different theoretical and empirical perspectives, including mapping out different approaches towards conceptualising vocational identities and investigating the meaning these can have for particular societal or occupational groups. The empirical studies, all of which present their own approach towards a theoretical foundation for the investigations undertaken, focus on bankers in Denmark, young mothers entering training programmes in Germany, tourism employees in Greece and skilled workers in Europe.

The *FAME Consortium* starts this section with an overview of how different national European research traditions connect theoretical concepts of vocational identity formation with empirical research and related theoretical concepts and topics. It outlines how 'identity' is conceptualised in psychology, psychoanalysis and sociology and delineates a new conceptual framework for the analysis of vocational identity. Furthermore, with examples drawn from Estonia, Greece and France it shows how the debate on vocational identity has been anchored in different national, empirically-based research traditions.

The presentation of three empirical studies follows this introductory overview in part one. Combining quantitative and qualitative methods, *Morten Smistrup* investigates the vocational identity of Danish bankers and the role it used to play in the past and currently plays in processes of becoming a committed bank employee. From the analysis of the banking sector he delineates some general aspects of vocation and vocational identity and the significance of these phenomena to society and the individual. The vocation herein is conceptualised as a formative collective organising principle as opposed to the self, which presents a subjective organising perspective.

Based on a German pilot project with young mothers, *Gwendolyn Paul* and *Uta Zybell* discuss the role of vocational training for an individual's vocational socialisation and the development of a vocational identity. For teenage mothers who break with the regular structure of status passages of German employees (i.e. general schooling, vocational training, gainful employment and then starting a family) being able to take part in a vocational training programme strongly confirms the value of a person learning a trade, becoming skilled and being involved in work contexts as a 'gateway to the world' and as an opportunity for societal participation. By following a considerable number of young mothers during the course of their training, they forcefully show how integration into and participation in work settings also influences the overall identity of these mothers, hence underlining the interdependence between work and family life in identity formation processes.

With a different focus *Nikitas Patiniotis* and *Gerasimos Prodromitis* introduce the issue of the 'double' vocational identity of self-employed owners of small, often family-run, businesses that are to some extent characteristic of people working on the margins of a number of sectors in the economy. Based on an empirical investigation, they discuss the situation of employees working in the Greek tourist industry and hypothesise that self-employed owners in this sector in particular develop a complex vocational identity that reflects responses to the demand for more flexible work practices and the low recognition of formal qualifications and training related to the field. Employees working in this sector find themselves challenged to deal with multiple, and sometimes ambiguous, vocational identities not only due to their position as being self-employed, but also because of the unstable, seasonal and sometimes precarious employment conditions, which are quite common across Europe, but in southern and eastern European countries in particular.

From the policy debate about whether an occupationally structured or a flexibility-based modular system of vocational training drives labour markets more effectively, *Felix Rauner* explores and discusses the future of vocational education and training systems in Europe and their role in fostering or inhibiting the development of a vocational identity. In his analysis vocational training systems in Europe can be structured according to two qualification scenarios: first, education and training for and by means of skilled work—the vocational education scenario, and second, the accumulation of skills necessary for employment—the market-driven employability scenario. He introduces a number of possible criteria that could support the assessment of vocational training systems in an international comparative perspective. One major finding in this comparative approach is that skilled workers trained according to the first scenario tend to develop a vocational identity in the course of their training process, which has the positive effect of strengthening employees' performance orientation and quality awareness.

Part two brings together contributions that thematise the dynamics between personal identity and work and employment, a strand of research that has received major attention since the first empirical investigations of industrial sociology and work psychology. The dominant theme here is how individuals deal with the flexibility demands of some modern work settings and manage to integrate diverse work experiences into a coherent self-image to generate continuities in their personal identity and career narratives. All three contributions take a subject-oriented approach by methodologically addressing these issues with the help of qualitative studies that present individual narratives from Switzerland, Australia, Germany and the UK.

Sabine Raeder and *Gudela Grote* explore personal identity in the context of work flexibility drawing on a psychological approach towards identity. Based on an empirical study with individuals who experienced career changes they conceptualise, according to Hausser's identity model, the dimensions biographical continuity and ecological consistency as aspects of the self-concept, locus of control and self-esteem. They conclude that their interview participants generally succeeded in integrating career changes in their identity through emphasising biographical continuity and a high overall ecological consistency. They argue that detailed analysis is necessary to capture the wide variety in individual biographies and personal identities and that in order to support personally valued vocational identities, individuals should be supported in establishing an appropriate balance within their identity construction.

Stephen Billett also looks at how individuals construct continuity in their lives under conditions of change that include re-directions in their careers and employment, and connects his approach with investigating individuals' motivations to engage in lifelong learning. He proposes that individuals' sense of self shapes and is shaped by their participation and learning throughout working life through a quest to become 'themselves' in the sense of creating a coherent self-image. In this process, individuals' agency and intentionality is likely to be directed by and towards their sense of self, which also includes the negotiation of identity as they engage in work. He concludes that in understanding the processes of learning and the remaking of work practice this individual sense of self needs acknowledging and to be accounted for, particularly in policies and practices associated with lifelong learning and when it comes to attempting to mobilise that learning.

What it takes for individuals to fulfil expected demands of becoming a 'flexible employee' is explored by *Simone Kirpal* and *Alan Brown* on the basis of three narratives. Some human resources departments and managers increasingly favour multi-skilled, mobile and adaptable employees who can potentially perform a variety of tasks as the 'ideal model' against which they wish to recruit. While this may put great pressure on some employees, others may regard themselves as actors who actively try to use flexibility, mobility and learning as instruments to foster their broader vocational goals and career prospects. To what extent this may conflict with or support the development of strong work identities and whether the increasing flexibility of skills, work and employment may negatively affect the development of forms of identification with work and an individual's overall personality is further explored.

The contributions to the third part of this volume connect vocational and professional identity formation with theoretical and empirical research on work and organisational commitment. The chapters presented in this section are either based on quantitative methods or larger qualitative empirical investigations.

Yehuda Baruch and *Aaron Cohen* start this section with a theoretical chapter introducing the concepts of organisational commitment and professional identity as two major constructs in behavioural and management studies. They deduce an integrative conceptual framework to clarify the association between organisational commitment and professional identity by relating those two constructs to each other, exploring their multi-dimensional character and the multiple constituent components of which they are comprised. By discussing the relevance and implications of commitment and professional identity for the working life of individuals, they hope to suggest a new perspective for further studies into the combined effect of both constructs.

Based on an empirical investigation in the German automotive industry *Bernd Haasler* explores young trainees' experiences of occupational and organisational commitment as they make their way through the German apprenticeship system. During this period young people typically are expected to meet various expectations of developing attachments and forms of identification with the company and the occupational field they train for at the same time as it is believed that the direction these processes take during this formative period also significantly influences the young people's subsequent work-based learning, competence development and career orientation. Although the

German vocational training system in the first place aims to foster apprentices' vocational identity formation the results show that during the first year of the training young people develop a much greater attachment towards their employing organisation than to the vocational field they are specialising in.

Looking at a broader European perspective, *Simone Kirpal, Alan Brown* and *M'Hamed Dif* discuss how individuals' attachments to more classical forms of commitment and identification with work may conflict with new flexibility and learning demands. They observe a general trend towards the 'individualisation' of employee commitment and work identities, which challenge the individual to develop a proactive and 'entrepreneurial' work attitude based on multi-skilling and flexibility. They argue that employees at the intermediate skills level in particular may in many contexts be over-challenged to fulfil increased demands of flexibility and continuous learning, because they may lack the necessary resources, skills and capacities on the one hand, and, on the other hand, are not sufficiently supported in their working environment to become equipped to meeting changing work demands. Especially when considered from a perspective of potential labour market exclusion this is highly problematic and may disadvantage a potentially high number of employees in Europe.

Taking a different perspective and methodological approach *Akihiro Ishikawa* challenges some contemporary stereotypes of Japanese workers by means of cross-cultural comparative study as well as longitudinal analyses. While Japanese workers are commonly assumed to develop their work identity and commitment largely in relation to the organisation they work for, his analyses reveal that attitudes of Japanese permanent full-time employees are not so work centralised, work satisfied and company dependent as compared to workers in other countries. The meaning of work and working, however, differs considerably between different job strata (i.e. between manual workers, administrative staff, supervisors and technical staff). The author regards the growing number of semi-unemployed Japanese youth as one major reason for the declining work-oriented life style in Japan.

Part four of this volume deals with how professional identities are actively shaped through organisational and institutional mechanisms. The two contributions present two case studies of how professional identities are institutionally being created or constructed as newly emerging job profiles or work demands that require new forms of work identity, for example, when professional tasks are being re-defined or require a new skills background or composition.

Monika Nerland and *Karen Jensen* address the role that initial education can play in constructing a new professional self. They analyse curricular and policy documents in order to demonstrate how new kinds of work identities are offered to students in Norway who want to become nurses or computer engineers. These documents, which recently have been newly adopted for both professional groups, also define, implicitly or explicitly, emerging visions and expectations of the professional self. Based on theoretical concepts introduced by Foucault the authors discuss how the formulation of goals, activities and evaluation procedures in the curricula impose new demands on the learning self as they view the students as creators of knowledge, boundary crossers and innovators of self and ethics.

The second case study, which *David Finegold* and *Robert Matousek* present, focuses on the bioscience industry in the US. While historically the diverse skills required in the sector were embodied in specialists from different disciplines such as biology, chemistry and computer science, who spoke different technical languages and had different approaches to solving problems, major advances in biotechnology require new types of professionals. The authors introduce two new types of bioscience professionals who embody a new combination of skill mix: computational biologists who are able to integrate programming skills and biological knowledge, and bioscience business professionals who can integrate science and business to help commercialise new products. The authors discuss some of the key labour market, organisational and individual-level factors related to the creation of new professional profiles and identities and identify processes that may also apply to similar developments in other forms of complex knowledge work.

Part One

Vocational Identity in Theory and Empirical Research

1

Decomposing and Recomposing Occupational Identities—A Survey of Theoretical Concepts

FAME Consortium

The following individuals contributed to this article: Alan Brown (University of Warwick, UK), M'Hamed Dif (University of Louis Pasteur of Strasbourg, France), Leena Helemäe (University of Tallinn, Estonia), Simone Kirpal (University of Bremen, Germany), Sokratis Koniordos (University of Patras, Greece), Gabriele Laske (University of Bremen, Germany), Nikitas Patiniotis (Panteion University of Athens, Greece) and Olga Strietska-Ilina (Czech National Observatory of VET & Labour Market, National Training Fund, Czech Republic)

1.1 Occupational Identities in Historical Perspective[1]

In Europe, the existence of occupations has a long-standing tradition deriving from the medieval history of the organisation of crafts, the formation of guilds with certain requirements for membership, the industrial revolution and the establishment of a mass system of compulsory education (Greinert, 1997; Stenström and Lasonen, 2000). Historically changing political and economic environments connect the

---

[1] Reference is made to 'vocational', 'occupational', 'professional' or 'work-related' identity as any kind of identity formation processes that develop through the interaction between the individual and the work context including vocational education and training. The most inclusive terminology may be applied when referring to 'work-related' or 'work identity', whereas 'vocational' or 'occupational identity' more specifically refers to certain features of the work context or a specific concept of work. For example, 'occupational identity' may be more applicable to labour markets and work concepts that are structured along occupational lines. However, the project partners reached a common understanding to use the different terminology in an interchangeable manner referring to the same kind of identity formation processes at work.

A. Brown, S. Kirpal and F. Rauner (eds.), Identities at Work, 13–44.
© 2007 *Springer.*

individual to the work context in very different ways and each period called for a different kind of identification with work. Thus, vocational and broader work-related identities are not constant over time; rather they need to be understood in a dynamic way.

In agricultural, pre-modern times organised around the feudal system each individual was socially, politically and economically dependent upon a work-and-bread giver. Work was closely linked to a person's social relations and status and identities were largely ascribed and attached to pre-defined social roles (Gellner, 1992). Under capitalist economic relations work became contracted whereby the person was politically free. However, the economic contractual relationships of early industrialisation still preserved a high level of interdependence between work and social status. It provided a newly emerging collective work identity that at least for the first half of the 20th century could be considered relatively stable. During that period the qualifications to perform in an occupation both in industry and crafts were mostly obtained through on-the-job training and usually served as the basis for a lifetime occupational specialisation.

With the establishment of modern welfare states, the relationship between work and social status became much more complex. As over the past decades working conditions have been constantly improved and legally regulated, work tasks and duties have become clearly defined in time, space and function marking a clear distinction from private time and leisure. The welfare state also provided for a harmonisation of life-styles across the hierarchy of occupations and the private sphere. 'The liberation from economic vulnerability and subjection' (Gellner, 1992, p. 142), the separation of work and the social life beyond it, and the homogenisation of life styles also brought about greater freedom in terms of how individual work identities are linked to social roles.

For hundreds of years apprenticeships in the crafts and trade business all over Europe had two main functions. First, to equip a person with some basic skills that would secure an income to sustain a family. The second function was to socialise a person into a community of practice whereby the person would acquire not only skills, but also internalise a certain kind of conduct and outlook. Both aspects, the establishment of an economic foundation and the internalisation of certain norms and behaviours, were geared towards the individual's smooth and successful transition and integration into society. At the same time, the socialising function of apprenticeships worked in two directions: from the individual's point of view as a learner it enabled her or him to become equipped and prepared to succeed in a given profession; and from the occupational community's point of view it helped to 'mould' a person to conform with the established norms and professional standards within this particular community (Heinz, 1995).

Two major historical developments lead to the reorganisation of communities of practice and the traditional forms of work-related socialisation: the emergence of an industrial work force and the expansion of formal schooling. These developments resulted, among other aspects, in an 'industrial culture' that dominated most Western societies until the 1970s. The extension of formal education, either in the form of a generalist type of schooling or in the sense of vocational or technical schools, to a certain extent replaced major socialisation functions that were formerly related to the work context. Today, secondary socialisation through formal education has largely replaced the former role of extended apprenticeships, which for some young people used to begin as early as at the age of 11.

Since the 1960s occupational communities with long traditions and which for decades relied on a high level of collective solidarity and relational interactivity like, for example, collectives of farmers or workers with a strong proletarian tradition and identity have become disembedded. Traditional forms of identity are increasingly challenged and are undergoing changes, whereas concurrently societal openness creates new opportunities for individuals to have and make choices in all aspects of life including work (Beck, 1986; Keupp et al., 1999). Structural factors and shifts like the incorporation of computer technology in industrial labour processes and the tertiarisation of the economy trigger labour market demands for greater flexibility and mobility of the labour force. For the individual worker this means fewer opportunities to identify with a clearly defined vocational milieu or community of practice, which the earlier arrangements cultivated and linked with the formation of occupational identities.

One characteristic of modern societies is the decomposition and fragmentation of structures and institutions that historically provided the individual with a framework of stability and pre-defined elements with which individuals could identify (Berger et al. 1975; Sennett, 1998). As a consequence, workers today are increasingly challenged to develop a more individualised type of worker identity (Kirpal, 2004). As 'actors' and 'agents' they need to respond to the intensification of competition, technological innovation, shifting skilling needs, new employment patterns and uncertain labour market developments. They are required to actively seek and select varying features and characteristics from different models of skill development, professional conduct and practices that have multiplied and have become more available and accessible. Workers today are challenged to actively shape and recompose their occupational identity.

In this process modern education systems play a key role as they are oriented towards the acquisition of formal certificates, which increasingly constitute a prerequisite for subsequent insertion into the labour market. The new role of formal schooling has considerably delayed job entry until late adolescence and beyond. In terms of identity formation this means a more open orientation making work-related identities nowadays rather the result of a personal trajectory than of something ascribed by a societal role occupied in one's late childhood or early adolescence. Longer and broader education exposes young people to a variety of influences that offer a wide range of opportunities, situations and practices with which to identify. When young people today enter the work setting most of them have already shaped, at least partially, an identity that is rooted outside the work context. Developing an occupational identity has become optional. Furthermore individuals are placed within a framework that gives them choices and opportunities for actively shaping structures and processes around them.

Choice and complexity are modern features not only with which individuals are challenged to deal, but they are also reproduced at the systemic and institutional level. Concepts of work and how vocational training, skills acquisition and insertion into work contexts connect vary across occupations, sectors and countries. Technological innovation and global market competition not only result in permanent changes of work organisation that put high demands on flexibility and mobility, but they also increasingly challenge formal education and training systems to supply modern qualifications and 'just-in-time' knowledge in response to the demands of the labour market. Looking at European countries today, we have to acknowledge that the institutional responses to those demands can be quite different and may range from a flexible to a highly formalised vocational education system (see Rauner in this volume). In any case, each strategy presents a different kind of solution and concept of work (Jaeger, 1989). While the Anglo-Saxon approach followed the path of a liberal and flexible system of labour market arrangements and vocational preparation that is output-oriented when it comes to skills acquisition and learning (Deißinger, 1996), other nations followed the tradition of combining practical work experience with school-based vocational training as is the case with the apprenticeship systems of Austria, Germany and Switzerland. While the first example builds in a high level of flexibility into its training and accreditation system, the latter emphasises the process of learning and becoming skilled supporting the formation of a vocationally-based identity through a socialisation process that focuses on becoming a member of a particular community of practice.

The general education and vocational training systems across Europe are challenged to respond to labour market demands that push for greater flexibility. Today, they need to consider and prepare young people to be able to master a whole range of work tasks and associated vocational roles. Multi-skilling, changing job profiles and employment patterns, competitive requirements on job performance and the creation of hybrid occupations (like, for example, the European job profile 'mechatronic') assume insertion of people into various communities of practice simultaneously and the development of a complex skill mix.

Modern forms of work organisation with highly complex internal structures (like teamwork, project-based teams that cross traditional organisational boundaries and interdisciplinary interdepartmental work) are increasingly combined with links to external and international communities of practice. Forming part of different communities, however, may not always be compatible and may demand conflicting loyalties (Cohen, 1994). The insertion of the Self into incompatible communities of practice certainly is not unproblematic, because the individual may encounter discomfort and conflict also at the level of his or her self-identity. This may not question the identification with a particular community of practice as such, but puts great challenges on the individual to integrate different expectations, professional roles and levels of identification into a coherent self-picture (Sennett, 1998).

1.2 Concepts of Identity—Contributions from Sociology, Social Psychology and Psychoanalysis

Identity is a relatively recent concept of the social sciences. It was introduced and further developed through two different currents: the tradition of American social psychology views identity as a principle of social organisation (Goffman, 1969; Mead, 1937), whereas in the tradition of psychoanalysis, primarily represented by Erikson (1970; 1973), identity is regarded as a principle of psychological organisation.

Goffman developed the concept of identity as a principle of social organisation the furthest. He refers to 'personal' and 'social' identities that are ascribed to the individual through interacting with others. Personal identity stresses the uniqueness of an individual, for example, through her or his distinctive and clearly identifiable biography, habits and attitudes. The individual obtains a social identity through the attribution of certain specified characteristics by others that have the nature of normative expectations (Huber and Krainz, 1987). The individual is expected to subordinate herself or himself to these expectations by acting accordingly, and behaving as others would do in the same social context. These expectations also imply performing very particular and clearly defined social and professional roles as they relate, for example, to being a 'good' mother or doctor.

The expectations are structured according to acting in conformity with a role within a given social context, such as a professional group. Benefits for acting in conformity with the expectations of the professional group may be, for example, recognition and acceptance by other members of the group. These processes of social acknowledgment act as an external guidance that helps the individual to build up certain dimensions of identity that can be shared with others.

> In the case of personal identity, by contrast, there is a demand to distinguish oneself from all others, i.e. to be like no other. These conflicting expectations require a balance otherwise there is a risk of non-identity in two ways. In one case the completely objectified blending into different depersonalized role contexts, in the other case stigmatization on the basis of behaviour deviating from norms (Huber and Krainz, 1987, p. 475).

The psychoanalytical concept of identity as a psychological organisation is rooted in the work of Freud. Erikson extended Freud's libido theory regarding development in early childhood. According to Erikson, shaping an ego identity or a psychosocial self-definition is a crucial developmental step that demands distinction from others. The awareness of having an identity is tied to the 'perception of one's own sameness and continuity in time and the related perception that others also recognize this sameness and continuity' (Erikson, 1973, p. 18). In this regard adolescence becomes the decisive phase 'during which the person looks for his place in some sector of the society through free role experimenting, a niche that is clearly outlined and, nevertheless, appears to be made especially for him' (Erikson, 1973, p. 139).

Psychoanalytical social research, as influenced by Marxist ideas, considers work as the most important medium for transforming the individual into a social being through socialisation processes (Leithäuser and Volmerg, 1988). Socialisation during formal education and in the work context plays a decisive role, because occupational categories provide a major offer of society to the individual for finding a 'clearly defined place' through vocational education and training and the entry into a vocationally structured world. This world offers predefined roles, which help the individual to create a concept of one's self as a specific role is taken up. Accepting a role also implies taking on an identity and helps the individual to become integrated into a community of practice and to display certain features that distinguish one group from another.

> In the classical approaches towards describing the formation of an identity during youth and early adult age the profession was always the focus as the anchor of one's view of oneself. Failing here was considered to be the key risk factor for what could be lifelong misadjustments (Silbereisen, 1997, p. 184).

In the German-speaking countries, Habermas (1976) in particular further developed the American concept of ego identity. He distinguishes between three types and stages of identity: in the first stage he defines a natural identity that stands for the identity of the biological human being as well as of all plant and animal organisms. The second type, the personal identity, is supposed to be maintained consistently throughout life despite the various and sometimes conflicting demands of different role systems to which a person belongs. Being part of these role systems in turn leads to the formation of a social identity. In the second stage Habermas integrates aspects of both the personal and the social dimension of identity. In modern societies this stage sometimes breaks down during the adolescence phase, before, on a third level, the ego identity is developed. This level is characterised by the ability of the adult to build up new identities and integrate them with those overcome.

In the context of occupational identity formation Habermas' third stage of identity is of particular importance as labour market demands for increased flexibility and mobility of workers challenge the individual's ability to build up new identities and integrate them with those overcome. This issue creates a linkage to the concept of bricolage identity, a term originally stemming from Levi-Strauss and adopted by Carruthers and Uzzi (2000). Bricolage identity 'involves the decomposition of existing identities into their constituent components and their recombination into a new identity' (Carruthers and Uzzi, 2000 p. 486).

Taking a bricolage, or third stage, identity perspective for delineating a theoretical framework of occupational identity formation, we must ask to what extent the actors themselves take part in shaping their own career paths. As research shows (Witzel et al., 1996), the status passage from school to work is not just a structurally determined, situated problem that assigns the individuals to their life paths. Rather it is co-shaped by the actions of the actors themselves and thus must also be examined as a complex socialisation process during which outside selection is complemented with self-selection. Whether and how individuals modify and shape their own occupational biographies in ways that do not follow exactly the paths suggested to them by their occupational choices is an interesting question for further research. The individual's ability to shape, modify and adjust her or his own career path is what Habermas has described as a highly cultural achievement: the ability of an adult to build up new identities and to integrate in them those left behind.

1.3 Occupational Identities and Culture: Social Anthropological and Ethnographic Perspectives on Identity Formation

Social anthropology and ethnography scrutinised the concept of identity, individuality and the Self in the context of society and culture. During the last decades of the twentieth century two schools crystallised among the traditions of scholars in social anthropology and related sciences. The two mainstreams can be roughly defined as ethnocultural and modernity schools, the former represented mainly by Anthony Smith, the latter by Ernest Gellner, Benedict Anderson, Eric Hobsbawm and others. Within these two traditions, the ethno-cultural school views identity as ascribed by 'objective characteristics', whereas the modernity school understands identity as a conscious construction of the individual resulting from modern socio-economic developments and the extended role of communication. This approach stresses the 'subjective characteristics'.

Transferring these approaches to aspects of occupational identity formation, we are confronted with the dynamics between the institutionalised structures of labour markets, vocational training systems and communities of practice, and the individual's ability to choose from and to combine certain elements of these structures for constructing her or his occupational identity. On the one hand, occupations are composed of a number of 'objective characteristics', which provide a framework for the individual to identify with when developing an occupational identity. They are typically linked to performance expectations and professional roles, which the individual takes up and internalises while undergoing a vocational socialisation process. Although the kind of division of labour that largely defines the structure and concrete features of work-related roles and functions is often rooted in long-standing traditions, most of these roles remain relatively stable even in post-modern work contexts (Palán, 1997). They are typically sustained by specific requirements in terms of learning, skills and work practice.

On the other hand, job profile and professional roles are not static, but they change and are modified according to changing work practice, work demands and skill requirements. While workers are challenged constantly to adjust and enhance their vocational skills, sometimes performing tasks that require a combination of skills completely different from the ones initially set out in their vocational preparation, they may entirely re-shape their work-related identities in response to the actual work practice. In so doing, the individual plays an active role in re-defining professional roles that may even lead to the establishment of new job profiles. Depending on the rigidity of the work situation, the workers may shape the duties and tasks imposed by the job thus being in a position to contribute significantly to re-conceptualising a formerly pre-defined occupational situation. From this perspective, occupations and professional roles are also shaped by individuals' 'subjective characteristics'.

As identity formation processes connect these two dimensions, the 'social' and the 'personal', they have to be understood in a dual way. The development of an identity is constrained, circumscribed and shaped by existing social structures and processes (Jenkins, 1996; Sarup, 1996). At the same time, identity formation implies an element of active engagement and self-definition on the part of the individual. From an external perspective society offers social roles and structures (family, gender, social status, etc.) to the individual, while as part of an internal process, the individual accepts or rejects aspects of the offer as he or she internalises certain roles and other societal elements (Giddens, 1984). From a sociological perspective this is described as the interdependence of structural and individual aspects of identity formation. Already existent structures like occupations with specific work profiles, qualification requirements, social acknowledgement and traditions exist and evolve. These structures may change over time and provide opportunities and restrictions. However, they do not necessarily force the individual into a given structural path as there is always scope for individual agency.

1.3.1   Collective Identities

Occupational categories and specialisations do not exist without individuals. In the context of group dynamics identity formation processes also function as a form of differentiation and separation from 'the other'. They are linked to a feeling of 'us' and 'them' generating a sense of sameness with some and difference from others (Tajfel, 1981). This process also includes the urge for reliable social relations and places to make the individual feel belonging to one particular group in distinction to other groups. Occupational identities in the sense of membership of a community of practice or as a form of collective social identity distinguish the members of one occupational community from another. They provide for continuity and stability in the work context and are based on vocational traditions. These traditions have long sustained biographic elements for individuals, which the mere job concept does not (Jaeger, 1989). One central aspect of collective identities therefore is to hold on to demarcations. These demarcations often exhibit highly regulated features leading to inflexibility when it comes to work organisation and innovation. To the extent to which they generate specific, rather narrow and closed professional cultures they can turn out to be highly resistant towards change (Kern and Sabel, 1994).

The collective dimension of occupational identities manifests itself as workers combine in associations and establish professional communities. The purposeful creation of occupational structures and specialisations may derive from workers' initiatives, but more often they tend to be the result of experts' and practitioners' interests. In this context, the creation of unifying symbols attached to a specific occupation plays an important role. These symbols typically become instrumental for occupational identity formation processes and often are developed in order to pursue a particular purpose like, for example, enhancing the prestige of an occupation. These mechanisms can also be transferred to the company level when promoting a corporate identity. Here, symbols and prestige may be artificially created, but they serve as powerful tools for the creation, modification, or redefinition of occupational identities.

Collective memory or nostalgia (Armstrong, 1982) is sustained by myths or symbols, which can easily be made instrumental to manipulate group dynamics and identity formation processes at the individual and collective level. Symbols may be real or false, but they always serve to promote the distinctiveness of the social group. As Hobsbawm (1992) puts it, the 'invention of tradition' by creating common myths can be very powerful. Once created and sustained, they are difficult to reshape, alter or abandon, because it is the 'symbolic rather than the material aspects of common fate that are decisive for identity' (Armstrong, 1982, p. 9).

1.3.2 The Active Construction of Work Identities: the Estonian Case

In Estonia, studies focusing on early life careers can look back at a tradition of more than 35 years. Studies at Tartu University initially focused on vocational counselling and the process of how individuals decide to follow a particular vocational track. Influenced by communist education one major concern was how to 'locate the right person to the right place' and to define 'a scientific direction of labour force allocation through individuals' occupational choices' (Titma, 1972, p. 22). Distinct from the official ideology, this concept emphasised the active role of young people showing some similarities with the American human resources approach of that time (Ginzberg, 1968; Ginzberg et al., 1951). In this context, the vocational orientation was linked to an individual's personal development assuming that occupational choices are dependent upon understanding the 'interconnections between society and individual as well as the ability to pursue socially meaningful goals' (Titma, 1972, p. 46).

The communist regime promoted a concept whereby work became the central element of life, connecting the society and the individual as a necessity and the basic sphere of self-realisation of every human being (Titma, 1972). That a person's skills, abilities, knowledge and experiences should match the specific requirements of a particular job was regarded as the main factor when making occupational decisions. In addition, work values were also assumed to have an impact on how people value and choose a particular occupational specialisation. Values as criteria for choices were conceptualised as being dynamic and subject to change. In the light of labour force allocation, these values should be 'consciously shaped' to help young people make 'the right' choices in the sense of being aware of one's own abilities and skills in combination with the chosen work context and socially acceptable goals.

Inspired by the American sociologist Ginzberg, occupational choice was conceived as a process of different stages that connects general education, vocational training and the chosen vocational track with the specific job or workplace. During the 1960s self-determination and 'subjective aspects' of occupational choice were emphasised like, for example, how an individual perceives and values the popularity and prestige of a particular occupational specialisation. In those early studies the meaning of work and individuals' attitude towards work were closely related to work ethics. The meaning of work was assessed in the context of life orientations by measuring a person's emotional, cognitive and behavioural attitude towards different spheres of life such as study, work, non-profit activities, family, leisure, etc., all of which were treated as values (Saarniit, 1997).

In the 1970s the attention shifted towards analysing the dynamics between work, occupational specialisations and inequality. As the Soviet institutional structure constructed society as an undifferentiated whole that in the first place valued the individual as part of a social entity, the level of self-realisation and individuals' autonomy at work were also conceptualised as being determined by social structures. Researchers started to focus on the 'objective aspects' of occupational identity formation and the influence of institutional structures upon the behaviour of a cohort instead of looking at an individual's value orientation. Life course approaches that were later introduced during the transition period in the 1990s also emphasised a structural perspective by conceptualising an individual's life course as a 'product' of social structures. However, it also acknowledged the interdependence between structure and individual agency as

> variations from institutionalized patterns not only affect subsequent events in the life of any given individual but also can, (. . .), generate new social structures and institutions. Social forces thus not only 'trickle down' from social institutions to individuals' lives but also 'percolate up' from individuals' actions to modify existing social patterns and institutions, and perhaps even create new ones (Mayer and Tuma, 1987, pp. 3–4).

This conceptual innovation was accompanied by the methodology of behaviour-centred, life event analyses.

When we connect the research phases described above with the political situation of Estonian society it is possible to delineate how the ideological pressure influenced the discourse on work-related identity formation. The official discourse and censorship placed work in the centre of existence. The meaning of work, work values and expectations of work performance were normatively constructed. In the context of socialism and the communist society work was considered not only to be the basis of existence, but also as a mediator between the society and the individual. It was perceived as a necessity and the basic sphere of self-realisation of every human being. During the 1960s scholars from socialist societies were given the opportunity to exchange ideas with Western scholars. Subsequently, Western theories and approaches influenced career studies and induced a new emphasis on value orientation and behaviour.

1.4 The Role of Vocational Training on Work-related Identity Formation: Experiences from Greece

Vocational training and skills acquisition highly influence the development of work-related identities. Drawing on empirical research, this section discusses the role that vocational education and training can play for identity formation using the example of skilled manual workers in Greece, who at some point became self-employed. The empirical research was carried out between 1988–1989 and 1998–1999. In total, 170 self-employed artisans working as machinists in the metal-working industry or in the garment industry were interviewed. The interviewees were grouped according to three categories: artisans, smaller employers and larger employers depending on the amount of managerial tasks that their work entailed. Interviewees had businesses that employed between one and 14 staff. Most of them considered skills acquisition and enhancement as their most important asset for ensuring the sustainability of their business. As for decades the required skills changed slowly, the specialised skills base provided a fundamental source of stability. Skills were typically acquired through on-the-job training, a long process that could take up to seven years and that was a major source for developing vocational identities. Today, rapid technological change make on-the-job learning and apprenticeships lose their 'enskilling' role thus decreasing their earlier importance for the shaping of work-based identities.

In Greece, the artisans-to-be on average began working at the age of 14. For the older generation it was even common to start an apprenticeship at the age of 9, 10, or 11 years. This implies that their work orientation was not in any way a matter of individual choice (Watson, 2001). Rather, they were obliged to work and, since they were minors, it was the adult guardian, who would set up a contractual agreement with the employer.

Most artisans had a poor peasant, worker, or marginal urban 'petit bourgeois' background. Coming from low-class families with restricted language codes most of them underachieved at school or had dropped out (Bernstein, 1975; Frangoudakis, 1978; Willis, 1977). The weak

level of school performance meant that many of them did not progress
through what Piaget designated the 'formal operational stage of cognitive development', which largely unfolds under the impact of formal
education during early adolescence (from 11 to 15 years) and involves
the development of the capacity to understand abstract and hypothetical
ideas (Piaget and Inhelder, 1973). Instead, on-the-job apprenticeships
largely consisted of 'learning-by-doing', and the repetitive performance
of routine tasks, making it very difficult for the trainees to acquire an
understanding of abstract and higher level work processes. This system
of vocational training operated a mechanism of exclusion that effectively channelled apprentices with a lower class background into manual jobs, while individuals with higher-level general education and of
middle class origin were favoured to become larger employers
(Koniordos, 2001).

1.4.1   Traits and Skills

'Traits' is a notion taken from psychology. It originally means 'dispositions', or 'enduring tendencies within the individual to behave in
certain ways' (Krech et al., 1962, p. 105). The concept has also been
applied in the context of dual and segmented labour markets, initially
developed on the basis of the U.S. experience.[2] It links ways and types of
skill acquisition to labour market segmentation. In the latter context,
traits have been defined as 'behavioural patterns, which will be reproduced in response to a given stimulus in a particular type of environment' (Piore, 1975, p. 130). They are differentiated into specific and
general traits.

A specific trait is a behaviour produced in direct response to a stimulus from the environment. It is acquired in a given environment by means
of imitation and socialisation. Thus a specific trait acquired in the workplace by the process of on-the-job training, i.e. a productive trait, may be
thought of as a habit. General traits are sets of rules from which

> behaviour may be derived which enables an individual to deduce
> from the environment and the stimulus [at hand] what the cor-
> rect response may be, although the particular combination of

---

[2] On primary and secondary labour markets and industrial dualism see Doeringer and
Piore (1971), Piore (1975) and Berger and Piore (1980).

circumstances may never have been encountered before (Piore, 1975, p. 130).

Traits of this kind are generated either by induction from a series of specific traits, or are taught at various levels of formal education. If, however, general traits are to be retained, they must be reinforced by continuous on-the-job usage. Otherwise they may degenerate into a set of specific traits.

Applying the traits concept to vocational training, on-the-job training and formal education respectively is decisive for the distinction between specific and general traits and, concomitantly, for the distinction between the lower (semi-skilled and skilled workers) and upper (professionals and managers) tiers of primary labour markets, which also resemble mobility chains:

> The concept of mobility chains represents an attempt to formalise the intuitive notion that socio-economic movement in our society is not random, but tends to occur in more or less regular channels. These channels are such that any given job will tend to draw labour for a limited and distinct number of particular points [stations]. As a result people hold jobs in some regular order or sequence. We shall term such a sequence a mobility chain (Piore, 1975, p. 128).

The concept of traits allows for deciphering the importance of education and on-the-job training for the formation of particular types of assets and skills profiles, which orient artisan apprentices in the selection of their subsequent vocational paths. It is useful to distinguish between specific and general traits as either crafts oriented or associated with administration, management and commerce. Accordingly, artisans as wage-dependent workers would have an abundance of specific technical traits that they picked up on-the-job, obtained some general technical traits by attending low-grade technical classes and some basic specific administrative traits by observing what others did (for example, their supervisors). The small employers would typically have acquired some low-level general administrative skills, mainly by experience and imitation, as well as specific technical traits on-the-job and in technical schools. Lastly, the larger employers would be imbued with general administrative traits picked up in enterprises with which they had a family connection, and/or in management training at college.

Confirming the traits hypothesis, the Greek investigation shows that the length of formal education (as one of the two ways of imputing general traits) correlates with the type of proprietor. The emergent pattern is that the longer someone attended formal schooling, the closer the person approaches the large employer type of entrepreneur. Inversely, decreasing numbers of years of formal education tend to correlate with the artisan worker type. Although the quality of education could not be considered, longer schooling also facilitates that students have the possibility to absorb more theoretical and general knowledge. A comparison of the average years of schooling between the two vocational specialisations investigated shows that (with the exception of the small employers) machinists in metal-working on average attended school about 1.5 years longer than the workers engaged in garment making. The greater differential in years of school attendance can also be attributed to the traditional role expectations of women that placed emphasis on assuming housekeeping and family responsibilities after completion of elementary education. Accordingly, the female interviewees working in the garment industry on average attended 6.6 years of schooling compared to their male counterparts, who attended on average 8.1 years (Koniordos, 2001).

Closer study also reveals that the majority of the independent artisan and small-employer machinists attended technical school courses at evening classes alongside working during the day. This combination exposed them to formal education and elementary general technical traits while practical on-the-job training provided them with specific technical traits and a chance to apply the more general knowledge learned at school. These people were trained as skilled craft workers. By contrast, practical technical education did not form part of learning the garment trade. Here, the character of the trade itself, its domestic environment and the overall state of the industry further supported the traditional role of women in Greece. Finally, most of the large employer type of entrepreneurs had followed high-school, college, or university courses. With their middle-class background and a considerably higher proportion of formal education they were being prepared for non-manual labour and supported to develop abstract thinking capabilities and administrative skills.

Since most of the artisans and small employers could not or only to a very limited extent rely on financial assistance from their families, their skills became their primary asset. Skills turned into the basic means for obtaining higher wages that would allow for securing some savings and eventually turn into capital for the individual to establish her or his own business. Once a business was set up, skills again became the crucial resource in order to safeguard know-how, technical independence and to keep down unit labour costs. The skills acquired during the artisan apprenticeship and working prior to establishing an independent workshop had to be fairly broad in order that the individual was prepared to tackle successfully new challenges at work (Piore and Sabel, 1984). By being skilled and successful, the artisan was able to attract customers and to acquire a good reputation in the trade. It would be extremely difficult to remediate the lack or insufficiency of skills in order to survive as an independent employer. The process of becoming an independent artisan, however, also implied a shift from accumulating specific technical traits to developing general technical traits. While, in the sample, the machinists showed a strong inclination towards combining a longer and higher-level technical schooling with on-the-job training, practical work experience was of paramount importance for skill acquisition in garment manufacturing confirming the notion that in garment manufacturing technical skills are mainly picked up on-the-job.

In summary, we can conclude that machinists in metal-working attended school much longer than skilled workers in the garment trade. Also, their on-the-job apprenticeships lasted twice as long as those involved in garment making, they worked more years as wage-earners and changed employers more often before becoming independent. This appears to imply that for becoming and surviving as an artisan a *sine qua non* is the acquisition of skills, particularly in machining. But the making of garments also requires expertise and knowledge of fabrics, designing, making prototypes, wholesaling and retailing, and the actual sewing implies mastery of operating the machines, fine finishing and ironing. It also extends to wholesaling and retailing of goods. Still, artisan and small-employer machinists who started their own business had a wider range of technical skills than the skilled workers in garment manufacturing. This may be due to the technology involved that obliged machinists to stay longer in education and to have more practical on-the-job training. This increases their chances of acquiring specific and general, mostly technical, traits type of skills. By contrast, skilled garment artisans, due to the greater division of labour in the trade, were more restricted in their range of work tasks. Small employers in garment making also displayed administrative skills as part of their qualification for becoming independent. The higher involvement of general traits combined with the fact that all of them are male gives them a profile distinct from that of the same trade artisans, and distinguishes them from the different types of machinist, among whom there are less marked disparities.

1.5   Research on Occupational Identity in France

Occupational identity formation has received considerable attention in the French research context during the past three decades. Since the introduction of the continuous vocational training (CVT) system in France in the early 1970s, the process of work-related identity formation has undergone an important structural change. This coincides with the end of Fordism as the dominant paradigm in the economy and the advent of an economy based on globalisation and a new flexibility paradigm (Dif, 1998). During the earlier period of sustained economic growth with a relatively low rate of unemployment (1965–1975) the French sociologist Renaud Sainsaulieu conducted major empirical investigations on work-related identity formation. On the basis of 200 qualitative interviews and 8,000 questionnaires that covered employees of different skill levels, who worked for public and private companies across a range of sectors, he developed a typology differentiating between four types of identity formation at work (Sainsaulieu, 1977, 1985).

The first type is characterised by 'community-based' relationships and applies to workers with basic qualifications typically performing routine tasks. It is built on a close relationship between the members of a collective based on affection, solidarity and cooperation. The collective identity among the group members serves as a refuge and a protection against divergences and clashes. A hierarchical authority in the form of a leader is accepted for guidance and mediation in cases of conflict. By contrast, the 'negotiation' type of vocational identities is specific to professionals and executives and is based on the acceptance of differences and the use of negotiation and open democratic debate to solve conflicts. Individuals with a 'negotiation' type of identity are highly attached to their profession and value autonomy and refuse any imposed hierarchical authority. They rather prefer a leader whose recognition is based on work expertise and mediating competencies in the context of group dynamics.

Third, Sainsaulieu identified an 'affinities' type of identity that is changing over time due to socio-professional mobility. It is found among self-directed learners (technicians and executives) within professions that are undergoing rapid change. The interpersonal relationships within the groups are selective and affective. A leader is accepted only as project promoter, but is generally considered a hindrance to individual professional promotion. Finally, the 'retreat' identity is typical for individuals who use work as an instrument to benefit other spheres of life, such as the family or leisure. These individuals may be socially excluded and marginalised employees due to their low level of qualification, their age (employees near retirement), their employment status or ethnic origin, for example. Within groups with these atomised identities a strong hierarchical authority is often instrumental for coordination and leadership.

These four types of work-related identities were conceptualised within the context of economic growth and a Fordist production model. Twenty years later Sainsaulieu and colleagues adapted and extended this classification to the requirements of the new post-Fordist economy. In the light of new empirical research (Francfort et al., 1995), Sainsaulieu's four forms of vocational identity were adapted taking into consideration simultaneously two types of interactivity: *sociability* (relational interactivity) and the mode of *interactivity with the organisation* (interactivity and engagement with work processes as opposed to the interactivity guided by established rules and regulations of the organisation). Based on a multi-dimensional study with a sample working in 296 occupational specialisations identified from 81 companies across different sectors the following changes could be observed (Sainsaulieu, 1996, 1997):

- The 'fusion' type of identity that was anchored in a strong attachment towards colleagues, the community of practice and a formally established occupational status has been declining. This development concerns all categories of employees who have accumulated a long work experience (generally over 15 years) within public and private organisations belonging to traditional sectors. Most of these sectors (such as the steel and automobile industries, banking and transport) are or have been undergoing rapid organisational and structural changes. As a result, the attached communities, which traditionally relied on a high level of collective solidarity and relational interactivity, are breaking down into micro groups.
- The 'retreat' identity is developing in two directions: On the one hand, it is extending by including a new category of employees who have been destabilised by technological change and the threat of labour market exclusion. As a means of protection against change and potential risks, they are holding on to an established work routine that is supported by administrative rules and regulations. On the other hand, half way between the original 'retreat'

identity and its extension to an 'administrative approach', we find the emergence of a new category of employees, who work directly with clients and assume counselling responsibilities within the developing public sector. They distinguish themselves as 'civil service professionals' who develop their own identity features.

- The adaptation of the 'negotiation' type of identities includes two related developments characterised by a high level of relational and work-based interactivity. The first development takes the emergence of professionals in the field of new technologies into consideration. They are highly attached to comradeship values based on a job well-done as well as autonomy, trustworthiness and solidarity between members of the profession. The second development concerns the emergence of a new category of dynamic managers, executives, sellers, etc. who possess competences that allow them to invest in change and collective mobilisation by being, at the same time, highly integrated in the organisation. Sainsaulieu calls this new form of occupational identity the 'entrepreneurial' or 'corporate identity' model.

- Finally, 'affinities' type identities have developed in a way whereby they now exhibit 'mobility of identity formation' based on a combination of a high level of interactivity with work and low sociability. As a result of a lack of opportunities for promotion due to the development of a flexibility-based mode of human resource management with flat organisational structures, a new generation of dynamic and 'mobile' workers (specialised technicians, executives and graduates) has evolved during the last three decades. They are more inclined to secure their professional career through project-based personal strategies founded on occupational flexibility and mobility. Their relational network investment is primarily oriented towards the achievement of their personal career projects rather than those of the professional group or the organisation.

On the basis of three empirical investigations conducted by different research groups during the 1980s, Claude Dubar confirmed in different terms Sainsaulieu's evolutionary four forms of occupational identities.[3] He explained an individual's work-related identity formation as a process

---

[3] The first field investigation on 'Socio-vocational Inclusion Programmes' was launched in 1982 and concerned unemployed young school leavers without qualifications in the region of Nord-Pas-de-Calais (France) (Dubar et al., 1987); the second field investigation was conducted between 1984 and 1985 and concerned a CVT programme for employees' career development within two production units of thermal

of double transactions: biographical and relational transactions (Dubar, 1991, 1994; Dubar and Engrand, 1986; Dubar and Tripier, 1998). The 'biographical transaction' refers to time-dependent identity formation of 'negotiating with oneself' by creating an identity for oneself and planning his or her occupational trajectory as a continuous re-creation of the past or as a succession of discontinuities. The 'relational transaction' concerns the individual's relational interactivity with the members of a given space of identification structured by a set of rules and ethics.

Both kinds of transactions are heterogeneous and interrelated. They are heterogeneous due to their different dimensions: as a 'subjective' and time-dependent dimension, the biographical transaction brings into play the aspect of continuity and discontinuity of the individual's socio-professional trajectory and a sense of belonging and commitment. By contrast, the relational aspect of the transaction triggers, as part of an 'objective' dimension, the process of recognition of identity. Through interactivity (negotiation, adjustment and compromise) the outcome of each type of transaction is dependent upon recognition by others. That is, the individual's success in his or her socio-professional trajectory is partly determined by the acknowledgement of others, who base their judgement on how the individual makes use of his or her biographical capacities.

Dubar somehow confirms and further develops Sainsaulieu's four types of occupational identity, but applies a different terminology. According to Dubar, a biographical transaction founded on continuity (within and between generations) allows employees to construct their own vocational trajectories according to a mode of continuous progression. When their claim for progression is recognised within the organisation and under the condition that the relational transaction with the employer is favourable, it is possible to speak of a 'corporate identity' as the principal element of socio-professional identification (similar to Sainsaulieu's 'negotiation identity'). The employees, technicians and executives consider themselves as members of the organisation and can easily adapt to new policies of human resource management. In contrast, without the desired stability or progression in the light of favourable recognition, their identity will become 'categorical' as a socio-professional reference for individuals, who identify with an occupational category at odds with the dominant mode of human resource management. In this case, the biographical and

---

electricity of EDF (Dubar and Engrand, 1986); and the third investigation covering the period from 1986 to 1989 concerned CVT policies and practice within firms that applied innovative modes of labour organisation, training and human resources management (Bel et al., 1988).

relational transactions do not positively coincide and the individuals' occupational identification is blocked (corresponding to Sainsaulieu's declining 'fusion'-based identity).

A biographical transaction based on a succession of intra and inter-generational discontinuities makes some employees construct their vocational trajectories without a referential sense of belonging to a particular occupational specialisation and/or organisation. If they succeed in getting recognition for their qualifications and/or in creating useful professional links, they form a 'network identity' as a means of seeking further socio-professional recognition and promotion (corresponding to Sainsaulieu's 'affinities' identity). By contrast, as the less qualified and/or employees who are lacking professional links experience job instability and a threat of marginalisation and labour market exclusion, they may identify with a socially undervalued non-professional sphere. When the biographical transaction is increasingly becoming structured along discontinuities and reinforced by negative relational transactions, individuals are progressively pushed to internalise an 'identity of exclusion', which Dubar calls an 'outside' work identity. This would correspond to Sainsaulieu's 'retreat' identity.

1.6   A Dynamic Approach Towards Occupational Identity Formation[4]

Any research tackling the issue of occupational identity formation processes needs to be sufficiently dynamic to account for continuities and changes of occupational identities over time. The processes whereby people develop an occupational identity, and learn the skills necessary to perform effectively in that occupation, are complex. The following framework seeks to identify some basic components in order to account for this complexity. It underlies the aspect of skill acquisition as a fundamental basis for any kind of work-related identity formation processes. The main assumption is that certain skills, knowledge and understanding of work processes have to be mastered before someone can be considered skilled.

A dynamic representation of occupational identity formation processes allows for changes to the body of skills, knowledge and understanding to be acquired and also recognises the longitudinal dimension to becoming skilled. In addition, the context-specific competences that

---

[4] This section is based on Brown (1997).

an individual develops over time are acquired in particular social settings. Individuals learn with and from others, and help others learn, and the significance of this means that the process of skill acquisition needs to be placed in a social context. Another presumption regards the individual as an agent in the construction of his or her own particular set of skills and understandings that he or she acquires. That is, each individual may pursue a very different approach by trying to achieve mastery of the different elements that comprise an occupational identity. Additionally, the process of acquiring an occupational identity takes place within particular communities of practice. There may be a broad community of practice at the occupational level, but there will also be more particular communities of practice associated with particular work organisations and education and training institutions in which skills are being developed. Indeed, one influence may be that of a particular workgroup within an institution or company that has very typical ways of working differentiating it from other groups.

From the above assumptions it is possible to delineate what may be required from a comprehensive framework of occupational identity formation in particular work settings. It needs to accommodate:

- A dynamic representation, allowing for change and development over time;
- The social dimension, whereby an individual learns, works and interacts with others;
- The individual as a significant actor in the construction of her or his own occupational identity;
- The existence of general and particular 'communities of practice' associated with particular occupations and organisations, which can operate at a number of levels.

Two aspects are important to keep in mind. First, the sets of activities at work and communities of practice and the identities they support are constantly changing. Second, not all aspects of these activities, practices and identities are passively received by those engaging in them while in the process of becoming skilled; rather individuals also actively engage in shaping them. An understanding of such dynamism is required if a fundamental tension about occupational identity formation processes is to be recognised: that is, there is both continuity and change in how these processes develop over time. The framework is further based upon some fundamental theoretical commitments.

1.6.1   Learning is a Social Process

An individual learns through interaction and communication with others. The process of learning though does not generate a single type of interaction. Rather learning takes place in contexts in which there may be multiple dimensions to the nature of the interactions: there may be a host of working and other relationships that have an influence upon the learning process. Individuals learn from a variety of sources and relationships. Not only are these relationships patterned differently, according to differences between individuals and contexts, but also the sheer variety in what, how and from whom learning occurs is sufficient to ensure that there is not a linear transmission of learning. Changes in the particular constellations and configurations of influence and different patterns of relationships are sufficient to ensure that learning as experienced can differ significantly for different individuals even within similar contexts. Thus learning is a social process, but with differential effects and outcomes on particular individuals.

1.6.2   The Occupational Identity Forms Part of an Individual's Overall Identity

When considering the formation of occupational identities, there are two traps for the unwary. The first is to assume a smooth transition into appropriate skilled work for those who complete their initial training. In some cases work would be found in a completely different area: in such circumstances the extent to which an individual feels he or she 'has' the occupational identity for which he or she has been trained is problematic. The second trap is in thinking that the vocational specialisation in which young people are training or people are working in always has particular significance for them. Particularly a young person may attach far greater importance to developing an identity in a broader sense than to developing a particular occupational commitment. The distinction could be portrayed as the difference between 'making a life' and 'making a living'. When expressed in that way, it can readily be seen that the former is of greater significance, and that the extent to which the latter (occupational) orientation is a central component of the former may vary between individuals and over time. The occupational identity is just one of a number of other, sometimes competing, identities that make up the overall identity of an individual.

The technical possession of the requisite skills, knowledge, under-standing and expertise necessary to be considered skilled is only one component to the development of an identity at work. Empirical research (Bash and Green, 1995) shows that one major distinction between young people becoming skilled is the extent to which they see themselves as active in constructing their own identity, and in how they perceive their developing occupational identity. Some young people rather passively accept their place at work. They see themselves as likely to be doing broadly similar work with their current employer for the foreseeable future. They are not operating with any progressive notion of career, nor do they have any great expectations of work. Their iden-tity at work seems bound up with being an 'ordinary' (rather than a 'special') worker: doing the job steadily, without entertaining thoughts of promotion or changing employers. On the other hand, there are examples of young people who are actively constructing dynamic iden-tities, in which occupational success and making a career are important factors (Stern and Eichorn, 1989; Weis, 1990).

1.6.3   Having a 'Skilled Worker' Status is Dependent upon External Recognition

The above arguments have indicated that becoming skilled is a social process in which a number of others also have a role to play. While acknowledgement of formal status as a skilled worker may come through completion of an apprenticeship or similar status, both the individuals themselves and others, may be wary of conferring the epithet 'fully skilled'. Indeed, somebody can only become an experienced skilled worker when the person and others recognise him or her as such.

The acquisition of experienced or skilled worker status is contested in the sense that it is not clear at what precise point of time an individ-ual reaches this status, because it is dependent upon judgements of a number of people, who may be using different criteria in forming their judgements. One sign of recognition may be that others (for example, clients, peers or trainees) turn to the individual for advice, because they acknowledge that the individual possesses valued skills, knowledge, expertise or experience. Another means of external recognition may come from management through job grading and/or the type of work or responsibilities allocated to the individual. Besides external recognition the individual itself also has to recognise the value of his or her own skills, to have a sense of self worth and a belief of owning significant skills.

How individuals are perceived by other working group members, managers, colleagues, clients and other member of associated professional communities can be very influential in the formation of an occupational identity for that individual. The judgements of others may not necessarily be consistent and, even if they were, people may ascribe different values to particular characteristics. For example, a thorough painstaking approach to work may be appreciated by trainees and clients as 'conscientious', but be seen as irritating by managers for being 'too slow'.

1.6.4   Entering into a Community of Practice is an Important Element of Forming an Occupational Identity

As mentioned above, the recognition of significant achievement and attainment of status is in itself a socially mediated process dependent on the recognition of others and a sense of self-worth. This also implies that learning and skills acquisition is embedded in relational social processes. When individuals develop work-related identities these need to be related to particular socially situated, contextually embedded practice and the work context. It is the community of practice that links the skilling aspect with the work context, the field of expertise and other social processes involved. Thus, a dominant theme in occupational identity formation is entry into a community of practice.

The process of entering a community of practice may be most evident in Germany, where the initial vocational education and training system is driven by the principle of 'Beruf'. Individual organisations, however, can have their own distinctive communities of practice around which they structure their work activities and which influence their attitudes towards training. This is perhaps strongest where a specialist group is set up within a larger organisation, with people from a mix of occupational backgrounds, a different set of work activities and a different pattern of inter-relationships with other work groups. Such groups may consciously define themselves as 'special'.

1.6.5   There Exists Mutual Interdependence between Structure and Agency

There may be a danger that the idea of a community of practice is elevated to a position whereby the individual is seen as 'becoming' a practitioner and learning the practice in a rather passive way. It is not simply a matter of taking on identities and roles, which are pre-existent and pre-structured. Individuals do not just attach themselves to particular communities, they may also take a pro-active role in becoming a full participant or even a change agent actively reshaping the community of practice. As has already been outlined in the previous sections, there is scope for individual agency to act upon the structures and processes in such a way that it does not only affect the respective communities of practice, but also other elements that form part of his or her work identity.

Individuals learn how to engage in the activities at work in the way they do. Company management may have very clear ideas about what they consider to be appropriate ways for their skilled workers to engage with their work, but individuals may react very differently to such expectations. Their behaviours and attitudes may range from complete rejection to complete engagement leading to very different types of work identity. However, the reaction of others can also have direct or indirect effects on perceptions that the individual and/or others have on that engagement and developing identity. This is perhaps most marked when the work activities themselves are changing rapidly. A battle between 'old' and 'new' ways of working, and ways of engaging with work, is common at all times, but is given greater impetus when there is major organisational and/or technological change in a workplace as has been the case in telecommunications during the past ten years, for example. This 'battle' may be given added spice, if the proponents of the different views represent an 'old guard' and a 'new wave', trained in different ways and with differing sets of skills and attitudes.

From the above it is clear that there exist a number of key tensions in any attempted explanation of occupational identity formation processes. First, there are always, sometimes conflicting, elements of continuity and change over time in the processes whereby occupational identities are formed. The formation, maintenance and change of an occupational identity are always influenced by the nature of the relationships around which they are constructed. Second, the individual is a significant actor in the construction of her or his own occupational identity, but the process is not wholly subjective. It is rather conditional upon external recognition and acknowledgement. Third, individuals and their interactions with others are constrained by the structures and processes of the work context and the respective communities of practice in which they take place. Over time these interactions may lead to modifications and reshaping of these same structures and the communities of practice. Fourth, occupational identities vary in the intensity with which they are held, and in the significance individuals ascribe to them. They may or may not be of great significance to an individual. On the other hand, the broader process of identity formation in the sense of 'making a life' is fundamental to all individuals.

These ideas can be linked to those of Lave (1991), whose general ideas are that changing knowledgeable skills are subsumed in the process of changing identity in and through membership of a community of practice and situated social practice emphasising interdependency of agent and world. She also points out that activity, meaning, cognition, learning and knowing are underpinned by inherent processes of social negotiation of meaning within a socially and culturally structured world. And finally, newcomers become old-timers as they develop a changing understanding of 'practice' through participation in an ongoing community of practice.

1.7 Concluding Remarks

Identity is not merely a complex notion but it is also a *synthetic concept*. As Cohen puts it, an individual's identity is 'a basket of selves which come to the surface at different social moments as appropriate' (Cohen, 1994, p. 11). The declaration of identities varies in different contexts and a person may identify herself or himself in a more general or a more specific way in any given environment. For example, the self-definition of a person's occupation may correspond to the most detailed level of specialisation in the work context or within a community of practice, but it may be very general in a non-work-related environment. This deviation does not mean that any of these identities are false or true. It only shows that identities are flexible and that there is not only one truthful identity. Any self-definition or kind of identification may be perfectly valid at any given moment. What is important to acknowledge is that identities are not static, but they are fluid, conditional and subjectively modifiable.

In this process the individual assumes a crucial role in actively shaping their work identity. While we recognise that individuals become agents of society that actively reflect upon external conditions (Giddens, 1991), we also acknowledge the close interdependence between sociality and individuality. This is also true for the work context: work shapes the individual, but at the same time the individual shapes work processes and structures. The self is not an autonomous agent, but it is socially and culturally constructed and certain elements of a person's identity will always be collectively imposed. However, the individual possesses the ability of a conscious, purposeful act, of a choice of roles and performances even under a situation of constraints (Cohen, 1994). Increasing flexibility of work processes and structures create new opportunities for the individual to become a change agent in the work context. Concurrently, other factors such as an individual's socio-economic background, the length and quality of formal education and/or on-the-job training or the socio-political context and the extent to which it makes occupational identities instrumental are structural variables that also have an influence upon how work identities are shaped.

Today, technological shifts and the tertiarisation of the economy, among other aspects, result in challenging labour market demands that are geared towards tacit skills, transversality, competition and a flexible work organisation. These developments do not only play a formative role at the macro-level, they also set a new framework for individuals to actively engage in shaping their work-skills profiles and linking them to their work-related identities. While newly emerging occupations typically involve new skills and/or new arrays of mixes of older and newer skills profiles, they often appear to play a generalist role and function in identity formation processes (see Finegold and Matousek, Chapter 14). This hybridisation character of modern work makes the development and reformulation of work identities particularly challenging.

While work remains a formative element of the overall identity of an individual, it has become being just one option among others. Still, being able to master a particular occupational specialisation plays a strong role in developing a social identity. Skilled work is regarded here as a medium for personal realisation of meaning and interpretation of existence and the implementation of biographic intentions and interests. The profession not only proves to be a normative horizon for one's entire life, but also at the same time represents one of the key links for conveying social relations. Thus, to be able to work in a chosen vocation occupies a special position between 'social structure' and action in the 'private sphere'. It remains important in social life as a defined passage for social and economic participation and can be regarded as a major source of the feeling of one's own value or one's view of oneself, and the means through which someone presents herself or himself to the outside world (Goffman, 1969). To a great extent the notion of skilled work continues to define work satisfaction, social and economic participation, social status, inequality and lifestyle. It co-shapes the socio-cultural personality and is an 'identity-supporting' socialisation factor that should not be underestimated.

References

Armstrong, J.A. (1982). *Nations before nationalism*. Chapel Hill: University of North Carolina Press.

Bash, L. and A. Green (1995). *World Yearbook of Education 1995: Youth, education and work*. London and Philadelphia: Kogan Page.

Beck, U. (1986). *Risikogesellschaft: Auf dem Weg in eine andere Moderne*. Frankfurt/M.: Suhrkamp.

Bel, M., C. Dubar. and P. Méhaut (1988). Les innovations en matière de formation. *Actualité de la Formation Permanente* 96(9–10), 74–79.

Berger, P.L., B. Berger and H. Kellner (1975). *Das Unbehagen in der Modernität*. Frankfurt/M. and New York: Campus.

Berger, S. and M.J. Piore (1980). *Dualism and discontinuity in industrial societies*. Cambridge: Cambridge University Press.

Bernstein, B. (1975). *Class, codes and control*. London, Kegan Paul: Routledge.

Brown, A. (1997). A dynamic model of occupational identity formation. In A. Brown (Ed.), *Promoting vocational education and training: European perspectives* (pp. 59–67). Tampere: University of Tampere Press.

Carruthers, B.G. and B. Uzzi (2000). Economic sociology in the new millenium. *Contemporary Sociology*, 29(3), 486–494.

Cohen, A.P. (1994). *Self consciousness: An alternative anthropology of identity*. London: Routledge.

Deißinger, T. (1996). Modularisierung der Berufsbildung—Eine didaktisch-curriculare Alternative zum 'Berufsprinzip'? In K. Beck, W. Müller, T. Deißinger and M. Zimmermann (Eds.), *Berufserziehung im Umbruch. Didaktische Herausforderungen und Ansätze zu ihrer Bewältigung* (pp. 189–202). Weinheim: Deutscher Studien Verlag.

Dif, M.H. (1998). Flexibilité du travail et ses implications pour l'emploi: réflexions sur les modèles émergents. *Economies et Sociétés, Economie du travail, Numéro 20, Série A.B.*, 231–246.

Doeringer, P.B. and M.J. Piore (1971). *Internal labor markets and manpower analysis*. Lexington, MA: Heath Lexington Books.

Dubar, C. (1991). *La socialisation: construction des identités sociales et profession- nelles*. Paris: Armand Colin.

Dubar, C. (1994). Le sens du travail: Les quatre formes d'appartenance professionnelle. *Sciences Humaines* 37(3), 22–25.

Dubar, C. and S. Engrand (1986). La formation en entreprise comme processus de socialisation professionnelle (LA): l'example de la production nucléaire à EDF. *Formation Emploi*, 12(16), 37–47.

Dubar, C. and P. Tripier (1998). *Sociologie des professions*. Paris: Armand Colin.

Dubar, C., E. Dubar, M. Feutrie, N. Gadrey, J. Hedaux and E. Verschave (1987). *L'autre jeunesse: des jeunes sans diplôme dans un dispositif de socialisation*. Lille: Presses Universitaires de Lille.

Erikson, E.H. (1970). *Jugend und Krise. Die Psychodynamik im sozialen Wandel*. Stuttgart: Klett Cotta.

Erikson, E.H. (1973). *Identität und Lebenszyklus*. Frankfurt/M.: Suhrkamp.

Francfort, I., F. Osty, R. Sainsaulieu and M. Uhalde (1995). *Les mondes sociaux de l'entreprise*. Paris: Desclée de Brouwer.

Frangoudakis, A. (1978). *Demotic School Reading Books: Ideological compulsion and pedagogical violance.* Athens: Themelio.

Gellner, E. (1992). *Reason and culture: The historic role of rationality and rationalism.* Oxford: Blackwell.

Giddens, A. (1984). *The constitution of society: outline of the theory of structuration.* Berkeley, CA: University of California Press.

Giddens, A. (1991). *Modernity and self-identity: self and society in the late modern age.* Stanford, CA: Stanford University Press.

Ginzberg, E. (1968). *Manpower strategy for the metropolis.* New York and London: Columbia University Press.

Ginzberg, E., S.W. Ginsburg, S. Axelrad and J.L. Herma (1951). *Occupational choice: An approach to a General Theory.* New York: Columbia University Press.

Goffman, E. (1969). *Wir alle spielen Theater. Die Selbstdarstellung im Alltag.* München: Piper.

Greinert, W.-D. (1997). *Das duale System der Berufsausbildung in der Bundesrepublik Deutschland.* Stuttgart: Holland + Josenhans.

Habermas, J. (1976). *Zur Rekonstruktion des historischen Materialismus.* Frankfurt/M.: Suhrkamp.

Heinz, W.R. (1995). *Arbeit, Beruf und Lebenslauf: Eine Einführung in die berufliche Sozialisation.* Weinheim: Juventa.

Hobsbawm, E.J. (1992). *The invention of tradition.* Cambridge: Cambridge University Press.

Huber, J. and E.E. Krainz (1987). Identität. In S. Grubitzsch and G. Rexilius (Eds.), *Psychologische Grundbegriffe. Mensch und Gesellschaft in der Psychologie. Ein Handbuch* (pp. 474–478). Reinbek bei Hamburg: Rowohlt.

Jaeger, C. (1989). Die kulturelle Einbettung des europäischen Marktes. In M. Haller, H.-J. Hoffmann-Nowotny and W. Zapf (Eds.), *Kultur und Gesellschaft. Verhandlungen des 24. Deutschen Soziologentags, des 11. Österreichischen Soziologentags und des 8. Kongresses der Schweizerischen Gesellschaft für Soziologie in Zürich 1988* (pp. 556–574). Frankfurt/M. and New York: Campus.

Jenkins, R. (1996). *Social identity.* London: Routledge.

Kern, H. and C.F. Sabel (1994). Verblaßte Tugenden: Zur Krise des deutschen Produktionsmodells. In W.v. Treeck (Ed.), *Umbrüche gesellschaftlicher Arbeit* (pp. 605–624). Göttingen: Schwartz.

Keupp, H., T. Ahbe, W. Gmür, R. Höfer, B. Mitzscherlich, W. Kraus and F. Straus (1999). *Identitätskonstruktionen. Das Patchwork der Identitäten in der Spätmoderne.* Reinbek: Rowohlt.

Kirpal, S. (2004). Researching Work Identities in a European Context. *Career Development International, 9*(3), 199–221.

Koniordos, S.M. (2001). *Towards a sociology of Artisans: Continuities and discontinuities in comparative perspective.* Aldershot: Ashgate.

Lave, J. (1991). Situated learning in communities of practice. In S. Behrend (Ed.), *Perspectives on socially shared cognition.* Washington DC: American Psychological Association.

Leithäuser, T. and B. Volmerg (1988). *Psychoanalyse in der Sozialforschung. Eine Einführung am Beispiel einer Sozialpsychologie der Arbeit* (Vol. 148). Opladen: Westdeutscher Verlag.

Mayer, Karl Ulrich and Tuma, Nancy Brandon (Eds.) (1987). Applications of event history analysis in life course research. Berlin: Max-Planck-Institut für Bildungsforschung (Series: Materialien aus der Bildungsforschung No. 30)

Mead, G.H. (1937). *Mind, self, and society.* Chicago: University of Chicago Press.

Palán, Z. (1997). Výkladový slovník vzdělávání dospelých: DAHA.

Piaget, J. and B. Inhelder (1973). *Die Psychologie des Kindes* (2nd ed.). Olten *et al.*: Walter.

Piore, M.J. (1975). Notes for a theory of Labour Market Stratification. In R. Edwards and M. Reich and D.M. Gordon (Eds.), *Labour market segmentation.* Lexington, MA: D.C. Health & Co.

Piore, M.J. and C.F. Sabel (1984). *The second industrial divide: Possibilities for prosperity.* New York: Basic Books, Inc.

Saarniit, J. (1997). Mitte-eesti noorte väärtusteadvuse spetsiifikast. Vene noored Eestis: sotsioloogiline mosaiik. *Avita*, 69–82.

Sainsaulieu, R. (1977). *L'identité au travail.* Paris: Presse de la Fondation Nationale des Sciences Politiques.

Sainsaulieu, R. (1985). *L'identité au travail* (2nd ed.). Paris: Presse de la Fondation Nationale des Sciences Politiques.

Sainsaulieu, R. (1996). *L'identité au travail* (3rd ed.). Paris: Presse de la Fondation Nationale des Sciences Politiques.

Sainsaulieu, R. (1997). *Sociologie de l'entreprise: organisation, culture et développement* (2nd ed.). Paris: Presses de Sciences Politique et Dalloz.

Sarup, M. (1996). *Identity, culture and the postmodern world.* Edinburgh: Edinburgh University Press.

Sennett, R. (1998). *The corrosion of character: the personal consequences of work in the new capitalism* (1st ed.). New York: Norton.

Silbereisen, R.K. (1997). Das veränderungsoffene und grenzenbewusste Ich—seine Entwicklung über die Lebensspanne. In E.U. Weizsäcker (Ed.), *Grenzen-los? Jedes System braucht Grenzen—aber wie durchlässig müssen diese sein?* (pp.180–198). Berlin, Basel, Boston: Birkhäuser.

Stenström, M.-L. and J. Lasonen (2000). *Strategies for Reforming initial vocational education and training in Europe.* Jyväskylä: Institute for Educational Research, University of Jyväskylä.

Stern, D. and D. Eichorn (1989). *Adolescence and work. Influences of social structure, labour markets, and culture.* Hillsdale, NJ: Lawrence Erlbaum.

Tajfel, H. (1981). The achievement of group differentiation. In H. Tajfel (Ed.), *Human groups and social categories* (pp. 268–287). Cambridge: Cambridge University Press.

Titma, M. (1972). *Professionaalne orientatsioon kõrgemat haridust nõudvatele kutsetele.* Tartu: TRÜ Kommunistliku kasvatuse laboratoorium.

Watson, T.J. (2001). *Sociology, work and industry.* London, New York: Routledge.

Weis, L. (1990). *Working class without work: High school students in a de-industrializing economy.* London, New York: Routledge.

Willis, P.E. (1977). *Learning to Labour: How working class kids get working class jobs.* Aldershot: Gower.

Witzel, A., V. Helling and I. Mönnich (1996). Die Statuspassage in den Beruf als Prozess der Reproduktion sozialer Ungleichheit. In A. Bolder, W.R. Heinz and K. Rodax (Eds.), *Die Wiederentdeckung der Ungleichheit. Tendenzen in Bildung für Arbeit* (pp. 170–187). Opladen: Leske+Budrich.

2

Tensions in the Vocational Identity of Danish Bankers

Morten Smistrup
Roskilde University, Denmark

2.1 The Trade of Banking

Economic (Baldvinsson et al., 2000) as well as sociological literature (Swedberg, 1987) share the basic understanding that the role of banks is to be propagators of saving funds for the purpose of investment. At the same time banks assume the risk that is related to the issuing of credit as well as to handling major parts of the payments in society. But the role and nature of the work in banks and the vocational self-understanding—vocational identity—of bankers has changed. The vocation of the banker has during the last couple of decades been subject to fundamental transformations due to deregulation, new technologies and an increasing level of globalisation. These changes have transformed the professional role of the banker from that of the teller to that of the counsellor—or even the seller (Regini et al., 1999).

The traditional role of banking might be described from three different perspectives (Swedberg, 1987). First, in a functional perspective, banks can be seen as institutions either for centralising societal capital in the form of savings or as propagators of capital in the form of loans or as both (i.e. Marx, Weber and Sombart). Second, from a perspective focusing on the role of banks in the social economy, banking is considered according to the nature of the relation to the customer—who is financing whom and for what purpose (i.e. Parsons and Smelser). Third, from a power perspective, a judgement is made of the extent of the influence of the financial institutions and how this is realised (i.e. critical sociology).

A. Brown, S. Kirpal and F. Rauner (eds.), Identities at Work, 45–68.

These different perspectives highlight different functions of banks as financial institutions, which are still valid even though some of those functions have developed and been differentiated over time. Historically, these different perspectives also highlight a number of problems banks typically face, some of which are constitutive for the nature of banks as institutions and the collective identities they generate. These problems address:

- The importance to demonstrate high levels of trustworthiness and reliability by which banks aim at minimising the risk of a so-called 'rush' where people in panic withdraw their money from the bank causing major crisis or even bankruptcy.
- To signal distance from the 'loan shark' and the historically and religiously founded disrespect for money lending and instead convey that banking is a respectable trade.
- To avoid being linked to any form of fraud or illegal transactions (even though banks are very often drawn into such) and assure that 'your economic secrets are well protected by us'.
- To neutralise the fear of some politicians and groups in the population that banks or financial capital could exercise too large an influence in society.

Even though national legislation as well as bank procedures themselves have made extensive efforts to reduce these problems they are still constitutive of the culture of banks and need to be considered in order to understand the banking environment and the physical arrangements in banks as well as the appearance of the individual banker.

Banking, as well as a number of other industries, has changed dramatically during the last decades due to fierce modernisation processes (Regini et al., 1999; Finansrådet, 2001). These changes are related to new technologies; deregulation of money markets and sharpened competition; and an increasing degree of globalisation.

New technologies have changed the forms of economic exchange in society as a whole: all salary and social welfare transfers are performed electronically as transactions from one bank account to another. The same goes for private savings in the form of retirement funds, etc. A major part of the day-to-day payments of households are made using credit cards, and a lot of operations traditionally conducted by bankers are increasingly executed through home-banking systems. This means that the banks do not have to actively motivate people to entrust their working capital by placing their savings into a bank account. While forty years ago the household economy for a large part of the population was based on cash (and maybe some minor savings), today nearly all household transactions involve banks. This means that almost everybody— from the unskilled worker to the manager—is interacting on a daily basis with banks and bankers must be able to interact with people from all social groups. Within the bank technological developments have brought about two major changes: first, the tasks related to the safe handling of cash have diminished and the importance of jobs related to this has decreased, and, second, a considerable number of administrative routines have vanished.

The deregulation of the monetary market has opened the way for broader competition between banks and made room for new actors on the financial market. This has lead to the creation of so-called 'financial supermarkets', whereby banks engage in providing a number of new products and services. For the individual banker this means that she[1] has to deal with new and changing products and that his or her role is changing in direction of that of the seller. The customer, on the other hand, is developing a growing consciousness about the importance of checking the different bank offers, and as such customers have gained a much greater market power while the authority of the banker has decreased.

In summary, the situation of the banking sector has been undergoing change in that the societal role of banks has changed from servicing the privileged to serving the public in general; the traditional status and authority of the banker has been shattered; and competition has sharpened with an increasing orientation towards selling products and services. However, despite modernisation processes having changed many aspects of banking, banks as institutions are still functionally based upon the gathering of free capital and redistributing this in the form of loans. But this takes place in new ways that have caused great changes in the work profile and the role of the individual banker.

2.2　The Research Project

In conveying the image of trustfulness and reliability, a precondition for the smooth functioning of banks, the financial sector relies on high levels of employees' identification with the values of banking. As such

---

[1] Since 60 per cent of bank employees are women I use 'she' when nothing else seems obvious.

a positive vocational identity is recognised in the sector as an important qualification for an individual banker, even though significant changes within the sector have changed the conditions for the formation of this identity. The duality between the importance of vocational identity and the fundamental changes of the conditions for forming identification with the banking profession was the background for developing my research question which was to examine the relationship between vocational identity and qualification demands in the late 20th century in the Danish banking sector.

Before entering into more detail on the above discussion I will outline the research project I am referring to in this chapter. The project was a single case study (Yin, 1994) of bankers but with the ambition to say something in general about what might be termed 'commercial service work', i.e. areas of work where a trusting, even empathic, relationship to the client/customer is realised for commercial purposes. Most of the empirical material was collected in the spring and summer of 2001.

On the meta-theoretical level the project was positioned within critical realism (Bhaskar, 1989). An important assumption in this position is that even though the social world is a product of human action and interaction and is socially constructed, it meets the individual as a reality. In this sense the individual does not produce these social structures, but it is through social practices that this social world is reproduced and transformed. Hence, it is the discourses and narrative constructions of meaning that largely determine the conditions for this reproduction and transformation. In a meta-theoretical perspective it means that I take on an ontological stance and not merely an epistemological one. As a consequence of this meta-theoretical perspective the project studied structural aspects of the social life in banks as well as how individual bankers on the subjective level produce meaning in an interaction with these social structures.

In the project several forms of data were collected. This included a thorough study of theories of identity especially in relation to work and, based on this, a survey was conducted of 1200 Danish bankers all working in customer related functions (line functions). This means that experts who were working as specialists in staff functions were excluded from the population. All the individuals in the population were members of the trades union for bankers, but since more than 90 per cent of those in customer related functions (including middle managers) are members of this organisation it was considered not to bias the material. The quantitative material was analysed and used in a traditional descriptive way.

Additionally, I conducted 15 thematic, narrative interviews of between 2 and 3 hours. The opening question was: 'Tell me everything from your life that you find important to understand the banker you are today'. Before putting this question forward I assured them that I considered them experts of their own lives and conditions of work and as such wanted them to narrate as freely as possible and that I would wait before asking more specific questions until late in the interview (this worked well with the female bankers, while the male bankers typically needed supporting questions after a rather brief presentation of their formal career). The interviews were analysed first from the perspective of individual life histories (Mishler, 1986; Alheit, 1994) and second with a focus on categories developed on the basis of the individual life histories methodologically inspired by grounded theory (Strauss and Corbin, 1990).

The two categories of empirical material, qualitative and quantitative, were only partly brought together. To a large extent they were presented as parallel approaches since the objective was not to follow a 'methodological triangulation', but rather that the different types of data should reveal different sides of reality and as such they could possibly tell different stories. This resulted in a multi-faceted and rich empirical description of the vocation of the banker that has generated broad interest as well as discussion.

2.3   A Sense of Vocation

The purpose of this chapter is to place the ideas of vocation and vocational identity as central concepts in the discussion about how to qualify the labour force to match the demands of late modern production. Given the limitations of space I will refrain from an extended discussion about the nature of the future labour market but just underline that the necessity of high level vocational skills based on a broad knowledge base, the competences to facilitate employees' flexibility and abilities for lifelong learning are central in the discourse about what is expected from the labour force in future.

Since the discussions in this chapter connect the concept of vocation to societal production as well as individual identity formation, it is necessary to clarify the basis of this notion. Briefly one might say that the concept of 'vocation' implies a *continuation*, a *specification* and a *demarcation*. Vocations are continuously developed over time through a historical and cultural process during which the division of labour is institutionalised in the form of physical and social structures. But vocations do not just develop. Being closely related to and founded on the social division of labour vocations designate specific, separated areas of work where specific things are done in ways that demand particular skills. And finally, a vocation creates demarcations within the labour force and as such constitutes an in-group and an out-group. This demarcation is based on internal coherence through the development of shared meanings and practices and a consciousness about how those meanings and practices differ from other vocations. This idea of the nature of the vocation can be illustrated through the following model (Figure 2.1).

The model suggests the need to understand vocations along three dimensions. First, vocations are the result of a historical and cultural process of social construction and institutionalisation. This means that they must be understood on the basis of their relation to the societal production process and the way this is organised as a result of tradition and the historical division of labour (Laske, 2001; Sigurjonsson, 2002) and the ways these are reified through processes of structuration and institutionalisation (Giddens, 1984; Berger and Luckman, 1966/1999).

Second, vocations are established as individuals perform work-based activities and 'do' specific things, i.e. concrete work tasks that respond to social needs. This is not to be understood in an abstract, decontextualised sense but is embedded in specific social structures, concrete physical surroundings, social relations and structures of power. The concrete work that members of the respective vocational community do plays

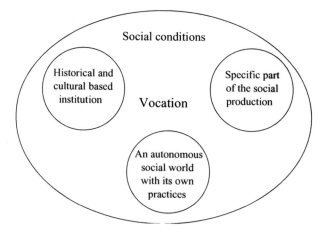

Figure 2.1   A diagrammatic representation of vocation

a formative role in relation to the vocation. This, however, is inseparable from and in a tensional relation to work in its abstract function as creation of value. As such the vocation inherits the contradictions that emerge form this. On the one hand, vocations give individuals the possibility of self-realisation that is a potential in most work (Dewey, 1963; Kerschensteiner, 1980), but on the other hand, the latent contradictions inherent in capitalist production create certain ambivalence (Becker-Schmidt, 1982; Weber, 2002; Salling Olesen, 2000).

Third, vocations establish demarcations between and internal coherence within different areas of working life. The vocation functions as a basis of social belonging and exclusion since it constitutes an exclusive, socially autonomous world that enables its members to distinguish themselves from other vocational groups and establish common understandings of the nature and meaning of what they themselves are doing. As such they are able to identify who is 'in' and who is 'out' (Turner, 1999; Wenger, 1998; Bourdieu, 1994, 1997). Those collective understandings or shared meanings that constitute this exclusive world can also solidly be found in the historical and cultural roots of banking. As they are perceived and integrated as part of the vocational self-understanding of the individual banker they function as a formative element in the daily work and constitute the basis that makes it possible for the individual employee to personify the confidentiality and trustworthiness that banks aspire to represent.

These three outlined aspects describe a vocation as a reality that is socially constructed, but meets the individual as a social reality that appears as a *collectively organising perspective*. When the individual assumes this perspective, certain practices, categories of meaning and normative expectations become apparent. To be accepted as a competent expert within the vocational field the individual needs to integrate this perspective in her expectations of herself in relation to work. This might, for instance, be those demands the employee in a bank meets that are generated from the societal function of banking as well as from the historical development of the profession. This also has to do with the ability to assume the role of the banker and as such meet the expectations of how to perform on different 'stages' (Goffman, 1992): interacting with colleagues, customers etc. This provides members of the profession as well as outsiders (especially customers) with the possibility to recognise a person as 'a banker', but it also places pre-established expectations from the same groups on the employee to perform and make judgements according to these role expectations. This is something the newcomer can only acquire through practical experience and which through a more or less troublesome process has to be integrated in relation to the dispositions and biographical experiences of the individual. This is a significant precondition to be able to comply with the expected performance in a competent way, but while understanding and learning to act according to the (semi-)formulated expectations, something implicit is also learned: the individual learns to take on the vocational identity of a banker.

2.4   How Bankers Describe Themselves

The above line of reasoning leads to a focus on the individual and shared ideas about *what you must be able to do, what you are expected to 'be'* and *what you are expected to do* in order to be recognised as a banker. While getting to the heart of these three aspects, the individual is learning and developing the self-image of a professional banker, which is established through participating in the dynamic relations of everyday life in the bank. These learning processes are closely related to the collective self-image of the members of the vocation. Empirically, there exists a remarkable coherence between the demands for integrative adaptation to the collective norms and standards in the bank and the experience of the individual bank employee, who experiences the bank as a suitable frame for individual self-actualisation. As such the 'meeting' between the two organising perspectives is fairly unproblematic. From my investigations, the following elements seem to signify the shared understanding among the bank professionals of what the vocation of the banker is from a collective organising perspective:

- As a banker you must be able to win the trust of the customer and possess the ability to establish a general view of the customer's problems and needs and be able to suggest professional solutions to these problems based on the products of the bank in a way that benefits both parties in the long run.
- In the interaction with the customer the banker must preserve a personal distance to the customer in such a way that what takes place remains within certain themes and follows the respective rules. These relations form part of the reproduction of the symbolic space of the bank. While doing so, the banker must be able to handle the existing demands for control and external regulation

and, despite this, nurture the intimacy that is necessary for the banker to assume the role of an adviser.

- The banker must be familiar with and live up to the role expectations typical for banking, including the maintenance of a personal front characterised by a subdued 'professional' appearance without expressive signs of individuality and visible expressions of needs and emotions. This means that at all times the banker must stay in control in any kind of situation since this is strongly related to the prevailing view of what expresses trustworthiness and reliability.

- Through participating in the general basic education shared by practically everybody in customer-related functions, the new banker acquires the ability to master what is accepted as the necessary knowledge and gets acquainted with the products and procedures. This is a central element in developing the professional ability to thematise and formulate problems in a way that is expected from a banker and becomes part of the social construction of meaning within the group.

- The new banker has to learn the norms and values that are functioning as the prescriptive and regulative basis for everyday behaviour in the bank and, not least, is the basis of the expectation to demonstrate loyalty that reaches far beyond the regular working hours.

Learning the collective perspective is a complex process even though typically perceived as a very natural one. The experiences developed while practising the vocation have to be integrated into the individual's self-image and related to her habitual resources as well as her biographical experience. As such the vocation also functions as a possibility to maintain and reproduce the individual self. This self must possess the ability to contain the meaningful as well as the contradictory side of the work in the bank. The habitual resources and the biographical experiences represent continuity and coherence in the sense that to the individual they are the basis for establishing a reasonably stable self-concept in relation to the surrounding world. But this is also related to change since the individual continuously integrates new experiences that demand transformation of this self-concept. This is elevating the importance of the vocation from being just a functional, societal institution to also becoming a subjectively enriching category. The empirical studies revealed that the following elements of the work of the banker contribute to enhancing personal satisfaction:

- The work enables bankers to satisfy the need to meet people and help them solve problems that are important in their lives. This enables them to experience that they are doing something of social importance and that can be significant in people's lives while at the same time they contribute to the success of the bank.
- The work creates the possibility for the banker to experience her personal and experiential knowledge gathered through her total life span and in life contexts different from work. At the same time the individual experiences that her needs and dispositions in work and personal life are not fundamentally inconsistent. As such most bankers experience a considerable level of coherence in their lives.
- The individual experiences that it is possible to realise her personal inclinations and dispositions within the limitations that are established by the socially expected personal front. She experiences that she can with very few problems adapt to the expected behaviour and identify the possible span of deviation from it to create some space for individuality and self-actualisation.
- In a rule-based work situation dominated by control and reporting systems the bankers establish the counselling situation as an area where they can exercise control. Within this space they have the sense of creating a trusting relationship with the customer and experience this as two-sided.
- The individual has the possibility to cover her social needs and enjoy the recognition from colleagues on the back-stage, as a relief from the privatised space for counselling that is dominant on the front stage, and that offers personal reinforcement.

The bankers experience that the bank fulfils their expectations in a way that can be the basis for a significant identification and as such they experience a high level of authenticity in their work, internally as well as externally. This establishes a relationship where the demands placed by the vocation upon the individual and the personally satisfactory sides of work coexist in a stable but fragile balance.[2] This balance

---

[2] This might be the result of a certain over-determination in the material caused by the construction of the research approach but despite this I consider the conclusions to be valid.

is only maintained through a constant effort to control the latent contradictions inherent in this situation. It also appears that this balance reaches further than just the narrow area of exchange between labour and the individual. It contains a personal attitude towards work, norms and expectations as to how tasks are completed and an understanding of one's own social role and position. These are important elements in the formation of a vocational identity.

2.5   Understanding Vocational Identity

Theoretically there is widespread agreement that identity describes learned ways of handling experiences of difference and concordance between the individual and the social surroundings (Hetherington, 1998). As such the understanding of vocational identity can neither be separated from the specific vocation that represents the source of identification nor from the individual, who experiences difference and concordance. This implies that all the aspects that constitute the vocation also contribute to the formation of a vocational identity. Learning a trade in all its dimensions cannot be reduced to training and skills development, because it also involves individuals identifying such differences and concordances and dealing with these while developing a vocational identity. If the acquisition of the relevant knowledge base and work practices are separated from developing a matching identity the individual will never reach a level of 'genuine understanding' (Gardner, 1993) or 'intuitive expertise' (Dreyfus and Dreyfus, 1991) that characterise the full member of a community of practice.

When a young apprentice or trainee enters the bank she meets the vocation as a pre-structured world constituted by established norms, institutions and shared meanings to which she has to adapt in order to be accepted as a legitimate participant (Lave and Wenger, 1991; Nielsen and Kvale, 1999; Wenger, 1998). This is a normative requirement for integration, which is executed more or less rigidly. As one banker states: 'we are all kinds of people (. . .) but, of course, (. . .) if someone is too provocative (. . .) and will not accept what it takes, then I am afraid she will not "survive" very long'. Others describe how newcomers are politely but firmly corrected when they deviate from the norms. The other side of this rigid integration is that the vocation functions as a field for self-realisation where the young person may enact and realise her individuality. Several young bank employees described, when talking about their work experiences, how they have the possibility to develop sides of themselves that they appreciate and that they are able to find ways to express their individuality. When the employees related to stories about how they as individuals evoked change in local practices, the sentence 'you must realise that I am not a typical banker' appeared frequently in the interviews. This statement relates to the fact that the recruitment of new trainees is based on trying to identify candidates who will fit smoothly into the organisation. Hence, we find a tendency towards a great uniformity in education, values and social background among those recruits, which is supported by quantitative (Smistrup, 2002) as well as qualitative data (Smistrup, 2003). In the ways described here the process whereby a newcomer is allowed participation and membership is a reproduction process (where she internalises the norms and expectations) as well as a transformation process (were she is seeking to establish space for her individuality within this), a process whereby the successful outcome is largely based on the existence of suitable habitual preconditions (Bourdieu, 1994).

An essential aspect of learning a trade is to learn what you are expected 'to do' in order to be recognised as a skilled employee or expert in the vocational field. This implies a shift in focus from the actualisation of an individual self and the significance of the individual to a collective understanding of what the individual is expected *to be*, is able *to do* and *how her actual practice is recognised by others*. This shift is a prerequisite to recognise herself as a banker. Identity is a concept that is highly suitable to conceptualise encounters between individuality and context since it is the result of a learning process that evolves in the space of tension between social norms and individual needs. Vocational identities are developed as a result of the learning processes that unfold in the borderland between 'the collective' and 'the subjective' while the trainees participate in, conduct and reflect upon the work practice and their work experiences. This is fundamentally based on conceptualising identity as relational and a learning process which takes place in the interaction between a structured social word that pre-exists the individual and faces her as a reality and a subjective world that has been structured by the totality of her biographical experiences and life conditions (Alheit, 1994; Dausien, 1998).

Developing an identity is characterised by continuity as well as change (Dewey, 1963). The source of change through learning is the social and material interaction (in its widest sense) under specific contextual circumstances (Mead, 1934; Goffman, 1992; Wenger, 1998), but the results of learning, and as such its significance beyond the specific context, is dependent upon the continuity of biographical experience

(Salling Olesen, 2000; Alheit and Bergamini, 1995; Dausien, 1998). When the trainee acquires the knowledge base and understands the work procedures, and integrates those into her existing knowledge base and former experiences, her conception of self as well as of the social world develops. When she at the same time learns the social practices of the vocation—how to act and interact in accordance to role expectations— and integrates these learning experiences as part of her orientation towards herself and the social surroundings, her self-concept and her concepts of the surrounding world are enriched. By learning a trade at a proficient or advanced level she also develops a vocational identity in the sense that the integration of the vocational context into her biographical experiences necessarily includes identifying differences and concordances, and this also involves learning processes in relation to how to deal with these. This is essential to the formation of identity in relation to the vocation and the work context. At the same time the trainee continuously enriches her personal experiences and integrates these into her vocational practices and in this way she contributes to the development of the collective self-understanding of bankers on the micro level.

There exists an intrinsic connection between *being good* at practising a vocation and having developed a *coherent vocational identity*. In saying so it is important to state that this does not imply the assumption of a static, well-defined, stable identity of 'the banker'. The weakness of most models of vocational identity is that they emphasise certain dominant norms characterising the vocational specialisation and certain elements of a common self-understanding established among the members of the respective community of practice. However, what those models fail to describe is the processes through which people become proficient in their vocation and how this is related to developing a particular vocational identity and the way this identity is reproduced and transformed (Brown, 1999).

Studying vocational identity inspired me to think about this type of identity as emerging from the interaction of two fundamentally different perspectives: the vocation as a collectively organizing perspective (Berger and Luckman, 1966/99; Bhaskar, 1989) and the self as a subjectively organising perspective (Stern, 1989). As outlined in the previous section of this chapter, as a collectively organising perspective the vocation describes a specific part of societal labour in relation to which specific social structures and institutionalisation processes develop. Within these a semi-autonomous social world emerges with its own vocational practices. The self might be understood as the specific mental structuring of the individual based on biological dispositions as well as biographical experiences. In my study, I conceptualised the self as a subjective structuring perspective founded on a combination of linguistic, narrative and non-verbal, bodily-embedded social and interpersonal experiences that the individual makes through interacting with her surroundings and which, simultaneously, is the basis of the individual's orientations towards herself and these social surroundings.

While working and, through vocational practice, developing her individual experiences and self-understanding, the individual contributes to the reproduction and transformation of the structural organisation as well as the shared understanding of the members of the respective community of practice. But while transforming and reproducing the vocational practices and its shared meanings the individual also reproduces and transforms her own self since this also involves the social experiences the person has gained through this process. Only analytically can the individual be separated from the collective processes of transformation and reproduction. The individual is not able relate to and act in this social context without understanding its structures and having internalised certain role expectations. But one can also ask whether these integration processes are the result of acting within these contexts. This, however, is not a conscious and rational process. It is, on the one side, affected by unknown or unrecognised conditions and effects in the social context (Giddens, 1984; Bhaskar, 1989) and, on the other, the self is characterised by narrative as well as embodied, non-verbal experiences (Stern, 2000). A psychosocial approach underlines this as well (Salling Olesen, 2000).

In spite of this mutuality societal and mental processes are fundamentally different. While social structures are not only the result of rational action, mental structures are far from being exact reflections of the real existing social and physical world. That both types of structures reproduce each other, but are at the same time fundamentally different, makes the mutual transformation possible, i.e. opens the possibility of learning processes. Since the social structures are not the result of rational planning and decisions, it is possible for people to have unexpected and surprising experiences. And as mental structures are not merely the reflection of the material surroundings it is possible for individuals to exceed this reality in the form of social imagination and visions. This understanding of vocational identity is presented in the model below (Figure 2.2). It is an attempt to illustrate the dynamic nature of vocational identity trying to bridge the gap between the subject and the social context while still exploiting the tension between the two. Vocational identity is developed in a process of interaction whereby the

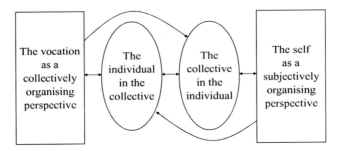

Figure 2.2   A diagrammatic representation of vocational identity

collective forms an integral part of the individual and visa-versa while at the same time each one is constitutive of the other. It is formed in a process of reproduction and transformation of the self as well as the vocation. As such vocational identity might be understood as the product of two processes.

First, the collective becomes part of the individual and reproduces and transforms this individuality. This is a process whereby the individual internally constructs aspects of identity shared with other members of the community of practice through social stereotyping and creates differences in relation to other groups through the social categorising of these groups (Turner, 1999). The result of this process is the establishment of similarities and differences based on characteristics, actions, values and practices that are established as desirable within the vocation and which individuals have embodied through vocational socialisation. These processes also function to produce a normative standard—the 'generalised other'. This embodiment is a learning process based on the individual's personal biography and general life conditions. It is realised through vocational training and participation in work processes and is thus the result of this socialising process (Salling Olesen, 2000). This socialisation process, however, does not just have the form of blind adaptation. In the reflective processing of experiences the individual not only identifies the normative demands but also the possibilities of deviation from these, and establishes what could be termed a 'collective other' that represents what is possible.

Second, the individual becomes part of the collective and as such contributes to its reproduction and development. In this process the individual presents herself within the work context as a unique person with an individual life history and a variety of personal experiences. It is in this confrontation that the individual finds the space for realising her potential and fulfilling her needs for social belonging, security etc. But it is also where she faces a situation that is ambivalent, needs compromising and forces her to devalue or silence a number of earlier experiences to survive as part of the community. Part of protecting one's own individuality within the vocational context can be understood in terms of back- and front-stage behaviour (Goffman, 1992) and the ability to comply with role expectations and the social identity formation process this implies. This calls for the development of tolerance of ambivalence (Becker-Schmidt, 1982) as a central quality of vocational identity. On the other hand, the individual to some extent affects the social surroundings through action and negotiation.

2.6   Banking and Bankers

In the empirical studies of bankers the social relation with the customer manifested itself very strongly. This relationship is characterised by a complex exchange of trust and reliability on a professional as well as personal level and is closely related to two aspects of the vocational self-understanding of bankers. They, on the one hand, see themselves as people who help customers solve important problems in their lives and, on the other hand, as bankers who, as business people, have the responsibility of not involving the bank in risky engagements. The first element of this self-understanding is based upon a solid vocational knowledge combined with having highly developed communication skills and possessing the ability to gain the confidence of others. Bankers typically perceive these skills as a part of their personality or as something they have learned from their parents during primary socialisation. The second element is connected to bankers being careful, sceptical and critical, which either derives from their vocational training and/or is related to personal traits and their work-life socialisation.

The elements of the collective and the subjective self-understanding (or organising perspectives) described in the previous section are partly contradictory. The way the individual banker deals with this contradiction is two-sided. On the one hand, she individualises and privatises the situations when she functions as a counsellor mixing professional judgements and normative personal understandings in making business decisions. On the other hand, she assumes a paternalistic role towards the customer. This attitude is apparent when bankers describe their task in relation to the customer as parallel to that of a doctor or when they attempt to 'mould' the customer to show economic 'responsibility' and in this way the bankers establish personal norms and values as criteria for the evaluation of the customer. This approach positions the banker in a similar role to that of the 'concerned parent', who acts according to what she thinks is best for her 'child', while at the same time this positioning makes it possible to administer a self-image as being loyal to the bank and meeting the business requirements.

Another important source of identity formation is the collegial relationship within the bank. Bankers as a professional group put in a lot of effort to maintain a stable social balance among themselves. A dominant feature of this relationship is to help and support one another and to have a relaxed and easy-going tone outside opening hours. But this is also a relationship where everybody maintains a distinct distance. Though habitually bank colleagues participate in company-organised sports and other leisure activities and to some extent engage in social exchange with other bankers, it is not a very close or empathic culture. A characteristic feature of this culture is that bankers are reluctant to criticise one another, to behave in ways that might be interpreted as confrontational or to express strong and explicit feelings (especially negative ones). This reflects an established norm of personal distance and emotional control that is also a key element in customer relations as described above, but is also a means to maintain the privacy of the counselling situation. Demonstrating emotional control combined with living up to a formal dress code forms part of the shared understanding of what constitutes the professional appearance. But the interviews also revealed that this is rather founded on the habitual dispositions of the employees than on corporate rules. As such those features of the professional appearance appear stable as an element of the shared vocational identity of bankers. However, it is also obvious that it is a fragile stability that might easily be shattered.

Any activity in the bank is subservient to strong front-stage backstage regulations and it is expected that the employee is able to handle the rules of these two scenes. The opening hours during which customers might be present are characterised by a rigid bodily and emotional control. This applies to the dress code, forms of behaviour, not to be seen eating or drinking etc. It is common understanding that a highly controlled appearance and behaviour expresses a sort of inner virtue and conveys a higher level of seriousness and precision. At the same time this kind of appearance and the symbolic signal of the social space are a precondition for the establishment of the paternalistic position in relation to the customers and to help maintain the desired balance between intimacy and distance. This is partly reproduced in an interaction between explicit rules and the dispositions of the individual banker, but it is also a highly efficient form of social control. Only very rarely are reprisals or corrections necessary to maintain this.

Loyalty towards the bank as an institution is also an important element in the self-understanding of bankers that is formative in relation to the development of their vocational identity. How this loyalty is understood and referred to, however, may differ. The expression of loyalty ranges from a very strong identification to a more reluctant and limited commitment. But the general picture is that employees believe that they are obliged to demonstrate their loyalty to the bank as an institution far beyond their regular working hours. Even if most ordinary employees are not going as far as seeing themselves as 'ambassadors of the bank' in their private lives (though many do) it is a widespread understanding that since they might be associated with the bank they should at all times be aware how they appear in public (not least in smaller communities) and refrain from making critical remarks about the bank at private social occasions.[3] But there were differences in attitudes. Several young employees, for example, expressed a strong identification with the bank most likely developed through their forming vocational training and the positive perception of having successfully made the transition from school to working life, feelings which were as yet less influenced by ambiguous organisational experiences. Among the older and more experienced employees a former strong identification with the employer seemed to have been replaced by more reluctant expressions of commitment that do not involve the same level of devotion. This change could be related to negative organisational experiences due to staff reductions, replacements, organisational restructuring, etc., which have made them develop a more complex and ambiguous relation to the bank. But since 'being loyal' forms an essential part of a banker's self-image and this is based on a high level of identification with the bank, these reservations do not take the form of criticism towards the bank. Instead, it is expressed as a more critical attitude towards management. This enables the individual banker to see herself as loyal even while dealing with the ambiguous experiences.

Summarising this section it seems that bankers in their personal orientations towards their work through a continuous effort balance a paternalistic orientation in their relations to the customer with a high level of loyalty towards and identification with the bank. They

---

[3] This form of identification might be related to the development of a corporate identity, but from the bankers' point of view there is no distinction between a corporate identity and 'being a banker' (i.e. relating to the vocation). Hence, I interpret this as an element of the vocational identity.

reproduce these attitudes within the social space they establish which is characterised by being kept 'pleasant' and free of conflicts and confrontational behaviour. These processes are based on personal orientations or dispositions as well as the bank-specific vocational socialisation. It is, however, a fragile balance since it is characterised by contradictory demands. These contradictions constantly challenge the employee to make decisions and negotiate to what extent and in what ways she complies with meeting the different expectations. What meets the eye as a high level of identification and balance reveals itself as a permanent struggle to maintain an identity that is able to mediate these contradictions. The combination of predictability and precaution that characterises the banker is a product of this and is combined with a degree of traditionalism that conveys the image of bankers as being 'boring'. The individual banker is aware of this stereotype, but accepts that this is the price that must be paid in order to appear as professional on the front-stage. This is contrasted by a much more multi-facetted social life 'back stage' than what appears on the 'front stage' and the fact that the safe and controlled social space with a minimum of visible conflicts also contains relationships between colleagues that are characterised by competitiveness. In this context competition is not necessarily expressed as an urge to win, but rather as a wish not to achieve less than the other employees in a similar job position. Also in this context it is important not to be or appear aggressive.

An important basis of the reproduction of the described social practices, through which the vocation acts as a collective organising perspective, is the recruitment of new trainees that possess habitual dispositions that mirror the existing ones and thus support the current social practices. This explains why the elements in the work of the banker that are valued and experienced as a possibility to realise individual needs in the work-context, at the same time have a reproductive function in relation to the vocation itself and as such are promoted and reinforced. In many aspects the values that the employees exercise in their private lives do not appear very different from those exercised in the bank. For instance, bankers' personal lives appear quite traditional with a focus on the family and their close social context preserving traditional family values (for example, most bank employees live in families with 2 or 3 children and have rarely been divorced). In their social life in general they mirror their distance to and interest in other people as well as the traditional and cautious norms that they value in their counselling practice.

2.7   The Significance of Vocational Identity

This chapter outlined how the development of a vocational identity and mastery within a vocational area are strongly related, not least within banking. I have tried to show that vocational identity is not a stable entity established during the period of vocational training. Even though the training is of fundamental importance for developing a vocational identity and becoming a part of the community of practice, the vocational identity is transformed and reproduced in the course of lifelong learning. This duality between constancy and development is an essential element of vocational identity as a vocational qualification, not the least during times of change. The constancy of vocational identity is fundamental for the individual in the practical dealing with hundreds of specific everyday situations. It is the basis that makes it possible for the banker to operate in most of these situations with only a minimum of conscious monitoring. The shared nature of vocational identity makes the individual banker recognisable as a member of the community of practice and makes it possible that her assessments and judgements most of the time are in line with what other members of the community would do. Finally, it also makes her recognisable and predictable to the customers as she meets their expectations and does not cause anxiety. Developing the vocational identity of a banker is the basis of internal predictability and as such leads to the mutual recognition of and between members of the vocation and the surrounding world as well. But vocational identity can only play this role if it constantly adapts to the changes of social situations and customer expectations. This means that the individual as a member of the vocational group has to be aware of those changes and continuously assess and evaluate her self-understanding as a banker in the light of change and adapt it accordingly. Identity is an ongoing learning process.

As underlined earlier the work situation of bankers is characterised by conflicting interests and demands. The individual banker continuously has to balance these divergent demands and deal with them in relation to her self-understanding as a banker. Thus, vocational identities are not coherent in themselves but they might be understood as socially acceptable ways for the individual to create some form of coherence or meaning in a working life that typically is characterised by conflicting interests. The role of vocational identity is to establish shared ways of containing contradictions and thereby create a common sense of coherence in the working life of bankers. As such tolerance of ambivalence has to be a basic quality of vocational identity. This role of vocational identity is important to make stressing and conflicting work situations bearable. At the same time this is also the reason why vocational identities have a 'conservative' connotation during times of change. Balancing the contradictions of capitalist work life demands requires immense efforts and a defensive attitude, because this balance is fragile.

That individuals develop a vocational identity in relation to their respective community of practice is also of importance in a broader societal sense. Besides creating internal coherence within the professional group it is also the basis for establishing and maintaining shared standards and norms for the quality of work. Through their vocational identity individuals create demarcations from other groups by which a shared understanding of the role of the vocation in relation to societal production and society as a whole are established. In times of increasing complexity of production professional groups cannot be regulated from one central institution but have to be decentralised. This moves an important part of control and regulation to the vocational institutions themselves. Hence employees' vocational identities must be considered central to the sustainability of production on a broader level.

Finally, vocational identity plays a key role in lifelong learning. Incorporating elements of situatedness as well as of biographical constructions of continuity, vocational identity can be considered as a basis of adult learning. Any learning process builds upon previous knowledge, which is negotiated and transformed within situated practices. But this knowledge is also situated within a biography that includes not only an individual's self-image of what she *is*, but also a vision of what she may *become*. In this sense a vocational identity is not just a construction of the present based on a reconstruction of the past but is also a forecast for the future. Since the motivation for adults to engage in lifelong learning is strongly related to how meaningful they consider the topics of learning in the light of their present lives and their future plans they will typically revert to their vocational identity. Maybe this identity must be enriched or maybe it has to be transformed, but it cannot be ignored.

Although these general conclusions about the significance of vocational identity are drawn from my investigation with bankers, I consider them to be of general relevance. The 'good' banker is expected to be able to juggle three balls at the same time: be helpful to customers, loyal to the bank and professionally recognised by colleagues. Meeting these divergent demands is only possible on the backbone of a strong vocational identity. But the banker today has to stretch her arms still further to catch the balls.

References

Alheit, P. (1994). *Taking the knocks. Youth unemployment and biography.* Arbejdstekster no. 11, Roskilde: RUC.

Alheit, P. and S. Bergamini (1995). Biographical and life-history research as a new qualitative approach in social sciences and education. An introduction. In S. Papaioannou, J.F. Lauridsen, P. Alheit and H. Salling Olesen (Eds.), *Education, culture and modernisation* (pp. 203–228). Roskilde: RUC.

Baldvinsson, C., T. Bender, K. Busck-Nielsen and F. Nytoft Rasmussen (2000). *Dansk Bankvæsen.* København: Thomsom.

Bhaskar, R. (1989). *Reclaiming reality: a critical introduction to contemporary philosophy.* London: Verso.

Becker-Schmidt, R. (1982). Modsæningsfyldt realitet og Ambivalens—kvinders arbejdserfaringer i fabrik og familie. *Udkast, 2*(10), 164–198.

Berger, P.L. and T. Luckmann (1966/99). *Den samfundsskabte virkelighed. En videnssociologisk afhandling.* Viborg: Lindhardt og Ringhof.

Bourdieu, P. (1994). *Centrale tekster inden for sociologi og kulturteori.* København: Akademisk Forlag.

Bourdieu, P. (1997). *Af praktiske grunde.* København: Hans Reitzel Forlag.

Brown, A. (1999). *A dynamic model of occupational identity formation.* Retrieved August 2005 from http://www.theknownet.com/renderXML.opendoc.fcgi.

Dausien, B. (1998). Education as biographical construction? Narration, gender and learning—a case study. In P. Alheit and E. Kammler (Eds.), *Lifelong learning and its impact on social and regional development. Collected papers.* Bremen: Donat Verlag.

Dewey, J. (1963). *Experience and education.* New York: Collier Books.

Dreyfus, H. and S. Dreyfus (1991). Intuitiv ekspertise: den bristede drøm om tænkende maskiner. Århus: Munksgaard.

Finansrådet (2001). Fremtidssyn for den finansielle sektor—et debatoplæg. København: Finansrådet.

Gardner, H. (1993). *The Unschooled mind. How children think and how Schools should teach.* London: Fontana Press.

Giddens, A. (1984). *The constitution of society.* Cambridge: Polity Press.

Goffman, E. (1992). *Vore rollespil i hverdagen.* Larvik: Østlands-Postens Boktrykkeri.

Hetherington, K. (1998). *Expressions of identity. Space, performance, politics.* London: Sage Publications.

Kerschensteiner, G. (1980). *Arbejdsskolen.* København: Nyt Nordisk Forlag.

Laske, G. (2001). Vocational Identity—a central element in the European concept of work. Retrieved August 2005 from http://www.theknownet.com/xml/forum_front/changing_identities/meat.html.

Lave, J. and E. Wenger (1991). *Situated learning. Legitimate peripheral participation.* Cambridge: Cambridge University Press.

Mead, G.H. (1934). *Mind, self and society. From the standpoint of a social behaviorist.* Chicago: The University of Chicago Press.

Mishler, E.G. (1986). *Research interviewing: context and narrative.* Cambridge, MA: Harvard University Press.

Nielsen, K. and S. Kvale (1999). *Mesterlære. Læring som social praksis.* København: Hans Reitzels Forlag.

Regini, M., J. Kitay and M. Baethge (1999). *From tellers to sellers. Changing employ-ment relations in banks*. Cambridge, MA: The MIT Press.

Salling Olesen, H. (2000). *Professional identity as learning processes in life histories*. Paper no. 12, Life History Project. Roskilde: RUC.

Sigurjonsson, G. (2002). *Dansk vekseluddannelse i støbeskeen: fra lavstidens mesterlære til moderne dansk vekseluddannelse*. Århus: Fællestrykkeriet for Sundhedsvidenskaberne, Århus Universitet.

Smistrup, M. (2002). *Mennesker og faglighed i danske banker. En statistisk profil af danske bankmedarbejdere*. Rapport til finansforbundet. København: Finansforbundet.

Smistrup, M. (2003). *Bankmedarbejderen—splittet mellem Varnæs og Scrooge. Om fag, faglighed og identitet blandt danske bankmedarbejdere*. Roskilde: RUC/Institut for pædagogik og uddannelsesforskning.

Stern, D.N. (1989). Developmental Prerequisites for the Sense of a Narrated Self. In A.M. Cooper, O.F. Kernberg and E.S. Person (Eds.), *Psychoanalysis: Toward the second century* (pp. 168–178). London: Yale University Press.

Stern, D.N. (2000). *Barnets interpersonelle verden*. København: Hans Reitzels Forlag.

Strauss, A. and J. Corbin (1990). *Basics of qualitative research: Grounded theory pro-cedures and techniques*. Newbury Park: Sage Publications.

Swedberg, R. (1987). *Sociologists look at banks*. Stockholm: Department of Sociology, University of Stockholm.

Turner, J.C. (1999). Some current issues in research on social identity and self-categorization theories. In N. Ellemers, R. Spears and B. Doosje (Eds.), *Social identity. Context, commitment, content* (pp. 6–34). London: Blackwell Publishers.

Weber, K (2002). Professionsuddannelserne i vadestedet eller Senmodernitetens paradoksale kvalificering. *Social Kritik*, 81, 56–83.

Wenger, E. (1998). *Communities of practice. Learning, meaning, and identity*. Cambridge: Cambridge University Press.

Yin, R.K. (1994). *Case study research. Design and methods*. London: Sage Publications.

3

The Role of Developing a Vocational Identity for Women—The Example of Young Single German Mothers

Gwendolyn Paul and Uta Zybell
University of Darmstadt, Germany

3.1   Introduction: The Role of Vocational Training in Germany

Skilled labour still has a high standing in German society owing to the dominance of the concept of 'Beruf' that reflects a structure of formally recognised occupations. This has to do with the Federal Republic's specific organised educational structure for skilled workers in the Dual System and the associated remarkable importance and predominance of specialised occupational labour markets. Here, the occupational concept turns out to be constitutive as far as vocational training in the Dual System is concerned. Furthermore it is the structuring principle for the job market. Occupational profiles and related vocational training schemes are the two as yet inseparable sides of vocationalism, which is oriented towards continuity and securing employment. Being trained in an occupation therefore relates not only to 'specialist expertise associated with a permanent activity based on the division of labour' [translated from German] (Negt, 2005, p. 23), but also to a personal lifestyle, which—in contrast to a job as casual employment—is constructed on the basis of continuity.

In Germany, the transition from school to gainful employment takes place in two stages. The 'first hurdle' that needs to be overcome is making the transition from school into vocational training. This transitional phase is societally organised and forms a substantial structural element

A. Brown, S. Kirpal and F. Rauner (eds.), Identities at Work, 69–90.

of a person's life story and trajectory. Vocational training as a form of socialisation for an occupation forms the basis and essential requirement for making the transition into the employment market even if it is no guarantee. It can be assumed that the occupation-related learning and development processes that individuals are undergoing in the course of a vocational training programme 'not only serve the purpose of qualifying for mastering work tasks, but they also influence the entire development of the personality' [translated from German] (Heinz, 1995, p. 12). Only when vocational training has been successfully completed does the 'second hurdle'—entry into the job market—need to be overcome.

Starting vocational training marks a considerable change of lifestyle and brings with it the challenge of new impressions and experiences. Young people are challenged to deal with work demands and stress, new norms and rules (including those of the workplace), and accept that formerly known freedom and free time have to be given up. At the same time, taking part in this new world of experience and receiving the first income while in training are found to be a first step towards financial independence from the parental home (or from reliance on state benefits). Those elements provide the opportunity to take on personal responsibility, expand one's scope of action and to design an individual life plan. In the course of dealing with the experiences of working life, the majority of trainees find their expectations of vocational training and of the tasks assigned to them in the company increasingly change in the direction of wanting to be given greater responsibility to carry out tasks independently, while their ideas for their career and own future take a more definite shape. The experiences gained from vocational training enable individuals to design a lifestyle and structure their life, for example in terms of time allocation. At the same time they learn to formulate their own ideas for shaping the arrangement of work situations.

Working (or completing an apprenticeship) involves acquiring specific categories of experience such as fitting in with regulated time structures, collaboration in pursuit of shared objectives, productive activities, social integration and recognition, all of which help the individual to develop a socially recognised independent lifestyle. 'As a result of occupational socialisation, these categories of experience become anchored in the personality with a differing sense of subjective obligation' [translated from German] (Heinz, 1995, p. 96). Consequently, the lack of employment or vocational training is personally experienced as a loss of elementary qualities of experience. Hence, the lack of regular and regulated gainful employment does not only have negative consequences for the material security of a person's livelihood. For unemployed people it also affects their social integration and psychosocial well-being. Not having a meaningful structure to the day in terms of time and content, and being limited in terms of leisure activities due to financial restrictions, often accompanies a drop in social status. This gains expression both in dependence on state benefits and in social isolation. Although socialisation processes in unemployment take a different direction depending on personal, social, occupational and regional circumstances, 'deficiency-creating socialisation processes' ['defizitäre Sozialisationsprozesse'] (*ibid.*) can often be observed.

3.1.1   JAMBA—a Pilot Project to Foster the Professional Integration of Young Mothers

The increasing number of supplementary (state-funded) measures to support vocational training opportunities for young people clearly shows that for a long time now the German vocational training system has been unable to meet current demands and requirements. This is demonstrated in particular by the continuous growth in support for disadvantaged people. Intending to prevent or at least reduce long-term unemployment among young people and the associated negative socialisation processes, such supportive measures have almost become an integral part of the system. An important factor in this respect is the integrative potential of the system, i.e. its aim and ability to integrate various social groups by taking into account equal opportunities requirements (cf. Nader, et al., 2003). The project 'JAMBA—Junge allein erziehende Mütter in der Berufsausbildung' (young single mothers in vocational training) of the German state of Hesse aimed at improving the opportunities for labour market integration of a specific group, which is disadvantaged in terms of participating in dual training programmes.

Initiated in 1998 by the Ministry of Economics, Transportation, Urban and Regional Development, initially for a duration of five years, the project tackled the disadvantaged situation in the training market of young single mothers below 27 years of age. It created a general set-up that would take into account the situation of young single mothers in connection with their vocational orientation. An important innovation here was (and still is) to give them the opportunity to take part in an in-company training programme that would take up less time than the usual programmes. This so-called part-time training corresponded with a reduction in training time of approximately 25 per cent compared with the standard scope of vocational training. Concretely, for the young mothers this meant they had to work for only six instead of eight hours in the company each day. The vocational school tuition was not affected by this arrangement and reduction in training time.

Within the framework of the project, new and until then unresearched organisational forms of basic vocational training were tested out. Until then only few experiences of young mothers in in-company training were available. The scientific monitoring of the pilot project (provided by the Technical University of Darmstadt) was based on the idea that the suitability of a vocational training system should be assessed in terms of its ability to integrate 'weaker people' into the system. This criterion meant it would be appropriate to review whether the German dual vocational training system provides opportunities for integration for previously excluded young people so that they can comply with the national vocational qualification standards. Concretely, this meant investigating whether the Dual System is suitable for young mothers or not.

During the four years of academic support, the sample comprised two groups each involving approximately 50 young mothers and at least 80 companies. The project discovered a step-by-step expansion in the area, i.e. each year approximately 100 young mothers take up a vocational training course at established and new locations. Participating in the state of Hesse are conurbations, small towns and areas with a very rural structure. By anchoring part-time training in law, it is now possible, in principle, to complete part-time training throughout Germany and independently of a pilot project.

The results of the project clearly demonstrate that the structure of the vocational training system is behind the times in terms of responding to and accommodating individual patterns of action and orientation. These results suggest that education policy should push for a much stronger differentiation of the Dual System. In this respect the *JAMBA* project has trodden new paths and opened new doors, which will provide an important stimulus for increasing the flexibility of the vocational training system.[1]

Based on the project's results this chapter investigates the vocational socialisation of women and the associated development of a vocational identity through their participation in a training scheme. Completing vocational training as a prerequisite for obtaining employment is of

---

[1] As a response to the unequal conditions for this group to participate in the German training system that the project disclosed, the new Vocational Training Act (*Berufsbildungsgesetz*), which came into force on 1 April 2005, incorporated the opportunity to make training schemes more flexible.

central importance in the development of an identity and the opportunity for social participation. Initially, the category of 'gender' shall be discussed as a deciding factor of influence in the German vocational training system and the resulting gender-specific differences in terms of access to the training market as well as to different kinds of training courses. This shall be followed by a discussion of the situation of young single mothers in vocational training. Although it is true that due to its particular situation this group represents a specific clientele within the vocational training system, those mothers are no different from other young women in terms of their professional orientation, that recognises completing vocational training is important as the basis for good prospects in professional and private life.

3.2   Different Sexes Take Different Transitional Routes into an Occupation

The prescribed structuring of people's curriculum vitae through school education—further education/training—gainful employment is applicable to women and men alike. The strict institutional structuring of a person's 'life course' in Germany is characterised by clearly organised transitions from primary school into a tripartite school system, and from there into a vocational training system (including *Fachhochschulen* [Universities of Applied Sciences] and universities) with each stage providing varying leaving certificates. This is followed by various realisable and positioning opportunities on the employment market. 'Social institutions such as the educational system (. . .) structure the life course by standardising individual labour market entries, positions, career paths, and long-term perspectives to a high degree' (Krüger, 1999, p. 192). Vocational training has a central significance for the 'structure of the life course as it forms a structural element of the curriculum vitae, a hinge between school and the employment market' [translated from German] (Heinz, 1995, p. 138). Thus it forms the 'first hurdle' that needs to be cleared on the job market track, and it is considered essential for the individual's occupational socialisation and the development of an occupational identity.

3.2.1   Job Orientation among Women

Despite the changes in the structure and significance of gainful employment, it can still be assumed that the occupation itself continues, to the greatest possible extent for *both sexes*, to be the decisive 'core of social identity ascription and personal self-identification' [translated from German] (Beck et al., 1980, p. 223), even if this happens in different ways for women and men. In recent years the labour force participation rate for women in Germany has risen to over 65 per cent (cf. Statistisches Bundesamt Deutschland, 2004), which indicates that women (and increasingly women with children also) give a high priority to gainful employment and are increasingly job-oriented. But it should be emphasised that despite this significant increase women's labour force participation remains relatively low in comparison to other countries. Furthermore, the level of labour force participation does not correspond to the desired level many women express.

'The individualisation of women's life contexts (high divorce rates, for example, compel women to build up their own material existence; single mothers account for a disproportionately high percentage in official poverty figures) is expressed in job-orientation gaining significance, but also in increased labour force participation (even if this is still considerably below the level of educational participation). At the same time, West Germany is bottom of the league in Europe when it comes to women's labour force participation rate' [translated from German] (Beck, 2000, p. 29).

Serious differences between the sexes also exist when it comes to opportunities for accessing the education/training and employment markets, as well as to the kinds of occupations entered and the positions held. For example, gender-specific principles of distribution in the education and training market remain largely unchanged when it comes to occupational choices and the share of vocational training places in the dual system (which is male dominated) and places in school-based vocational training courses (which are female dominated). Even though around 90 per cent of young women today, just like young men, attain a formal qualification in the vocational training system (cf. Cornelißen et al., 2002, p. 43), their participation in the various forms, routes and qualifications in the vocational system continue to differ very strongly from those of male trainees. The sex ratio as a symbolic order and social condition determines the social placing of the sexes in society, which consequently also affects access to (vocational) education.

The social ratio into which the sexes are yoked is the result of a complex process: polarising differentiation, discriminating assessment, disparate treatment and unequal positioning of people according to gender all interact with each other [translation from German] (Becker-Schmidt, 2000, p. 61).

3.2.2   The Double Structure of Vocational Training

The splitting of the German vocational training system into a dual apprenticeship route and a school-based route is one of the most powerful configurations to uphold this polarising differentiation. Whereas historically, school education was oriented towards bridging the period until young women were married and, on the other hand, towards supporting activities necessary in society that could not be provided by the trades or industry, the Dual System was expressly designed for young men to integrate them long-term into gainful employment and into society. Even today, young women are under-represented in the Dual System and in spite of having better school leaving grades their chances of securing a vocational training place are much worse. They frequently have to relinquish their original wish to enter an occupation in favour of following a school-based course. School-based training routes on the one hand generally require a higher investment in education than company-based routes, as they often have a longer duration, do not include any remuneration while attending the course, and, on the other hand, usually mean lower salary expectations and worse promotion opportunities in the job market.

Owing to the 'historical legacy of the double structure of vocational training' [translation from German] (Krüger, 2004, p. 27), there exists a structured assignment of men's and women's occupations, which is associated with unequal valency and a negative label being applied to what are held to be 'women's jobs'.

> Whereas, for some time, the significance of an occupation has been growing more equal with respect to the life courses of the two sexes (. . .), the old assumptions of normality concerning male and female life courses have remained stubbornly engrained in the structure of the transitional system (. . .) [translated from German] (*ibid.*).

The rigid institutional structuring of people's vocational development in Germany and the structuring of the sex ratio that has become embedded within it have proven resistant to normative transformation processes, with the result that discrimination continues even under changed conditions. Although the composition of students in the school-based vocational system is changing due to the change from an industrial to a service society, and men are now also present in these areas, the structurally conditioned discrimination against this transitional route persists. Krüger (2004) impressively demonstrates institutions' power of resistance with respect to structural change:

> The SVE system (5 school-based vocational educational system, *comment by G.P.*) also shows that the cultural historical gendering has become 'structure', i.e. that it today operates according to a gendered logic, but indifferently to the actual sex of their participants. Women who escape SVE benefit from the VED (5 vocational and educational dual system, *comment by G.P.*) advantages, and men who enter SVE will have to fight its disadvantages (Krüger, 1999, p. 224).

Although vocational training turns out to be equally important for women and men, an unequal concern for the question of life development has to be noted. Job-centeredness in the male curriculum vitae, despite wide-reaching changes in the sex ratio, still retains its validity, and family commitments are fundamentally compatible with this. For women, however, the family-centred life course has lost its validity; its place is taken by the new guiding principle of the so-called 'double lifestyle' [*'doppelte Lebensführung'*] (Geissler and Oechsle, 1994, p. 147). In other words, making a career and building a family are no longer alternatives, but have become equally relevant life spheres, which have to be combined (individually!).

> For young women, a biographical perspective that focuses only on the deployment of the worker in the workforce is too limited. Unlike young men, they are still—as previously—not available for company-based gainful employment for their whole life [translated from German] (Geissler and Oechsle, 1994, p. 147).

Accordingly, creating a link between relative work autonomy and family presence constitutes a specific feature of the female life context. The relationship between private life and work that is sought, and how this is brought into a reconcilable solution, i.e. whether a continuous equal balance, a series of phasing one after the other, or a weighting in favour of one sphere or the other is preferred, ultimately also depends on how the individual gets to grips with normative and institutional rules: 'Life design (. . .) develops amid the conflicting forces of society's requirements, one's own orientations and the concrete context' [translated from German] (Geissler and Oechsle, 1994 p. 164). It should still be noted that the horizon of women's life design today necessarily includes their occupation, and that within this they wish to realise their own secure existence, a personal endowment of meaning, and also social status.

Despite the rapprochement in educational participation and qualifications gained, and women's increased job orientation, the category of gender turns out to be an enduring determining factor of different life courses and life opportunities. The acquisition of educational and vocational qualifications does not necessarily mean the lifting of the sex-specific segmentation of the education and employment market and a change in the sex ratio, which is rooted in the structure of organisations.

Over the following pages, the completion of vocational training is considered as the basis for the social and occupational integration of young mothers. Here our interest turns to the development of an occupational identity in vocational training and the freeing from conditions of dependency—as a result of unemployment—that previously characterised the lives of the young mothers. The acquisition of an occupational identity evidently has an important function for the stabilisation of a personal construction of identity.

3.3 Vocational Training as a New World of Experience for Young Mothers

Despite trends of transformation, social expectations of a normalised life development pattern continue to exist, comprising the biographic sequence of the successive passage towards a new and higher status. Anyone who differs from this course will run into difficulties when it comes to integration:

> The education and training market scarcely offers any opportunities for young women who do not stick to the socially prescribed route of school, training, commitment to a partner, children. Thus, despite all the observed individualisation processes, standardisations in the CV are still to be considered the norm [translated from German] (Paul-Kohlhoff, 2002, p. 146).

Even with high motivation for education and suitable schooling conditions, young mothers come up against insurmountable barriers in their search for vocational training places, because they are assumed to have deficiencies and limitations as a result of their responsibility to bring up children. They belong to that group of young people who fall through the net of vocational training positions and who only have very slender chances of obtaining vocational qualifications. In view of the great importance of vocational training for long-lasting occupational integration, the lack of education means worse life opportunities overall and only a very low level of participation in society.

The outcomes of the pilot project JAMBA conducted throughout the German state of Hesse are presented and discussed here. The project aimed at the occupational integration of this group, which as a result of early motherhood has broken society's prescribed curriculum vitae structure of school education, vocational training/education, gainful employment, and then starting a family. The project

> takes effect at a point that almost no other measures reach: young mothers are encouraged and supported to take an in-company training course, and companies are encouraged to take them as trainees. Young single mothers in fact face cumulative disadvantages that result in them being excluded from vocational qualifications if they do not receive systematic support [translated from German] (Zybell, 2003, p.12).

3.3.1   Design and Objectives of the JAMBA project

Methodologically, the cognitive interest and research objective of the JAMBA project were geared towards investigating how young single mothers successfully cope with their participation in a vocational training course while at the same time raising their children, what conditions need to be created to make this arrangement possible, and how the individual women organise their daily lives. Furthermore, the project was concerned with the question of how new organisational structures of vocational training are gaining acceptance by companies and vocational training institutions as well as by the young women themselves.

The evaluation- and practice-based accompanying research attached great value to the empirical method in the development of academic knowledge. Data collection was designed as an inductive procedure with individual cases and project-related contexts forming the basis for generating conclusions that could be generalised. Qualitative methods in the form of interviews, discussion groups and verbal (expert) surveys facilitated access to an as yet little researched area of reality by focusing on assessing the individuals' perspectives. This material was supplemented by quantitative data. The research design was based on the procedure of triangulation, which offers a multi-perspective view on the phenomenon under investigation. In order to record and analyse the situation and interpretation of vocational training of young mothers from various standpoints, the survey extended not only to the young participating mothers, but also to companies offering training and the participating vocational schools as well as to selected experts.

As regards surveying the young women in the project, equal importance was attached to quantitative as well as qualitative methods in order to supplement the research of cross-individual contexts with the subjective interpretation of these contextual factors. Partially standardised, written questions on the circumstances of the mothers' lives, their experiences at work and the vocational school and their employment prospects were applied in a three-stage process at the beginning, in the middle and at the end of their training. A second qualitative line of data collection was performed, on the one hand, via textbook-supported interviews and, on the other hand, via moderated group discussions in order to gain insight into common orientations and coping patterns. Analysis and evaluation were based on qualitative and comparative hermeneutic procedures.

The two partners of dual vocational training—companies and vocational training schools—were surveyed on the basis of a universal written questionnaire prepared by means of textbook-supported individual interviews. Since implementing such a pilot project or even establishing a new transition model for regular training would not be possible without the companies' willingness to provide training places, some experiences were recorded with greater differentiation at selected companies by way of interviews. Here, the central themes were the clientele of young mothers as well as the new organisational form of part-time training. An overall telephone survey was performed subsequently in order to assess retrospectively the general view of the companies that offered training.

Theme-centred and textbook-supported expert interviews complemented the data. These experts were representatives from the Ministry, social administrative authorities and the chambers of industry and commerce. As a whole, the evaluation was understood as a continuous process of reflection and feedback that was constantly fed into the training process in the sense of a results transfer so that the training conditions could be continuously improved.

3.3.2 Skilled Work in Contrast to Housework and Upbringing Children

Whereas before the training courses began, the young mothers' lives were heavily characterised by isolation and little contact with the 'outside world', the results of the project clearly demonstrate that participating in a vocational training programme is experienced as forming a link with society. For the young women, vocational training 'with children' means taking a route that leads to independence. In addition to opening up an additional area of life to them, in which they are active and which is intended to secure their future, the training situation also reshapes their perceptions and their relationship with themselves. After all, they used to identify to a high degree with their situation as caregivers, which generally implied dependency on state transfer payments and their family of origin. It also entailed a certain separation from people of the same age group owing to their different way of life.

That social recognition of the mother role only has a short range is seen in the contradictory requirement of being a full-time mother on the one hand, while at same time young people are expected to go out to work and provide for themselves. In German society housework and bringing up children are attributed only a diffuse value. In contrast, skilled work and gainful employment enjoy a high level of esteem. The young mothers do not beat about the bush when describing the contrast between the two forms of working: 'You don't get much recognition as a housewife and mother. The fact that you get a salary makes you part of the working society. Otherwise you're 'not worth as much', so to speak.' Especially when women receive social security benefits, they can feel that they have a lower status because they are non-workers. Their dissatisfaction with the monotony of everyday life in their various dependent situations is expressed in statements such as 'I thought life was just passing me by, that nothing was happening. And I'm so young, it's not right, that can't have been all that there was.' Thus the 'single-lane' life context, oriented primarily towards the responsibility for childrearing, is no longer sufficient for women, neither generally in society nor individually.

The process of moving into the world of work through training has the function of setting the course for the subsequent development of identity. 'For younger people, pride at their achievements at work is an important medium for strengthening their self-esteem and creating social bonds' [translated from German] (Negt, 2005, p. 23). This is particularly true for young mothers, who as trainees, school students and workers enter into new relationships from which they draw a great deal of self-confidence and confirmation. For them, their occupational work always stands in contrast to or rather in addition to their work as a mother and head of the household. As a result of the expansion of their repertoire of behaviours, their relationship to themselves and to others also changes.

The young women stress how important it is for them that they have left behind their old routine thanks to their training and that they have a new task that gives additional meaning to their day: 'It's just great. I have to get up in the morning, and I know why. I am there for me, not just for my child.' In addition to helping them overcome a phase of aimlessness and 'going with the flow', participating in vocational training also allows the women to move themselves back closer to the centre of their everyday life. Self-realisation and responsibility for oneself are powerful arguments for vocational training for young mothers with children. One young woman expresses this in the following way: 'But it's also such a good feeling because at that moment you're not a mother, you're simply yourself.' This 'being oneself' gains a new dimension as a result of the vocational training. For the young women, gainful employment does not just mean making a proven and positively valued contribution to society. It also means developing skills that are not directly related to home and child.

In the assessment of the meaning of skilled work in contrast to the work of reproduction, what the young mothers say in the JAMBA project tallies with the values that were also found in other studies. Stauber (1996), who has analysed the life development of single mothers in rural regions, states:

> The vocational sphere is a social context for these women, which because of the social status of gainful employment from the outset stands in a different evaluation context. But it also stands apart from other social contexts as a result of its different rules—responsibilities that lie elsewhere, different communication structures. This difference—namely with respect to the types of contact that are made in the family context—is described as being liberating [translated from German] (Stauber, 1996, p. 121).

The company environment challenges people in a completely different way; it is precisely the contrast to the work of reproduction that appeals to the young mothers. This, however, also does imply one particular requirement, namely the maintenance of an inner consistency despite external changes. Keupp (1999) defines identity as the 'permanent job of making adjustments between inner and outer worlds' [translated from German] (Keupp, 2001, p. 808). With this statement he describes the idea of a process that is not necessarily linear and continuous, but which is carried out in the form of a project. The young mothers in vocational training have to integrate the newly arrived tasks and relationships into their existing concept of self—and this is something they do not always find particularly easy.

3.3.3   Developing a Vocational Identity Despite of New Lines of Conflict

Ambivalent feelings, i.e. having conflicting attitudes and feelings at the same time form part of the everyday life of young working mothers. Positive and negative components are often simultaneous and irreconcilable. The central, irresolvable contradiction relevant to all young mothers in the project is that between attachment to the child and the ability to let go at the same time. Coping independently with new tasks outside the family context, which is only possible in temporary separation from the child, also provides an opportunity for self-awareness, self-confidence and confirmation, but also for uncertainties, deep-felt worries, fears, conflicts of conscience and self-doubt. The participants describe their route through training as being spurred on by motivation and optimism, but also held back by problems and inner conflicts.

For example, most young mothers in training are accompanied by daily feelings of insufficiency and of being torn between the two spheres of life. They permanently experience the feeling of not having sufficient time and energy to react appropriately to demands and needs. Their stress and guilty conscience relate most strongly to their children, as it is here that they experience the greatest changes compared to previously. But in their jobs, too, the young mothers frequently want to demonstrate more flexibility and commitment than they are actually able to give. They have to struggle to persevere with training not just at the level of real reconcilability, but also at the level of disapproval and criticism from their social environment and at the level of their own opinions, beliefs and wishes, where there are potential lines of conflict. They live amid the conflicting forces of profit and loss, opportunities and risks, enrichments and irritations, and each must cope with this conflict in her own way. Determining the relationship between the two poles, or between all the facets, is ultimately crucial in the development of an identity.

As 'commuters between two worlds', for which their personal and social identity is just as important as their vocational one, they share their fate with all working mothers. In view of the contradictory expectations that various reference groups or persons direct towards the young mothers and which demand autonomous decisions, Lempert (1998) states that 'role conflicts are a significant 'driving force' towards improved moral development' [translated from German] (Lempert, 1998, p. 185). Owing to these crises, young mothers also have the opportunity to redefine the norms of their roles.

The interviews demonstrated that all participating young mothers go through transformation processes that can trigger immense dynamism, which may take different forms depending on their actual situation. If the women succeed in using the conflicts and tensions to their benefit, they make significant progress in terms of gaining independence, self-determination and emancipation. However, if the woman suffers experiences of failure and severe frustrations, she may withdraw from the training programme, which can mean further gaps and hindrances in her curriculum vitae.

It is remarkable how strongly identification with work is linked to professional activity. This is demonstrated in the young mothers' linguistic expressions when they talk about their situation in relating conspicuously to 'work' rather than 'training'. Just by their choice of nomenclature, it becomes apparent that vocational development signifies membership of the 'community of practice'. The status of learning is pushed into the background against that of working. The training is being connected with being a participant in the world of work and achieving occupational success or being occupationally capable. It pays to take up an important position in the company. As a result of the practice-oriented vocational training that closely links working and learning, the young women feel genuinely needed through directly participating in the company's work processes. One trainee proudly reported that the company 'counts on us.' Through carrying out useful activities, they can demonstrate the concrete results of their work, interact with the customers and offer services. In this way they are integrated both into the organisational structure and time schedule of the company and the social structure it provides (cf. Zybell, 2003, p.159). To be integrated as a staff member and thereby being able to prove and strengthen their social skills is extremely important for the young mothers, too.

All these elements foster the development of a vocational identity. The young women know that they are cogs—even if small ones—in the work process. This means that if they are absent, there is a gap, and if they are present, their contributions are at least recorded. At any rate, they are in a certain way responsible and this bolsters their self-esteem: 'Working for a company you have to be accountable for the work that you do. And I also can prove to myself, somehow, that I can do it. And not be left standing like a loser.' In this respect, the young mothers regard their training as fully fledged work. Earning their own money, even if the trainee wages are still minimal and not sufficient to live independently, also contributes to their high level of identification with their work. Although not entirely accurate as far as training is concerned, they associate with this the dimension of recognition in the form of being rewarded for their contributions.

> Hence the women (. . .) are more strongly oriented to the concept of gainful employment instead of to training as socialisation into an occupation. Rather, they see training as preparation and integration into work [translated from German] (cf. Zybell, 2003, p. 162).

It should not be forgotten that following a training programme and having children can also put women under enormous pressure to be successful. They want to prove in their working and social environments that they are worth the investment that is being made in them and that they can meet the expected demands. The strongest pressure to succeed is felt in the vocational school and in the company. Hence this directly concerns their concrete performance in training and only indirectly their overall situation. The fear of not fulfilling expectations is present in many ways. Although being grateful for having the opportunity to obtain a vocational qualification, this can also lead to a fear of failure.

3.3.4   Route Towards Independence

All project participants were aware of the relevance the vocational training had for their future employment prospects. They knew that as an unskilled employee, they would be badly paid and more likely to lose their job. 'I want to achieve something in my life. I want to plan a future. The traineeship gives me the basis to do that.' The prospects for their future life gain defined contours and promising aspects as a result of the vocational training. Added to this is the motivation to be a positive role model for their own children: 'I want my daughter to be proud of me one day and not have to say: my mother is a cleaning woman.'

For the young mothers undergoing a vocational training course with having children means taking a route that leads to independence. This independence involves various dimensions. In the first place, there is the prospect of *financial independence*. The young mothers stress how they feel the strain of reliance on state benefits or the financial support of their family of origin. They feel extremely restricted and regimented and wish they had more self-determined financial scope. Closely linked to the desire for financial independence is increased *independence from the family of origin*. Detachment from their parents is often not yet as complete as desired. Their own motherhood often has a contradictory effect due to the need for help and assistance. The parent-daughter ties conceal the risk of making boundaries and independence more and more difficult. Vocational training can make a considerable contribution to removing the young mother from the parents' influence for the medium term. Furthermore, training allows the young mothers to become *more independent of negative social labels*. Experiences of stigmatisation as young mothers, lone parents and recipients of social security benefits often cumulate to a negative image in the social environment. As trainees they experience more (and more positive) recognition. Being a trainee also promotes their self-image to the extent that the women become *more independent of their children*. The primary self-definition of the mother role is extended to the vocational context and their work performance. The dimensions of independence do not mean that complete independence in all areas can be achieved by completing vocational training. Rather the young mothers are treading a path towards greater independence and are equipping themselves with what is needed to continue this path. Ultimately, it is gainful employment that will determine their path towards achieving full independence.

At the end of the training, the young women were extremely proud of having achieved their qualification. Under difficult conditions and through various different crises they have achieved something that 'no-one can take away from them'. Being accredited as a skilled worker means more than having a particular activity profile or having improved ones capabilities to secure a livelihood. The vocational qualification also means a gain in self-determination and stability and the attainment of a higher social status. 'Now that I've passed the exams I feel that I have climbed above the background I came from.' Some women even found that an across-the-board improvement in their life took place, from their living situation to their relationship with a partner. The vocational training does not only have significant impact on their career prospects, but also affects their entire attitude towards life. 'I've been mixing with people and taking an active part in life again. These are things where I can say that it was the training that brought them to me'.

The relationship to the world of work creates a new sense of esteem, as the occupation forms the 'eye of the needle through which individuals are able to transcend the immediate private circle of their family and their affairs' and share in societal practice (cf. Schelsky 1965, quoted after Beck et al., 1980, p. 222).

3.4 Conclusion

Germany is a vocationally-oriented society in which 'career and vocationalism have a central normative and regulative importance for social integration' [translated from German] (Baethge, 2000, p. 375). This vocation centeredness can readily be seen in everyday situations when people respond to the question of 'What are you?' by mentioning the job they do. In Germany, we still define ourselves via our occupational specialisation—in so far as we have one. The strong socially integrating force of the occupation has its downside in the exclusion and marginalisation of those who do not have a vocational background and are not participating in gainful employment or work in forms other than full-time schemes. Baethge (2000) delineates the partial exclusion women experience and the loss of privilege among the uneducated and part-time workers (cf. Baethge, 2000 p. 377ff). Girls and women generally demonstrate high levels of job orientation, which is sustained by the increased level of female labour participation. This clearly indicates the social recognition that labour participation generates and its importance in terms of forming an identity attached to performing skilled work. On the other hand, women's comparatively low labour force participation rate in Germany in international perspective cannot be explained by women's lack of job orientation, but is an indicator of the persisting influence of sex-specific structural, normative and also individual factors on work biographies.

With regard to the everyday life of young mothers, who tend to be highly disadvantaged on the training and employment market, working gains a high significance. With a successfully completed vocational training they can proudly state that they 'are something' and offer something to society that gives them special recognition. Furthermore, they can engage in conversations relating to the world of work, their experiences in the workplace, conflicts arising there and how they enjoy performing particular work tasks, thus exchanging ideas with colleagues and becoming socially integrated. Taking part in these domains means some kind of 'normality' and therefore a 'link' to a world that remained closed to them as housewives and mothers.

Numerous empirical studies demonstrate the change in demands of work and career postulating that employment should have subjective meaning and its content should be interesting. Such expectations of personal fulfilment that the career is supposed to meet, is expressed mainly among young employees and women.

Among three-quarters of employees subjective demands of work predominate. These are concentrated either on the content of the work activity or on the network of communicative relationships at work (. . .): people want to be inwardly involved in work, be able to play a personal part in it and gain from work a confirmation of their own competencies [translated from German] (Baethge, 1991, p. 7–9).

Integration into the world of work also means integration into a social network. This generally relates to the direct work context and less to anything beyond that.

From the JAMBA project we can see that the occupation shapes both the personal and the social identity of a person in its interweaving of cultural and content structures with personal lifestyle (cf. Albrecht, 2002, Sprache: Geschlecht—Identität—Beraf. Zum Einfluss der Sprache auf geschlechts-bezogene Berufsorientierungsprozesse, unpublished essay, p. 7). To have an occupation means much more to the young mothers than acquiring a set of skills and expert knowledge. They are now a member of the working society and therefore have access to a cultural area that offers a different kind of recognition than that of being a mother only. Skilled work gives a new direction to their life, a different meaning and ultimately also more structure. The young mothers see themselves increasingly as active participants and as equal members of a community of practice who enjoy equal rights. Increased self-awareness, new frameworks of reference and realms of experience change their scope for action and their self-definition.

For these women, their career is even less separable from the rest of their life context than it is the case for working men and women who do not have children. In their particular life situation, the young mothers are not only crossing the border between working and family life, but they also build bridges as they (have to) link the two spheres together. As a result they develop an

> extended concept of work, which is characterised by two boundaries: with respect to people of the same age and with respect to working men. The statements made by the young women revealed that they contrast training not with free time but with family work [translated from German] (Zybell, 2003, p. 162).

First, the young women hardly have any free time to themselves, and second they see their private time also as being work. One woman formulates this double work reference as follows: 'Work actually gives me a chance to rest. The exhausting part only begins in the evening, when I get home.' The specific nature of their situation compared to people of the same age lies in the fact that the latter do not yet face the demands of raising children and family work, and compared to working men in that, to these men, family does not require any special effort of reconciliation.

The results of the empirical study we presented confirm the importance of a person's occupation as a 'gateway to the world' (Beck *et al.*, 1980, p. 222) and as an opportunity for societal participation. The young mothers have successfully been able to develop a distinctive vocational identity, even if they have not in all cases been able to enter their 'dream occupation'. They transfer their occupational sense of belonging into a general membership of society. The majority of the project participants could no longer imagine not being in employment. 'I have to say that I now wouldn't want to give up work and go back to where I was before. Work has given me a great deal in life.'

Despite being in circumstances that initially seem to be incompatible with undergoing a vocational training programme, the example of young mothers shows the continued strength of vocational identification. The specific characteristic of the group of young mothers lies in the fact that they became mothers 'too early' and *not* that, just like other young women, they attach great value to vocational qualifications. Despite the tendencies for individualisation, their motherhood acts as a decisive obstacle in the way of obtaining a training place in the German Dual System. This continues to be the typical route by which most young men and women become integrated into the labour market in Germany, even though it has been characterised by a series of crisis symptoms for many years.

References

Baethge, M. (1991). Arbeit, Vergesellschaftung, Identität—Zur zunehmenden normativen Subjektivierung der Arbeit. *Soziale Welt*, 1, 6–19.

Baethge, M. (2000). Gesellschaftliche Integration—Jenseits von Beruf und Beruflichkeit? Oder: Zum Gegensatz der soziologischen und qualifikationsstrukturellen Dimension in der Berufskategorie. In F.-J. Kaiser (Ed.), *Berufliche Bildung in Deutschland für das 21. Jahrhundert. Dokumentation des 4. Forums Berufsbildungsforschung 1999 an der Universität Paderborn* (pp. 275–382). Beitrag zur Arbeitsmarkt- und Berufsforschung no 248. Nürnberg: IAB.

Beck, U. (2000). Wohin führt der Weg, der mit dem Ende der Vollbeschäftigungsgesellschaft beginnt? In U. Beck (Ed.), *Die Zukunft von Arbeit und Demokratie* (pp. 7–66). Frankfurt/M.: Edition Zweite Moderne.

Beck, U., M. Brater and H. Daheim (1980). *Soziologie der Arbeit und der Berufe. Grundlagen, Problemfelder, Forschungsergebnisse.* Reinbek bei Hamburg: Rowolt.

Becker-Schmidt, R. (2000). Frauenforschung, Geschlechterforschung, Geschlechterverhält-nisforschung. In R. Becker-Schmidt and G.-A. Knapp (Eds.), *Feministische Theorien zur Einführung* (pp. 14–62). Hamburg: Junius Verlag.

Cornelißen, W., M. Gille, H. Knothe, P. Meier, H. Queisser and M. Stürzer, (2002). *Junge Frauen—junge Männer. Daten zu Lebensführung und Chancengleichheit. Eine sekundäranalytische Auswertung.* DJI 'Gender' series, Vol. 12. Opladen: Leske+Budrich.

Geissler, B. and M. Oechsle (1994). Lebensplanung als Konstruktion: Biographische Dilemmata und Lebenslauf-Entwürfe junger Frauen. In U. Beck and E. Beck-Gernsheim (Eds.), *Riskante Freiheiten* (pp. 139–167). Frankfurt/M.: Suhrkamp.

Heinz, W.R. (1995). Arbeit, Beruf und Lebenslauf. Eine Einführung in die berufliche Sozialisation. Weinheim: Juventa.

Keupp, H. (2001). Identität. In H.-U. Otto and H. Thiersch (Eds.), *Handbuch Sozialarbeit / Sozialpädagogik* (pp. 804–810). Neuwied: Reinhardt Ernst.

Krüger, H. (1999). Gender and Skills. Distributive Ramifications of the German Skill System. In P. Culpepper and D. Finegold (Eds.), *The German skills machine: sustaining comparative advantage in a global economy* (pp. 189–227). New York/Oxford: Berghan Books.

Krüger, H. (2004). Der Institutionenansatz in der Geschlechterforschung am Beispiel der beruflichen Bildung. In A. Paul-Kohlhoff (Ed.), *Berufsbildung und Geschlechterverhältnis* (pp. 17–33). Bielefeld: Bertelsmann.

Lempert, W. (1998). *Berufliche Sozialisation oder was Berufe aus Menschen machen. Eine Einführung.* Hohengehren: Schneider Verlag.

Nader, L., G. Paul and A. Paul-Kohlhoff (2003). An der Zeit—Zur Gleichzeitigkeit von Selbstständigkeit und Begleitung aus Sicht der Betriebe, der Berufsschulen und der Bildungsträger. Münster. Lit.

Negt, O. (2005). Bindungen. *Frankfurter Rundschau*, 25 February 2005, p. 23.

Paul-Kohlhoff, A. (2002). 13 Thesen: Teilzeitausbildung als Reformperspektive für die duale Ausbildung—eine effektive Förderung der Integration von Frauen in die Berufsausbildung. In Bundesanstalt für Arbeit (Ed.), *(Teilzeit-) Ausbildung für junge Mütter und Väter. Modellprojekte aus der Praxis. Informationen für die Beratungs- und Vermittlungsdienste* (pp. 146–148). Vol. 2, Nürnberg: IAB.

Stauber, B. (1996). *Lebensgestaltung alleinerziehender Frauen. Balance zwischen Anpassung und Eigenständigkeit im ländlichen Regionen.* Weinheim/München: Juventa.

Statistisches Bundesamt Deutschland (2004), retrieved from www.destatis.de/basis/d/erwerb/erwerbtab1.php (as at 24/2/2004).

Zybell, U. (2003). An der Zeit—Zur Gleichzeitigkeit von Berufsausbildung und Kindererziehung aus Sicht junger Mütter. Münster: Lit.

4

The 'Double' Vocational Identity of the Working Population in the Greek Tourist Industry

Nikitas Patiniotis and Gerasimos Prodromitis
Panteion University of Athens, Greece

4.1   Introduction

Human identity presupposes a relation between the individual and both, the other and the self. Every form of identity, including the vocational one, is expressed as a 'symptom' (Lipovatsz, 1991, p. 273), as an incident experienced by the other through particular forms of behaviour and social relations accomplished by the individual. In the present chapter, we trace the particular forms of behaviour and social relations that employees working in tourism display alongside their vocational identity.

The tourism industry in Greece has been rapidly expanding in the last 40 years due to the prosperous post-war economic period in Europe. It is remarkable that during the period of tourism rise in the south of Europe, a reciprocal migration movement from the South towards the industrial countries of the North started to evolve. The workforce started moving from parts of Italy, Spain, Greece and other southern countries in order to seek employment in the more industrialised North. Till today, the emigrants' remittances and the tourist exchange are welcome since they contribute to the relief of the commercial deficit, help to reduce the economic crisis, and therefore, alleviate poverty in the South, particularly after those countries became full members of the European Union.

Tourism and migration led to a radical transformation in the countries of the South including Greece (Patiniotis, 1979). This transformation has affected the social structures but also the people living in these countries in

A. Brown, S. Kirpal and F. Rauner (eds.), Identities at Work, 91–114.
© *2007 Springer.*

terms of personality and identity formation. While today migration to other countries has lost its former importance, tourism has become very important. The increase of tourist activities does not only have economic but also social, cultural and environmental implications. When tourism takes place in traditionally organised societies, it lays down new rules and influences the social attitude and behaviour of people in their ways of living and interpersonal relations within the family and the neighbourhood, but also within the communities of practice and how they practise their trade.

In relation to our subject of research a series of questions arose: Do employees working in tourism develop a particular vocational identity? Do they believe that it is worthwhile pursuing permanent employment in this field or do they regard the arduous but profitable jobs in the tourist field as a means to make quick savings in order to invest in other economic fields or activities? In other words, does their employment in this field form part of their life plan or not? Due to the seasonal employment patterns in the sector, people typically work for half the year only, whereas during the other half of the year they either remain unemployed, work in other fields or engage in other activities while waiting for the next tourist season. Thus, we ask whether employees working in tourism develop a vocational identity in this occupational area or rather build forms of 'identity bricolage' (Carruthers and Uzzi, 2000, p. 486) deriving from their diverse employment opportunities. Or are those people deprived of developing any form of stable vocational identity because of their diverse activities?

The above-mentioned research questions arose in the context of the 5th EU Framework Project 'FAME—Vocational Identity, Flexibility and Mobility in the European Labour Market' (for further details see Kirpal, Brown, and Dif in this volume). In the framework of this project, the small sample Greek study applied qualitative methods for data collection with semi-structured interviews conducted in two geographical regions: on the island of Crete and in a small town in mainland Greece. Both regions possess different socio-economic features and have a completely different tourism development background. The data on the tourism employees interviewed are presented in the compact format of a detailed table in the appendix of this chapter (Yin, 1994, p. 136f). We choose to present the data in this format since a more detailed presentation of the individual cases would exceed the limits of this chapter.

We believe that the analysis of employees' vocational identities in Greek tourism enables us to engage with a sector that is continually expanding in the present period of time. The economic situation in modern tourism is characterised by uncertainty in the annual course of this field and, consequently, an uncertainty regarding the future of employment, the very long working hours, the flexibility of working relations and the interchange between periods of intense employment and unemployment. These are representative examples of the modern 'risk society' (Beck, 1986). For this reason we consider tourism as a typical field of modernity.

In Greek tourism, very frequently we find the 'self-employed employer', a unique form of employee. This form of small business owner can be met in every European economy. This type of employee is owner and employee at the same time, working alongside the small number employees he or she may employ. He or she often works hard, perhaps harder than the other employees. This type of 'self-employed employer' is met in restaurants, travel agencies, car rentals, small hotels and similar forms of businesses and is actually very common across Europe. However, although a considerable proportion of the workforce is employed in such forms of services and small businesses, it has not been considered much in current international research.

In our study, we tried to trace and analyse the real situation of employees working in tourism hence the 'self-employed employer' is well represented. Furthermore, we considered the vocational identity of these people to be an interesting case.

In order to provide an integrated presentation of our research outcomes, this chapter has adopted the following structure: First, we refer to the parameters that determine the Greek tourist industry and the social effects of this successful sector of the Greek economy. We proceed with the presentation of the functioning parameters of the tourism sector and the skills and competences that employers expect from their employees. In the majority of cases those skills are not acquired from a particular kind of formal vocational education. In the next section, we introduce some semantic and theoretical considerations regarding the study of vocational identity and then present our empirical findings on the vocational identity of people employed in this sector. Apart from the regular employees, employment in tourism is largely characterised by self-employed owners of small tourist businesses, so we can observe the emergence of flexible vocational practices, which lead to the mapping of multiple vocational identities for the tourism industry employees.

4.2   Employment in Greek Tourism

In Greece, tourism is a substantial economic sector that has been growing constantly since the 1970s. The sector has recently created approximately 20 per cent of the Greek GDP employing about 17 per cent of the country's workforce. In 2005, the number of foreign tourists is expected to rise to approximately 14 million, which is 1.5 times higher than the Greek population. The number of tourists should even increase when the millions of Greek tourists who spend their holidays in Greek tourist destinations are included.

Greek tourism is characterised by seasonal employment mainly restricted to the summer season. Tourist businesses usually operate from April to October. They remain closed for the rest of the year and dismiss their employees in order to hire them again next year. Although slowly rising, winter tourism is very low and addressed to Greeks only. Agro tourism has been greatly supported in the last twenty years in an endeavour to combine agricultural and tourist activities (Jacovidou, 1991; Portalidou and Jacovidou, 2002), but this had a relatively low impact.

The sector comprises different types and sizes of companies ranging from very small and one-person businesses to large hotel chains. Also foreign companies are continually gaining ground, particularly foreign tour operators, which move massive numbers of tourists (Sheldon, 1986; Zacharatos, 1992). They typically aim to satisfy simple tourist expectations that could be fulfilled in every sunny coastal region on the planet. Turner and Ash (1970) called these expectations the '4s': sun, sand, sex and sea (Turner and Ash, 1970, p. 11). Those massive numbers of tourists are influenced in their decision concerning their destination by low prices, the advertisement of foreign tour operators and their friends' opinions, who have already visited the chosen destination (Tsartas and Thanopoulou, 1995, p. 119). Tourists of this type often have very little social interactions with the employees working in tourism. They typically spend their holidays in all-inclusive resorts isolated by the surroundings and have no contact with the local population. In such tourist 'ghettos' (Tsartas, 1998) like the clubs Méditerranée in Greece, for example, social interaction between tourists and locals does not occur. However, there is closer contact in other forms of tourism such as cultural, ecological and discovery tourism, although these forms are still largely the province of fringe groups not only in Greece, but also all over the world.

At any rate, 'the more mass tourism expands, the more the transition from a "face to face" relation to a distinctively commercial relation between the tourists and the locals is evident' (Tsartas et al., 1995, p. 21), a reality with obvious impact on the vocational identity of tourism employees. The vocational identity of employees working in tourism is obviously affected by the social influence stemming from the tourist industry as well as tourists' behaviours and the opportunities to meet locals. We should not disregard the fact that this contact takes place at a time when tourists are on holiday while the employees are working hard.

4.2.1 The Social Effects of Tourism

The social effects of the tourist industry affecting the formation or the transformation of employees' vocational identity working in this sector may be encoded, in no particular evaluative order, as follows (Stott, 1978, p. 81; Andronicou, 1979; Jafari, 1974, p. 238; Tsartas et al., 1995; Tsartas and Thanopoulou, 1995; Tsartas, 1998; OECD, 1980):

- Tourism as we can observe in Greece leads to the rapid transformation of agricultural areas into areas that offer mainly tourist services. People live in opulence owing to high earnings and income poured into the area under tourist development.
- The level of income becomes the principal indicator of social status diminishing the importance of factors such as family traditions, educational background or political power. Pursuing higher earnings becomes a personal strategy leading to individualism, competition and superficial social relations based mainly on personal interest and selfishness. The ostentatious showing off of wealth and the consumer goods owned by the 'successful' undermines the role of altruistic relations.
- The practices of local tradition are adjusted and commercialised to be compatible with the tastes and aesthetics of the foreign tourists. This leads to an estrangement from tradition.
- Tourists bring with them their own way of life, consumption, entertainment and food habits, which are imitated by the locals who aspire to be considered successful. Thus, there is a decline or even a rejection of local habits and a prevalence of foreign ones.
- The environmental effects from the rapid growth of tourism can be registered, especially in areas considered as 'traditional settlements' or areas of 'exceptional natural beauty'. The effects may concern the natural environment as well as buildings, arbitrarily built settlements, advertisements, etc. that spoil the landscape.
- Young people and women become financially independent by means of employment in tourism.
- The seasonal nature of employment and long working hours blur the distinction between work and leisure affecting employees' relations with family, friends and colleagues.

- The economic dominance of tourism makes employees leave traditional sectors and areas of employment that do not offer equally high earnings. Furthermore, the development of the sector leads to long working hours and the employment of large numbers of foreign, often illegal, workers.

4.2.2   Employment Patterns in Tourism

Like other countries with a significantly growing tourist sector, Greece experiences serious problems due to the lack of a specialist labour force. However, differentiating from developments in other European countries with prosperous tourism, Greek employers do not consider that employees need to be well trained in order to be hired. This is a general trait of the Greek economy: the phenomenon that business activities do not rely upon well-trained and specialised employees, who would be more productive and, as a result, better paid by the employers. As we have outlined in another paper:

> the predominant form of Greek private business is the small-sized, family-owned enterprise. Companies are often run on an emotional basis, managers usually reaching business decisions amateurishly, through instinct and intuition instead of market investigation. On the other hand, entrepreneurs, in general, appear reluctant to undertake expansion activities, albeit profoundly profitable, without state support. Moreover, many Greek entrepreneurs tend to view their vocation as temporary, often becoming engaged in short-run, speculative gains. This propensity seems to stem from the unstable institutional and economic environment. Data indicate that businessmen have accumulated substantial profits, but these profits have come mainly from exploitation of favourable legal devices, as well as from the squeeze on employees' salaries. Research has shown that labour wages and salaries in Greece tend to increase at a markedly lower rate compared to other EU and OECD countries (Patiniotis and Stavroulakis, 1997, p. 192).

To better understand the functioning of the Greek labour market and the sector in the promotion of employees' vocational identities, we repeat something formerly mentioned in another publication:

> The saying of the famous painter Jannis Tsarouchis that 'in Greece you are whatever you declare' seems to apply to the practice of most companies with the exception of those requiring a high

level of specialization. This means that a person can virtually practise any occupation he or she wishes, regardless of his or her education, training or other qualifications. The only requirement is his or her intention to practise in the area. In Greece, many people with different educational qualifications practise the same occupation alongside another. The lack of correspondence between peoples' fields of training and employment is also exacerbated by the practice of 'multi-employment'. In such cases, wage earners work for two (or even three) employers, sometimes in completely unrelated occupational fields (Martínez Cellorio, Ferran, and Patiniotis, 1997, p. 33; see also Mihail, 2003; Kufidou and Mihail, 1999).

Due to the seasonal nature that characterises Greek tourism, it is expected that large numbers of employees consider their employment in the tourism sector as seasonal and non-permanent. Most hotels and tourist shops or services only operate between six to eight months per year. Employees who work in tourism only over the summer have several options: for the rest of year they may be unemployed, live on their savings or the unemployment benefit from the State Manpower Agency, which they are entitled to receive for a period of up to six months, or they may work in other economic areas. From our research, we found that other employment opportunities range from the primary sector (e.g. working as farmer or fisherman) to the tertiary sector (e.g. instructor, insurer). The seasonality of tourist jobs as well as the awareness that even without special training it is easily possible to find a job may be two key reasons why employees typically do not pursue further training and qualifications.

Employers in tourist enterprises reckon that most of the graduates from training institutions specialised in tourism do not have the necessary knowledge to practice their profession. As a consequence, they hire mainly non-specialist employees who cost the employers lower salaries. Because of their low salaries, their compensation is also lower in case they are made redundant. As a result of this strategy most tourist employers prefer not to hire employees who graduated from schools of tourism. Hence, 'the graduates of tertiary tourism education institutions, who work in the tourist industry, are considerably fewer than their respective counterparts in other European countries' (Igoumenakis, 1992, p. 48).

It is remarkable that research projects and publications after 1981 did not show great concern for professional expertise or work process knowledge, skills, competences or the quality of the workforce to support the development of this industry, although strenuous efforts were being made in order to boost tourism. It seems that during the 1980s macro-economic, land-planning and advertising policies were considered sufficient to secure tourism development and its transformation into an 'industry' (Zacharatos, 1980, 1986; Komilis, 1986a, b). This still seems to be the attitude today. In their papers on the future of tourism and the factors that can lead to its qualitatively improved development, political executives from the two biggest Greek parties referred only briefly to improving the employees' vocational training. With this situation in mind, students of the Greek polytechnics only rarely specialise in tourism. This is verified from the fact that the fewest preferences and, therefore, the lowest pass grades in the university entrance exams for 2005 were achieved in the departments of 'Tourism Studies' of five Greek polytechnics.

The employers' attitude even makes it difficult for graduates from tertiary tourism education institutions to find employment in the sector. Thereby, they are often forced to change employment, while employers, especially those of small tourist enterprises, continue to hire non-specialist workers who do not have special salary requirements and pressing demands for permanent employment.

The aforementioned surely has striking effects on the vocational identity of tourism employees. These effects can be documented by studying the tourism employees' biographies (Patiniotis and Prodromitis, 2002) and will be analysed further below.

4.3   Theoretical Considerations in the Study of Social Identity

The main issues in the context of theoretical analysis and empirical pinpointing of 'social identity' relate to the individual and collective components of identity. These issues include the psychological mechanisms that influence self-definition, the 'external' social forces that determine the normative framework for the constitution of identity as composed of both similarity and difference, and the form and orientation of emotional investment involving implications for identity, as well as the corollary of this investment on the social discourse and the behaviour of social actors.

It is noticeable that social identity comprises conjunctions between the individual and the social on the one hand, and the psychological and the sociological on the other hand. This phenomenon has often been empirically registered either as a mere addition to some sociological and central parameters of psychological research or, as use (and in some cases misuse) of non-conventional psychological mechanisms, from the researchers' point of view, used in an effort to analyse widespread phenomena. The outcome that ensues from such options is the preservation, feedback and disguise of the scientific bipolar 'methodological holism—methodological individualism' or, in other words, the reproduction of sociological and psychological reflections and the failure of transcendence beyond this approach due to a superficial and 'supplementary' conjunction between psychology and sociology (Papastamou, 2002).

On a theoretical level, these one-sided choices of explanatory principles are connected to the preservation of a deceptive distinction between the individual and the society. In terms of modern sociological theory this distinction is expressed as a problem of tracing the relations between the social authority of action and the social structure (Mouzelis, 1991, 1995; Giddens, 1990). The selection of psychologically reductionist explanations gives maximum autonomy to subsystems of social integration at the expense of social structure, whereas recourse to sociologically reductionist explanations results in the detachment of the systemic structure at the expense of a relative autonomy of the social action authority. In consequence of this second option, we have, on the one hand, the image of a 'highly socialised' puppet-individual, and on the other hand, an anthropomorphic image of society in its entirety, in which meanings such as 'principles of social values', 'collective consciousness' or 'collective soul' have a value in themselves as entities that control everybody and everything in society.

Integration into social groups and differentiation from others form the basis for the formation of a social identity through a procedure of recognition and self-attribution to in-group specific characteristics and, at the same time, the adoption of original views (Tajfel, 1979; Tajfel, 1982; Turner, 1982; Turner, Oakes et al., 1994). Thus, social identity could be simultaneously deemed to be a cognitive structure related to the management and classification of social information, and a structure of emotional and judgmental investment on both the individual and collective level. In short, social identity could be considered as an organisational principle of: the definition of social groups; the regulation of the relations between the individual and her or his reference group; and the regulation of in-group relations. This specific approach provides the framework for concepts and formal theoretical analyses, which could be evaluated in empirical research regarding the social identity of workers in the tourist industry. Therefore, in our research, we have studied the formation of the social-vocational identities of Greek tourism industry employees. We have adopted the basic theoretical principle according to which the constitution of social groups is directly linked to the individual's need for a distinctive identity, which enables individual differentiation from others.

4.4   Method of Investigation

In order to provide a theoretically rich and methodologically rigorous approach to the study of vocational identity, we need to consider further a number of issues related to individual and collective aspects of the constitution of identities. In this way, it is possible to dodge, on the one hand, the overuse of the paradigm of methodological individualism which orientates research unilaterally towards the study of individual cognitive and affective procedures and, on the other hand, the excessive first order magnitude attribution of those macro-social factors that result in the disregard of intermediate levels in the formation and interaction of relationships.

In order to reach this goal we considered Doise's (1982) distinction of four analytical levels of socio-psychological reality as particularly useful. This distinction between 'in-group', 'out-group', 'inter-group' and 'ideological' levels of analysis provides a useful framework for the classification of individuals' expression, in the course of their self-definition procedures, as personalities and members of a professional group at the same time. Furthermore, this framework is useful for the study at the level of the individuals' convergence with the group, the relations they promote with other members of the group and the in-group and out-group power structures. Finally, turning this context to advantage, there is the potential to pinpoint the main ideological principles that intervene in the individuals' discourse and analyse their self-definition as personalities and members of social groups during the formation and elaboration of social relations on various levels.

4.4.1   Data Collection

With these theoretical principles for data collection (realised in the summer of 2002) we adopted the method of semi-structured interviews. We modelled the thematic guide for data collection in a way to avoid possible sociological or psychological reductionism. The individuals' discourses were classified in such a way that different levels and keynotes in the definition of vocational identity could emerge. In a complementary fashion, we followed a common approach to analyse vocational identity formation as identified by the collaborative research team of the FAME project (see Kirpal, 2004). This approach identified different aspects in the socio-psychological processing of the experience of work of the employees who participated in the research. These aspects included: integration into and satisfaction with the work environment; the meaning of work; feelings of integration into a group with reference to the organisation and in relation to other workers; recruitment, organisation of work and the experience of hierarchy; and broader implications in relation to the wider environment and the subject of work.

The model guide for the realisation of the semi-structured interviews with employees in the Greek tourism industry was outlined as follows:

1. Initially their individual-demographic characteristics were assessed (length of time in tourism industry, description of tasks in the present position, motivation to choose to enter the tourist industry, motives for the choice of the present position, educational qualifications, education considered compulsory in order to achieve maximum productivity in their present position, employment status (permanent or temporary) and the degree of satisfaction and evaluation of material and symbolic benefits).

2. The second keystone of the model guide covered the individual's experience and evaluation in relation to the work environment (the firm's profile, hierarchy, evaluation of horizontal and vertical relations, the degree of commitment to both the work and the employer and the firm, initiative potential, feelings of job self-autonomy and elements of satisfaction and dissatisfaction).

3. The next keystone studied in-field or inter-field manpower mobility either existing or as perceived by the employee.

4. The fourth keystone concerned the way in which employees comprehended and evaluated their area of employment (e.g. hotel sector) to assess their experiences in terms of collaboration, competition and institutional structures.

5. The 5th keystone investigated employees' evaluation of the Greek tourism industry.

6. The sixth keystone was linked to the previous one in assessing employees' definition and evaluation of the macro-social factors that influence the tourism sector.

A total of thirteen employees working in the tourist industry were interviewed, of which eight worked on the island of Crete. Crete is one of the most developed tourist places in Greece and different types of tourist-related jobs and occupational profiles can easily be spotted. The remaining five participants were interviewed in a coastal town in North-western Greece known as a holiday resort for Greeks who come from the area. This place can be classified as a tourist area 'under development'. The comparison of the data between this town and Crete not only take account of the various rates of tourist growth in Greece, but also of the different degrees of consciousness of the vocational identity of the interviewees. The imbalance in consciousness is attested by the fact that only three out of five latter interviews were included in the analysis, since the remaining two interviews did not provide sufficient data relevant to the objectives of the present study.

4.5 Data Analysis—The 'Double' Vocational Identity in the Greek Tourism Industry

The occupational profiles of the eleven people interviewed are listed in the annex, which also details the codification of the data affecting vocational identity formation. The codification takes into account the following parameters: (i) the present position (legal relation); (ii) reasons for choosing to enter the tourist industry; (iii) the educational level of the interviewee; (iv) special training; (v) supporting factors in the sense of positive aspects of the tourist occupation; (vi) barriers and obstacles (to employment in tourism); (vii) forms of individual professional mobility; and (viii) life plans. The research data emerging from the interviews were evaluated according to the method of thematic content analysis, which was conducted on the principles mentioned above.

In six cases the interviewees were either self-employed owners or managers. The 'double vocational identity' of somebody who considers herself or himself as a manager/employer and employee at the same time is an interesting element of the work identity of people working in the Greek tourist industry. We believe that this aspect should be a key issue in related research projects since it is a widespread phenomenon not only in Greece, but also in large numbers of other countries, especially at the European periphery. Focusing on regular employees only would for the tourist industry present a one-sided, distorted and misleading image ignoring the facets of 'complex' or 'mixed' identities typical of the self-employed manager. A first result of our data analysis is that the distinction between employee and employer in Greek tourism is not always explicit. As a sector with many small businesses, self-employment in personal or family-run units is widespread where personal labour input along with other employees is combined with managing the unit.

Apart from the self-employed owner we also find other types of employees working in tourism. Their perceptions and statements were analysed in the context of the nature of seasonal employment in the Greek tourist sector. Some seasonal employees hold down two jobs and employments at the same time, of which one might not be related to tourism, or, 'out of season' they work in another completely different area. Other employees have a permanent job in tourism only and do not work 'out of season'. Their earnings from tourist activities are often so high or the needs of the people of this category are so simple that working very hard for six or seven months can cover the living needs for the whole year.

These employees seem willing to search for permanent employment in tourism under more favourable circumstances. For them, it is a desirable field of occupation, because they regard the relatively high earnings compared to what they would earn in other segments of the economy as a positive element. Furthermore, they value the symbolic rewards, which emanate from the communication and interpersonal relations with tourists.

The data analysis revealed that people with a positive inclination towards their vocational identity in terms of developing a self-understanding as 'tourism people' are, apart from the self-employed owners, those who underwent vocational education and training related to tourism. Hence, specialised vocational training seems to be a dynamic factor for employees working in tourism developing a distinctive vocational identity. However, the self-definition of an individual as a 'tourism person' not only has to do with the specific training and formal qualifications, but also with on-the-job acquired practical knowledge, skills and competences a person has obtained by means of professional practice. These elements count besides the symbolic benefit people gain from rich interpersonal communication opportunities with large numbers of different people.

Taking into account that, from the interviewees' point of view, the tourist sector is a field of uncertainty which is vulnerable to imponderable and uncontrolled factors,[1] which can influence the annual number

---

[1] From our research such factors involve the economic crisis in the country of origin, inflation due to introduction of the EURO, natural disasters in tourist resorts and wars and conflicts in countries around the tourist resorts.

of tourist arrivals and the composition of the population of tourists, a number of personal strategies towards a personal vocational stability can be identified. Such strategies have to do with both vocational mobility and movement into fields other than tourism, as well as strengthening their current job position in the tourist sector. This last strategy is related to personal efforts at creating a 'non-formal curriculum vitae' based on the good reputation the person has acquired at the workplace. This involves forms of symbolic capital that the employee has accrued and which can be evaluated positively on the grounds of interpersonal relations and immediate communication with employers from the specific area.

4.6   Tourism as an Example for the Implementation of Flexible Labour Practices and the Acquisition of Multiple Labour Identities

Self-employment can be regarded as a common trait of the Greek economy. Since 1945, at least 25 to 30 per cent of the active working population in Greece have been registered as self-employed. Tourism in particular is a sector characterised by widespread self-employment in small family-owned businesses. Hence, making a distinction between employers and employees in the Greek tourist industry is extremely difficult. In their economic function family businesses, which typically operate with a simple allocation of duties and division of labour among the members of the family, seem to present a particularly interesting case. This allocation is ruled by the hierarchy of age and starts off the younger members of the family in the business without taking into account their educational level. In large family businesses, the 'self-employed employer' could be either the father or the mother with the members of the family being the full-time or part-time employees (Tsivakou, 2000, p. 358). Female employers comprise approximately 25 per cent of all employers in Greek enterprises (Greek Observatory of Employment, 2000). The Greek Statistics Service (ESYE) registers the non-formal employees, who are family members and work for the family business, under the classification 'assistants and non-paid members'.

Employees, who display a positive attitude in terms of their vocational identity, consider themselves as 'tourism people'. Apart from the self-employed owners these are typically professionals who have undergone special training related to tourism. However, the self-definition of a 'tourism person' refers to a lesser degree to the training received, and to a much higher degree to the on-the-job acquired practical knowledge and competences accumulated in the course of professional practice as well as the symbolic benefits from the interpersonal communication with a large and diverse number of people in the tourism field. This is due to the relatively low prestige of vocational education, whereas work experience is widely recognised in the Greek economy and facilitates integration into the professional field.

The multiple characteristics of personal strategies and elements of self-definition that could be identified in this field lead to a distinct and specific form of vocational identity of people employed in the Greek tourism sector. When taking into consideration the multiplicity of incentives in tourism, the different levels of educational backgrounds and vocational training, the negative and positive aspects of working in the tourist industry as well as the sumptuousness of the life and the personal mobility plans of some workers (illustrated in the annex) it becomes apparent that the vocational identity of tourism employees does not constitute a clearly framed and strictly recorded network of self-attributed traits, but rather a dynamic field of elements that are activated by the individuals themselves.

According to a dynamic socio-psychological approach towards social identity (Sennett, 1998; Castells, 2003; Brown, 1997; Mike, 1996; Wenger, 1998; Niethammer, 2000; Zavalloni and Louis-Guérin, 1984; Kirpal, 2004) the incorporation into social classes and individuals' active involvement in reference groups lead to the framing of social representations, which facilitate particular social orientations of employees in tourism. At the same time, individualistic practices are developed by means of individual involvement, experience and understanding of social knowledge in relation to both personal experience and social history in the broad sense of the term.

The focus on social identity with a special concern with its vocational component requires, on a first level, the recording of patterns of the individual's self-presentation and self-definition concerning 'self-image' and 'vocational identity' as a dynamic process between individuality and social relationships at work. The pinpointing and practical evaluation of the interrelationship between socio-psychological identity and the professional component of work are important to understanding the development of the vocational identities of tourism employees.

Using these concepts and interrelationships, the data analysis can be undertaken from two different standpoints. According to an individual-centred approach, the focus can be on elements of the participants' individual self-definition in relation to personal mobility strategies in terms of moving within or outside the tourism sector. From a more holistic or sociological perspective, attention can be focused upon the dynamics between structural demands and needs, which influence in a subsidiary way job entry, job satisfaction and the organisation of employment in the tourism field.

Combining these two interpretative approaches it is possible to identify factors affecting the interrelationship between employees' vocational identity and a broader socio-psychological identity. First, the lack of a tourism infrastructure due to its seasonal nature impedes the establishment of a structured, conscious and well-developed vocational identity of the 'tourism employee'. At the same time, the existence of organised tourist enterprises requiring large numbers of seasonal employees results in an oversupply of labour. In addition, tourism is a sector that reacts sensitively to the conjuncture of economic and political factors that are beyond the control of those involved in the sector. Easy access to tourism jobs regardless of the individual's educational level and training background and workers employing multiple and flexible 'survival' and mobility strategies are dominant features of work in this sector. Second, the diminishing social presence of arrangements for joint employer-employee collaboration and the declining role of trade unions (Esser, 1982; Müller-Jentsch, 1988; Kassimati, 1997; Alexiou, 1994) result in the marginalisation and factionalism of Greek tourism employees. Not being organised in professional groups for the expression of joint interests also undermines the development of tourism employees' vocational identities in traditional sociological terms.

4.7   Epilogue

The material generated in this research is amenable to analysis and interpretation from differing standpoints. One can evaluate the results on micro-sociological grounds shedding light on the individual biographies of the interviewees. On the other hand, one has the potential to contrast the individuals' stories with macro-sociological data to delineate that tourism is a non-cohesive and contradictory segment of the economy. At any rate, due to the inability to infer the 'ideal' or 'stereotypical' employee in the Greek tourist industry, researchers may be discouraged from attempting further theoretical finishing touches based on a wide-ranged empirical study.

Annex 1   Factors Affecting the Vocational Identity of the Employees

Job profile of the Interviewee	Occupational status	Reasons for choosing to work in the sector	Educational background	Specialised training	Supporting factors	Obstacles (experienced and considered)	Forms of professional mobility	Life plans
Restaurant waiter of Albanian origin (male)	Paid work	Securing livelihood; Easy access to find a job	Psychiatry student in the 3rd year	No	Balance between material and symbolic reward; Self-commitment	Difficulties in the first steps of social and economic adjustment	In-tourism mobility to improve income; Working conditions and interpersonal relations with the employer; Self-realisation	Repatriation; Practising the subject of studies; Acquisition of personal property
Self-employed (goldsmith) (male)	Self-employed owner	Family tradition	Secondary education	No practical work in sales	Reward from the 'aesthetic of the commodity'	Ambiguity; Insecurity; Unpredictability of the sector, which is perceived as chaotic	No	Overarching approach of personal mobility potential; Orientation towards establishing own business
Hotel receptionist (female)	Regular employee; Heir to the Business	Family tradition	Secondary education	State school for tourism studies	Commitment, personal involvement, affective investment, interpersonal relations	Uncertainty regarding the future of the tourist industry	Temporary transfer in the past to a similar position; Return to present position due to affective reasons	Possible mobility but only in the field of tourism; Final return to the family business for sure

Continued

Annex 1 Continued

Job profile of the Interviewee	Occupational status	Reasons for choosing to work in the sector	Educational background	Specialised training	Supporting factors	Obstacles (experienced and considered)	Forms of professional mobility	Life plans
Restaurant Manager (male)	Self-employed owner	Family tradition; Personal suitability and sense of superiority	Secondary education	Intensive training in 'Tourism business Organisation'	Sense of individual superiority	Problems with interpersonal relations with customers and colleagues; Limited personal free time	In the context of family business regarding an hierarchic allocation of tasks, according to age	
Self-employed restaurant owner (male)	Self-employed owner	Favourable period of tourism in the 1980s		No	Balance of relationships/ mutuality between owner and customers	Indifference of the central government policy on tourism; Absence of infra structures and central planning	Mobility to the tourist industry 15 years ago; Previous jobs as technician and commercial representative	Enjoyment of personal free time after the end of the tourist season; Occupation compatible with his personal agricultural property

Office clerk in car rental services (female)	Paid work	Supplement income during the summer period	Music teacher	One month of non-formal training in the specific post	Seasonal work supply; foreign languages; interpersonal relations; job satisfaction at a symbolic level; Recognition of work; liberal management	Lack of free time	Seasonal jobs in tourism	Desire of making a career in the tourist sector; Concerned about future employment insecurity; Exams for a permanent position in the public sector
Restaurant waiter (female)	Paid work	Tourist occupation totally compatible with personality	Higher education	Graduate of the higher institution for tourism vocations	Satisfactory earnings; Liberal management; Interpersonal relations with employer; Pre-condition for efficiency in work is a positive, balanced personal and	No negative elements	Continuous employment in the tourist sector; Seasonal jobs as industrial worker in the dull period for tourism	Continuous employment in tourism all year round; Retirement at the age of 45

Continued

Annex 1 (Continued)

Job profile of the Interviewee	Occupational status	Reasons for choosing to work in the sector	Educational background	Specialised training	Supporting factors	Obstacles (experienced and considered)	Forms of professional mobility	Life plans
Tourist guide of Austrian origin (male)	Paid work	Practical reasons associated with personal life	Higher education	Not mentioned	Contact with Greek civilisation and the Greek way of life; Good relations with management	Problems of adjusting to the Greek culture	Previous occupation in an airline in his country	Intention to stay in Greece
Campsite manager (male)	Self-employed	Alternative for summer employment	Secondary education	No	Personal gratification from 'intercultural exchange'; Exploitation of the Greek tradition in the provinces	Lack of infrastructure on the local level; Intensive employment, both personal and for the family members	Previous occupation as car mechanic; Seasonal employment in tourism; Works in the dull period of tourism in a family cattle-breeding unit	

Waiter at a coffee shop (male)	Paid work	Tired of previous work as a sailor; Decision to return and live in his homeland	Secondary education	No	Homeland is a way of life; Life perspective totally compatible with the particular job	Substantial absence of tourist organisations in the field	Moved into tourism due to tiredness with his previous occupation as a sailor
Captain of a tourist vessel (male)	Self-employed owner	Tired of previous work as a sailor; wanted to live in his homeland; Supplement income	Lower education level	No	Gratification on a symbolic base (interpersonal relations, mutuality, recognition); Balance between loneliness and peace during winter time	Income is not satisfactory; Unbearable costs	Return to homeland and permanent position as a fisherman (previous occupation as a sailor); Tourist occupation is clearly seasonal

The presented research results provide useful and accessible evidence for the planning of multiple political interventions. Questions include whether such interventions should have, for instance, an individualised character or whether, within the individual's micro-field, they should aim to raise employees' job satisfaction and to improve human resources development strategies. Interventions should emphasise (i) the marked preference of research participants for a liberal form of management (Bourantas and Papalexandris, 1999; Stavroulakis, 1997; Tsiganou, 1991; Raftis and Stavroulakis 1991; Szell, 1988) and (ii) the key role of direct interrelationships in the tourism field. In addition, these research data could form the basis for macro-structural interventions to support labour supply in the tourism field and foster employees' confidence in their vocational identity. Finally, interventions could aim to sustain the tourism family businesses and to promote the rationalisation of tourism-related education and training programmes.

References

Alexiou, A. (1994). *Zur Frage der Entstehung und Formierung der griechischen Arbeiterbewegung.* Frankfurt/M.: Lange.

Andronicou, A. (1979). Tourisme à Chypre. In E. de Kadt (Ed.), *Tourisme: Passeport pour le développement?* Paris: UNESCO and BIRD.

Beck, U. (1986). *Risikogesellschaft. Auf dem Weg auf eine andere Moderne.* Frankfurt/M.: Suhrkamp.

Bourantas, D. and N. Papalexandris (1999). Personality Traits. Discriminating between Employees in Public and Private Sector Organizations. *International Journal of Human Resource Management,* 10(5), 858–869.

Brown, A. (1997). A dynamic model of occupational identity formation. In A. Brown (Ed.), *Promoting vocational education and training: European perspectives* (pp. 59–67). Tampere: University of Tampere.

Carruthers, B. and B. Uzzi (2000). Economic sociology in the new millennium. *Contemporary Sociology,* 29(3), 486–494.

Castells, M. (2003). *Die Macht der Identität.* Opladen: Leske + Budrich.

Doise, W. (1982). *L'Explication en Psychologie Sociale.* Paris: Presses Universitaires de France.

Esser, J. (1982). *Gewerkschaften in der Krise.* Frankfurt/M.: Suhrkamp.

Giddens, A. (1990). *The consequences of modernity.* Stanford, CA: Stanford University Press.

Greek Observatory of Employment (2000). *Structural image and developments in the labour market.* Athens: EPA (in Greek).

Igoumenakis, N. (1992). Education and employment in the tourism industry. In: Th. Papatheodosiou (Ed.), *Greece and European labour market* (pp. 45–52). Athens: TEI Athens (in Greek).

Jacovidou, O. (1991). Employment in tourism: A way out for the agricultural population in Chalkidiki. *The Greek Review of Social Research*, 83, 32–47 (in Greek).

Jafari, J. (1974). Socio-economic costs of tourism to developing countries. *Annals of Tourism Research*, 1(3), 227–262.

Kassimati, K. (1997). *The Greek trade-union movement in the end of 20th century*. Athens: Gutenberg (in Greek).

Kirpal, S. (2004). *Work identities in Europe: Continuity and change. Final Report of the 5th EU Framework Project 'FAME'*. ITB Working Paper Series No 49. Bremen: Institute Technology and Education/University of Bremen.

Kirpal, S., A. Brown and M. Dif (2006). The individualisation of identification with work in a European perspective. In A. Brown, S. Kirpal and F. Rauner (Eds.), *Identities at work* (pp. 285–313). Dordrecht: Springer.

Komilis, P. (1986a). *Tourist activities*. Athens: KEPE (Planning Issues Series No. 10) (in Greek).

Komilis, P. (1986b). *Territorial analysis of tourism*. Athens: KEPE (Planning Issues Series No. 20) (in Greek).

Kufidou, S. and D.M. Mihail (1999). Decentralisation and Flexibility in Greek Industrial Relations. *Employee Relations*, 21(5), 485–499.

Lipovatsz, Th. (1991). Greece: a dual identity. In Th. Lipovatsz (Ed.), *Political psychology issues* (pp. 266–284). Athens: Exandas (in Greek).

Martínez Cellorio, X., M. Ferran and N. Patiniotis (1997). Placing the current roles of vocational education and training professionals in national contexts: Spain and Greece. In A. Brown (Ed.), *Promoting vocational education and training: European perspectives* (pp. 25–36). Tampere: University of Tampere.

Mihail, D.M. (2003). Atypical working in corporate Greece. *Employee Relations*, 25(5), 470–489.

Mike, M. (1996). *Constructing identities*. London: Sage.

Mouzelis, N. (1991). *Back to sociological theory—the construction of social orders*. London: MacMillan.

Mouzelis, N. (1995). *Sociological theory—What went wrong? Diagnosis and remedies*. London: Routledge.

Müller-Jentsch, W. (Ed.) (1988). *Zukunft der Gewerkschaften—Ein internationaler Vergleich*. Frankfurt/M.: Campus.

Niethammer, L. (2000). *Kollektive Identität*. Reinbek: Rowohlt.

OECD (1980). *L'impact du tourisme sur l'environnement*. Paris: OECD.

Papastamou, S. (2002). Pourquoi. *Nouvelle Revue de Psychologie Sociale/New Review of Social Psychology*, 1, 8–29 (in French).

Patiniotis, N. (1979). *Abhängigkeit und Arbeitsemigration*. Ph.D Thesis. Frankfurt/M. (in German).

Patiniotis, N. and D. Stavroulakis (1997). The development of vocational education policy in Greece: A critical approach. *Journal of European Industrial Training*, 21(6/7), 192–202.

Patiniotis, N. and M. Prodromitis (2002). *Vocational identity in the Greek tourism sector*. Final report for the FAME Project. Patras: University of Patras.

Portalidou, M. and O. Jacovidou (2002). Quality as a condition in the development of agricultural tourism. *The Greek Review of Social Research*, 108/109, 325–345.

Raftis, A. and D. Stavroulakis (1991). Attitudes towards workers' participation in Greek industry: A Field Study. *Spoudai*, 41, 290–15.

Sennett, R. (1998). *The corrosion of character.* New York: Norton.

Sheldon, P. (1986). The tour-operator industry: An analysis. *Annals of Tourism Research,* 13(1).

Stavroulakis, D. (1997). Quality circles autonomy. Evidence from a Japanese and a western subsidiary. *International Journal of Quality and Reliability Management,* 14(2), 261–287.

Stott, M.A. (1978). Tourism in Mykonos: Some Social and Cultural Responses. *Mediterranean Studies,* 1(2), 72–90.

Szell, G. (1988). Participation, workers' control and self-management. *Current Sociology,* 36(3).

Tajfel, H. (1979). Individuals and groups in Social Psychology. *British Journal of Social and Clinical Psychology,* 18, 183–190.

Tajfel, H. (1982). Social Psychology of intergroup relations. *Annual Review of Psychology,* 33, 1–30.

Tsartas, P. (1998). Sociability and tourism: An analysis of the characteristics in different forms of tourism. *The Greek Review of Social Research,* 96/97, 111–132 (in Greek).

Tsartas, P. et al. (1995). *The social implications of tourism in the prefectures of Corfu and Lasithi.* Athens: EKKE (in Greek).

Tsartas, P. and M. Thanopoulou (1995). A proposal for the investigation of the role of tourism in the socialization of the Greek youth: the cases of Ios and Serifos. *The Greek Review of Social Research,* 86, 114–128 (in Greek).

Tsivakou, I. (2000). *The adventures of the identity in the labour field.* Athens: Themelio (in Greek).

Tsiganou, H. (1991). *Workers' participative schemes—The experience of capitalist and plan-based societies.* New York: Greenwood Press.

Turner, L. and J. Ash (1970). *The golden hordes: International tourism and the pleasure periphery.* London: Constable.

Turner, J.C. (1982). Towards a cognitive redefinition of the social group. In H. Tajfel (Ed.), *Social identity and intergroup relations* (pp. 15–40). Cambridge: Cambridge University Press.

Turner, J.C., P.J. Oakes, S.A. Haslam and C. McGarthy (1994). Self and Collective: Cognition and Social Context. *Personality and Social Psychology Bulletin,* 20, 454–463.

Wenger, E. (1998). *Communities of practice.* Cambridge: Cambridge University Press.

Yin, R. (1994). *Case study research—Design and methods.* Thousand Oaks: Sage.

Zavalloni, M. and C. Louis-Guérin (1984). *Identité Sociale et Concience.* Montreal: Montreal University Press.

Zacharatos, G.A. (1980). *Tourist development program for the area around the Lake N. Plastira (Megdova).* Athens: KEPE (Planning Issues Series No. 23).

Zacharatos, G.A. (1986). *Tourist consumption.* Athens: KEPE (Planning Issues Series, no 25).

Zacharatos, G.A. (1992). *The organization of the package-tour and the tour operator as a producer of holiday travel.* Athens: EOT.

5

Vocational Education and Training—A European Perspective

Felix Rauner
University of Bremen, Germany

The debate on the further development of national vocational training traditions focuses principally on how to qualify the workforce for the intermediate skills sector (see Figure 5.1). In industrialised countries this segment accounts for 60 to 70 per cent of all employees (Tessaring, 1994; Grubb, 1999).

This figure explains why the European Council in the Lisbon Declaration (2000) has attributed such a great economic relevance to vocational education and training (VET) and in the context of implementation why it pursued the strategic goal of 'making the Union the most competitive and most dynamic knowledge-based economy in the world' by 2010. It was from these ideas that the European Ministers of Education formulated the far-reaching aim that 'the systems of general and vocational education [in Europe] shall become a worldwide reference for quality'. As a consequence of this aim, the establishment of a common European area for vocational education and training by 2010 in accordance with the package of measures defined in the so-called Copenhagen Process, ranks high on the political agenda. This process includes:

- Establishing a common European structure of vocational education and training on the basis of the rather open and flexible European *VET area*. Such an area ensures both the adaptability and integration of the national VET systems in the ongoing convergence process.

A. Brown, S. Kirpal and F. Rauner (eds.), Identities at Work, 115–144.

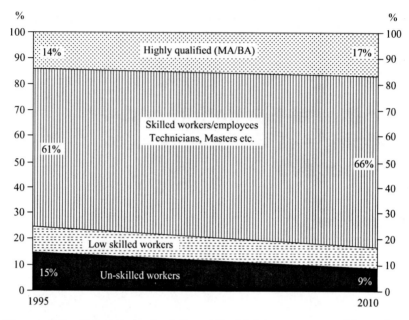

Figure 5.1 Development of the skilled labour segment (Tessaring, 1994; Schüssler et al., 1999)

- Facilitating a structure that allows for *transparent* and mutually recognised qualifications.
- Developing a European *qualification framework* from which the laterally and vertically differentiated skills that engender transparency can be defined. On this basis, the *European Credit Transfer System for VET (ECEVET)* ensures the recognition of formally and informally acquired skills all over Europe—sustained by a certification scheme to be implemented throughout Europe (European Commission, 2003).

This European vocational education project initiated by the Copenhagen Process assumes that it will

- Ensure a high level of flexibility resulting from the interplay between the different employment systems and the qualification of employees.
- Allow for qualifications 'à la carte' in the sense that individuals will have the opportunity to determine their qualification profile.
- Detach vocational education from the highly divergent structures of national VET systems and convert vocational education and

training into a European qualification market, which will be regulated through a European certification system, the European Qualification Framework (EQF).

- Increase the mobility of employees in the European labour market.
- Significantly reduce the reaction time with which the qualification systems can respond to the changing qualification demands of the employment system.

During the introduction of vocational training programmes minimal standards will be defined. Whether these can be defined in a similar manner to those which occurred during the introduction of the Europe-wide Bachelor and Master courses when a European area of higher education was established is an open question. The answer reached depends on which one of two competing traditions of vocational education and training is accepted. These traditions differ on how vocational competence development and vocational identity formation are connected. Rousseau's novel 'Emile' made us aware of the importance of a radically subjective perspective on education. Since then, it has been commonly accepted in pedagogical science that competence development is inseparably linked to the formation of vocational identity.

> Er muss seine spezifische Berufsrolle antizipieren und sich mit ihr identifizieren—anders würde keine Kompetenzentwicklung denkbar sein [He has to anticipate his specific professional role and identify with it—otherwise competence development would not be possible]; this is how Herwig Blankertz interprets Rousseau's educational utopia (Blankertz, 1983, p. 140).

In this context Heinz (1995) observes that empirical findings of vocational socialisation research show that

> die Tätigkeitsanforderungen und die Karriereoptionen eines Berufes in Verbindung mit den darauf bezogenen Qualifizierungsprozessen für die Entwicklung der sozialen Identität von zentraler Bedeutung sind [the job tasks and career prospects of an occupation together with the respective qualification processes are of crucial importance for the development of a social identity] (Heinz, 1995, p. 104; cf. Brose, 1986; Mönnich and Witzel, 1994).

Where competence development is disconnected from occupationally organised work and the related vocational qualification processes, the relationship between vocational identity, commitment and competence development becomes loose and fragile. In which case, modularised systems of certification function as regulatory frameworks for the recognition and accumulation of skills that are largely independent from each other and disconnected from genuine work contexts.[1] Here, commitment and performance orientation are driven by the risks that derive from the liberalised, non-regulated qualification and employment system. The alternative—represented by the central European tradition of vocational education and training—is founded on principles concerning the organisation of work and division of labour along occupational categories. Here, vocational education and training aims at developing vocational competence and identity. However, how vocational identity translates into commitment, performance and quality awareness is a question of concern. Indeed, it is one that theory and research on commitment have as yet been unable to answer (cf. Kirpal, 2004; Brown, 2004).

Historical ramifications of a European employment market and a common European area of vocational education and training are of vital importance for the future development (Copenhagen Process). This chapter will further analyse these ramifications and the consequences for the employees and the employment systems in Europe. This approach, however, requires defining and applying evaluation criteria. Whether modern VET research allows for this, and how possible gaps might be filled by referring to examples of excellent national VET practices and examples from the European VET Leonardo programme shall also be discussed in this paper.

5.1   Vocational Education Versus Employability

The diversity of European VET systems can be structured according to two qualification scenarios[2] (see Figure 5.2): first, education and training which is both undertaken for the purpose and achieved through the practice of professional work (vocational education scenario), and

---

[1] One attempt to establish a national qualification framework on this basis is the UK system of National Vocational Qualifications (cf. Young, 2005).
[2] These scenarios shall henceforth be referred to as 'vocational education' and 'employability'.

Features	Vocational education scenario	Employability scenario
1. Position within the educational system	Part of the educational system	Training market
2. Qualification model	Work-readiness for skilled labour and autonomy in the performance of tasks	Employability, flexibility
3. Educational contents	Occupational profiles and curricula	Modularised certification systems
4. Target groups	Graduates from the general education system	Not specified
5. Training concept	Regulated dual apprenticeship programmes of three to four years	Training and qualification 'à la carte'
6. Support structures	VET research and VET planning	Institutions for accreditation and assessment

Figure 5.2 Alternative qualification scenarios for Europe

second, the accumulation of skills necessary for employment (employability scenario).

According to the Department for Economic Change and Employment at the Wissenschaftszentrum Berlin for the analysis of employment, vocational education and innovation (see Soskice and Hancké, 1996; Hall and Soskice, 2001) these alternative traditions of qualification correspond to the features of coordinated market economies (CMEs) on the one hand, and liberal market economies (LMEs) on the other hand. More specifically, in CMEs advanced VET systems are embedded within them. Whilst characteristics of LMEs include qualification strategies that leave it to the individual to decide upon the portfolio of their skills and qualifications, and to acquire those in an education market to increase their employability, all of which is typically sustained by modularised certification systems.

The vocational education scenario has a high affinity to the VET systems of central European countries like Switzerland, Germany, Austria and Denmark, which are also characterised by CMEs. The employability scenario, on the other hand, can be found in LME countries, of which the United Kingdom and the United States are prominent examples.

5.1.1   Scenario 1: Education and Training Achieved through and for the Purpose of Skilled Labour (Vocational Education Scenario)

Initial vocational education and training is integrated into the secondary level of the educational system or located at the post-secondary level if trainees are already in possession of an upper secondary level qualification (e.g. 'Abitur' in Germany). It is not uncommon that even graduates with a Bachelor's degree undergo a dual apprenticeship programme in order to improve their employment opportunities. The basis for vocational education is training programmes of three to four years, which are oriented towards occupational profiles ('Berufsbilder'). The vocational qualification allows for pursuing a higher education degree at a vocational college or university. The business sector actively participates in the planning of vocational training via its industrial associations and trade unions. They jointly shape and define the occupational profiles, develop the training plans and curricula and guide the implementation of the practical training in companies. This qualification model integrates in-company training with a component of theoretical vocational education in vocational schools, which complements the work experience.

The *objective* of the apprenticeship training is occupation-specific employability ('Berufsfähigkeit'). Upon completing their apprenticeship the trainees are expected to have the competences of skilled workers and be able to perform work tasks without any additional training at the workplace. The integration of initial vocational education and training into the education system leads to the formulation of objectives that are also oriented towards general education. A pioneering example in this respect is the learning objective adopted in 1991 by the Conference of Education Ministers in Germany, whose aim is to enable trainees to participate in shaping society and the world of work with a sense of social and environmental responsibility (KMK, 1991). This is a pioneering example insofar that it comprises initial vocational training with a mission relating to general education. However, the proper response to the tension between education and qualification is regarded as a particular pedagogical and didactic challenge.

The *training contents* are derived from the characteristic tasks and qualification requirements of the respective occupational area on the one hand, and by making reference to the educational goals on the other hand. The educational contents represent action-oriented and action-reflective knowledge. The structure of these contents represents action-oriented knowledge, and is based on criteria of competence development or, respectively, on the novice-expert paradigm. The training forms part of an integrated context, which is constituted by the respective occupational profile.

The *target group* of initial vocational education and training normally has a lower secondary level qualification. However, since apprenticeship training is a method of qualifying adults for skilled work, it is open to everyone who wants to learn a specific trade.

The training period lasts between three and four years and is spent, as far as the practical part is concerned, in practical work settings according to the apprenticeship model. The accompanying school-based instruction helps to reflect upon and systemise the practical work experiences in order to transfer the work process-oriented knowledge that is necessary to enhance the vocational competence. The competence development is evaluated by appropriate assessment procedures. Vocational training goes in line with the integration into the respective community of practice.

The (further) development of occupational profiles and vocational training programmes requires *VET research* and a complementary scheme of *VET planning*, which involves, in addition to the public authorities responsible for education, experts from the respective professional associations and trade unions. What is of crucial importance for this model of vocational education is the higher education background of vocational teachers differentiated according to occupational domains, and the pedagogical qualification of in-company trainers.

5.1.2 Scenario 2: Accumulation of Competences for Employment (Employability Scenario)

In this scenario, the qualification of employees for the labour market cannot be systematically located within the educational system since it is the employees themselves, who determine whether and when to qualify for a specific task. Whether they resort to the qualification certification offered by a college or another training provider, or whether they acquire the necessary skills through self-learning—for example, in the work process—is in this scenario not subject to regulation. Vocational qualification can therefore be regarded as a part of the *training market*. Demand and supply are regulated by the market mechanisms of the training service sector. Within the companies the qualification of employees is the responsibility of human resources management and development. Human resource development is thus a dimension of organisational development. A distinction between initial and continuing vocational training does not exist.

From a macro-economic perspective, *employability* and the realisation of a flexible labour market are being emphasised. Enterprises' entry requirements are generally oriented towards a high level of general education of new employees, and towards their ability and willingness to participate in continuing vocational training—according to the company's needs. In this scenario, the employees pursue their own goals. Which goals they pursue will depend on the individual's background; goals can be geared towards employment, attractive job tasks (self-fulfilment), making a career or increasing one's income. As a consequence, a cohort of semi-skilled workers frequently emerges below the level of skilled workers.

In this scenario the *contents of the educational programmes* are neither regulated by an occupational profile nor by a vocational training plan. Instead, they result from the qualification needs of the companies and economic sectors. Only the professional requirements for health and security-sensitive tasks are regulated.

A differentiated regulation scheme for the CVET market seems to act as the certification system; this defines the entirety of vocational skills by means of verifiable module descriptions. The qualifications to be certified represent single basic skills, which can be accumulated individually according to qualification profiles.

This scenario offers qualification to all employees. It does not draw a distinction between different target groups of initial and continuing training. A particular target group, however, which should be considered individually, is the unemployed. Particularly, their employability can be improved by customised qualification measures that result from this scenario: qualification 'à la carte'.

This qualification scenario can be established on different regulatory levels: as a free and deregulated (or unregulated) market or as a more regulated market for further education. Although in reality, it is usually established in a manner very similar to the latter possibility. This ensures that new competences that are relevant for employment can be documented and are thus accepted in the sense of a certificate of qualification. The accumulation of certificates can ensure access to formal continuing education at technical colleges and universities. In order to improve the customer orientation of this system, it offers some forms of guidelines to the target groups. These include:

- An independent evaluation tool for CVET programmes, which follows the model of good quality test development.
- An assessment and certification system for the recognition of the acquired qualifications.
- Guidelines to orient oneself in the CVET market.

Formal regulations for the education of vocational teachers and trainers are not needed. CVET providers (e.g. community colleges) will instead establish their own professionalisation standards in a bid to achieve competitive advantage.

5.2 Evaluation Criteria

Within their educational programmes the European Union has introduced evaluation criteria of 'good' and 'best' practice. The criterion of 'bad practice' was sacrificed because of the opportunistic aim not to explicitly discredit national VET traditions. This procedure challenges research investigating in educational innovation programmes to adjust their evaluative procedures to identify such 'good' and 'best' practice examples, and to re-define assessment criteria accordingly. Current evaluation practice is far from able to rank practices as better or worse than one another. To date, establishing all-encompassing criteria of better or worse practice of vocational education and training has been beyond the scope of scientific methodology. A particular problem is the large numbers of criteria because ultimately they can only be justified on a normative basis. What research can contribute to this process is to make the scientifically and normatively justified criteria transparent, and thus increase the rationality of the discourse on best, better and bad practice.

In the following paragraphs a number of criteria shall be outlined, which are subject-oriented, economically and socially relevant, and which explicitly or implicitly serve as theoretical foundations of pertinent reports and publications on international comparative studies of VET systems (see e.g. Descy and Tessaring, 2001; Deißinger, 2001).

5.2.1   Education and Qualification Opportunities

The right to education is a social achievement, which, as far as the industrialised countries are concerned, includes the upper secondary level. Accordingly, every young person has the right to obtain an upper secondary level qualification, usually by the age of 18 years. In countries with an established dual vocational training system the vocational training schools form part of compulsory schooling. In countries with a school-based VET system, compulsory education also extends to initial vocational education and training, which is completed together with a state diploma. Regardless of how the national upper secondary school level is structured, the vocational training at this level improves the opportunities for further education and qualification for all young people. However, countries which do not extend their compulsory education to the upper secondary level restrict the right to vocational education.

Approximately 80 million citizens in the European Union do not have an upper secondary level qualification. They are considered low skilled. According to the objectives of the European Council (2003) at least 85 per cent of 22-year old European citizens should have completed an upper secondary level qualification by 2010.

5.2.2   Career Prospects

From a macro-economic point of view, the vocational 'career' is ultimately determined by the respective labour markets. For the intermediate skills segment these are predominantly the local labour markets. Statistically, a higher level of educational attainments improves an individual's career: university graduates have better career prospects than skilled workers with a completed vocational qualification, and the latter have better career prospects than unskilled or semi-skilled workers. However, when the number of university graduates exceeds the absorption capacity of the employment system for the highly qualified (see Figure 5.1), then those graduates have to qualify for the intermediate sector of the labour market despite the fact that they are holding a university diploma. The proportion of apprenticeship trainees holding a university degree is increasing to up to over 50 per cent, this is in most part because of the increasing number of students in higher education. In contrast, systems that are characterised by a high vertical permeability between initial and continuing vocational education and higher education allow for career plans that are adapted to individual interests and market opportunities, and are less endowed with the inherent risks discussed above.

5.2.3 Employability and Youth Unemployment

Different models of organising and shaping the transition from school to work can either increase or decrease the employment opportunities for young people. At the first threshold of the school-to-work transition in many countries young people with a lower secondary level qualification still have the opportunity to opt either for pursuing a vocational track or for continuing their general school education. In the case where the initial vocational education is school-based and integrated into the upper secondary level, access to the vocational track is unproblematic.

It is the second threshold that determines whether the newly qualified young workers will make the transition into the employment system or not. At this stage the mechanisms of the labour market, more specifically the interplay between the education and the employment system, come into play. Hence, the rate of youth unemployment subsequent to the completion of the vocational training period or the acquisition of an

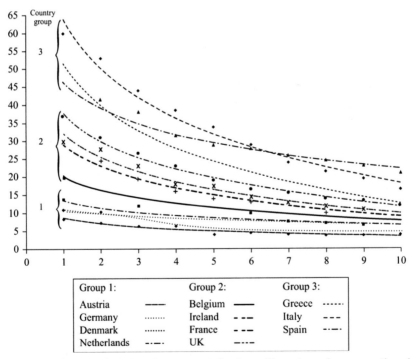

Figure 5.3 Youth unemployment at the transition stage from vocational training to employment in EU member states (Descy and Tessaring, 2001)

upper secondary level qualification can be considered an important indicator of the *functionality* of the VET system.

An analysis of EUROSTAT data on the transition from vocational training to gainful employment shows that countries with a well-developed apprenticeship system have relatively low rates of youth unemployment (cf. Figure 5.3). In contrast, the entrance barriers are relatively high in countries with school-based vocational education or market-based qualification schemes. For example, youth unemployment directly after completion of a vocational training is between 20 and 38 per cent in Belgium and France, and even in the UK, it is significantly higher than in those countries from cluster 1. Moreover, in Greece, Italy and Spain, the youth unemployment rate subsequent to upper secondary school education is about 50 per cent, and it takes at least ten years before this unemployment rate is reduced by labour market mechanisms to near the levels of cluster 1.

5.2.4   Income

The type of initial vocational education also affects income during and after the training period. Traditionally, apprenticeship training includes remuneration on the basis of the amount of training that has been completed. For instance, the allowances paid within the Joint Apprenticeship Programmes in the U.S. usually reach about 50 per cent of the wages of skilled workers during the first six months, and up to 92 per cent in the last year of training. However, in other countries, the training allowances are considerably lower, particularly when the school-based education covers up to 50 per cent of the overall training programme. In Germany, the training allowances amount on average to 25 to 30 per cent of a skilled worker's salary. Where the vocational training takes place in vocational schools and state-owned training centres the trainees are students of the upper secondary school level and do not receive any remuneration.

From the companies' point of view apprenticeship training is profitable when, as a consequence of work-based training, apprentices engage in value-added work processes. Private training centres, which offer training programmes comparable to dual apprenticeship schemes, charge tuition fees of up to 500 Euros per month. This segment of the training market emerges when there is a shortage of in-company training positions and attractive programmes of school-based vocational training are unavailable.

5.2.5 Competence Development

In regulated VET systems the vocational competences which individuals are expected to acquire within an initial vocational training programme are, for the most part, already defined by the occupational profiles and training curricula. On the one hand, this guarantees a minimal standard of qualification. On the other hand, however, it limits the vocational competence development of each trainee insofar as the competence scope is already pre-defined according to the vocational track. One criterion important for the overall competence development is the possibilities of further qualifications, and the possibility of obtaining a formal qualification from higher education together with a vocational certificate. In countries without a developed VET system the market for continuing training and further qualification offers individual qualification opportunities, which can be adapted according to the learner's specific needs and interests. Making successful use of these opportunities depends strongly on the self-initiative of the individual and on the possibilities and restrictions in accessing the appropriate programmes.

General education on the upper secondary school level predominantly prepares individuals for university studies. Therefore, the acquisition of vocational skills is in competition with the acquisition of the aptitude for higher education. This competition contributes considerably to the 'stigmatisation of vocational education' (Lim, 2005). From a theoretical point of view, this conflict is addressed with the concept of 'education within the medium of occupational work' ('Bildung im Medium des Berufes'), which advocates the integration of vocational and general education. Only if such integration is realised will it be possible to avoid the further development of the belief that vocational competence within the upper secondary education level leads to a dead-end road, and to halt the academic drift between the two skill sets.

5.2.6 Markets for Skilled Labour

Countries with established systems of vocational education and training that are aiming at domain-specific work-readiness and vocational proficiency ('Berufsfähigkeit') normally also have well-developed markets for skilled labour, which are largely defined and structured along occupational profiles. The dual vocational training systems, as training markets, form an integral part of the markets for skilled labour. They are integral because within developed VET systems the

qualification of skilled workers takes on average three years; this qualification period then acts as a barrier against the emergence of a low-
wage sector and to some extent against societal poverty.

Well-functioning markets for skilled labour are a crucial precondition for innovative employment systems. Therefore, to what extent VET
systems are able to respond dynamically to the increasingly variable
demand of domain-specific competences is decisive for the future
development of those systems. A major concern for companies in
this context is the question of whether qualifying their workforce for
occupation-based work profiles provides good grounds for organisational development and innovation, or whether the effects are in fact the
opposite, and lead instead to the emergence of internal demarcations
through occupational role models (Kern and Sabel, 1994).

5.2.7   Innovation and Competitiveness

Innovation and competitiveness seem to depend to a degree on the
skills and competences of the workforce. However, even though this
connection is intuitively transparent, it is empirically difficult to prove.
A differentiation between the company, regional and national level does
at least allow for a better classification of the relevant research findings. At the company level, the realisation of a business process-
oriented work organisation relies on both the decentralisation of
responsibilities, and a high level of vocational competence on the part
of those employees who are directly involved in value-added work
processes, that is, on the part of the skilled workers. This is particularly
true when the principle of open and dynamic occupational cores has
been implemented (Heidegger and Rauner, 1997). Of equal importance
are the criteria of performance orientation, quality awareness and commitment. These, however, are only investigated as a consequence of
either occupational or organisational commitment.

Regional innovation systems and milieus are based on networks of the
sectoral communities. Here, regional dialogue between employees',
employers', chambers' and regional policy-makers' associations, industries and companies, and local and regional training providers are all
linked through some kind of informal pact. Innovation research has
shown that a developed apprenticeship system and the ensuing tradition
of skilled workers and engineers promote the emergence of innovative
development and production settings (Ruth and Rauner, 1991). This generated tradition, which helps to establish innovative communities of
practice, is characterised by mutual recognition, understanding and trust.

National innovation systems are heavily influenced by the qualification of employees for the intermediate sector. In his study on the 'Competitive Advantage of Nations' Michael E. Porter (1990) emphasises the relevance of the form and structure of vocational education and training systems to his theory of innovation. As an outstanding example in international comparison Porter mentions Switzerland with its highly developed apprenticeship system. This system integrates about 70 per cent of young people into dual vocational training, and also features an internationally renowned engineering track. The highly competitive German industry, according to Porter, is also due to the excellent qualification standards and volume of skilled workers:

> While weak in national endowments, Germany enjoys other advantages decisive to upgrading industry. One is a pool of highly-paid but highly educated and motivated workers. German workers take unusual pride in their work, particularly in producing quality goods (Porter, 1990, p. 369[3]). Porter identifies 'the well-developed and distinctive apprenticeship system [as a] factor-creating mechanism' [. . .] whose importance is hard to overestimate (Porter, 1990, p. 369).

Innovative know-how, which is fundamental for competitiveness in high-tech key industries, is based on the *interplay between experience-based, practical and scientific knowledge.* The duality of reflected work experience and the acquisition of scientific knowledge is outlined in the first scenario on the level of initial vocational education and training, and is also increasingly demanded at the level of higher education. From the perspective of learning and development theory, this duality is considered an ideal-type for the appropriation of professional skills (Chi et al., 1988; Ericsson and Smith, 1991).

5.2.8   Social Integration

The multitude of research projects on both the social integration and exclusion of young people during the transition from school to work points to the particular relevance of the criterion of social integration for the evaluation of VET systems and the corresponding VET practices.

---

[3] 'On the other hand the lack of managerial education contributes to German weakness in many marketing-intensive consumer good and business service industries', (Porter, 1990, p. 369).

If it turns out that VET systems cannot satisfy the demand for training positions, then the consequences with regard to the social disintegration of young people might actually be more severe than a future lack of skilled workers. Statistical data on juvenile delinquency suggest that the successful integration of young people into a company-based or dual vocational training programme is a valuable step toward their integration into society.

5.2.9   Costs and Benefits

Methods and procedures to determine, or at least improve estimates of, the costs and benefits of vocational education and training are only available to a limited extent at present. Quantifying the benefits poses particular difficulties. If one applies a somewhat simplified procedure to assess training costs and benefits (see Beicht et al., 2004), then it is possible to demonstrate that the productivity of a trainee reaches a level of about 80 per cent of that of a skilled worker by the end of only their second year of qualifying for an occupation in the tradition of apprenticeship training (see Figure 5.4).[4]

If the proportion of time spent between school-based and work-based learning is about 1:3 respectively, then it is possible to calculate the appropriate payment for apprentices on the basis of empirical studies about the productivity of 'trainees' work'. Given the fact that, in international terms, the training allowances in Germany are rather moderate, it is clearly feasible to organise a reasonable self-financing VET system according to the vocational education scenario. Indeed, costs would *only* be caused by the part of the training programme that takes place in vocational schools.

5.3   A European Perspective

Vocational education and training in Europe finds itself in a paradoxical situation. The majority of the EU member states extend the ban on the harmonisation of the education sector (Article 150 of the Maastricht

[4] According to a study by Wolter et al. (2003) there are net profits of dual apprenticeship training in Switzerland of 800 euros per trainee on average. In contrast, in Germany there are reported net costs of 8.500 euros per trainee per year. Approximately only 30 per cent of all companies offering training report that the benefits of apprenticeship training exceed the costs (see Walden and Herget, 2002; Beicht et al., 2004).

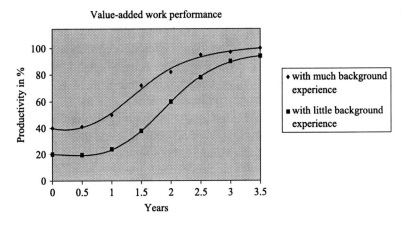

Figure 5.4 Productivity of apprentices relative to the productivity of skilled workers

Treaty) to vocational education. Yet, at the same time European institutions undertake great efforts to use the initial and further training of skilled workers as a strategic resource for the European economic area. The instruments required for this lay the foundations necessary to establish a common area of vocational education and training. This is by virtue of the 'open structural design', which nevertheless shows all features of a new VET system. The scenarios discussed in part 1 of this chapter demonstrate that Europe finds itself at a crossroads in terms of how to design this open VET architecture. The 'vocational education scenario' involves a strategy that allows for *actively shaping* a new pathway, whereas the 'employability scenario' favours an *unstructured path* that leaves the production of vocational qualifications to a liberalised service market. This was stipulated in the General Agreement on Trade in Services (GATS) in 1994 (von Kopp, 2002; Scherrer, 2003; Hennes, 2003). The criteria developed in Section 2 make it possible to assess the strengths and weaknesses of those competing scenarios from a subject-related, economic and societal point of view.

5.3.1 Vocational Education and Training as a Part of the Education System

The models of vocational education and training currently established in the different EU member states can be categorised according to the two qualification scenarios, but only to a first approximation. In some countries we find mixed systems, where school-based, in-company and outside-company training as well as informal vocational training tracks coexist or are combined in some way. Countries where forms of dual training in the tradition of apprenticeships prevail, or exist at least as a sub-system, have established different versions of this model. Roughly speaking, the differences in the design of the training process can be classified according to the amount of learning undertaken in qualifying work processes or, alternatively, according to the amount of practical training which is shifted to external or in-company training workshops (see Figure 5.5).

In the Anglo-Saxon countries, modern apprenticeship programmes are oriented towards the tradition of master craftsperson's training. Vocational competence development takes place through learning in work processes and by becoming a member of the community of practice of the respective company (Rauner, 2002). From the very beginning of their training, apprentices are actively involved in the company's value-added work and production processes. During the first half of the 20th century (initially in central European countries) the dual organisation of apprenticeship training developed: training comprised of components of course-based training attached to training workshops. Since then, systematic practical course-based vocational training, especially in the first year, is considered to be an advanced model of vocational learning. This systemised method for acquiring basic vocational skills is the foundation necessary for the later specialised training in real work processes. Finally, the third variation of apprenticeship transfers virtually all practical training into workshops and training centres. An aspect of this variant is that the transfer of practical skills becomes largely

In-company ⟵ *Practical training* ⟶ *outside-company*

Modern apprenticeship	Dual apprenticeship model	Practice-oriented training
Scotland	Switzerland	France
Australia	Germany	Sweden
USA	Austria	Netherlands
Canada	Denmark	

Figure 5.5 Models of apprenticeship training—classification according to the extent of learning taking place in practical work processes

independent of the unforeseen events of the daily work routines and business processes of real-world companies.

In school-based VET systems the opportunities for formal education normally improve. This improvement stems from the fact that vocational education is organised as an integral part of the education system and therefore vertical and lateral permeability up to college or university level is enhanced. At the same time the government and general administration have the opportunity to restrict this permeability: they may wish to do so if they felt it necessary to counteract problematic levels of academic drift within the education system. When evaluating these competing models of vocational education according to their efficiency of transfer of work-readiness and vocational proficiency, it is found that the quality of training declines with the increasing distance from the real work processes in companies (Grubb, 1999; Hamilton and Hamilton, 1999). However, if evaluated according to their integrating potential and the permeability between vocational and general education, school-based models prove to be more useful; they are particularly successful at facilitating their students' pursuit of further education at schools and universities.

5.3.2 Education and Career Opportunities

VET systems do not completely determine educational opportunities and career prospects but they do influence them considerably. If the success of VET systems is measured according to the proportion of young people who obtain a school-leaving certificate that gives them access to higher education and the proportion of university students, then Australia, Finland, Sweden, Poland, Hungary and Norway are at the top of the ranking with a proportion of students entering HE of between 60 and 75 per cent. By contrast, Switzerland, Germany and Austria are at the bottom with figures hardly reaching 30 per cent (see Figure 5.6).

If instead we gauge success in terms of number of career opportunities corresponding to training undertaken then the results bring out a totally different picture. As the employment systems of developed national economies can only absorb between 15 and 20 per cent of highly-qualified employees (i.e. holding a university degree), the majority of graduates in countries with a high or very high proportion of university students move into the intermediate employment segment, which would otherwise be supplied by the VET system. Furthermore, the graduates'

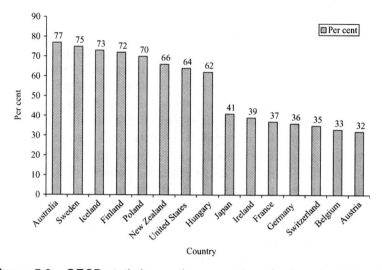

Figure 5.6   OECD statistics on the proportion of university students

academic qualifications are not appropriate for work profiles at the inter-mediate level, which means that graduates frequently have to undergo a programme of vocational training subsequent to their degree. An increasing percentage of graduates thus face the paradoxical situation that with a Bachelor's degree they are rated at 'level 4', according to the European framework for the recognition of vocational qualifications, but have to undertake dual vocational training, rated at 'qualification level 2', in order to *improve* their vocational skills and employability (KOM, 2004, p. 317).

There is a similar picture in relation to educational opportunities. For example, if our first scenario is detached from the education system, as is the case with the traditional dual system of vocational education and training in Germany, and if the educational track that prepares individuals for higher education is largely separated from the track leading to vocational certificates, as with the German *Gymnasium*, then the decision to pursue dual vocational training, after obtaining a lower secondary school qualification, acts as a considerable restriction to entry to university education and thus of further career opportunities. However, if on the other hand, vocational education is linked to acquiring entry qualifications for higher education, as prac-tised with increasing success in Switzerland, then vocational education and training becomes particularly attractive because the initial training not only conveys a comprehensive qualification for a labour market-relevant occupation, but also facilitates access to the opportunity of further qualification at technical colleges and universities (compared to the alternative of actively restricting such access outlined above). A glance at the transition from school to vocational education, the first threshold of school-to-work transition, reveals quite divergent figures for the different EU member states. Whilst this threshold is relatively low in Austria with its plural VET systems, it has risen increasingly in Germany, over the past two decades, with its distinct dual system. This rise was ultimately caused by the reduction of training positions because this precipitated an extension of the training programmes between lower secondary school completion and the commencement of a vocational training programme. The increase in the average age of trainees, from 16.6 years old (1970) to at present nearly 20 years old, is regarded as one of the major weaknesses of German apprenticeship training. This weakness is predominantly attributed to the fact that German apprenticeship training has become detached from the core feature of dual vocational education and training; *learning in qualifying and productive work processes* (Rauner, 2004).

5.4 Competence Development and Vocational Identity

The results of research concerning the development of vocational competence in different VET systems can be summarised into three parts.

1. The key to qualifying skilled workers for the intermediate employment market is to teach them domain-specific vocational competences and not abstract 'core skills' or general education (Gerstenmaier, 2004). Domain-specific work process knowledge is thus the pivotal point for developing vocational competence. International competition over the quality of goods has led to a revaluation of the skilled work in direct value-added work processes, and has thus enhanced the status of the work process knowledge of employees. Additionally, this competition had also led to 'the flattening of hierarchies, the elimination of supervisory layers and the tendency for employees to have more responsibilities and to interact with a wider circle of other employees' (Grubb, 1999, p. 177). Yet, this tendency towards developing broader job profiles (core occupations) and scaling down the vertical division of labour

has not resulted in the de-professionalisation of occupation-based work, as one might have expected, but instead has led to an actual enhancement of such work (Grubb, 1999, p. 187; Rauner, 2000).[5]

2. Vocational learning about work processes is superior to school-based learning providing the development of the vocational skills and competences are attained through a process of acquiring membership in an appropriate community of practice, that is, through situated learning (Lave and Wenger, 1991). This therefore requires occupation-based work to be oriented towards modern occupational profiles and for work tasks and processes during training to have the character of development tasks (Havighurst, 1972). To illustrate this point let us consider W. Norton Grubb who quotes a typical statement from the director of a milling tool manufacturer: 'I don't think the technical colleges necessarily can give the depth of training which can be learned in the industry itself' (Grubb, 1999, p. 176). Equally, another manager from a mechanical engineering company said:

The difference [between our apprenticeship programme and education programmes] is that we base our instruction on real-life situations and not on the theory behind it. We bring in actual parts. We bring in actual prints. We talk about real-life situations. I don't think you get that necessarily in a school situation (Grubb, 1999, p. 176).

A comprehensive study among trainees in the German automotive industry has shown that a shift of their training to workshop settings and the reduction of their training in actual work processes distinctly impeded

---

[5] The emergence of the academic system, with its highly diversified structures for research and teaching, and the privileges associated with a university degree have together increased demand for higher education on the international scale. At the same time industrialisation and the subsequent establishment of *scientific management* in the early 20th century engendered a far-reaching devaluation of operative work and therefore a de-qualification of the majority of employees. The result was a worldwide reduction, and sometimes discontinuation, of the pre-industrial tradition of apprenticeship training. It was only the emergence of process-oriented business strategies in the late 20th century which produced work that once again required highly qualified and highly motivated employees. The consequence was the re-establishment of comprehensive initial vocational education and training schemes as outlined by the vocational education scenario.

the building of their vocational competences. In their study, Bremer and Haasler refer to what they call 'hospitalisation effects' (Bremer and Haasler, 2004, p. 180). However, these effects are (partly) combated in the third year of training when the apprentices are challenged 'on the spot' to make up for competence deficiencies 'to which they come naturally through their work experience, but which also involve an element of crisis' (Bremer and Haasler, 2004 p. 176). The majority of trainees with an occupational profile achieve a sufficient vocational proficiency to be considered 'work-ready' after a training period of three years; provided that the development potential of qualifying work processes is fully exploited.

Studies of competence development typically make a distinction between three characteristic development paths within a three-year dual vocational training course. According to type A, the qualifying work processes aspect of the training amounts to 140 days per year, which is two thirds of the overall available training time; the final third is assigned to school-based vocational education. Trainers estimate trainees' prior work-related experience and knowledge to be at 25 per cent on average of what was required. This figure varies between 10 and 30 per cent according to the particular occupational profile. Training instructors agree that, when the 140 days of practical training are indeed used for learning in qualifying work processes, then the objectives of work-readiness and vocational proficiency are achieved in principle. Moreover, they also concur that apprentices, upon the completion of their full training, are in possession of competences which are equivalent to those of fully skilled workers. If, instead, apprentices spend most of their training time in training workshops (type B), then it is found that the development of vocational competence and proficiency is delayed. This delay is particularly illustrated by their proposed solutions to occupation-specific tasks; they are often impractical (Figure 5.7).

In a comparative study, two groups of trainees, one who underwent training according to type A (group A) and one according to type B (group B), were given an evaluation task to master (see also Haasler, Chapter 10). 60 per cent of the trainees from group A considered the assigned task to be a typical skilled worker's task, while the other 40 per cent of trainees considered it to be an engineer's task. In group B, this judgement ratio was exactly the opposite: in spite of twelve months training, the majority (60 per cent) of these apprentices' suggested solutions which indicated that they had not developed an accurate conception of the occupational expertise that is required of the toolmaker that they were training to become. The comprehensive basic training in

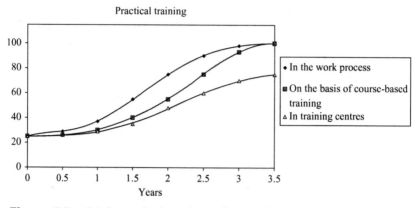

Figure 5.7 Attainment of work-readiness depending on the training amount in qualifying work processes

metalwork that these apprentices had received in their first year of the apprenticeship, which although course oriented, took place predominantly in training workshops and laboratories, did not contribute much towards professional growth, and is therefore responsible for their failure to develop and understand occupation-specific solutions (Haasler and Meyer, 2004, p.145). In addition to these meta-trends, there was clearly also diversity within the training types (A and B); this is assumed to reflect the different learning environments and training methods within the type of training because of the different companies involved.

If vocational training is completely detached from actual work practice, then the qualifying effects of practical work experience are renounced (type C). This considerably delays the formation of vocational competence.[6] If practical work experience is integrated into the training process, as is the case with traditional apprenticeship training, a particularly effective learning method, which also shortens training periods, is achieved.

A study by Haasler and Meyer (2004) compared trainees from SMEs (small and medium-size enterprises), who had been largely trained in practical work processes, and trainees from large companies, who had

---

[6] All forms of vocational education require a two-year period of practical education for students to be deemed to have sufficient occupational aptitude. Consequently, even vocationally-related courses taught at universities, such as medicine, law and teaching, have had to be supplemented with additional periods (about two years) of practical training in order for students to be regarded as professionally proficient.

instead been largely trained in workshops during their first year. The study identified huge differences in the development of both vocational competence and vocational identity. Trainees from SMEs developed elements of vocational identity specific to their chosen occupational domain after the first year of training. Whilst,

> Im Gegensatz dazu stehen die Befunde aus der Untersuchung der Auszubildenden der Großindustrie. Sie verfügen weder über eine vergleichbare berufliche Kompetenz noch hat sich eine nennenswerte berufliche Identität entwickelt [The findings concerning the trainees from large companies contrast this picture. They did not develop a comparable level of vocational competence, nor did they develop anything at all one might wish to call vocational identity] (Haasler and Meyer, 2004).

The authors attribute this contrast to the varying learning environment and training methods within different companies (this has already been identified as an important factor, see above).

Providing that a skilled worker's chosen occupational specialisation meets their interests and inclinations, then those trained according to the first scenario tend to develop a vocational identity during the course of that training process. The development of this identity strengthens their performance orientation and quality awareness, particularly when they are working in the occupational domain for which they have trained. If, instead, vocational identity is under-developed, or even non-existent, in the employees of a company because of the absence of an initial vocational education, the Human Resources Management department of that company has to undertake a great deal of effort to compensate for the ensuing lack of commitment. Frequently, this compensation is achieved by mechanisms which increase the employees' extrinsic motivation, such as a distinctively performance-based wage system, which comes together with the threat of cutting back underperformers. Mechanisms at the societal level, such as a divided labour market and mass unemployment, can also affect employees' extrinsic motivation: the potential threat of unemployment strengthens the work ethic of employees (see Jaeger, 1989, p. 569).

Competence and qualification research show that competence development and the formation of vocational identity are in fact closely connected (Raeder and Grote, 2005, p. 337). Conversely, adherence to a social system which sticks to the normative ideal of the work ethic, as in European societies, entails the risk that those economies will lose their competitive edge and capacity for innovation (Jaeger, 1989, p. 566).

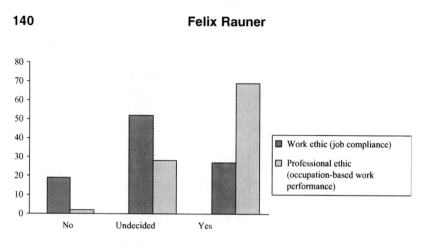

Figure 5.8   Work ethic and professional ethic in two Swiss enterprises

A work ethic which consists of a disciplined performance of professional duties without reflection is inconsistent with corporate culture that emphasise professionalism. The latter corporate culture aspires to an ethic which leads employees to participate in shaping their own work and structures. Indeed, it is just such a culture which has been a key feature of all the developed national economies ever since the late 20th century. Employees' cooperation and communication, responsibility for, and holistic understanding of, their work contexts are all also characteristic of the ethic to which corporate culture aspired and achieved. Indeed, such characteristics were also important to developed economies in the late 20th century; because of the high diversity of such economies they were particularly crucial to the dynamics of these societies. Two case studies by Jaeger (1989) provide support for this thesis (see Figure 5.8). When employees were questioned in these studies, the vast majority (69 per cent) believed that occupational commitment results from a professional ethic, and that the traditional normative ideal of a work ethic only plays a minor and somewhat vague role (Jaeger, 1989, p. 569).

5.5   Conclusions

Using the economic, social and subject-related criteria from the Copenhagen Process to evaluate two competing development scenarios has provided a strong argument for Europe to adapt its old tradition of vocational education and training, its *apprenticeship* system, so it is suitable for the conditions of a modern economy.

Vocational training that is integrated into actual work processes can make an important contribution to the social integration of young people; it teaches individuals how to participate in social situations, and other general social competences. These outcomes are not only important for the world of work but in fact have ramifications for the very cohesion of our societies. The experience of mastering a work task in real work settings can be valuable to the development of a young person's personality. The assumption that people who perform complex and challenging tasks at work will tend to develop and apply a similar approach to other spheres of life is widely supported by empirical research. Accordingly, the EU member states assign high social and political relevance to the connection between vocational training and social cohesion. This is illustrated by their decision to allow the free movement of employees in the European labour market because it helped to erode formerly closed regional labour markets and local milieus. In terms of cultural diversity vocational education has a strong integrative potential. This is because vocational education can utilise the previous work experiences of its young pupils as a resource for the development of vocational identity. Now, given many of these pupils have different cultural backgrounds—up to 50 per cent of all vocational pupils in German cities have a migration background—they will most likely have also had different work experiences. Therefore, the discussion of culturally diverse work experiences can simultaneously develop vocational identity and increase understanding about other cultures, thereby facilitating the beginnings of social integration.

Vocational education which is based on the development of vocational competence *and* identity contributes to a professional ethic. This ethic is indispensable in pursuit of Europe's ambitious target of preserving itself as a prospering economic area.

References

Beicht, U., G. Walden and H. Herget (2004). *Kosten und Nutzen der betrieblichen Berufsbildung in Deutschland.* Reihe: Berichte zur Beruflichen Bildung, Heft 264. Bielefeld: Bertelsmann.

Blankertz, H. (1983). Einführung in die Thematik des Symposiums. In D. Benner, H. Heid and H. Thiersch (Eds.), *Beiträge zum 8. Kongress der Deutschen Gesellschaft für Erziehungswissenschaften vom 22–24, März 1982 in der Universität Regensburg* (pp. 139–142). Zeitschrift für Pädagogik, 18. Beiheft. Weinheim/Basel: Beltz.

Bremer, R. and B. Haasler (2004). Analyse der Entwicklung fachlicher Kompetenz und beruflicher Identität in der beruflichen Erstausbildung. *Bildung im Medium beruflicher Arbeit. Sonderdruck, Zeitschrift für Pädagogik*, 50(2), 162–181.

Brose, H.-G. (Ed.) (1986). *Berufsbiographien im Wandel*. Opladen: Westdeutscher Verlag.

Brown, A. (2004). Engineering identities. *Career Development International*, 9(3), 245–273.

Chi, M.T.H., R. Glaser and M.J. Farr (1988). *The nature of expertise*. Hillsdale, NJ: Erlbaum.

Deißinger, Th. (Ed.) (2001). *Berufliche Bildung zwischen nationaler Tradition und globaler Entwicklung. Beiträge zur vergleichenden Berufsbildungsforschung*. Baden-Baden: Nomos.

Descy, P. and M. Tessaring (2001). *Kompetent für die Zukunft—Ausbildung und Lernen in Europa. Zweiter Bericht zur Berufsbildungsforschung in Europa: Zusammenfassung*. Cedefop Reference Series. Luxemburg: Amt für amtliche Veröffentlichungen der Europäischen Gemeinschaften.

Ericsson, K.A. and J. Smith (Ed.) (1991). *Toward a general theory of expertise*. Cambridge, MA: Cambridge University Press.

European Commission (2003). *Enhanced cooperation in vocational education and training*. Stocktaking Report of the Copenhagen coordination group. October 2003. Brussels.

Gerstenmaier, J. (2004). Domänenspezifisches Wissen als Dimension beruflicher Entwicklung. In F. Rauner (Ed.), *Qualifikationsforschung und Curriculum. Analysieren und Gestaltung beruflicher Arbeit und Bildung* (pp. 151–163). Bielefeld: Bertelsmann.

Grubb, W.N. (1999). The subbaccalaureate labor market in the United States: Challenges for the school-to-work transition. In W.R. Heinz (Ed.), *From education to work: cross-national perspectives* (pp. 171–193). Cambridge, UK: Cambridge University Press.

Haasler, B. (2006). Apprentices' experiences of occupational and organisational commitment: An empirical investigation in the German automobile industry. In A. Brown, S. Kirpal and F. Rauner (Eds.), *Identities at Work* (pp. 261–283). Dordrecht: Springer.

Haasler, B. and K. Meyer (2004). Kompetenzentwicklung von gewerblich-technischen Berufsanfängern in Großindustrie und in kleinen und mittleren Unternehmen im Vergleich. In K. Jenewein, P. Knauth, P. Röben and G. Zülch (Eds.), *Kompetenzentwicklung in Arbeitsprozessen—Beiträge zur Konferenz der Arbeitsgemeinschaft gewerblich-technische Wissenschaften und ihre Didaktiken in der Gesellschaft für Arbeitswissenschaft am 23./24. September 2002 in Karlsruhe*. (pp. 137–146). Baden-Baden: Nomos.

Hall, P.A. and D. Soskice (Ed.) (2001). *Varieties of capitalism: The institutional foundations of comparative advantage*. Oxford: Oxford University Press.

Hamilton, S.F. and M.-A. Hamilton (1999). Creating new pathway to adulthood by adapting German apprenticeship in the United States. In W.R. Heinz (Ed.), *From school to work. Cross-national perspectives* (pp. 199–213). Cambridge/New York/Melbourne: Cambridge University Press.

Havighurst, R.J. (1972). *Developmental tasks and education*. New York: Longman & Green.

Heidegger, G. and F. Rauner (1997). Reformbedarf in der Beruflichen Bildung. Gutachten für das Ministerium für Arbeit, Gesundheit und Soziales des Landes NRW, Bremen/Düsseldorf.

Heinz, W.R. (1995). *Arbeit, Beruf und Lebenslauf: eine Einführung in die berufliche Sozialisation.* Weinheim/München: Juventa.

Hennes, S. (2003). Bildungsdienstleistungen im Welthandelsrecht. *RdJB*, 51(4), 449–465.

Jaeger, C. (1989). Die kulturelle Einbettung des Europäischen Marktes. In M. Haller, H. J. Hoffmann-Novottny and W. Zapf (Eds.), *Kultur und Gesellschaft.* Verhandlungen des 24. Deutschen Soziologentags, des 11. Österreichischen Soziologentags und des 8. Kongresses der Schweizerischen Gesellschaft für Soziologie in Zürich 1988 (pp. 556–574). Frankfurt/M.: Campus.

Kern, H. and Ch. Sabel (1994). Verblaßte Tugenden. Zur Krise des Deutschen Produktionsmodells. In N. Beckenbach and W.v. Treeck (Eds.), *Umbrüche gesellschaftlicher Arbeit* (pp. 605–625). Göttingen: Schwartz.

Kirpal, S. (2004). Work identities of nurses: Between caring and efficiency demands. *Career Development International*, 9(3), 274–304.

KMK—Kultusministerkonferenz (1991). Vereinbarung über die Weiterentwicklung der Berufsschule. Bonn.

KOM (2004). Richtlinie über die Anerkennung von Berufsqualifikationen.

Kopp, B. von (2002). Globalisierung, Liberalisierung, Deregulierung, GATS: Gefahr für das öffentliche Schulwesen? *TIBI (Trends in Bildung international)*, 2, 1–6.

Lave, J. and E. Wenger (1991). *Situated learning. Legitimate peripheral participation.* New York: Cambridge University Press.

Lim, D. (2005). Removing the stigma: Vocational education and training in Hongkong. Presentation: Shanghai Education Forum 2005 (June 22–23, 2005). Conference Proceedings p. 185–189.

Mönnich, I. and A. Witzel (1994). Arbeitsmarkt und Berufsverläufe junger Erwachsener. *Zeitschrift für Sozialisationsforschung und Erziehungssoziologie*, 14, 262–277.

Porter, M.E. (1990). *The competitive advantage of nations.* New York: The Free Press.

Raeder, S. and G. Grote (2005). Berufliche Identität. In F. Rauner (Ed.), *Handbuch Berufsbildungsforschung* (pp. 337–342). Bielefeld: Bertelsmann.

Rauner, F. (2000). Zukunft der Facharbeit. In J.-P. Pahl, F. Rauner and G. Spöttl (Eds.), *Berufliches Arbeitsprozesswissen* (pp. 49–60). Baden-Baden: Nomos.

Rauner, F. (2002). Berufliche Kompetenzentwicklung—vom Novizen zum Experten. In P. Dehnbostel, U. Elsholz, J. Meister and J. Meyer-Henk (Eds.), *Vernetzte Kompetenzentwicklung. Alternative Positionen zur Weiterbildung* (pp. 111–132). Berlin: edition sigma.

Rauner, F. (2004). Reform der Berufsausbildung. Expertise im Auftrag des Ministeriums für Wirtschaft und Arbeit des Landes Nordrhein-Westfalen. Download: http://www.itb.uni-bremen.de/downloads/Publikationen/expertise_nrw.pdf

Ruth, K. and F. Rauner (1991). Perspektiven der Forschung zur Industriekultur. In E. Hildebrandt (Ed.), *Betriebliche Sozialverfassung unter Veränderungsdruck* (pp. 172–203). Berlin: edition sigma.

Scherrer, C. (2003). Bildung als Handelsware. *RdJB*, 86–100.

Schüssler, R., K. Spiess, D. Wendland and M. Kukuk, (1999). *Quantitative Projektion des Qualifikationsbedarfs bis 2010.* Beiträge zur Arbeitsmarkt- und Berufsforschung Nr. 221. Nürnberg: IAB.

Soskice, D.W. and B. Hancké (1996). *Von der Konstruktion von Industrienormen zur Organisation der Berufsausbildung. Eine vergleichende Analyse am Beispiel von Großbritannien, Deutschland, Japan und Frankreich.* WZB Discussion Paper FS I 96–310. Berlin: Wissenschaftszentrum Berlin für Sozialforschung.

Tessaring, M. (1994). Langfristige Tendenzen des Arbeitskräftebedarfs nach Tätigkeiten und Qualifikationen in den alten Bundesländern bis zum Jahre 2010. Eine erste Aktualisierung der IAB/Prognos-Prognose 1989/91. *Mitteilungen aus der Arbeitsmarkt- und Berufsforschung*, 27(1), 5–19.

Walden, G., U. Beicht and H. Herget (2002). Warum Betriebe (nicht) ausbilden. *Berufsbildung in Wissenschaft und Praxis (BWP)*, 31(2), 35–39.

Walden, G. and H. Herget (2002). Nutzen betrieblicher Ausbildung für die Betriebe—erste Ergebnisse einer empirischen Erhebung. *Berufsbildung in Wissenschaft und Praxis (BWP)*, 31(6), 32–36.

Wolter, S.C., S. Mühlemann and J. Schweri (2003). *Why some firms train apprentices and many others do not.* IZA Discussion Paper No. 916, Oct. 2003.

Young, M. (2005). *National qualifications frameworks: Their feasibility for effective implementation in developing countries.* Discussion Paper, Skills and Employability Department. In ILO Skills. Working Paper No. 22, Geneva.

Part Two

Work and Personal Identity

6

Career Changes and Identity Continuities—A Contradiction?

Sabine Raeder and Gudela Grote
ETH Zurich, Switzerland

6.1   Introduction

Current assumptions concerning the consequences of increasingly demanded work flexibility on personal identities are contradictory. Some researchers question whether people can develop a personally valued identity if the work environment does not remain stable and the individual cannot control the changes. Sennett (1998) even assumed that high work flexibility may cause the disruption of identities. Other researchers emphasised new opportunities for the individual. Keupp (1997) pointed out that it will be necessary to challenge the assumption of stability as a prerequisite for a healthy identity development, and to adapt the current approach towards identity by focusing more on continuous processes of identity construction.

Three empirically derived typologies analysing the interrelation of work and identity support the assumption that individuals can deal with flexibility. The typologies of the European FAME Consortium (Kirpal, 2004b), the Special Collaborative Centre 186 (Heinz, 2002; Witzel and Kühn, 2000) and developed through our own research (Raeder and Grote, 2004) consist of types characterised by different degrees of flexibility (cf. Table 6.1). All types show different patterns of adaptation to demanded flexibility and of shaping individually desired flexibility, none of them leading to identity disorders. The typologies present an overview by abstracting from the individual cases. They do not provide detailed information on what flexibility means to individuals, how individuals interpret it and integrate it into their personal identity. They also

A. Brown, S. Kirpal and F. Rauner (eds.), Identities at Work, 147–182.

Table 6.1   Empirical studies on work and identity discussed in this chapter

Research team	Discipline	Approach	Key findings
FAME Consortium (Kirpal, 2004a, b)	Vocational Education Research/ Sociology	Typology of work identities in the context of work flexibility	Continuum of forms of work identities ranging from 'classical' to 'flexible'
Heinz (2002), Witzel and Kühn (2000)	Sociology	Typology of modes of biographical agency (longitudinal study)	Six modes of biographical agency in three categories: (1) *Status Arrangement* with the modes 'Company Identification' and 'Wage-worker Habitus'; (2) *Advancement Ambition* with the modes 'Career Orientation' and 'Optimising Chances'; (3) *Autonomy Gain* with the modes 'Personal Growth' and 'Self-Employment Habitus'
Raeder and Grote (2004)	Work psychology	Identity types in the context of work flexibility	Four types of vocational identity: (i) Continuous, (ii) Job-centred, (iii) Critical-flexible and (iv) Self-determined
Hoff et al. (1991); Hoff (1990)	Work psychology	Locus of control of skilled workers (longitudinal study)	Due to individual options, situational constraints and experiences of conflict, the participants developed an integrationist locus of control

do not consider the underlying desire to present their individuality in the biographical narrative and personal identity construction. In order to show the complexity of decisions in one's life course and of processes of identity formation, it is necessary to reveal individuality beyond the information given in these typologies.

In this paper, we first present these three typologies and introduce the concept of personal identity on which our research is based. With the aim of describing vocational identity in the context of flexibility in detail, we present a qualitative analysis of the identity of persons with career changes, people who have been working in two or more occupational areas (Sheldon, 1995). Vocational identity is thereby understood as part of the overall personal identity specific to the sphere of working life (Hausser, 1995). Our research is based on psychological concepts and theories.

6.2 Typologies of Work and Identity

The European FAME team (Kirpal, 2004a, b) analysed vocational identities in considering the context of vocational education and training, historical developments and economic features. The study produced a continuum of forms of work identities leading from a classical to a flexible, individualised work identity. The classical form was characterised by high identification with the company and the work tasks. Employees with few resources like qualification, motivation or self-esteem typically perceived work-related changes as a threat. People with a more flexible identity were more able to use flexibility and competence development for achieving their goals. Commitment towards the company or the occupation was subordinated to these goals. Most study participants, however, developed forms of adaptation to flexibility demands somewhere between these poles of the continuum.

In a longitudinal study, Heinz (2002), Witzel and Kühn (2000) developed a typology of six modes of biographical agency belonging to three categories. The category 'Status Arrangement' comprised people who emphasised continuity in their career characterised either by high loyalty to the employer or by looking for job security and a reasonable salary. This category included the modes 'Company Identification' and 'Wage-worker Habitus'. The category 'Advancement Ambition' consisted of individuals who either intended to climb the career ladder or to gain responsibility without aiming at the next career step. The respective modes were 'Career Orientation' and 'Optimising Chances'.

The category 'Autonomy Gain' described people who concentrated on their development with a focus either on their own personality or on setting up their own business. This category subsumed the modes 'Personal Growth' and 'Self-employment Habitus'. These six career types varied in their experiences of discontinuity, and flexibility, in the course of their biography. People of the modes 'Personal Growth' and 'Optimising Chances' decided for a temporary time-out for travelling or learning languages. People of the modes 'Career Orientation' and 'Optimising Chances' invested time in further training or higher education. People of the mode 'Personal Growth' used periods of unemployment for a vocational reorientation. Women of the modes 'Company Identification' and 'Wage-worker Habitus' interrupted employment for their family.

Our own typology resulted in four types of identity: the 'Continuous', the 'Job-centred', the 'Critical-flexible' and the 'Self-determined' (Raeder and Grote, 2004). Compared to the other types, the continuous type was characterised by the most prominent golden thread drawing through the work biography. The job-centred type reported the lowest consistency between the spheres of life often caused by a dominance of working life. The self-determined type showed high internal locus of control attributing control to personal factors as opposed to the interactionist locus of control attributing control to situational and personal factors. The latter was predominant in the other types. The critical-flexible type did not show specific features concerning identity. The identity types differed in their position in working life. Many people with a continuous career, including managers, appeared in the continuous and job-centred type. In the critical-flexible and self-determined type were more employees without managerial functions, employees working in highly flexible companies and more people with a career change. Opposed to all other types, the critical-flexible type assessed the flexibility demands of employers negatively. The results showed that the widely postulated high individual flexibility does not enhance a successful career.

The typologies refer to two different aspects of flexibility. On the one hand, employees search for flexibility in their working life for pursuing their personal goals. Such flexibility ranges from flexible arrangements in working time and place to portfolio work and career changes (cf. Sheldon, 1995). On the other hand, employees have to adapt to the flexibility demands of employers or the labour market (cf. Reilly, 1998). Personal biographies and work identities interact with these processes of flexibility. The national context of educational and occupational structures delimits or opens up the range of flexibility. Flexibility may be restricted by a system that requires specialisation in an occupation and a specified vocational training for working in an occupation (cf. Kirpal, 2004b). Under such circumstances, individually desired job changes are only possible after having acquired the necessary competences.

With the aim of presenting individuality beyond such typologies, it is necessary to consider the definitions of identity used. The existing variety of approaches towards identity can be roughly distinguished by the definition of identity as outside perception or as self-perception (cf. Frey and Hausser, 1987). The first perspective uses the term identity for describing someone's position in the social context by referring to the social role, the identification with social groups and one's occupation or work task (e.g. Ellemers et al., 2002). The FAME team (Kirpal, 2004b) followed this approach. The typology of the Special Collaborative Centre 186 (Heinz, 2002; Witzel and Kühn, 2000) can be added to this approach as it applied similar information although not drawing on the term identity. The latter perspective understands identity as a self-reflexive process of an individual. We applied this approach in our research, because it allows—as the study of Hoff (1990; Hoff et al., 1991) shows—a more detailed analysis closer to the subjective and individual self-perception of the person.

In a longitudinal study, Hoff *et al.* (1991) analysed the development of locus of control—one dimension of personal identity (Hoff, 1990)—in a sample of skilled workers (cf. Table 6.1). The authors decided to extend the bipolar locus of control concept that concentrates on internal and external control (cf. Rotter, 1966). They distinguished deterministic, i.e. internal (events are determined by the person), external (events are determined by the situation) or fatalistic (events are determined by chance of fate) locus of control and interactionist locus of control (events are determined by an interaction of person and situation). In the first wave, internal, additive-deterministic (events are determined either by the person or the situation) and interactionist locus of control were equally distributed in the sample. Only a few participants expressed a fatalistic locus of control. In the second wave six years later, the fatalistic locus of control vanished and some people adopted an additive-deterministic or interactionist locus of control. The authors concluded that the variety of individual options and situational constraints as well as experiences of conflict fostered the development of an interactionist locus of control.

While the three typologies turn towards researching flexibility, Hoff *et al.* (1991) focus on the interrelation between work and identity in line with Sennett's (1998) assumption that work should both remain stable over one's life course and allow personal development. Although they limit their study to the dimension of locus of control, they show that this perspective of identity as self-perception can lead to a detailed description of identity. The identity model of Hausser (1983), Hoff (1990) refers to, does not call for such a narrow perspective as it conceptualises identity in three components and several sub-dimensions. The use of this identity model would allow analysis of the complexity of personal identity constructions while maintaining their individuality.

Table 6.2   Psychological identity concepts discussed in this chapter

Researcher	Approach	Key assumptions
Erikson (1959)	Identity theory	Identity achieved in adolescence remains unchanged during adulthood. The perception of continuity in time and consistency across contexts is crucial for personal identity.
Marcia (1980)	Model of identity development	Identity develops during one's lifetime going through four identity states: • Identity Achievement • Foreclosure • Identity Diffusion • Moratorium
Hausser (1983, 1995)	Model of identity structure and development	Structural model with three dimensions: • Self-esteem • Locus of control • Self-concept (with the aspects: biographical continuity; ecological consistency, consequence in the relation of attitudes and behaviour, authenticity in the relation of emotion and behaviour, individuality and equality)

Three more reasons support applying Hausser's model (1983, 1995). Hausser referred to the tradition of identity researchers like Erikson (1959) and Marcia (1980) and integrated a variety of aspects of a personal self-definition and conceptualised identity structure and development. To introduce the identity topic, we first show how the model of Hausser relates to the tradition of identity theory particularly to the work of Erikson and Marcia. Table 6.2 summarises their key assumptions.

6.3   The Concept of Personal Identity

Hausser followed Marcia in understanding personal identity as 'self-constructed' (Marcia, 1980, p. 159). Identity is part of the self-perception and cannot be completely captured from an outside perspective as is the case with personality or social roles. Identity does not comprise all facets of self-perception but only those, which are subjectively meaningful and which affect the person. Thus, personal identity is defined as a self-reflexive process of an individual that is structuring and relating a variety of personal experiences (Frey and Hausser, 1987).

Hausser drew on Erikson's assumption that identity comprises the perception of continuity in time and consistency across contexts (Erikson, 1968 as cited in Kroger, 2000). Continuity, however, does not stand for limiting the process of identity development to youth and adolescence and assuming that the personal identity once achieved remains unchanged during a lifetime (Frey and Hausser, 1987). Like Marcia, Hausser conceptualised identity as a life long developmental process and did not support the normative assumption that continuity is a prerequisite for healthy identity development.

Although Hausser agreed with Marcia in defining identity as a developmental process, he did not support the notion of attaining the goal of an 'ideal' identity status. Marcia adopted Erikson's ideal status of achieved identity and further differentiated it into four identity states, which a person may go through once or more often during lifetime. Marcia (1980) described these four stages as follows:

Identity Achievements are individuals who have experienced a decision-making period and are pursuing self-chosen occupation and ideological goals. Foreclosures are persons who are also committed to occupational and ideological positions, but these have been parentally chosen rather than self-chosen. They show little or no evidence of 'crisis'. Identity Diffusions are young people who have no set occupational or ideological direction, regardless of whether or not they may have experienced a decision-making period. Moratoriums are individuals who are currently struggling with occupational and/or ideological issues; they are in an identity crisis (p. 161).

Frey and Hausser criticised the idea of setting normative criteria for a normal and personally valued identity and argued for not normatively assessing individual identities. Hausser's developmental model, therefore, is not bound to stages that are to be achieved. Based on the circular model of identity process by Whitbourne and Weinstock (1979), Hausser assumed a life long developmental process by which current experiences are continually integrated into one's general self-conception.

Frey and Hausser (1987) pointed out four core topics of the dynamic of identity: the relation of the perspective from the inside and from the outside (problem of reality); the relation of the various elements of identity (problem of consistency); stability and change of these elements (problem of continuity); and the creation and presentation of a unique identity (problem of individuality). Hausser's (1983, 1995) identity model aimed at treating these four core topics. In his structural model, he succeeded in integrating three usually separated research fields concerning the self: self-concept, self-esteem and locus of control. With these dimensions of self-perception, self-evaluation and personal control, he covered a cognitive, an emotional and a motivational dimension of identity. He further divided the self-concept into six aspects: biographical continuity, ecological consistency, consequence in the relation of attitudes and behaviour, authenticity in the relation of emotion and behaviour, individuality and equality. Hausser followed Hoff *et al.* (1991) in defining locus of control as comprising internal, external, fatalistic and interactionist locus of control, as he assumed the bipolar control concept of internal and external locus of control (cf. Rotter, 1966) to be unrealistically simplistic. Thus, Hausser addressed the problem of reality in defining identity as self-perception and discussing its relation to reality. The aspects of the self-concept biographical continuity, ecological consistency and individuality cover the problems of consistency, continuity and individuality. The problem of individuality refers to the assumption that a person attempts to present an individual identity construction, and this is the main focus of this chapter.

Like Marcia (1980), Hausser assumed that identity may differ with respect to different spheres of life. Vocational identity, one of the identities specific to a particular sphere of life, refers to one's working life.

6.4   Research Question

The main objective of this chapter is to analyse the personal identity of people with career changes. In order to consider the complexity of individual identity constructions we developed a system of categories for describing such identity constructions. Furthermore, we analysed whether the career changers use specific strategies within their personal identity construction.

Drawing on the identity definition of Hausser (1995), we confined our qualitative analysis to four dimensions of identity, i.e. biographical continuity, ecological consistency, locus of control and self-esteem. We chose these dimensions, because they are especially important in the context of changing careers. The first two reflected the main identity concern of Erikson (1959) further elaborated and discussed by Marcia (1980), Frey and Hausser (1987) and Keupp (1997). We assumed that continuity is not anymore assured through the golden thread of the occupation, and that consistency between spheres of life is questioned if people have to invest a lot of time in their qualification. The dimension of locus of control referred to processes of decision and control in the context of biographical changes. Self-esteem was included for evaluating the other identity dimensions (cf. Hausser, 1995).

6.5   Methods

6.5.1   Sample

The sample consisted of 18 men and 12 women, who had worked in two or more occupations, i.e. had changed their career at least once (cf. Sheldon, 1995). At the time of the interview, they were living in Switzerland and were aged 40 to 50. In the sample, we considered as many different occupations and combinations of occupations as possible. Occupations were classified according to a German classification system (Statistisches Bundesamt, 1996). Careers within an occupational direction in terms of a further qualification in the same area (e.g. technical school after an apprenticeship in a technical occupation) were not included in the sample. In the context of the Swiss education system and labour market with a clear occupational orientation, working in a different occupation implies to acquire the corresponding formal competences and qualification. Individuals completing three levels of education were considered in the sample: secondary level II with a

'Lehrabschluss' (equivalent to a completed apprenticeship) or 'Maturität' (equivalent to A-levels); tertiary level I with a degree from a 'Höhere Fachschule' or 'Berufsprüfung' (equivalent to a tertiary technical or vocational institution); and tertiary level II with a university degree. In comparison to the Swiss population as a whole, participants with higher education were slightly overrepresented in the sample.

This sample formed part of the sample used for developing the identity typology (Raeder and Grote, 2004), which was based on quantitative data of employee surveys and on qualitative data of these 30 people with a career change, and of another 29 people with a continuous career in one occupation. The more detailed analysis in this chapter aims at revealing additional information on personal identity constructions.

6.5.2 Procedures

We conducted semi-standardised interviews. The interview guide comprised questions concerning the vocational biography, reasons for work-related decisions, competences, resources and the importance of working life in relation to other spheres of life. The interviews were transcribed.

The data analysis proceeded in three steps. In the first step, the data was analysed by means of qualitative content analysis (Mayring, 2000). This method was chosen so as to include the data of all cases in one procedure and find out similarities as well as common patterns. In the process of systematic analysis, the interview data was divided into content analytic units. A content analytic unit was a statement consisting of one or several sentences. These content analytic units were then assigned to the identity-related categories determined by the identity model.

In the second step, the results of the qualitative content analysis concerning personal identity were validated communicatively (Lechler, 1982) for verifying that the participants accept their personal results as a description of their identity. In the process of communicative validation, the participants assigned their statements, which were coded for a category and printed on cards, to a continuum within each category (cf. Figure 6.1). They could add new information, put aside cards and decide at which point of the continuum they wanted to locate their statements. They could, therefore, choose the appropriate classification for every identity category. Their classification did not always agree with our coding, but was respected as their individual interpretation of their personal life story.

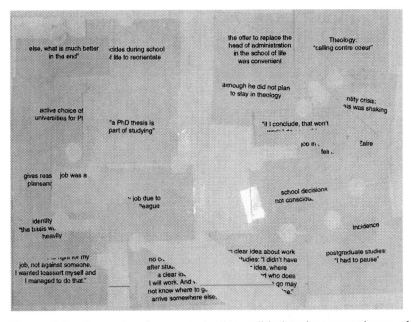

Figure 6.1   Example of communicative validation (category locus of control)

As self-esteem was used for evaluating the other identity dimensions, the participants were asked to locate cards representing these dimensions on a continuum leading from low to high self-esteem (cf. Figure 6.2).

In the third step, the continua of the categories were divided into three sections corresponding to a high, medium or low level. The cards assigned by the participants were thus divided into three groups. The data was further differentiated by inductively developing subcategories as recommended by Mayring (2000). We derived the subcategories from the data assigned to each category and revised them in the process of analysis. Each subcategory represented high, medium or low values within the category. In order to reproduce the statements of the participants as accurately as possible, we applied a highly differentiated system of categories. This system of subcategories completely represented the data, because all content analytic units were coded for subcategories. Our coding and the coding by the participants during the communicative validation did not always correspond. Example: a participant coded his statement that he has an artist's soul as highly

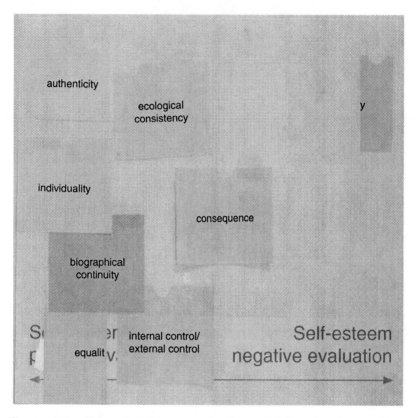

Figure 6.2 Example of communicative validation for the category self-esteem

continuous, but rated his statement as moderately continuous in that he had been interested in the work of a policeman from childhood onwards. Both statements represented a golden thread in his vocational interests and goals, but he assigned them to different levels within one category.

6.5.3 Categories

In this paper, we present the results concerning the identity categories 'biographical continuity', 'ecological consistency', 'locus of control' and 'self-esteem'. Below, we provide the definitions and examples of coding of these main categories as well as the subcategories and examples of coding of the subcategories (cf. Tables 6.3–6.9).

Table 6.3 Subcategories and examples of coding for high biographical continuity

High biographical continuity (subcategories)	Examples of coding
Golden thread in tasks	'I have always worked with young occupation, job or work people.'
Golden thread in non-work spheres of life	'I have always had relationships that resembled my job situation.'
Recurring pattern in working life	'It is always like that: I get some kind of input. Something fascinates me. And then, that's what I want, I exactly want to go there.'
Permanent vocational training	'I'm finishing this [vocational training] and have already enrolled for the next course.'
Permanent vocational interests and goals	'I have always been interested in history.'
Golden thread in vocational competences	'The logic is that I could always use later on what I had learnt in an earlier phase.'
Stable importance of work and private life	'I want to work while I'm living and to live while I'm working. That's a statement I made very early.'
Continuity in one's personality	'The big stumbling block, that always accompanied me, really was: "You are incapable".'
Abstract pattern of continuity	'To be precise, because I again and again experienced, when I let myself in for something, something new, when I had the feeling that's my next step, something became possible as a step after the next that I could not see at the moment. It only became possible, because I said yes to the next.'

Table 6.4   Subcategories and examples of coding for low biographical continuity

Low biographical continuity (subcategories)	Examples of coding
Changes in working life	'For a long time, I didn't set goals actively. For the first time, when I took this job.'
Changes in non-work spheres of life	'It always sounds brutal when you say the family is over. But this responsibility is gone.'
Clear-cut phases in working life	'The aspect of staying someplace for a longer time, 10½ years. Compared with the periods before where I did nothing for more than three years.'
Clear-cut phases in non-work spheres of life	'I really have the feeling as if I had different lives. And I remember the first very poorly.'
Break in working life	'At the same time, the price of dropping out. You have to start from anew. And you behave as if you were really good in your job. It takes you a long time until you are good in your job.'
Break in non-work spheres of life	'I had a baby very late, which is radically cutting in one's life. Suddenly, the whole organising. Flexibility is enormously cut in.'
Developmental process in working life	'There, I gained my first work experiences. In a team and a big organisation, it was an important experience. (. . .) First you don't think you can do it and then you just have to do it. Then you grow into it and that's okay.'
Developmental process in non-work spheres of life	'With every step I took I added something to that, what I am today, what I do today.'
Exception in working life	'This education is not focused that way [like my other education]. This education does not lead to a new occupational specialisation.'

Table 6.4   Continued

Low biographical continuity (subcategories)	Examples of coding
Exception in non-work spheres of life	'In South Wales, it had been the only time I had to pack my bags without wanting to.'
Ongoing search for a new challenge in working life	'I always need a new challenge.'
Variety in the occupation or job	'That's why I changed [the job] that often, because as soon as I knew it inside out, it was boring to me. I always needed something multi-faceted so that I'm faced with a challenge.'
Change in vocational competences	'By handcraft. By producing something where you have to look carefully. That's training for the eyes. (. . .) I remember that I made this development. I wasn't able to see at the beginning of my apprenticeship.'
Change in vocational interests and goals	'At home, it was not important what we women did, what kind of education we had. (. . .) What we achieved at school was not appreciated. Therefore, I made no efforts and I didn't learn anything. (. . .) I wanted to show that I am able to learn and I wanted to have a basis of general knowledge.'
Personality development	'I experienced a lot more ups and downs than today. I was less even-tempered.'
Changed importance of work and private life	'The job isn't as predominant as it has been in the past.'
Abstract pattern of change	'zigzag way'

Table 6.5 Subcategories and examples of coding for high ecological consistency

High ecological consistency (subcategories)	Examples of coding
Spheres of life influence one another	'Obviously, I had another field of experience (. . .) that's the field of family. (. . .) There are always relations back and forth [between family life and working life].'
Non-work spheres of life influence work	'I'm not going to have children, to have a family, and I will work till the age of 65. Therefore, I really want to do something what absolutely satisfies me.'
Work influences other spheres of life	'A good occupation is the basis for all sorts of things you can develop in your life.'
Balance between spheres of life	'Private and working life are totally interwoven in my life.'
Development in working life	'Well, I'm working well in such a cultural field. Before, I was lacking all that, because it was so uninspiring. I was dying like a flower. (. . .) Here, I have the feeling that I can develop, even when I have stress. It's much better mentally.'
Personality development in working life	'And in the phase of design, there comes stability in. (. . .) Designing myself through designing, that was of course closely connected. The designing of something and designing myself and finding my shape, who am I.'
Personality development in non-work spheres of life	'More and more clearly, being able to perceive more and more clearly what really matters. I learnt that best in my psychotherapy. (. . .) It was about reflecting what happens and how I can understand that and accept it. That really was a very important additional thread for seeing more and more clearly for myself.'
Support from non-work spheres of life for working life	'For now about 18 years, I'm living with the same partner and it is really permanent. I needed something like a secure anchor and there was always someone earning money.'
Vocational competences are applicable in various spheres of life	'For me it's always like that, things I'm learning somewhere go into all other fields and are realised there.'
Similar behaviour in different spheres of life	'Due to my age and my experiences, I had other demands. I would have expected that a professor of fundamental theology satisfies on the personal level, too.'

Table 6.6 Subcategories and examples of coding for low ecological consistency

Low ecological consistency	Examples of coding
Separation of spheres of life	'As police chief I managed a wonderful separation (. . .) between private and business.'
Discrepancy between spheres of life	'If I wouldn't have to work anymore, mustn't work anymore, for me it is an intellectual challenge. That's no use at home. (. . .) There are a lot of challenges you don't have at home.'
No development in working life	'And I was disappointed that I was of no importance as a person.'
No support from non-work spheres of life for working life	'Friends [supported me] not that much. They didn't realise (. . .) that people said, you draw well, it would be good, if you did something like that. (. . .) I would never have had the idea of doing something in this area. I wouldn't have known where to find an apprenticeship. (. . .) My parents didn't know a lot about that.'
Vocational competences are not applicable in other spheres of life	'In my job always [use my competences]. (. . .) In my private life to a lesser extent.'
Importance of working life	'I enjoy working, it's enriching my life.'
Dominance of working life	'My job got enormously important to me. A great deal actually happens in my job.'
Importance of private life	'Several love stories absorbed me more than the work content.'
Dominance of private life or other spheres of life	'School was a substitute for the family.'
Different behaviour in different spheres of life	'I am politically committed, but in my job I do not fight.'

Table 6.7 Subcategories and examples of coding for internal locus of control

Internal locus of control (subcategories)	Examples of coding
Personal choice or decision	'I knew for a long time when I've had enough, I'm going and then I'm travelling.'
Self-responsibility	'You are responsible for your own life yourself.'
Actively pursuing interests or goals	'When I intended something, I actually made it.'
Personal activity	'Yes, I attended a lot of courses to really find out, what [which occupation] belongs to me.'
Strong personal influence	'In an organisation like the police, few is made possible, you have to fight for a lot.'
Matter of course	'Into theology studies, the way was absolutely obvious to me.'
Actively shaping the situation	'I formed a department, that's called urban planning. (. . .) And then with my department urban planning and tourism, I began to take the public spaces in our town into my own hands.'

Table 6.8 Subcategories and examples of coding for interactionist locus of control

Interactionist locus of control (subcategories)	Examples of coding
Interplay of personal and situational factors	'At that time, I accepted the role of leader, because nobody was there and because I thought I could gather some experiences.'
Personal decisions depending on situation factors	'Actually I had the idea of making the technical school after the [apprenticeship as a] draftsman. But family came in between.'
Personal decisions coordinated with other people	'I come to a decision myself, but I like to coordinate myself with others.'
Personal decisions adapted to other people	'It was a period during which I would have wanted to set up a family and have children, but my partner never wanted to.'

Table 6.8   Continued

Interactionist locus of control (subcategories)	Examples of coding
Personal decisions adapted to situation factors	'Now you are certainly in family obligations, you get older. That you have to confine yourself to and say "you have to do something with that, what you are now and what you can do". And I'm just staying on this track and I'm looking at what's coming next.'
Influence of other people	'I made my "Matura" [i.e. A-levels]. At first, I didn't really want to start. She [girlfriend] pushed a little bit.'
Negotiating	'I had a really good supervisor, whom I esteemed. She was 15 years older than me, but had no training for teaching. She thought if I made the vocational training for teaching, she would have to leave. I could prevent that by motivating her to attend this training, too. She made it part-time. Then we did job sharing.'
Conditions allow realising personal concerns	'I could realise a lot of things with this colleague and later on with other people too, launch projects, really concrete equal opportunities projects.'
Seize an opportunity	'I'm a strategist, too. (. . .) It was a good opportunity, which I seized.'
Adapting to the situation	'It's not a pressure to communicate like I'm experiencing it with teachers. You always have to talk to one another and come out of your shell. And at the beginning that was a problem for me. (. . .) But you learn it somehow, that it is just all part of it. That's the rule. That you can talk about commonplaces, the discourse, language, communicate, approach the other. That's something fundamental in this world, in the area of education. That's something I had much pain learning it at all.'

Table 6.9   Subcategories and examples of coding for external and fatalistic locus of control

External and fatalistic locus of control (subcategories)	Examples of coding
Determined by situation factors	'That is, basically, I already focused on the aim, which I reached now, in infancy. (. . .) It has been inhibited by, the way I perceive it today, a difficult situation at school, which probably had to do with the family situation.'
Determined by other people	'That [apprenticeship as a bricklayer] was decided over my head.'
Strong influence of other people	'You can't talk of conscious decisions as regards vocational choice. With hindsight, let's say, you are simply in an environment, where there are certain options, where something like that happens, where you can't say you are the master of one's fate.'
Not able to take over control	'The company was very conservative. Just after my entry, the managing director changed. Under the old managing director, I would never have entered. (. . .) At this time, no one realised that finally I am too informal, frank and unconventional, than the company could ever change to. After a half year, it came to a breach due to leadership questions. (. . .) I started in April in this position and interviewed my co-workers for understanding how they work, what their goals personally were, where they wanted to go. Then, the personnel manager told me that this procedure is basically wrong, because appraisal interviews are to be conducted in November within the annual cycle and limited to the performance of the employee and salary questions. Then, I had to say "sorry, I don't agree".'
No personal control	'Theology came out of the inner feeling that I had to do that. You would call it a calling. Namely "contre coeur".'
Indecisiveness	'(. . .), because I didn't know, what I wanted.'
Helplessness	'At that time, when I was a teacher, I didn't like

Table 6.9 Continued

External and fatalistic locus of control (subcategories)	Examples of coding
	to stay in the village over the weekend. I lived in the same district as half of my pupils. (. . .) When I went out, the children would call me "Madame". That was awful for me. I found that awful at the age of 20. That was like running the gauntlet.'
No clear intention	'I didn't feel a pressure, because I didn't know what I really wanted.'
Luck	'Luckily, it worked that I could change my job.'
Fate	'I was always short-listed, destiny always selected. I never decided that.'
Chance	'By chance, I found a job in the city I was living.'

Biographical Continuity

Definition: 'the immediate perception of one's selfsameness and continuity in time; and the simultaneous perception of the fact that others recognize one's sameness and continuity' (Erikson, 1959, p. 23 as cited in Hausser, 1995). Examples of coding: 'The logic is that I always could use what I had learnt in an earlier phase' (high biographical continuity); 'I suppose from the age of 35 on I had an idealistic period. It was changing into an economic period. It got more important to earn good money and to have a good job' (low biographical continuity).

Ecological consistency

Definition: 'perception of coherence of one's own behaviour in different spheres of life' (Hausser, 1995, p. 29). Examples of coding: 'At that time, I could realise a lot of things, which were important to me in my life. To live and shape my own life' (high consistency); 'I am politically committed, but in my job I do not fight' (low consistency).

Locus of Control

Definition: 'generalized, subjective explicability, predictability and influenceability' (Hausser, 1995, p. 42) of events concerning oneself. Subcategories, which were theoretically defined in advance, were 'internal', 'external', 'fatalistic' (chance or fate) and 'interactionist' (interplay of external, internal and fatalistic factors) locus of control. These subcategories were refined in the process of data analysis. The continuum prepared for communicative validation led from internal to external control, as it was only possible to consider two dimensions. The interactionist locus of control was situated in the middle and the fatalistic locus of control merged with the external (cf. Rotter, 1966).

Examples of coding: 'I am now at the peak of what I do. I have a lot of work. I earn good money. If I changed my occupation again, I would have to start all over again. Then, I realised I do not want that at the moment. I try to carry on, but thought I have to do something for me, which gives me suspense and some challenge. Two years ago, I started a master's course in philosophy in England and I am studying part-time in England' (internal locus of control); 'I had to learn that the community is important in a city council. It is a collegial board and you have to support decisions you personally do not approve. (. . .) I learnt to guide the team processes' (interactionist locus of control); 'It is getting unpleasant. I am in New York nearly every two weeks. That is for nearly three years. It is still escalating. I am not the only one in the department, simply 250 per cent overburdened' (external locus of control); 'By chance, I found a job in the city where I was living' (fatalistic locus of control).

Self-Esteem

Definition: 'self-esteem is usually thought to be the evaluative component of a broader representation of self, the self-concept' (Blascovich and Tomaka, 1991, p. 115). As the participants assigned cards representing biographical continuity, ecological consistency and locus of control to the self-esteem continuum, no sub-categories were developed (cf. Figure 6.2).

6.6   Results

The subcategories show the broad spectrum of statements and explanations given. It was not possible to find patterns or strategies across subcategories. We, therefore, present the data for the whole sample along the categories 'biographical continuity', 'ecological consistency', 'locus of control' and 'self-esteem' based on the respective subcategories. The results are illustrated with the examples of seven individuals focusing on the most frequently assigned subcategories.

In visualising their identity in the process of communicative validation, the participants seemed to look for a balanced image of their identity. They laid emphasis on the pattern of all their statements and not on the exact position of each card. The participants made use of a broad range of interpretations. They reinterpreted episodes of their biography and decided upon the importance they should assign to the different aspects of one story. They, therefore, assigned their statements differently than we did. An interviewee, for instance, told that he got his first job by chance after having obtained his doctorate. In the process of communicative validation, he assigned this card to the category internal control instead of external or fatalistic control.

6.6.1   Biographical Continuity

The participants put more emphasis on high continuity than on low continuity, but no one assessed oneself as completely continuous or discontinuous. All participants chose some subcategories indicating low continuity, some subcategories indicating high continuity and some subcategories somewhere in between. The participants found high biographical continuity in:

- the golden thread in their occupation, job or work task,
- the vocational interests and goals they permanently pursued,
- a recurring pattern in working life,
- the golden thread in their private life or other spheres of life.

They expressed low biographical continuity in describing:

- clear-cut phases in their working life or other spheres of life,
- disruptions experienced in working life,
- changes in working life.

For illustrating these subcategories, we present two interviewees. The first gave examples for all the subcategories indicating high biographical continuity, the second for all subcategories indicating low biographical continuity. We present examples of either high or low continuity, although overall the two interviewees showed elements of both. The subcategories, to which we assigned the content analytic units, are provided in brackets.

Person 1: After finishing school, he underwent his apprenticeship in business and administration. He then preferred working as a social worker, attended a school for social work and studied psychology after some years of work experience. With the degree in psychology he started working as a process and business consultant. He is now self-employed as a partner in a consultants' network, teaches at a college and is preparing for his master's degree at a foreign university.

He explained his high biographical continuity as follows: he tried to integrate the economic and the social phase of his past into his present job as a consultant and succeeded in doing this (golden thread in working life). He always had the motivation to change society, but his aims altered. During his studies, he decided to stop working 'reactively' and to start consulting preventatively (permanent vocational interests and goals). As a social worker, he experienced symptoms of fatigue, as he had the feeling that his working days were all similar and he had to do the same kind of work every day (recurring pattern). He regularly left for some months for travelling around the world (golden thread in non-work spheres of life).

Person 2: She started her working life with an apprenticeship in gardening, which she quit due to the monotony of the work tasks. She then followed an apprenticeship as a physician assistant and worked for several years in this occupation. Between her various jobs, she was always travelling for some months. Not being satisfied in her job, she decided to attend a school for occupational therapy. After having worked for various institutions, she decided to become self-employed running her own practice.

She reported the following elements of low biographical continuity: she described the period of working as a physician assistant as a phase now concluded. At that time, she did not have any influence on decision-making. Today, she is more critical and decides on her own (clear-cut phases). After working for a homeopath, she decided to quit her career as physician assistant (break). She explained that she adopted a more realistic stance during the years as an employee. She realised that structures in institutions cannot be changed easily and that a lot of effort is required to change them (change). After having completed the school for occupational therapy she needed a time-out, which she used for travelling. At a certain point in time, she realised that the time had come to look for a job in the city where she was living (clear-cut phases in private life).

6.6.2 Ecological Consistency

The participants described themselves as predominantly consistent. They mentioned few aspects or examples of low ecological consistency. No interviewee assessed herself or himself as completely consistent or inconsistent. In the participants' descriptions high ecological consistency referred to:

- the influence of non-work spheres of life on their working life,
- the influence of their working life on non-work spheres of life,
- the support they got from non-work spheres of life for their working life,
- the balance between spheres of life.

They characterised low ecological consistency by:

- the influence of non-work spheres of life on their working life,
- the separation between spheres of life,
- the dominance of working life.

Person 3:   He started his working life with an apprenticeship as a carpenter and as a draftsman. He was then working as a carpenter, married and started building a family. Due to health problems, he could not continue working in this occupation and decided to study architecture at a technical college. He then worked as a self-employed architect constructing buildings for disabled people. In the meantime, he attended theology courses for laypersons and after some years started to study theology at university. He is now working as a pastor in a catholic church.

He reported the following elements of consistency: in general, he explained that his career changes were closely related to his personal development during lifetime and gave several examples. His private life had an influence on the decisions in his working life. He started his contact with the occupation of the carpenter through his family and then decided to follow that path. He decided to study architecture due to his health problems, which did not allow him to continue working as a carpenter. His theology hobby nurtured his decision to study theology. He assessed his present job as consistent, because he personally wants to stay in contact with people (influence of non-work spheres life on working life). Besides, he admitted that his private life had changed through learning processes in his working life (influence of working life on non-work spheres life). His family supported him in studying theology while working as an architect (support from private life for working life). He perceived work and non-work as balanced, as he finds compensation for work in handcraft and meditation. He is only employed 80 per cent, thus having more time for his family life. In his job, his personal life and his working life converge (balance between spheres of life).

Person 4:   He decided to start an apprenticeship as a laboratory assistant against the will of his parents. Because he set up a family, he decided to attend the police school for one year. Then he worked as a police officer and advanced in his career. In his spare time, he started painting and furnished a studio in his house. Having reached the top of the career ladder, he decided to quit the police and to work as an artist.

He mentioned the following elements of low ecological consistency: he reported two examples in which his private life had an influence on his working life. He was interested in the occupation of the policeman as his father was an auxiliary policeman. Setting up a family led to his career change and to the decision to attend police school. In the process of communicative validation, he judged both influences as low in consistency (influence of non-work spheres of life on their working life). He explained that he had managed to separate work and family life completely when he assumed a chief position at the police (separation between spheres of life). During his police career, he had clearly focused on his professional life and was not in power of control over his life and time management (dominance of working life).

6.6.3   Locus of Control

Overall, the interviewees mentioned as many examples for internal, as for external or interactionist, locus of control. No interviewee could be assigned to one specific category of locus of control, i.e. internal, interactionist or external locus of control. The participants described internal locus of control by:

- personal choice or decision,
- actively pursuing interests or goals,
- self-responsibility.

They characterised interactionist locus of control by:

- personal decisions depending on situational factors,
- adapting to situational factors,
- the interplay of person and situational factors.

They explained external or fatalistic locus of control as:

- determined by situational factors,
- determined by other people.

For illustrating these subcategories, we present three interviewees. The first has given examples for all dimensions of internal locus of control, the second for interactionist and the third for external locus of control. All three of them showed elements of the other categories, too.

Person 5:   After having left school, she started an apprenticeship as a secretary. She was working as a secretary while she was continually searching for her true vocational interests, as she was not content with the various jobs she had. During a course of photography she felt convinced that photographing could become her future occupation. She applied for studying at a school of art and design. She is now employed part-time at this school working as a self-employed photographer.

She mentioned the following elements of internal locus of control: After her apprenticeship, she decided to move to the city, because she wanted to live there with her friend (personal choice or decision). For finding out which occupation was the right one for her, she attended several courses. In one of these courses, she realised that she wanted to become a photographer (actively pursuing interests or aims). During the process of communicative validation, she added two aspects. She described her work as independent, because she is self-employed and only depends on the clients. She can plan her future self-responsibly according to her own aims (self-responsibility).

Person 6:   She started her working life with an apprenticeship as a draftsman. After having worked for some years on this job, she decided to study architecture at a technical college. She left college due to an attractive job offer. After some years of being politically active, she decided to work in the field of equal opportunities at a labour union. She attended a grammar school for adults in order to be admitted to a master's course.

She showed the following elements of interactionist locus of control: after her apprenticeship, her parents did not allow her to move alone to the southern Italian-speaking part of Switzerland. She, therefore, decided to go to Lausanne, a city in the western French-speaking part, where a friend of her sister was living. For studying architecture, she preferred Berne to Zurich, as she could continue living in Lausanne. She described being discriminated against in her job as a very illuminative experience. She had become aware of the antagonistic behaviour patterns and had to find ways to act against these patterns (personal decisions depending on situational factors). She judged male dominated industries and labour unions as a demanding work context, as she had to restart anew with every project. After she had quit her position in this labour union, internal structures were modified according to her suggestions. Due to her child, her own flexibility is very limited, as she has to organise the child-care for her working days (adapting to the situation). The labour union with which she was employed provided opportunities for directly influencing the equal opportunities policies in the companies (interplay of person and situational factors).

Person 7:   Her parents decided that she had to attend grammar school, which she left with a diploma as a primary school teacher. After some years of working and travelling around the world, she started an apprenticeship as a goldsmith. She is now working in her own studio and offers vocational training courses.

She mentioned several examples of external locus of control: while she was attending grammar school, she often felt left alone. She always had to cheat and to pretend that she had done her homework (determined by situational factors). Her parents decided that she had to attend grammar school, although she disagreed (determined by other people).

6.6.4   Self-Esteem

In the communicative validation, the participants assigned most cards to a high or medium degree of self-esteem. They arranged only a few cards at a low level of self-esteem. The participants assessed their self-esteem on average as medium or high. They, thus, seemed to be content with their identity construction. Dissatisfaction with their biography or identity was only tied to certain aspects. For instance, an interviewee expressed dissatisfaction with her career because she did not find a part-time job corresponding to her qualifications. However, when considering her overall life course, she was very content.

6.7   Discussion

The results show that the participants generally succeeded in integrating the career changes they experienced into their identity construction; the overall high level of self-esteem indicates that they felt content with their identity construction.

Biographical continuity appeared in the occupation, job or work task and in their vocational interests and goals. The participants also used abstract patterns and their private sphere of life to explain continuity. Low biographical continuity was expressed in clear-cut phases experienced in working or private life, and in breaks or changes experienced in working life. Continuity did not evolve over the whole life course, but included periods and sequences of years. It was rare that one golden thread would lead through their entire life, but several smaller golden threads covered some years, themes or events. Those typically were tied together and let continuity appear. Discontinuity did not vanish, but was not threatening the personal identity construction.

The participants reported a high level of overall ecological consistency. They explained high ecological consistency with influences between working life and non-work spheres of life, with the support they got for their work and with the balance between different spheres of life. Low ecological consistency appeared through the influence of private life on working life, the separation between spheres of life and the dominance of working life. The participants interpreted the influence of private life on working life as an indicator for high as well as low consistency. Although consistency was high in the sample, most of the participants invested a lot of time in their job or education and training. They attempted to fulfil their personal interests, dreams and goals in their working life. Many of them did not achieve a better work-life-balance, as the sphere of work was predominant in their life.

The statements of the participants were equally distributed across the categories 'internal', 'external' and 'interactionist' control. The participants carefully reported the various influences that led to their decisions. They described personal control by examples of personal choice or decision, of actively pursuing their interests and aims and of acting self-responsibly. They characterised interactionist locus of control by personal decisions, which were adapted to or even depending on the situation, and by the interplay of person and situational factors. In the case of external control, decision-making was determined by the situation or by other people.

The results reveal that limiting control to an internal and external dimension (cf. Rotter, 1966) is not sufficient to adequately describe vocational identities (Hausser, 1995; Hoff et al., 1991). In the process of communicative validation, the participants reinterpreted the events reported before and weighted all aspects of control. The interactionist locus of control should, therefore, be considered in research and integrated into the locus of control concept. We conclude that differentiation is needed concerning the interpretation process, in which a person assesses a factor as internal or external, its importance and the resulting locus of control.

Although some topics of identity were more frequently mentioned than others, the participants did not rely on consistent strategies. Individual differences were, therefore, limited to using specific explanations. Individuals could not clearly be distinguished by the pattern of subcategories they used. The participants seemed to deal effectively with the career changes. Our results show communalities with the findings of Billett (cf. Billett in this volume), who illustrates how the five individuals of his study adapted well to transformations in their working life. They succeeded in developing their sense of self through changes in their working life and through the interplay of work and private life.

In our study, it has to be considered that the participants were qualified and could rely on their education and vocational training. Additionally, they could benefit from the favourable conditions on the Swiss labour market, as they had the opportunity to find adequate employment in a new occupation, although they had few experiences directly relevant for the new job. Only few were employed below their qualification level, e.g. a psychologist working in her former occupation as a nurse. Considering the research on self-esteem and unemployment (cf. Wacker and Kolobkova, 2000), it has to be assumed that someone assesses the personal identity in a less favourable employment situation more negatively. The assumption of the development of the identity construction implies that this personal assessment may also change over the years. For example, during personally difficult periods of their biography, the participants may have assessed their identity more critically indicated by a lower self-esteem. For analysing this developmental process and its personal evaluation, it would be necessary to follow the individual identity development over the course of years. An aim would be to find out, in which way the identity construction is affected by life events and whether people regain their balance in coming to terms with what has happened.

The participating individuals looked for explanations and past events that supported their present identity construction. In our retrospective analysis, it is not possible to reconstruct the importance of past experiences and events for the personal identity in the past. For example, an interviewee explained that she always had the desire to cooperate. This explanation fits to her present view of her biography. Asked twenty years ago, she possibly may have given another explanation.

The analysis of personal identity based on a biographical narrative includes a variety of experiences, which cover a broad range of aspects within the identity dimensions. It therefore has to be assumed that such an identity construction is less focused than an identity construction mainly referring to the present point of view. Although reported retrospectively, events experienced during adolescence or early adulthood differ from events in recent years. The analysis of the dimension locus of control showed, for instance, that a considerable number of examples for external locus of control took place during youth or adolescence. This fact may be explained by parental restrictions during this period.

The differences between our coding and the perspectives of the individuals conveyed in the communicative validation indicate that there is a broad range of interpretation between the extreme values of the categories. It was a matter of interpretation whether there is a tiny or a prominent golden thread, how much time is a lot of time for the family and to what degree one's own control can be exerted. The participants chose the balance between the poles that was appropriate for them. They achieved resolution in constructing and reconstructing their identity and managed to redefine events in a way that meant they could accept them as an important part of their biography. They integrated inconsistencies that appeared in the interpretation process, i.e. chance was redefined as internal control into their life stories. They, thus, developed their identity in an ongoing process of interpretation and construction by which they integrated current events and experiences (cf. Hausser, 1995; Keupp et al., 1999).

In the course of the active process of identity construction, the participants continuously defined and redefined the golden thread in their life, although continuity in their working life was not necessarily evident. Occupation and work played an important role in their lives, but the many changes experienced did not lead to a disruption of identity. They found continuity in their work. Even in those cases where what was required by the employment situation was not desired by the person, career changes did not pose a threat to personal identity constructions (cf. Billett in this volume; Keupp, 1997; Sennett, 1998). The participants developed manifold interpretations and constructions, which all seemed to be viable for them. Considering this portfolio of interpretations and subcategories, it did not prove to be necessary to normatively assume an ideal identity status (cf. Marcia, 1980).

The typologies of the Special Collaborative Centre 186 (Heinz, 2002; Witzel and Kühn, 2000) and of the FAME Project (Kirpal, 2004b) support the assumption of a reciprocal relationship between work flexibility and identity. The first typology puts emphasis on the interaction between personal options and goals and the work setting. The latter leads to the conclusion that flexibility raises the necessity to constantly reinterpret one's identity construction (cf. Kirpal, 2004b). Our results mirror these findings, as the participants in our study adapted their identity construction to what had happened and decided on options that fitted their identity construction. Furthermore, the work biographies of our participants corresponded to the flexible type of work identity of the FAME typology. While the flexible type of work identity, representing a concept of social identity (cf. Ellemers et al., 2002), focused on the way people deal with requirements of and adaptation to work flexibility, the analysis emphasised how work flexibility is experienced and integrated into one's self-perception.

In following the personal desire to present identity as individual, our analysis revealed a broad spectrum of aspects describing identity. The results showed the complexity, the details and the differentiation within personal identity constructions. It would therefore be useful to continue analysing identity constructions based on the presented system of analysis and to develop it further.

Our results did not provide arguments against work flexibility. Considering the classical type in the FAME typology (Kirpal, 2004b) and the critical-flexible type in our typology (Raeder and Grote, 2004) working flexibly appears to be more demanding than working in a standard employment. A well-considered amount of flexibility is useful for employers and individuals. Although the participants succeeded in finding their adequate balance, the results indicate that it is advisable to support people in finding such a balance between elements of continuity and discontinuity, in the relation between spheres of life as well as between controlling and accepting the need to be controlled.

In the context of the present employment situation, employers and individuals should positively assess career breaks and changes in individual's biographies and provide career opportunities despite these disruptions. Employers should facilitate the process of establishing links from present to past work characteristics and events as well as bringing in and realising vocational interests and goals. The possibility of change and development as well as finding one's own position in these processes should be offered. Individuals should be enabled to find an appropriate balance between work and non-work spheres of life.

In the context of counselling, within or outside the employment relationship, this would imply the need to provide a setting for discussing personal interests and goals, personal choices, decisions and responsibilities. The interaction of these elements with restrictions and opportunities of the context should be regarded as well as considering the variety of possible interpretations. In order to enhance self-esteem, support should be offered in finding an adequate understanding and a positive evaluation of individuals in developing their own biography.

Acknowledgments

We gratefully acknowledge the financial support by the Swiss National Science Foundation (SNF-Grant 4043-58298) and the assistance of Katrin Good, Nathalie Portmann and Ricarda Seidel in conducting the study. We also thank the colleagues of our research group for their very helpful comments on an earlier version of this article.

References

Billett, S. (2006). Exercising self through working life: Learning, Work and identity. In A. Brown, S. Kirpal and F. Rauner (Eds.), *Identities at Work* (pp. 183–210). Dordrecht: Springer.

Blascovich, J. and J. Tomaka (1991). Measures of self-esteem. In J.P. Robinson, P.R. Shaver and L.S. Wrightsman (Eds.), *Measures of personality and social psychological attitudes*, Vol. 1 (pp. 115–161). San Diego: Academic Press.

Ellemers, N., R. Spears and B. Doosje (2002). Self and social identity. *Annual Review of Psychology*, 53, 161–186.

Erikson, E.H. (1959). *Identity and the life cycle*. New York: International Universities Press.

Frey, H.-P. and K. Hausser (1987). Entwicklungslinien sozialwissenschaftlicher Identitätsforschung. In H.-P. Frey and K. Hausser (Eds.), *Identität. Der Mensch als soziales und personales Wesen* (pp. 3–26). Stuttgart: Enke.

Hausser, K. (1983). *Identitätsentwicklung*. New York: Harper & Row.

Hausser, K. (1995). *Identitätspsychologie*. Berlin: Springer.

Heinz, W.R. (2002). Transition discontinuities and the biographical shaping of early work careers. *Journal of Vocational Behavior*, 60, 220–240.

Hoff, E.-H. (1990). Identität und Arbeit. Zum Verständnis der Bezüge in Wissenschaft und Alltag. *Psychosozial*, 13(3), 7–23.

Hoff, E.-H., W. Lempert and L. Lappe (1991). *Persönlichkeitsentwicklung in Facharbeiterbiographien*. Bern: Huber.

Keupp, H. (1997). Diskursarena Identität: Lernprozesse in der Identitätsforschung. In H. Keupp and R. Höfer (Eds.), *Identitätsarbeit heute. Klassische und aktuelle Perspektiven der Identitätsforschung* (pp. 11–39). Frankfurt: Suhrkamp.

Keupp, H., T. Ahbe, W. Gmür, R. Höfer, B. Mitzscherlich, W. Kraus and F. Straus, (1999). *Identitätskonstruktionen. Das Patchwork der Identitäten in der Spätmoderne*. Reinbek bei Hamburg: Rowohlt.

Kirpal, S. (2004a). Researching work identities in a European context. *Career Development International*, 9(3), 199–221.

Kirpal, S. (2004b). *Work identities in Europe: Continuity and change. Final Report of the 5th Framework Project FAME*. ITB Working Paper Series No. 49. Bremen: Institute Technology and Education/University of Bremen.

Kroger, J. (2000). *Identity development. Adolescence through adulthood*. Thousand Oaks: Sage.

Lechler, P. (1982). Kommunikative Validierung. In G.L. Huber and H. Mandl (Eds.), *Verbale Daten. Eine Einführung in die Grundlagen und Methoden der Erhebung und Auswertung* (pp. 243–258). Weinheim: Beltz.

Marcia, J.E. (1980). Identity in adolescence. In J. Adelson (Ed.), *Handbook of adolescent psychology* (pp. 158–187). New York: Wiley.

Mayring, P. (2000). Qualitative content analysis [28 paragraphs]. Forum: qualitative social research [on-line journal], 1(2), retrieved August 30, 2004, from http://www.qualitative-research.net/fqs-texte/2002–2000/2002–2000mayring-e.htm.

Raeder, S. and G. Grote (2004). Flexible und kontinuitätsbetonte Identitätstypen in flexibilisierten Arbeitsverhältnissen. In H.J. Pongratz and G.G. Voss (Eds.), *Typisch Arbeitskraftunternehmer? Befunde der empirischen Arbeitsforschung* (pp. 57–72). Berlin: Edition Sigma.

Reilly, P.A. (1998). Balancing flexibility—meeting the interests of employer and employee. *European Journal of Work and Organizational Psychology*, 7(1), 7–22.

Rotter, J.B. (1966). Generalized expectancies for internal versus external control of reinforcement. *Psychological Monographs*, 80(1), 1–28.

Sennett, R. (1998). *The corrosion of character* (7th ed.). New York: W.W. Norton.

Sheldon, G. (1995). *Berufliche Flexibilität im Spiegel der Zeit* (Vol. 19). Bern: Bundesamt für Statistik.

Statistisches Bundesamt. (1996). Klassifizierung der Berufe, Ausgabe 1992, Berufsbereiche, Berufsabschnitte, Berufsgruppen, Berufsordnungen. In Statistisches Bundesamt (Ed.), *Bevölkerung und Erwerbstätigkeit, Fachserie 1, Reihe 4.1.2, Beruf, Ausbildung und Arbeitsbedingungen der Erwerbstätigen 1995 (Ergebnisse des Mikrozensus)* (pp. 317–323). Stuttgart: Metzler-Poeschel.

Wacker, A. and A. Kolobkova (2000). Arbeitslosigkeit und Selbstkonzept—ein Beitrag zu einer kontroversen Diskussion. *Zeitschrift für Arbeits- und Organisationspsychologie*, 44, 69–82.

Whitbourne, S.K. and C.S. Weinstock (1979). *Adult development. The differentiation of experience.* New York: Holt.

Witzel, A. and T. Kühn (2000). Orientierungs- und Handlungsmuster beim Übergang in das Erwerbsleben. *Zeitschrift für Soziologie der Erziehung und Sozialisation*, 20(3. Beiheft 2000), 9–29.

7

Exercising Self Through Working Life: Learning, Work and Identity

Stephen Billett
Griffith University, Australia

7.1 Part I: Learning, Self and Work

7.1.1 Exercising Self through Working Life

This chapter seeks to understand how individuals engage in and learn through work and throughout working life, for what purposes and how they are motivated to learn effortfully. Without such an understanding there can be little certainty about whether the expectations placed on individuals by government and employers about individuals' helping themselves will be fulfilled, in the ways they intend. So it is important to know more about how individuals participate in and learn throughout their working life, how they exercise their agency in participating in and learning through work, and for what purpose, and how these are linked to their values and beliefs. In short, what is it that directs individuals' learning throughout working life? In what ways will the goals of government, industry groups and enterprises likely to be achieved through the actions of workers as actors and learners.

It is advanced here that an individual's sense of self and its exercise, through her or his agency and intentional acting, does much to direct and shape this learning and also the ongoing remaking of the practices enacted at work. It proposes a greater acknowledgement and consideration of the interdependence between individual and social agency of employees, not just the actions of employers and government. This is warranted within current conceptions of learning throughout working life and, in particular, the role of individuals' quest to 'be themselves'.

183

A. Brown, S. Kirpal and F. Rauner (eds.), Identities at Work, 183–210.
© 2007 *Springer.*

This quest includes the re-shaping of that sense of self as individuals participate in and remake their work practice (Billett et al., 2005; Billett and Somerville, 2004). This may well lead to contradictions and complexities among the intentions of governments, employers and individuals. The contributions of both social agency, in the forms of suggestion provided through societal cultural practices and norms, the complex of social factors comprising the situated experiences of the workplace, and also individual agency, in the form of intentions, gaze and engagement, are held to be interdependent. There is mutual reliance or interdependence between these contributions for sustaining their respective continuities and development in the remaking and transformation of the cultural practices that constitute paid work and in the development of individuals' capacities or learning. Central to both of these forms of continuity and their interdependence, yet less understood and acknowledged, is the agentic and transformative role of self as an element of identity in forming and energising this interdependence. To explore, illuminate and understand further this interdependence, a study of five individuals working life and life outside of work is discussed.

This study sought to identify bases of engagement by individuals in their working lives and the role played by their agency, intentions and sense of self in their work and learning within their working lives (Billett and Pavlova, 2005). Each of these five individuals confronted significant change at work and with their work during the period of the investigation. It found that, against expectations, in each instance these individuals' exercise of their agency and intentionality was directed towards 'being themselves', as they negotiated their place in changing work environments and work tasks. For four of the five, these actions and negotiations lead to improving, supporting or easing their standing in the workplace. In the fifth instance, it was not a lack of workplace support as much as the over exercise of agency that resulted in a less than satisfactory outcome. By different degree, for each worker, there was evidence of interdependence between their needs and the affordances of the workplace, but with the negotiations directed by their agency and goals. While governments are expecting individuals to be responsible for their own lifelong learning and helping themselves (Edwards and Boreham, 2003), the learning may not be directed in the ways that government and their employers envisage. So there may be inconsistencies among what individuals, employers and government want to arise from this helping themselves, because it is directed towards personal goals, albeit negotiated and reshaped through working life experiences. This suggests that policies and practices associated with aiming to secure particular kinds of working life outcomes need to be considerate of or consonant with individuals' agency in securing their sense of self. This includes the negotiation between the individual and the workplace in transforming and reshaping that sense of self. The conceptual premises and their embodiment in data about individuals' working lives are used to argue that while governments, education institutions and workplaces are keen to mobilise workers as learners throughout their working lives to serve economic and civic purposes (Field, 2000), such mobilisations are inevitably mediated though individuals' sense of self and intentions: their agency. These need accounting for in consideration of policy and practice.

To elaborate these propositions, this chapter initially outlines and discusses the relational interdependence between social and individual agency as a means to understand learning through and for work, and the role that individual agency and subjectivities play in that interdependence. Following this, the procedures for, participants in and findings of a study that investigated the five workers' working lives are described. The findings are elaborated in sections that discuss the alignments among the changing work of these individuals and their interests and intentions. It also elaborates how individuals' goals, preferences and intentions are intertwined with their work and working life and the central role of their personal agency in shaping how they work, and the interdependence between the changing nature of work and their 'sense of self'.

7.1.2 Learning throughout Working Life in Times of Change

Interest in learning through and for work seems to be on many minds at the moment. Much of this interest is motivated by government, industry and enterprise concerns about the availability and level of skills within national, industry sector and enterprise workforces and maintaining or developing these workforces through times of changing demand and requirements for workplace competence. Yet, while focusing on a common concern about the levels and quality of workplace skills, the goals of government, industry, enterprises and individuals and their preferred means to address these goals may be quite different and even divergent. Governments are interested in the provision of a workforce that can adapt to changing demands of an increasingly globalised and uncertain economic environment and can also resist unemployment

(Green, 2001). Industry representatives and leaders are likely to be primarily concerned about the maintenance and development of skills for that industry sector, which includes competing for public funds for educational provision, for instance, against other sectors. Enterprises are more likely to be concerned with the specific set of skills required for the continuity and development of their products and services. Individuals may be most concerned about their continuity of employment or progression along a career path.

These different purposes lead to distinct acts of agency. For governments, the aim seems to be to mobilise individuals to participate energetically and resourcefully in a global competition against counterparts in other countries (Field, 2000). This mobilisation is to be focused on individuals taking responsibility for their own learning—helping themselves— with government enabling their engagement rather than providing (Edwards and Boreham, 2003). Industry groups develop skills standards, develop and endorse courses to generate industry-specific skills and arrangements for their certification. They also implement schemes to attract or retain workers in the sector and identify skill shortages and relay these concerns to government. Depending upon their needs, enterprises might act to encourage or restrict training opportunities, facilitate enterprise specific certification, engage with national schemes or not bother with either. Enterprises also elect how they distribute and expend their resources for employee development, and often in ways impervious to government mandate (Brunello and Medio, 2001). They may deny more portable skill recognition and will likely not accentuate the complexity of the work to be learnt (except in advertising their wares), lest this be used to undermine the enterprises' capacity to control their labour costs. More than a lack of consonance, there are also contradictions in these distinct actions. The strategic goals of government may not always be consistent with those of the industry sector. Similarly, enterprises, where the engagement in and learning from work occurs, may have different priorities from those of both government and the industry sector. Somewhere in here sits the individual whose role in achieving any of these goals is central to their success, yet whose contributions appear to remain misunderstood and/or under-acknowledged.

And therein lies a key problem. These diverse and contradictory goals and processes may well misunderstand and underplay the role of the individuals, who are to be subjected to them. They seem to downplay the likelihood of individuals having their own interests and intentions, which may or may not coincide with others goals and concerns (Billett et al., 2004). So there may well be contradictions between individuals' goals and those of government, industry groups, and their employers, which may be exercised when they help themselves. This can lead to negotiated, and possibly contested, bases for interaction between individuals and the intents of their workplaces (Billett, 2001), industry or government (Billett, 2000). Individual interest and engagement is far from a secondary or peripheral consideration. Because of its role in learning and remaking of work practices, individuals' sense of self, their agency and intents are central to the prospects for government, industry and enterprises ever achieving their goals.

More than learning through their participation in work, individuals also actively engage in the remaking of the kinds of participation, vocational practice and skilled performance that governments, industry groups and enterprises seek to secure. How individuals elect to be mobilised through the exercise of their agency to secure governmental goals, engage with industry-designated attributes of their work, and enterprises' priorities are in some ways personally dependent. In part, they are an outcome of individuals' construal of, engagement with and construction of these goals and their associated practices in their working lives (Billett, 2006b). Yet, what initiates and directs individuals' learning throughout working life and the role that individuals' agency and intentions play, their consequences for their workplaces and the strategic goals of industry and government are far from being fully understood. Central to elaborating this understanding is individuals' sense of self.

7.1.3 Working, Learning and Identity

Work is a key element of adult life and, for many individuals, it is the means through which their identity is shaped and exercised (Noon and Blyton, 1997; Pusey, 2003). So more than engaging in work being solely about exchanging time and labour for remuneration, there are potentially important outcomes for individuals that arise from engaging in work activities and interactions. The salience of work to individuals' identity appears also to be more than positioning within different socially privileged forms of work. If this were the case, presumably only those employed in the most prestigious and highest-paid jobs would enjoy any sense of fulfilment in their work. The rest would be disillusioned and disempowered by their relative standing on such an externally mediated measure. Yet, workers engaged in what many would classify as low status and lowly paid work have been shown to exercise significant agency and pride in their work, and in ways associated with localised recognition and personal satisfaction (Billett, 2003a). This suggests powerful personal motivations for participation in work that might not be highly regarded in the wider community. One way to understand the importance of and links between self and work is that the process of engagement in activities is central to ongoing and moment by moment individual learning (Rogoff, 1990). The engagement in work of any kind leads to particular and possibly significant legacies in terms of individuals' development, in ways that are generative of close links between individuals' sense of self and their work. Consequently, work and learning are so intertwined as to almost inevitably link individuals to their work activities in some way.

Concepts, procedures and values are often learnt, reinforced and transformed through engagement in work activities. The workplace provides an environment that is rich in its contributions to individuals' learning as they engage in work activities and, in doing so, remake the cultural practices that comprise paid work (Hodkinson and Hodkinson, 2003; Somerville and Bernoth, 2001). The privileging of environments in which learning takes place should not be according to whether they are sites claiming to promote learning as their key purpose. Instead, it should be according to the degree to which they provide the inter-psychological experiences of activities and interactions that underpin substantive learning. It is through these that knowledge is experienced, accessed, engaged with and constructed. Development of knowledge and understanding is perhaps most effectively achieved when supported by the assistance of a more experienced partner who understands that knowledge and can make accessible what is otherwise inaccessible, and support and monitor learning and development (Billett, 2006a). Such affordances or invitational qualities are central to what constitutes a learning environment.

Nevertheless, central to this process of learning and what constitutes a learning environment is also the degree to which individuals act agentically in the process of constructing knowledge (Billett, 2005b). This epistemological agency likely comprises individuals' construal of what they experience (e.g. what constitutes welcome or unwelcome affordances), the degree of, and intent in, their engagement with those affordances (e.g. activities and interactions) and their construction of meaning, procedures and values. This process is shaped by and premised upon individuals' agency, through the focus and expenditure of conscious thought and action, and their intents—the particular focus and direction of that agency. These processes are shaped by individuals' sense of self and their subjectivity: how they view the world. The concept of individuals' gaze can be seen as a metaphor for the enactment of a sense of self and subjectivity. It is this gaze that shapes how individuals construe and construct the immediate experience they encounter at work. So individuals' learning, albeit the refinement of what is already known or its reinforcement, arises through their engagement in everyday conscious thought through what constitutes their personal epistemology (Bauer et al., 2004; Smith, 2004), notwithstanding that epistemology is itself being shaped iteratively and relationally through a history of engagements with the social world.

Transformational learning can also arise through engaging in new activities and interactions. These are particularly plentiful in turbulent times of employment, or when other experiences confront individuals with perturbations requiring new insights (Rogoff, 1990), novel procedures or diverse values (Somerville, 2002). These learning processes have parallel and analogous consequences for the cultural practices that comprise paid work. That is, as individuals engage in even the most routine form of learning they are participating in the active process of remaking cultural practices. Culture and society are remade and transformed as individuals engage with their practices, learn and construct them at particular points in their personal histories and points in time as they engage with a battery of social suggestions and norms (Billett and Somerville, 2004). It follows that central to individuals' learning and their remaking of culture is the degree to which their agency directs, engages and constructs what they experience: their epistemological agency which both shapes and is shaped by their sense of self (Billett and Pavlova, 2005). Consequently, both continuities and transformations in work and individuals' learning are linked to how individuals construe, engage in and construct the activities and interaction that comprise the historical, cultural and situational contributions that collectively constitute the gift of the social (Archer, 2000): that is, the norms, values and practices that are accessible in and projected by the social world.

7.1.4 Interdependence Between Social Suggestion and Individual Agency

There is interdependence between both individual and social agency in the dual process of two kinds of change: individuals' learning and remaking culture. Given this relational interdependence between the social (e.g. geneses of subjectivities, cultural demands and situational requirements) and individual (e.g. intentionality and agentic action) contributions to thinking and acting, and therefore learning (e.g. Valsiner and van der Veer, 2000), individual agency and intentionality play central roles in both kinds of change.

The key premise behind this relational interdependence is that neither the social suggestion nor individuals' agency alone is sufficient to enact the desired learning and the remaking of the cultural practices that constitute work (Billett, 2006b). The social suggestion or press of the social comprises societal norms, practices and values, and their enactment, albeit shaped by local factors in particular ways. However, this press or suggestion is unlikely to ever be complete or comprehensive enough in workplaces to secure complete socialisation: the unquestioned and unquestionable transfer of knowledge from the social world to the individual. As Newman et al. (1989) propose, if the social world was able to extend its message so unequivocally, there would be no need to communicate. This is because understandings would be implicit, not requiring further communication to be construed and comprehended. However, as Berger and Luckman (1967) propose, the social suggestion is not amplifiable in ways that lead to complete socialisation, because individuals engage with the suggestion with greater or lesser reception. For no other reason, because of the limits of the social suggestion, individuals have to be agenetic and active in the construction of meaning. Meaning and practices arising from the social world require interpreting and construing. Yet, even beyond simply attending to, engaging with and comprehending what is being suggested, importantly individuals also bring possibly unique bases of conceptions, procedures and values to their engagement with social forms and practices. These considerations lead to some premises for the central role of self in the learning of and remaking cultural practices that comprise work.

So, the first premise is that there is an inevitable and important interdependency between the agency of the social world in projecting or pressing its suggestion and that of the individuals in making sense of what is suggested to or afforded them. This is particularly salient for learning the cultural practices that constitute paid work. Much vocational knowledge has its origins in cultural practices and historical precedents (Scribner, 1985). This genesis is important because it arises from a cultural need and has been refined over time through enactments of the practices. Consequently, to access this knowledge with its historical and cultural legacy requires engaging with the social world, as this knowledge does not arise from within the individual. Rather when individuals engage with this knowledge and reconstruct it, in addition to their individual development, they are also remaking these cultural practices at a particular point in time and through particular relationships to the social suggestion.

From the ideas advanced above, the remaking of cultural practice and individual learning is not through some faithful process of reproduction. Instead, there is a remaking through individual's engagement with and construction of those practices, albeit mediated by the exercise of social and cultural norms and practices whose needs have to be met at particular points in time in individuals' personal histories. Moreover, the exercise of this personal agency is essential in transforming cultural practices as new cultural needs arise, such as those brought about by changing times or technologies. Wertsch (1998) distinguishes between mastery (i.e. compliant) learning and appropriation. Compliant learning is superficial and may well be the product of forceful or compelling social suggestion of the kind which Valsiner (1998) identifies. Appropriation is the socially derived learning in which individuals engage willingly that leads to a concurrence between what is experienced and individuals' values and beliefs. In this way, compliant learning may be superficial or appropriated depending upon the degree to which they are aligned with individuals' beliefs and values. Given that richer or deeper kinds of learning likely require effortful engagement buoyed by interests and intentionality (Malle et al., 2001), this kind of learning may arise more frequently when it engages individuals' interests and agentic action.

The second central role of individuals' agency in learning and the remaking of culture is that there is likely to be some degree of person-dependence in these processes. Individuals' construal of what they encounter is socially shaped, through a personally unique set of negotiations with the social suggestion, in a way that comprises their organic growth or life histories. These negotiations are encountered continuously through the myriad forms of social practices that individuals engage in throughout their lives that contribute microgenetically— moment-by-moment—to their ontogenetic development. From the earliest age, those processes that Piaget (1968) referred to as securing equilibrium, and more recently von Glasersfeld (1987) refers to as maintaining viability, comprise an enduring personal epistemological venture. As well as confronting novel experiences, individuals' construals are premised on an expectation of variability and inconsistency in the response from the social world as well as aspects of certainty and consistency. For instance, Baldwin (1894) noted that from the earliest age, children learn to expect inconsistency in their dealings with the social world. He notes how a request for a biscuit will be fulfilled on one day, but rejected on the next, by the same person. In this way, individuals' ontogenetic development arises through a personally agentic epistemological process that is shaped through ongoing interactions with the social world, whereby individuals come to expect and therefore monitor for inconsistency. In turn, this process subsequently influences how they engage with new experiences. These experiences are likely to be in some ways unique to individuals, are highly formative in ways that Vygotskians describe as inter-psychological, and link to intra-psychological attributes. As a consequence there will inevitably be personally distinct conceptions as well as areas of commonality or shared understanding with others in their process of knowledge construction and remaking of cultural practices (Billett, 2003b).

The third premise then is that, because of the ontogenetic legacy and personal epistemology, consideration needs to be given to individuals' pre-mediate experiences—those that come earlier and, in turn, shape subsequent construals. These construals shape their conceptions and subjectivities—gaze, if you like—and, consequently, how they construct subsequent experiences. It is these conceptions and subjectivities that shape individuals' intentionality and agency in the processes of their learning and the remaking and transformation of cultural practices. Because these pre-mediate experiences are themselves shaped by, yet contribute to, unique personal epistemologies, even the most apparently uniform social experience, which affords its contributions seemingly equally to all parties, will be the subject of a partly individualised process of interpretation, construal and construction. This leads to particular and possibly unique personal kinds of epistemological bases, albeit that they are socially shaped. So life histories comprising individuals' prior social experiences stand as an important premise on to how they engage with the contributions of the social that they encounter in the immediate experience (i.e. workplace activities and interactions).

The final premise is that the relationship between individual and social agency is not mutual or reciprocal, it is relational. Just as the social suggestion can be either weaker or stronger, so too can be individuals' engagement with a particular social suggestion (e.g. situated practice, cultural norm or cultural practice). The prospects for the coming together and contributions of the individual and social being enacted in equal parts or ways that are equally shared is quite remote.

The very interactive processes arising will be individually unique in some ways, and individuals may be selective in their reading of a particular social suggestion or simply be unaware of it (Billett, 2006b). So central to issues of the interdependence between social and individual agency is the fact that it is rendered relational as individuals encounter social experiences projected in multitudinous and diverse forms and construct meaning through ontogenetically diverse bases.

This relational interdependence is continually being negotiated between both social and individual intentions, and their relations are transformed. Within these ongoing negotiations a key role is the agentic exercise of individuals' sense of self or identity. Rose's (1990) concept of the 'enterprising self' provides an instance of this kind of agency. Here, the focus and direction of the individual, as an entrepreneur, is towards self-regulation and individualisation aimed at securing the employer's economic goals and, therefore, securing their relations as an employee. Yet, an inherently individually constructed set of intentions may also be characterised by resistance to or the clever manipulation of the regulatory practices of the workplace (Grey, 1994), as much as either unquestioning compliance to them or their expedient reproduction in the self. That is, the exercise of agency may not always be directed towards securing further social subjugation or faithfully reproducing existing subjectivities. Instead, it may focus sharply on securing more personal goals.

7.1.5 Appraising the Individual within Interdependencies at Work

In emphasising the individual and granting their agency as being distinct from the social experience, the issue arises of on what bases individual agency should be evaluated. Through a privileging of individual agency and intentionality the risk of a different kind of relativism emerges, that of the 'anything goes' kind. Beyond acknowledging the descriptive and personal-dependent phenomenological construction of self, there is a need to identify bases from which to discuss and evaluate the role of individual agency and intentionality in and for work. Social forms advance an objective valuing of work, which while flawed, reflects particular views of privilege and elitism (Wright Mills, 1973), and provides a basis for critique and evaluation, which is less easy from within a highly individualistic or personal-dependent form. For instance, such an objective account of what constitutes worthwhile work might be premised on benefits to the individual in terms of pay or advancement to higher status and paid positions. Of course, it is possible to propose that whatever the self in work means to individuals should suffice. However, some commentators would be quick to suggest that individuals are being duped into false consciousness (Ratner, 2000) or an incomplete or unsatisfactory sense of self. O'Doherty and Willmott (2001) hold that individuals are entangled with the social world and that they are working to identify a 'sense of self' in their work. Given the negotiated relationships between individuals and workplaces, and the need for individuals to engage in practices constructed by others, they propose it is more useful to view personal agency in terms of individuals securing a 'sense of self' within contested and negotiated relations. Even when able to exercise high levels of freedom, this offers a device for individuals to secure a sense of well-being and satisfaction that is associated with the goals of the work, rather than the allegedly more problematic humanistic conception of individual agency of 'being themselves' (O'Doherty and Willmott, 2001, p. 117).

So, a starting point for an evaluation of individual agency might be the capacity of individuals to negotiate and construct a 'sense of self' from what is encountered, rather than 'being oneself', which is held to be unrealistic in such socially saturated times (Gergen, 2000). This does not imply some chaotic privileging of a highly individualised epistemology. Instead, it reflects a constantly shifting and uncertain foundation of what comprises the self, but implies being agentic in securing a sense of self. This suggests that interactions between the individual and the workplace are negotiated, contested and above all are highly relational. It follows that individuals may attempt to construct a sense of self within the socially-derived constraints of their work.

It follows that as work requirements and the means of participation in work are transformed, there are direct consequences for individuals' subjectivities and identities, and possible renegotiation of the self. Understanding these consequences may be enriched through a consideration of the enactment of individuals' agentic action. In this way, learning throughout working life can be viewed as a transformative journey as individuals selectively negotiate their engagement in work, and with changing work requirements, work practices and the shifting bases for participation in work. Throughout, individuals' identity, subjectivities and actions will likely be subjected to selective, yet contested, and interdependent engagement.

7.2   Part II: Relations Among Work, Identity and Learning—Five Narratives

7.2.1   Studying Self, Learning and Work

The investigation described and discussed here attempted to identify the bases by which five individuals engage in their working lives and what guides their practices and decision-making. The data gathering comprised a series of sequenced tape-recorded conversations with the participants during a series of semi-structured interviews. The initial interviews were used to identify what constituted the work of these five individuals, through an analysis of their work activities and interaction, and then their personal histories including their working lives. These initial interviews were followed by conversations occurring every two months over the next twelve months. They were used to elicit data about work, working life, life outside work and transitions in working life. The aim here was to map changes in working life, subjectivity and decision-making over the twelve-month period. Specific questions were used to elicit data and refine and extend it beyond the initial analyses. The analysis included identifying the trajectories of participants' working lives and life outside of work. To appraise, verify and validate initial analyses, the data from each interview and its initial analysis and deductions were discussed with participants in subsequent interviews. A key concern of the investigation was to continue the conversations through a process of refinement and extension of data over a yearlong period.

7.2.2   Five Workers

The selection of the five participants was premised by a concern to include individuals engaged in different kinds of work (e.g. technically mediated), modes of engagement with work, and with diverse work histories (e.g. migrant, part-time worker). There was, however, no attempt to select participants who were well positioned to exercise personal and autonomous agency. The participants were as follows. Carl arranges insurance quotes and sells insurance to customers working on a commission-only basis as a broker for a large national insurance brokerage company. He is essentially a sole operator business within a large enterprise. Ken is a manager of an information and communications technology unit within a corporatised state government department. His unit has particular responsibilities for electronic security across the department. Lev is an electronics engineer working in a large multinational corporation, which designs and manufactures rail transportation systems. Lyn works part-time in a wholesaling business in the metropolitan fruit and vegetable market, as a member of small team of workers. Commencing at 2:00 a.m., she works two or three days a week, continuing until the day's orders are complete and dispatched. Mike works as a supervisor and customer service coordinator in a large motor vehicle dealership, working with the workshop and sales departments and with customers. He is a car mechanic by training and extensive practice. Collectively, these five individuals engage in diverse forms of work embracing different kinds of performance requirements and means of engaging in work.

Diverse and circuitous routes are common to each of these five individuals' working lives. Carl, the insurance broker, was a professional sportsman before retiring and developing a career in insurance brokering. So there is significant discontinuity between his original and current career. Ken, the manager of an information technology unit, grew up in and remains part of a Christian community. His first work experiences were church-related activities. After this, he worked in a range of service-oriented occupations (e.g. retail, restaurant management, pest eradication) before developing expertise with electronic security systems. It was through this expertise that he eventually became the manager of an information technology unit within a recently corporatised government department. Lev, the electronic engineer, learnt his electronics skills through a structured program of study during service in the Russian military. Later, he was employed as an electronics engineer in the Russian railway system. However, upon migrating to Australia, because of low levels of English language proficiency, he had to find employment in work that he described as being menial and demeaning (e.g. hospital night time orderly). Only when his English language competence improved was he able to secure employment in electronics. Lyn, who works in the fruit and vegetable market, had worked in forms of employment that would be classified as being low-skill and low paid (e.g. retail work, detailing cars in sales yards and factory work) while continuing to be the sole parent and provider for her three children. Mike's move into a supervisory role is relatively recent in the dealership in which he works. He had worked as a motor mechanic, throughout his working life. However, he had spent much of that time as a road-side service mechanic assisting motorists whose vehicles had broken down, which is quite different work than being in an automotive workshop.

So, of the five participants, only Mike has had a continuous vocational focus as a car mechanic, although his interests in customer servicing saw him engage in roadside emergency assistance work. The others, by different degree, have experienced discontinuities or transformations in their working lives and occupational identities. For Lyn, who works part-time in the fruit market, unlike the others, that work identity still remains unclear, uncertain and immature. Yet, she is quite intentional in working to transform her identity from that of a caregiver to her children to that of a worker. These diverse and meandering working life trajectories suggest that lifelong learning and learning throughout working life are focused on more than the development of skills. These processes also included the making and remaking of occupational identities and subjectivities through uncertain pathways that comprise these individuals' work life histories. As will be elaborated below, each pathway is marked by evidence of intentions and the exercise of their agency in attempts to secure those goals. Noteworthy in these pathways is the contrast with the linear developmental journey that was advanced by Erikson (1968). Rather than negotiating psycho-social crises that were primarily sourced within individuals as they negotiate their sense of identity and worth at socially sanctioned life stages, these five workers' trajectories emphasise the need to secure their sense of identity or self through disruptive and uncertain working lives. To understand the context in which these negotiations occurred, it is helpful to elaborate the changes to work and work practices and their consequences for these individuals.

7.2.3   Changing Work

There was transformation and change in each individual's work and work requirements in recent times, including during the yearlong data gathering period. Yet, instead of being disruptive and disarming or marginalising, as some accounts predict (e.g. Bauman, 1998; Beck, 1992; Rifkin, 1995), these five individuals largely adapted well to the transformation in their working life. Further, rather than being an impediment, in some instances, these changes were quite instrumental in bolstering their career progression and sense of self in their work.

The work of insurance brokers, such as Carl, had experienced considerable change because the Australian government had recently introduced regulations and legislation that demand greater evidence and transparency when advising clients about insurance quotes. Each quote now requires to be documented more fully and meticulously and, therefore, takes far longer. Consequently, small insurance quotes and policies have become less attractive to Carl because of the additional work and relatively minimal return. These small quotes are now passed on to the company's clerical employees. Carl's preference is to work on high value insurance policies and provide services to large policyholders by nurturing interactions and relations with these clients, and subsequently he has directed more attention to these kinds of projects. He reports being successful in this venture. This kind of work suits well his work preferences and it is profitable. The legislated changes also directly supported him in the second half of the year in a quite different and unanticipated way. He became involved in a lawsuit in which a potential client claimed malpractice and a failure to insure a property that was subsequently destroyed by fire. However, the more meticulous record keeping required under the new legislation provided clear documentation that no agreement had been concluded. So, these changes have ultimately served Carl's interests well in terms of his preferred business focus and the capacity to add greater probity to his practice.

Recently heightened global concerns about security have done much to enhance the standing and permanency of Ken's work in the information technology unit. This work comprises establishing and maintaining informational technology-based security systems within and outside the government department for whom he works. In particular, because of his rather itinerant early working life, now his primary work goal is to secure employment that will take him through to retirement. Consequently, changes that have brought about the requirement for heightened levels of security in his department and elsewhere are assisting him achieve this goal. A significant change in the global environment and sentiments of workplaces has served to bolster and make secure his work, and indeed elevated his work.

In recent years, the Russian electronics engineer Lev held a technical position in a large Australian enterprise that, upon being taken over by a multinational company, had centralised its maintenance work elsewhere, thereby rendering him redundant. However, this redundancy saw him move to a more prestigious and well-paid job in a multinational transportation corporation. The downturn and crisis in the global aviation sector following the 2001 attacks on New York and Washington deleteriously affected this corporation. However, because he works in the division associated with rail transport Lev has been spared redundancy again, unlike some clerical workers whose contracts were not renewed. Moreover, the corporation shifted its focus away from aviation, and the rail transport division was given primacy, thereby securing his employment.

Lyn is a relatively new employee at the fruit and vegetable market, and is aiming to secure and develop a niche role for herself. Yet her workplace, like the other wholesale businesses in the fruit and vegetable market, tends to have high employee turnover. Changes in this workplace include staff leaving or going on holidays and a new task of exporting fruit and vegetables by airfreight to retailers in Papua New Guinea. Lyn's employment seems buoyed by her interest in, and the capacity to undertake, new tasks and those conducted by others during their periods of leave. This has been exercised through her interest in managing the export orders, which includes her becoming solely proficient in customs processes. As Lyn is in the process of seeking and forming an occupational identity based upon her work in the fruit and vegetable wholesaler, opportunities afforded by new requirements in the workplace (i.e. export orders) to bolster her place in the work team and make more secure her position are greatly welcomed.

Mike works as a supervisor in a large vehicle dealership, coordinating relations between clients and the workshops. This position exists in large part as a response to the extended warranty periods offered by automotive manufacturers to customers purchasing new vehicles. These warranties tend to wed customers to the dealership. The purchase of a new vehicle is now the beginning, not the end, of the relationship between the customer and the dealership. Nevertheless, this change has particular consequences for workshop staff. Interacting with and maintaining clients have become a key focus for dealerships, because clients might purchase another new vehicle at the end of the warranty period. Mike, it seems, possesses the combination of automotive and interpersonal skills and values required to address customers' needs and coordinate work activities to support the continuity of positive relationships between the dealership and its customers. Moreover, he enjoys this kind of work as it brings together a range of professional interests associated with automotive engineering, customer service and some personal preferences about dealing with people and precision in one's work. So these changes to his work have directly served to meet his needs.

Although changes to work bring about challenges for those seeking to meet these requirements, in the case of these five workers it has also supported the continuity and development of their work-related goals. Only one participant experienced major disappointment over the twelve-month period of the study. This arose when Lev, the electrical engineer, on returning from a training course, became highly proactive and corresponded with each of three departmental heads about how his newly developed skills could transform the profitability of their departments. His invitations were treated with silent dismissal, not even acknowledgement. This suggests his agency had brushed up against and possibly contravened the workplace's regulatory practices and set himself outside of these practices. He also recounted angrily how the national human resources manager had failed to acknowledge his existence on a visit to the office where Lev worked. These incidents threatened his sense of self, and he responded accordingly. He resented the status afforded to others, such as his manager, while his own contributions went unrecognised. This may well have been the motivation for his pro-activity in promoting his services to senior management. Yet, his exuberant agency led not to his desired promotion, but to him being reassigned to other work duties.

In sum, against the researchers' expectations and predictions in the literature, the churning and transformations that have impacted these five individuals' work have broadly served to buttress their employment and standing. That is, changes in work assisted rather than inhibited these individuals' work goals. In at least three instances, there is a clear coincidence between their work goals and the changing requirements of their workplaces. Moreover, as discussed below, these changes permit the projection of their personal values into their work. Certainly, elsewhere in the transport corporation, for whom Lev the electronics engineer works, there have been significant job losses, career truncation and dislocations. Still, the experience of these five randomly selected participants suggests that generalised claims about changes in work leading to disempowerment, marginalisation and the generation of anxiety are not supported. Instead, a more nuanced and less prescriptive account of the relationships between changes in work and individuals' continuity and identity may be required. This account should comprise an engagement between both individual and social agency in the conduct of their work. To consider this relationship in more detail it is useful to identify the role that these individuals' identity, motivation and goals played in how they engage with changing workplaces, and how that affected their sense of selves.

7.2.4 Identity, Motivation and Goals

Interests outside their working lives were proposed by each participant to be of greater importance than their work and working lives. The insurance broker Carl emphasised the importance of his family life, his good relationship with his wife and his interest in his children and their development, and involvement in coaching junior sports teams. He noted the need for a balance between work and family life. Carl referred to some colleagues' divorces that were a product of focusing too much time and energy upon their work and neglecting their home life. Ken, the manager of the information technology unit, was quite insistent that his family and church represented the key goals towards which his work efforts were directed. This commitment was evident in the weekly tithe he pays to his church and the senior role he plays in its governance. He stated that upon retirement he would never think about his paid work. For Lev, family life, aesthetic pursuits and a small business installing security equipment were claimed as important goals beyond the corporate transport workplace in which he worked as an engineer. He directed efforts into his small business, and looked to this and his salary to generate the income he required to maintain his lifestyle and to educate his son. He stated that he would readily change jobs if it could secure him greater financial benefit. As a single parent, Lyn's goal for her work in the produce market was to provide more for her family through work. Her existing rental home was too noisy and she needed to move somewhere far quieter for the sake of herself and her children. She was also hoping to secure enough money to take her children on a holiday to the beach. Rather than working in the automotive dealership, Mike stated that he would much prefer to spend his time messing around with computers. His home life was claimed, in part, with working on computers and he referred to purchasing two exotic spiders, for which he cared and had established video technology links to monitor and record their lives. His home life was used to exercise other vocations. These activities were taken seriously. These, and his family, were the ends to which his work efforts were directed.

In this way, all five participants stated that life outside work was the major focus point of their lives. That is, work was not the only source of securing individuals' sense of identity and self. The participants referred to specific cultural activities, interests and communities that played a significant role in who they are, in how they see themselves, and provided evidence of the exercise of agentic action in their lives outside work. This is akin to them wanting to 'be themselves'. Dewey (1916) held that vocations are individuals' directions in life and not constrained to paid employment, however high or low in societal standing. The opposite of vocations, from the Deweyian perspective, is not leisure, but activity that is aimless, capricious and involves dependence upon others (Quickie, 1999). In their lives outside work, the participants demonstrated the exercise of their vocation as parents, local sport coach, church leader, technology enthusiast, entrepreneur, etc. However, Dewey (1916) argued that each of us is not restricted to just one vocation. This seemed to be the case here. Their engagement with work was premised on different goals and as such was relational.

Yet, while emphasising their life outside of work, each participant also acknowledged the significance of their working lives to their identity and sense of fulfilment: their sense of self. Commonly, each referred to being required to be competent at their work, in order to secure their employment. Each also referred to the importance of being respected as being effective and valued by their peers and other workers, and being identified as a person from whom others would seek advice and be valued for their counsel. Underlining this concern about respect were issues associated with identity and sense of self. There was also a rich intertwining between individuals' sense of self in the workplace and outside of it and that elaborated the significance of its exercise. Their work roles provided quite diverse bases for the exercise of their sense of self.

After a successful career as a professional sportsman, Carl now views himself as a successful insurance broker. He enjoys the interactions with people his work brings, the freedom to develop his clientele and contacts, to manage his own time and capacity to watch his business grow. So, aspects of his working life were claimed to be highly consistent with his sense of self and through his interactions with clients he is often able to get close to 'being himself'. Given the freedom he enjoys in his job and his indebtedness to the brokerage company in making this opportunity possible, Carl is in no hurry to achieve his ultimate goal of owning his own brokerage. Ken finds his work in the information technology unit rewarding, because it is an area of growth and employment security and stability, elements that did form part of his earlier working life. His current employment stands to provide him with engaging and well-paid work until retirement. He claims that any stable, well-paid work will suit his needs, because he does not associate his identity with work. Nevertheless, he takes pride in his efficient management of a unit within a government department, which reinforces his sense of self. So his work identity is shaped by a more general employment goal of security of employment, not the particular kind of work. His working life in the public sector is positioning him to support and direct his energies towards his church community and family. Yet, he works hard to secure this goal.

Quite openly, Lev referred to his electronic engineering work as providing him with respectable middle class status as well as the financial freedom that a good salary provided for him and his family. That is, the professional standing of his work afforded him a particular level of status in the community that is regulated by his occupational identity. Since arriving in Australia, Lev has worked agentically and intentionally to become proficient in English and realise fully the application of his electronics knowledge in well-paid, high status and productive employment. However, this came only after a period of engaging in menial work roles, constrained by his poor English language. His current job provides a sense of self that is more closely aligned to 'being himself' insofar as it represents a step towards the ideal he is trying to achieve: that is, higher levels of remuneration, autonomy and discretion at work. Nevertheless, he remains frustrated at not being able 'to be himself' in his approach to work and his conduct in the workplace, his dress and work habits have been questioned. He also feels under-utilised in his current position and believes he has the capacity to contribute more and is deserving of much higher remuneration and better conditions. Also, he regrets his work has not provided close friendships with his colleagues. For Lev, positive relationships with others are an important part of his identity and sense of being. Elsewhere, he realises these through socialising in the local Russian émigré community. This suggests a sense of work identity and agency that is strong, yet frustrated by a lack of potential fulfilment, acknowledgement and respect. Through not being allowed to 'be himself', Lev feels his 'sense of sense' is threatened.

For Lyn, work in the fruit market provides an opportunity to demonstrate a capacity to perform roles, other than being the caregiver to her children, outside of the home. She consistently reported having a strong sense of industry and organisation, and a desire to build a further financial foundation for herself and her children. These intentions were the basis of her being energetic and proactive in her work, 'being herself'. Becoming a paid worker and having sole responsibility for an area of work seems to fulfil an urgent need to re-affirm her identity outside the home. Her intentionality and agency here was evident throughout the yearlong period of the interviews. In the first interview, she expressed an interest in becoming proficient in the purchasing and transportation of fresh herbs. This arose from an opportunity in previous employment. By the second interview, her intentions and agency were being directed to another opportunity, being responsible for export orders. This requires understanding and responding to quarantine and custom requirements in which she alone was knowledgeable. As the year progressed she reported and was observed as having established herself well within the workplace, not only in a further specialist role, but also as a keen, proactive and reliable worker. Her intention was to become indispensable in the workplace and she pursued this agentically and with some success. She was buoyed by the owners' positive comments and gestures towards her and offers of additional work. Towards the end of the interviews, she had been offered a job to manage a plant nursery in an attractive coastal city about 100 kilometres north of where she lived and worked. Surprisingly, given her stated goals, she refused this offer. It also offered a living environment quite different from the one in which she had expressed constant dissatisfaction. However, the intertwining between her work and home lives may have influenced this decision. Such a move would disrupt her children's lives, she claimed. Also, she had met a man who operated a forklift at the fruit market, and they became engaged. So while exercising her agency in establishing herself within the workplace, there is also an intertwining between the workplace and her life outside of work, which in this case sought to reject a job offer that seemed to meet other of her stated intentions.

At the commencement of the interviews, Mike was experiencing difficulties with another supervisor in the automotive dealership over who had line authority within the workshops. This conflict threatened his commitment to the workplace. Subsequently, it was reported that this matter had been resolved in his favour. Then, despite claiming his home interests were the primary ones, he began to spend more and more time at his workplace. He went in early and came home late, sometimes driving to and from work in a car that had a persistent or difficult fault to diagnose. In earlier interviews, he claimed to have no career ambitions beyond his current supervisory position. There were more important things to do with his time. However, by the later interviews he had changed his mind. He noted his intention to apply for a more senior position in the future. A key purpose for Mike's practice in the dealership is to provide service to others, in which he found satisfaction and personal fulfilment. He referred back to his earlier career as a mobile service operator assisting stranded motorists, often holidaymakers, whose vehicles had broken down. He reported satisfaction in being able to assist these individuals and minimise disruption to their holidays. In this way, his new role in providing a high level of service is consistent with key personal intentions and subjectivities; of 'being himself'.

In these ways, the process of self-construction for each of these workers relates to and represents an entwining or interweaving of both working life and that outside of it; this is reflected in seeking to secure the self, and possibly 'be themselves'. The degree of relative or particular importance of 'being themselves' differs across these individuals and possibly fluctuates over time as particular events or priorities arise in their lives. For instance, Ken is not interested in securing his self through work in the public sector information technology role, although he wants to exercise a 'sense of self'. Yet, he is not alone. Common to all participants was a strong desire to exercise their sense of self in the workplace; and where possible for these individuals to 'be themselves', which encompassed both life inside and outside work, which is edging closer to the humanistic conception that O'Doherty and Willmott (2001) so strongly deny. There were differences between the role work plays for male and female participants.

However, for each of the five individuals work relates to their identity: they are identified as an engineer, supervising mechanic, effective worker, diligent and trusted insurance broker and manager. Moreover, all five participants were able to exercise in part personal agency. If the exercise of individual agency through personally fulfilling activities is a measure of the link between individuals' identity and their work, it might be concluded that all five individuals were exercising their 'sense of self' and engaged willingly and interdependently in their work. That is, part of their identity and construction of self and the exercise of agentic action is being directed and remade through interdependence with their work. This sentiment reflects what Pusey (2003) concludes is the role of work for middle Australia: 'For nearly everyone work is a social protein, a buttress for identity and not a tradable commodity' (p. 2). Each participant referred to the importance of being able to exercise their agency in their work activities. Perhaps Lev over exercised his. Whether it was the ownership of the work undertaken, the possibilities of trying to do new things, being able to manage oneself, being able to exercise standards of work and discretion that reflect individual goals, or the exercise of personal licence, the significance of the exercise of agency was amplified by each informant. So while they claimed work not to be as important as their life outside work, the evidence holds that these five workers' sense of self is negotiated, shaped and sustained in the workplace.

All this suggests the significance of agentic action in assisting and directing individuals to exercise their 'sense of self' through their work, with a goal beyond that of being able to 'be oneself', albeit through work or life outside work. Moreover, that sense of self changes over time and through negotiation with work. Somerville notes how aged care workers often engage in aged care work through convenience, rather than particular interest (Billett and Somerville, 2004). However, once engaged in this work they form identities as aged care workers and even carry emblematic back injuries of aged care workers with pride (Somerville and Bernoth, 2001). In this way, the transformation of self arises through engagement and negotiation with their work, as was the case with Lyn.

7.2.5   Self, Agency and Learning at Work

In conclusion, through the intertwining of work and life outside of work, these individuals are held to exercise a sense of self in efforts to 'be themselves' and, therefore, in how they engage in and what they learn through work and throughout working life. For some of the participants this was more readily achievable than for others. For Ken, his family and church community and relative lack of interest in the specific focus of his work meant that workplace conflicts were less significant to him than for Lev, for instance. So although both these individuals worked in large organisations that exercised regulatory practices (Bernstein, 1996) they were relational, seemingly having less impact upon Ken, the public servant, than upon Lev, the disgruntled electronics engineer. Ken was able to work around a new boss' agenda, for instance. Lev's sense of self seemed more violated by having his suggestions and existence being summarily dismissed. In these two cases, employees in large organisations prescribe a set of rules that regulate employees' behaviour and relationship towards others, their regulatory practices. True, the practices were not as prescribed as others have recorded (e.g. Grey, 1994). However, what is amplified in this study is how these individuals' sense of selves influences how, and for what purposes, they engage with work, and how they negotiate their sense of self accordingly, as exemplified by Lev and Ken's distinct responses.

Against some predictions and expectations about changes adversely affecting workers, it was found that change for these five workers had either buttressed or facilitated their standing in the workplace and their vocational goals. While all five participants claimed that their working life was merely a means to an end, the evidence suggests their identities, agentic actions and subjectivities were exercised in their work in consideration of securing their 'sense of selves'. By different degree, there was evidence of interdependence and intertwining between their work and life outside work. In particular, it seemed that these individuals' capacity to exercise their agency at work was strongly associated with how they valued that work and identified with it as permitting them to exercise a 'sense of self'. It reflected how they might exercise their efforts in participating in and learning through their working life.

This suggests that for lifelong learning to be successfully enacted consonance between the qualities of work and individuals' identity and interests may be required. Otherwise, there would be a contested ongoing negotiation between individuals' sense of self and the goals of the work practice. What the evidence suggests here is that because of these negotiations, the humanistic and perhaps unlikely goal of 'being themselves' may not always be possible to drive individuals' intentions and agentic action at work. However, for individuals to exercise a 'sense of self' in their work, they need to go on engaging in ways that sees the attainment of their interests and intentions. The consonance between individual and workplace goals that are identified in the study may well lead to unreflective, uncritical and limited learning outcomes. The sense is that, in some ways, Lev has had the richest of learning experiences. While not fully accounted for in Wertsch's (1998) account of appropriation and mastery, Lev's contestation with the corporate workplace had likely generated rich learning for him, albeit not the kind of learning he intended. At the commencement of the interviews he celebrated living and working in Australia, because he could exercise his agency and intents to their full in ways not possible in Russia. By the final interview, his sense of self and, perhaps overly idealistic, views about his adopted country were being tested. This suggests that learning throughout working life arises as much from dissonance, as cognitivists have long claimed, than through appropriation where shared values exist between the learner and the social practice.

It seems that from this small study that there is a need to consider lifelong learning in terms of individuals' drive towards securing a 'sense of self' and 'being themselves', both in their work and lives outside of work. Therefore, the quest of achieving the ambitious government, industry and enterprise goals of lifelong learning should be directed as much by individuals and thier identities and goals, as by government and employers. The mobilisation of the self will be likely realised in ways that are commensurate with the self, and directed towards individuals 'being themselves'.

Acknowledgements

The author acknowledges the research assistance provided by Ray, Dimitri and Margarita in the original study. Also, the contributions of

Alan Brown and Simone Kirpal assisted the revision of the chapter. This research was funded through the small grants scheme of the Australian Research Council.

References

Archer, M.S. (2000). *Being human: The problem of agency*. Cambridge: Cambridge University Press.

Baldwin, J.M. (1894). Personality-suggestion. *Psychological Review*, 1, 274–279.

Bauer, J., D. Festner, H. Gruber, C. Harteis and H. Heid (2004). The effects of epistemological beliefs on workplace learning. *Journal of Workplace Learning*, 16(5), 284–292.

Bauman, Z. (1998). *Work, consumerism and the new poor*. Buckingham: Open University Press.

Beck, U. (1992). *Risk society: Towards a new modernity* (M. Ritter, Trans.). London: Sage.

Berger, P.L. and T. Luckman (1967). *The social construction of reality*. Harmondsworth, Middlesex: Penguin Books.

Bernstein, B. (1996). *Pedagogy, symbolic control and identity: Research critique*. London: Taylor & Francis.

Billett, S. (2000). Defining the demand side of VET: Industry, enterprises, individuals and regions. *Journal of Vocational Education and Training*, 50(1), 5–30.

Billett, S. (2001). *Learning in the workplace: Strategies for effective practice*. Sydney: Allen and Unwin.

Billett, S. (2003a, 1–3 December 2003). Individualising the social—socialising the individual: Interdependence between social and individual agency in vocational learning. Paper presented at the 11th Annual International conference on post-compulsory education and training: Enriching learning cultures, Gold Coast, Queensland.

Billett, S. (2003b). Sociogeneses, Activity and Ontogeny. *Culture and Psychology*, 9(2), 133–169.

Billett, S. (2006a). Constituting the workplace curriculum. *Journal of Curriculum Studies*, 37(1), 31–48.

Billett, S. (2006b). Relational interdependence between social and individual agency in work and working life. *Mind, Culture and Activity*, 13(1), 53–69.

Billett, S. and M. Pavolva (2005). Learning through working life: Self and individuals' agentic action. *International Journal of Lifelong Education*, 24(3), 195–211.

Billett, S. and M. Somerville (2004). Transformations at work: Identity and learning. *Studies in Continuing Education*, 26(2), 309–326.

Billett, S., M. Barker and B. Hernon-Tinning (2004). Participatory practices at work. *Pedagogy, Culture and Society*, 12(2), 233–257.

Billett, S., R. Smith and M. Barker (2005). Understanding work, learning and the remaking of cultural practices. *Studies in Continuing Education*, 27(3), 219–237.

Brunello, G. and A. Medio (2001). An explanation of international differences in education and workplace training. *European Economic Review*, 45(2), 307–322.

Dewey, J. (1916). *Democracy and education*. New York: The Free Press.

Edwards, R. and N. Boreham (2003). 'The centre cannot hold': Complexity and difference in European Union policy towards a learning society. *Journal of Educational Policy*, 18(4), 407–421.

Erikson, E.H. (1968). *Identity, youth and crisis*. New York: Norton.

Field, J. (2000). Governing the ungovernable: Why lifelong learning promises so much yet delivers so little. *Educational Management and Administration*, 28(3), 249–261.

Gergen, K.J. (2000). *The saturated self: Dilemmas of identity in contemporary life*. New York: Basic Books.

Green, F. (2001). Its been a hard day's night: The concentration and intensification of work in the late Twentieth Century Britain. *British Journal of Industrial Relations*, 39(1), 53–80.

Grey, C. (1994). Career as a project of the self and labour process discipline. *Sociology*, 28(2), 479–497.

Hodkinson, P. and H. Hodkinson (2003). Individuals, communities of practice and the policy context. *Studies in Continuing Education*, 25(1), 3–21.

Malle, B.F., L.J. Moses and D.A. Baldwin (2001). Introduction: The significance of intentionality. In B.F. Malle, L.J. Moses and D.A. Baldwin (Eds.), *Intentions and intentionality: Foundations of social cognition* (pp. 1–26). Cambridge, MA: The MIT Press.

Newman, D., P. Griffin and M. Cole (1989). *The construction zone: Working for cognitive change in schools*. Cambridge: Cambridge University Press.

Noon, M. and P. Blyton (1997). *The realities of work*. Basingstoke, Hants: Macmillan.

O'Doherty, D. and H. Willmot (2001). The question of subjectivity and the labor process. *International Studies of Management and Organisation*, 30(4), 112–133.

Piaget, J. (1968). *Structuralism* (C. Maschler, trans. and ed.). London: Routledge and Kegan Paul.

Pusey, M. (2003). *The experience of middle Australia*. Cambridge, UK: Cambridge University Press.

Quickie, J. (1999). *A curriculum for life: Schools for a democratic learning society*. Buckingham: Open University Press.

Ratner, C. (2000). Agency and culture. *Journal for the Theory of Social Behaviour*, 30, 413–434.

Rifkin, J. (1995). *The end of work: The decline of the global labor force and the dawn of the post-market era*. New York, NY: Ajeremy P. Tarcher/Putnam Book, G.P. Putnam's Sons.

Rogoff, B. (1990). Apprenticeship in thinking—cognitive development in social context. New York: Oxford University Press.

Rose, N. (1990). *Governing the soul: The shaping of the private self*. London: Routledge.

Scribner, S. (1985). Vygotsky's use of history. In J.V. Wertsch (Ed.), *Culture, communication and cognition: Vygotskian perspectives* (pp. 119–145). Cambridge, UK: Cambridge University Press.

Smith, R.J. (2004). *Necessity in action: The epistemological agency of the new employee*. Unpublished Master of Education, Griffith University, Brisbane.

Somerville, M. (2002). *Changing masculine work cultures*. Paper presented at the Conference on Envisioning practice—Implementing change, Gold Coast, Queensland.

Somerville, M. and M. Bernoth (2001). *Safe bodies: Solving a dilemma in workplace*. Paper presented at the Knowledge Demands for the New Economy. 9th Annual

International Conference on Post-compulsory Education and Training, Gold Coast, Queensland.

Valsiner, J. (1998). *The guided mind: A sociogenetic approach to personality.* Cambridge, MA: Harvard University Press.

Valsiner, J. and R. van der Veer (2000). *The social mind: The construction of an idea.* Cambridge, UK: Cambridge University Press.

von Glasersfeld, E. (1987). Learning as a constructive activity. In C. Janvier (Ed.), *Problems of representation in the teaching and learning of mathematics* (pp. 3–17). Hillsdale, NJ: Lawrence Erlbaum.

Wertsch, J.V. (1998). *Mind as action.* New York: Oxford University Press.

Wright Mills, C. (1973). The meaning of work throughout history. In F. Best (Ed.), *The future of work* (pp. 6–13). Englewood Cliffs, NJ: Prentice Hall.

8

The Much Vaunted 'Flexible Employee'—What Does it Take?

Simone Kirpal* and Alan Brown[†]
*University of Bremen, Germany;
[†]University of Warwick, UK

8.1   Introduction

Work identities vary in the intensity with which they are held and in the significance individuals ascribe to them. They may have more or less significance for an individual at different times depending upon other interests as identities change in their meaning for the individual over the life course and depending upon the personal occupational trajectory (Heinz, 2003). This perspective, on the one hand, underlines that work identities are highly dynamic (Brown, 1997) and dependent upon a variety of factors and conditions. On the other hand, as work identities closely interlink with aspects and elements of work with which individuals identify (Kirpal, 2004b) we can assume that some level of identification with work is inherent to any kind of successful job performance. As research has shown, even under the most severe and restrictive working conditions a certain level of identification with work is still recognisable despite the ambiguity the experience might entail (Hoff et al., 1985). It is primarily identification with the work environment, the company, the company's objectives or the work-based tasks which individuals perform that make individual and collective productivity possible and functional, not only for the company, but also for the individual. These forms of identification with work typically generate some kind of work-related identity.

In countries with occupational labour markets such as Germany, occupational socialisation through apprenticeship training typically used to attach employees to specific occupational specialisations and largely

211

A. Brown, S. Kirpal and F. Rauner (eds.), Identities at Work, 211–238.

determined future skills development, career progression and company attachment over long periods of time, if not a lifetime (Greinert, 1997). Although the defining image of the Dual System as guaranteeing permanent skilled employment and carrying the possibility of further firm-based career progression is increasingly difficult to sustain (Kutscha, 2002), the concept of 'Beruf' persists as the dominant organising principle for the German vocational education and training system and national labour market (Reuling, 1996). In those systems that closely link skills acquisition with institutionalised training structures and labour markets, the formalised vocational training and the socialisation into acquiring an occupational specialisation form essential elements of developing an occupational identity (Heinz, 1995). Complemented and further supported by company-based socialisation, both elements are directly linked to belonging to particular work-based communities through occupationally defined categories with which individuals identify.

Modern work arrangements and flexible employment patterns increasingly mean that such classical forms of work-related identity formation are often undergoing significant change (Brown, 2004; Dif, 2004; Kirpal, 2004a). Classical occupational socialisation in some contexts is losing significance and organisational commitment is taking new forms as some of the earlier commitment and identification patterns are being questioned (Baruch, 1998). What this implies for the individual employee in terms of work orientation and commitment is still an open question. Some authors postulate that the 'entrepreneurial' employee will become the new prototype, gradually substituting for the Fordist worker, who used to rely on a standard set of occupational, predominantly technical skills and stability of work settings (Voß and Pongratz, 1998; Pongratz and Voß, 2003). This new 'entrepreneurial' type of worker is characterised by individualised sets of skills, internalised control mechanisms and the prioritisation of generic over technical skills while emphasis is given to the individual's responsibility to produce and market those competences in order to increase his/her own employability when changing employers.

The studies in this volume draw attention to how aspects of the model of the 'entrepreneurial' employee is no longer restricted to highly qualified professionals or employees working in certain sectors (such as ICT or multi-media). Indeed, where modern working practices have been introduced this increasingly puts pressure on the 'ordinary' skilled worker to adapt to new 'norms' in both manufacturing and service sectors (Holman et al., 2005). Of particular relevance to this trend is the finding that human resources (HR) development specialists and managers increasingly favour this entrepreneurial type of employee as the 'ideal model' against which they wish to recruit (FAME Consortium, 2003). Although studies of management and behavioural sciences confirm the interdependence between employees' identification with work and their work commitment (Steers, 1977; Cohen 1993; Whetten and Godfrey, 1998), strong work identities may, on the other hand, be perceived as a barrier to enhancing the flexibility of economic processes as companies are under pressure to respond to increased international competition and flexible labour markets with complex organisational restructuring (Herrigel and Sabel 1999; Finegold and Wagner, 1999). These developments mean that many employers in aggregate require a mobile, adaptable and flexible workforce making the 'flexible employee' highly desirable for an increasing number of employers.

In what way high levels of mobility and flexibility may conflict with or support the development of strong work identities shall be further explored in this chapter. Sennett (1998) postulates that the increasing flexibility of skills, work and employment negatively affects the development of forms of identification with work and, ultimately, has disruptive affects on an individual's overall personality. Employees, however, pursue different strategies as they try to make sense of their constantly changing work agenda and to integrate their diverse work experiences into a coherent self-image. Although the number of employees who are not adequately prepared and supported to respond to the new challenges may be potentially high, for some individuals mobility and flexibility can become important tools for pursuing their broader vocational goals. This chapter concentrates on looking at individuals who regard themselves as actors who actively try to shape their own work identities by using flexibility and mobility as instruments to foster their vocational development and broader career prospects. It is seeking to illuminate some basic features of the work attitude of the much vaunted 'flexible employee'.

8.2   Images of Identity in a Time of Change

The ideas presented in this article build on experiences and findings from the EU 5th Framework project 'Vocational Identity, Flexibility and Mobility in the European Labour Market'. The issue of flexibility presents a pressing topic to employees, because it can be expected that future economic and technological developments will influence the restructuring of labour markets and employment patterns in many sectors and work settings all over Europe. In some countries there has been a shift towards more flexible, temporary and short-term employment contracts and new emerging forms of self-employment in some contexts (Gottlieb et al., 1998). This shift is most marked in the transition economies (Loogma, 2003), but is also in evidence in particular contexts in Germany (Heinz, 2002a; Pongratz and Voß, 2003), Italy (Tomassini and Brown, 2005) and Spain (Marhuenda et al., 2004). Interestingly, however, in the UK where labour markets are less regulated permanent employment is still very much the norm (Moynagh and Worsley, 2005). Whether there has been a significant shift towards greater flexibility is an empirical question and needs to be raised in relation to particular contexts rather than being reified into a universal trend beyond the scope of organisational choice and human agency. The project tried to gain insight into how these developments affected employees' work attitudes, work identities and career orientations in particular sectors in seven countries. If the hypothesis is that greater flexibility and mobility result in looser employee commitment towards the workplace, the occupation, the company or the community of practice, it is of topical interest to identify what individuals perceive as essential factors of the work context they relate to and that potentially can generate motivation and effective work performance.

The restructuring of work and uncertainties over prospects of obtaining work in the field for which individuals have trained have increased the importance of transitions discontinuities and shifting contexts of career development in those countries such as Germany (Heinz, 2002b) that had clearly demarcated well travelled pathways into the labour market via a training system based upon clearly defined occupations (Reuling, 1996) and those transition economies that were previously centrally planned. In economies such as Greece, Spain and the UK, for a variety of reasons associated with labour market functioning, there were already uncertainties over prospects of obtaining work in the field for which individuals had been trained in a number of sectors. While Heinz (2002b) looks at how the processes of increased transitions discontinuities and shifting career development contexts affect the biographical shaping of early work careers, our study examined the effects on experienced workers, who would be expected to have more established work identities. The investigation of work identities extended beyond company attachment to include other sources of identification with work. These could vary and include not just the organisation or occupational specialisation, but could relate to a specific work group (Baruch and Winkelmann-Gleed, 2002), a particular work environment, a set of work activities, interaction with colleagues or clients and so on, all of which may change over time, as may the significance individuals ascribe to them (Brown, 1997; Ibarra, 2003).

Connecting to Giddens' (1984) structuration theory, the project emphasised the reciprocal relationship between social structure and individual agency in particular work settings. The project partners anticipated that, at the individual level, emerging new demands, with their implications for shifting skill needs, generate a potential for conflict with traditional work orientations and associated values, norms, work ethics and work identity patterns of employees. One focus of the analysis was therefore placed on identifying individuals' strategies for dealing with such conflicts. In those contexts where work-related identities are becoming increasingly unstable and disrupted (Carruthers and Uzzi, 2000), what kind of mechanisms and strategies do individuals develop in order to compensate for instabilities, fragmentation and uncertainties of work and employment structures? In which way do structural changes and individual strategies interact in the work context and what role does this interaction play in occupational identity formation processes? Are some individuals better equipped than others to handle instabilities and uncertain working conditions?

In line with theories of socialisation and identity formation (see Heinz, 1988; Wahler and Witzel, 1985; Heinz and Witzel, 1995; Heinz, 2002a), the process of developing forms of work-related identities was regarded as dynamic, influenced by structural conditions on the one hand, and individual orientations and resources on the other hand. This means that work identities develop in the course of complex negotiation processes at the interface between personal resources, attitudes and values and structural variables of the work setting. As they manifest themselves in the interplay between individual dispositions and structural conditions of the work context, they influence an individual's concept of work and relationship to, for example, his or her job, the work environment and the employing organization. If we look at the individual variables, these encompass ascribed attributes such as socio-economic background, gender and age, but also achievements like qualifications, skills and the capacity to learn and to cope with changing work requirements. The individual employment trajectories, part of the individual's 'strategic biography' (Brown, 2004), integrate and structure these variables in very specific ways by further incorporating personal interests, commitments and career plans. Taking into account individuals' responses and adaptations to, and interpretations of, work situations one major objective of the research project was to identify individuals' strategies for coping with changes and new demands at work and how these affect their work identities.

This shift in focus towards negotiation processes, thus underlining an interactive perspective, also acknowledges scope for individual agency. As individuals become more independent from socially defined stratifications such as social classes, they also become more dependent upon institutions such as education and training systems, employment structures or social welfare institutions. At least, this is what Beck's individualisation hypothesis (Beck, 1986) postulates. Through this process, individuals take on new roles as coordinators of their own personal work biographies: they become actors who actively shape their individualised work values, commitment patterns and career orientations, which a few decades ago used to be shaped much more on a collective basis (see also Carruthers and Uzzi, 2000). At the same time individuals are constrained by the institutional embedding of their actions and also higher-level structures as institutions interlink with the broader socio-economic and political systems to which they refer. Work identities and career orientations also need to be interpreted in this way.

Ultimately, any identity formation process is an achievement of the individual. The process of acquiring an occupational identity takes place within particular communities of practice where socialisation, interaction and learning are key elements. In these processes, however, modern socialisation theory regards the individual as an 'actor' or 'agent'. Individuals are agents of society who actively reflect upon external conditions (Giddens, 1991). This means that work shapes the individual, but at the same time the individual shapes work processes and structures. When it comes to the formation of work identities, it is not simply a matter of taking on identities and occupational roles, which are pre-existent and pre-structured. Nor do individuals just attach themselves to particular professional communities. Rather they may also take a pro-active role in becoming a participant or even a change agent, actively reshaping the community of practice (Brown, 1997). Hence there is scope for individual agency to act upon the structures and processes. As in some settings work structures that formerly provided continuity and pre-defined elements with which individuals could identify decompose and become fragmented, this active role is reinforced (Sennett, 1998; Beck, 1994; Beck and Felixberger, 1999). Workers are increasingly required to seek actively and select from models of skill development, professional conduct and practices that have multiplied and become more available and accessible. These demands can be quite stressful though in view of labour market volatility.

As people have and make choices work identities need to be understood in a dynamic way. They are not constant over time, but they may vary in the significance individuals ascribe to them and this significance is most likely to change over an individual's life course. The formation, maintenance and change of an occupational identity are always influenced by the nature of the relationships around which they are constructed. Over time these interactions may lead to modifications and reshaping of these same structures, the communities of practice and the individual's work identity. There is always a fundamental tension between the elements of continuity and change over time in the processes whereby occupational identities are formed. In addition, work identities have multiple levels and their meaning for individuals varies, so, for example, a young person may attach far greater importance to developing an identity in the broader sense than to developing a particular occupational or organisational commitment. The distinction could be portrayed as the difference between 'making a life' and 'making a living', and it can readily be seen that the former is of greater significance, and that the extent to which the latter (occupational) orientation is a central component of the former may vary between individuals and over time. The occupational identity is just one of a number of other, sometimes competing, identities that make up the overall identity of an individual (Brown, 1997).

8.3   Methods

The following analysis is based on narratives, covering the strategic biographies of three individuals, who formed part of the data generated for the research project 'Vocational Identity, Flexibility and Mobility in the European Labour Market'.[1] The project adopted a qualitative research approach, using semi-structured, problem-centred interviews (Witzel, 1996) and case study methods on the basis of common interview guidelines that were agreed by the project partners and slightly adapted according to the particularities of the respective national contexts. In order to assess the manifestation and formation of work identities in different work settings, the research covered various occupations across six contrasting sectors and seven different national economies. The research involved both manufacturing and service sectors, including metalwork/engineering, timber and furniture production, health

---

[1] For more detailed information about the project see Kirpal; Brown and Dif in this volume, FAME Consortium (2003) and Kirpal (2004b).

care/nursing, telecommunications, IT and tourism.[2] The project consortium consisted of partners from the Czech Republic, Estonia, France, Germany, Greece, Spain and the UK, a combination of countries that represented different cultural, socio-economic and political embeddings of work concepts and occupations in Europe. The core partners, Estonia, France, Germany, Spain and the UK, conducted large sample interviews, while the Czech Republic and Greece assumed the role of critical observers carrying out small-scale empirical investigations.

In total, the project partners interviewed 132 managers and representatives of human resources departments and over 500 employees, mainly employed at the intermediate skills level. Those interviews were conducted in two research phases in 2001 and 2002. While the first phase interviews with managers and HR experts were geared towards exploring structural variables such as work organisation and organisational changes, job profiles, skills requirements, career opportunities and recruitment strategies, the larger second part of the empirical investigation aimed at assessing employees' perspectives in terms of forms of identification with work, work attitudes, commitment patterns, performance of work roles and how they deal with changing work and skills demands. The objective of this research phase was to investigate the social-psychological dimension of occupational identity formation in order to complement and contrast the findings on the structural embedding, in particular work settings and expectations of managers, by connecting them to employees' individual dispositions, conditions and resources (see also Kirpal et al. in this volume).

The narratives presented here were generated through individual, in-depth interviews that took about 60 minutes each and were tape-recorded and transcribed verbatim. They are presented as case studies in order to explore in particular the individual-biographical dimension of work identities that takes account of an individual's occupational history and career development on the one hand, and the individual's perception of the work context and personal work attitude on the other. The case studies were developed so as to assess the developments and features of work, which the individual perceives as being important for his or her personal and professional development. These features include the meaning of work, a sense of belonging, an individual's work attitude and commitment, learning, the performance of occupational roles and work tasks, and how the individual relates to others in the work context.

---

[2] The findings structured along sectoral analyses are published in *Career Development International*, vol. 9, no. 3.

By analysing narratives, these elements are assessed from a subjective point of view; that is, how the individual perceives them over time.

8.4 Examples of Employees with a 'Flexible' Orientation to Work

One way of considering an occupational identity, to which we are adjusted and that is relatively stable over a period of time, is as a psychological 'home'. 'Home' in this context is a 'familiar environment, a place where we know our way around, and above all, where we feel secure' (Abhaya, 1997, p. 2). Dewey (1916) had seen an occupation as giving direction to life activities and as a concrete representation of continuity: a 'home' with clear psychological, social and ideological 'anchors'. But what drives those individuals who seek change and challenge rather than the security of a 'home'? These people 'move on' following an urge for change that seems to influence their orientations towards work much more than the potential risk of feeling the sense of loss and dislocation that Sennett (1998) identifies as occurring with some people when faced with discontinuities in their working lives. Religion, literature and film abound with stories of people 'breaking free' and 'loosening attachments to "homes" of many kinds, be they psychological, social or ideological' (Abhaya, 1997, p. 2). In this sense, after a period of stability, the attachment to a particular occupation or employer may come to be viewed as a confinement from which the individual longs to escape. That is, what is initially experienced as interesting and stabilising may, with the passage of time, lead to 'a sense of profound dissatisfaction with the comfortable limits' (Abhaya, 1997, p. 8) of the existing way of life.

It was this sense of looking for fresh challenges that was a dominant theme of interviews with employees who actively pursued the continual adjustment of their work identities in the light of flexibility that involved changing jobs, employers or their vocational specialisation. In fact, some of them conveyed the notion that flexibility itself formed an essential part of their work identity instead of forming medium- or long-term attachments that would produce greater continuity in their working life. The challenge was then to represent this change in the way an individual regards the work they do in a dynamic rather than a stable way. Thus, we needed to develop a representation of occupational identity that can theorise change as well as continuity, and one that allows individuals to move between the poles of regarding aspects of their work-related identities as 'anchors' or 'chains'.

Typically, when individuals seek to change their occupation and/or employer, because they want (or see themselves forced) to change direction, they are confronted with undergoing some kind of personal re-definition. The examples given below give us insight, among other aspects, into how such processes of re-definition develop. Martina from Germany started off as a bank clerk in pursuit of job security, but left the job due to limited career and development opportunities for women who worked at the bank at that time. Over the last 20 years she has experienced several re-directions of her professional trajectory that often represented a complete break with her former job tasks and work-based skills profile. When we conducted the interview in 2002 she was working as an IT project manager, but possibly saw herself changing direction again in the near future. Sally from England represents not only a substantive personal re-definition, but also involves a role re-definition from an organisational perspective. This is an example of someone undergoing a major career change: it is a case of a woman who became very purposeful about her own career development after the age of 30. It is also an example of a woman with highly developed communication skills and organisational skills challenging the company stereotype of the background expected of a production manager. Her gender and lack of a technical background led her to re-define the role of production manager in an engineering company. Finally, we have the example of Richard, an engineering graduate, who moved between sectors, functions and eventually moved away from the technical side into general management. Although his biography does exemplify a strategic career with changing work attachments, it also emphasises that individuals displaying a flexible attitude towards their work over time is not a recent phenomenon as it was a common route for those seeking to move into senior management positions in large organisations. All three seem able to switch between very different types of work, applying themselves with a will that leads to mastery of their work before looking for fresh challenges.

8.4.1 Martina from Germany Working in the IT Sector: from Bank Clerk to Textile Technician to IT-project Manager

Martina is a woman in her mid forties. After having completed the 'Abitur' (school leaving certificate for university entry) she did not know what occupation she wanted to follow or even the general direction her career should take. She had a vague interest in studying mathematics, something that was not very common for girls at that time (in 1977). Since her father was working at a bank, she decided to do an apprenticeship as a bank clerk. After having completed the apprenticeship she stayed on working with the bank for a couple of years to gain some initial work experience. She attained a small promotion during that time, but it was clear to her that women did not have great possibilities to make a career in the bank. In the beginning, she liked her work but became bored when work tasks became routine. She finally quit the job without having any other job offer. Her friends and colleagues could not understand that move, because working at a bank provided a well paid, relatively secure job, which at that time was thought to guarantee lifelong employment.

For the following eighteen months Martina worked and lived on a farm that was producing textiles in a traditional way. Initially she only intended to work there for a few months to take a break and to think about her vocational interests, but with time she developed a deeper interest in textiles and fabrics and decided to stay on. She particularly enjoyed the work atmosphere that was breaking with the common division between work and private life. This was a new experience and a very contrasting way of working compared to the job at the bank. Following her interest in textiles and fabrics, Martina studied for five years on a university course on textile and clothing technology with a specialisation in threads and fabric development. The course had a very technical orientation and, as a consequence, had only a very small proportion of female students (most women at that time preferred to study textile design). After completion of the course in 1988, it took some time before Martina finally found a job with a textile company. She stated that it was very difficult to find something corresponding to her qualification and that she felt discriminated against as a woman who wanted technical work in the textile industry.

The textile company hired her to work with the new, and at that time innovative, Computer Aided Design (CAD) systems, which started to revolutionise the whole textile industry. Working with the new computer systems and introducing them in the different departments presented a real challenge. Martina found this task very interesting and enjoyed her work, but soon started to encounter problems with the rather conservative and inflexible attitudes of staff reluctant to accept the new technology. She was struggling against a lot of resistance and felt that things were not moving fast enough leading to dissatisfaction with her work. In addition, after some years most work processes became routine once she had become familiar with the CAD systems, which became gradually established and she started to become restless. As a consequence, Martina decided to quit her job and to look for something else.

For personal reasons, she moved to a new town and started to look for a new job in the textile industry. Since in the region there were very few jobs in this sector, Martina started to develop a broader orientation and, after one year, got a job at a small software company producing software solutions for the tourist industry. They were looking for somebody with computer expertise and managerial skills. Although Martina had no background in tourism, she was recruited to help build up and systemise the project work. She started off working on project documentation, the development of project cycles, and project coordination and management. Today, she is holding a team leading position supervising about 20 employees and several projects. She is responsible for organisational tasks and for the management and recruitment of personnel, but is also to a lesser extent still involved in project work.

Although learning and skills development have not systematically evolved and been linked due to several career changes, Martina feels that there are many elements from her first and second occupations that she can apply today. Knowledge about accountancy and finance from her time with the bank helps her in her current position when working with budgets and introducing a new product cost accounting system. From her studies of textile technology it is the application of strategic and analytical thinking and problem solving that she can apply to systemise project work. From her former employment she brought with her the required technical understanding for working with computer systems. Interpersonal and managerial skills are competencies that she considers as being a combination of common sense and her own strong points. She feels that in her work as a project manager she has the function of a 'translator' between the client and the computer expert, who is developing the software system for the client. In this function, she has to understand what the client wants and translate it into a technical language for the programmer. At the same time she has to be able to translate the technical aspects of software development to make it understandable for the client when selling the product.

With time, Martina has found out that what she really likes doing and what she is good at is organising and shaping work structures and processes. She needs to be in a work environment that allows her to be creative and innovative. Thus, the work environment (the work atmosphere and the interaction with colleagues and supervisors) and how the work is organised are the most important aspects to her largely determining her motivation and performance. For her, these two elements are subordinated to work content or the actual work tasks. For example, she is now working in tourism and had to acquire a lot of knowledge about the tourist sector although she does not have a particular interest in it. But she likes the sector, because it is dynamic and gives room for bringing in new ideas. She feels that she could easily and flexibly adapt to different kinds of work structures, processes, or sectors as long as the work situation provides room for creativity and professional self-realisation.

To be able to change is a key aspect here. In her perspective it only takes 1–2 years of work experience to be more or less able to master a new job. After having reached the level of mastering a job, Martina usually very soon comes to a point where she wants to optimise processes and bring in her own ideas. She experienced that if the structures are too rigid for innovation or the staff are not open and flexible so that progress cannot really be achieved, she will soon become frustrated and dissatisfied. She may then still continue for some time, but if she feels that things are not moving, she would rather leave the job and, if necessary, the profession and look for something else.

The aim for professional self-realisation is the key element of her occupational identity and ranks higher than her commitment to a particular company, an occupation, a professional community or the perspective of making a career. And it also ranks higher than her personal life, social ties, family or being bound geographically. Thus, she does not only feel that she is a flexible person who can easily adapt to different work settings and tasks, but she needs the challenge of changes and flexibility in order to be satisfied at work. 'When I like what I'm doing, it is not important if I work 8, 10, or 14 hours'.

She does not see herself remaining with her current employer or in the sector, but thinks that she will soon move on. She can imagine herself starting again in a totally new field and from her side she is not tired or lacking the energy to start something new. It is only that she feels that with increasing age the opportunities become less as employers are more critical and reluctant to recruit employees who are older than forty. She would like to start again working in a smaller company with maybe 20–30 employees and striving to grow. She would also prefer to work in a dynamic sector like, for example, IT or tourism, because here things are moving and structures are still open and easier to modify. People working in these sectors are younger giving generally more room for innovation and developing new ideas.

The original wish for job security that once guided her when opting for an apprenticeship in the bank has been replaced by accepting a high risk level when leaving a job in order to find something more suitable.

She is now trusting in her skills and competencies and feels that she can always find a new job, only that maybe the time between two employment situations will become longer with increasing age. Martina is aware that her attitude towards work and employment is not and never has been compatible with building a family. The high level of personal flexibility and risk taking is probably only possible, because Martina has no family responsibilities, but is only responsible for herself.

8.4.2 Sally from England Working in Engineering: from Sports Teacher to Production Manager

Sally went to university straight from school and completed her degree in Sports Science. After graduation she went to work in outdoor pursuits, before returning a year later to study on a one-year full-time Physical Education teacher training course with Biology as a secondary subject. She chose the course because she was having problems getting a decent job, and did not know what else to do: 'it was a way of putting things off for a year.'

After completing her teacher training, she took a teaching post. It was short-lived. 'I discovered I didn't like kids.' She did not complete her probationary year, but took a job instead with local authority leisure provision. Through the next five to six years, she held various posts starting with life saving in a public baths and moving up into junior management in baths and parks facilities fairly quickly as posts became available. She gained membership of the Institute of Baths and Recreational Management during this period.

She left her last post with the plan to live abroad, but this plan did not work out. She was now 30 and needed work, so did some temping (involving temporary office work) for a couple of years. One of these jobs was with a small automotive company that is a first-tier automotive components manufacturer, specialising in the design, production, installation and testing of a particular set of components. She started as a temporary clerical worker. She asked for a permanent post, and was taken on in 'Customer Scheduling'. The job consisted of calculating and costing customers' requirements and keeping track of what was being produced and what had been dispatched. She took the job on a permanent basis because she needed the work and it seemed to be a reasonable company. Her starting salary was very modest.

Sally encountered no difficulties in undertaking the tasks of this job. She was promoted, and was eager to leave her first job as she felt it was not utilising all her skills and did not give her the level of responsibility she wanted. After three years, she was offered promotion to the post of 'Head of Logistics'—'which was not as grand as it sounds'. In this post, she managed the work of the clerical staff doing the jobs she had previously been doing herself. She managed six people. The only company training she received at this time was at her own instigation; she asked to go to Head Office abroad for a two-week period to orientate to the work of the company. They gave her this time, but it was left to her to structure this period for herself. She spent the time walking around the factory and talking to people, finding out for herself what was being done by whom and why. She found this period very informative and helpful.

After four years with the company, it was reorganising, and she was offered another promotion—as a 'Logistics Specialist', 'which was a non-job; I had no role'. Her salary for this 'non-job' was now double her initial salary. The following year she was given a further promotion to 'Production Manager' for a major customer group. Her job involved complete responsibility for resourcing the production and delivery of orders for this car manufacturer. In this job, she manages 100 permanent, mostly full-time, staff on a three shift system, plus 7 support workers based in the office. Her work involves the ordering and control of all materials, and responsibility for the production process itself, health and safety issues, staff management and customer liaison.

When the post became vacant, she had been encouraged to apply for it by her then bosses, and Sally was pleased to get this promotion. 'It was a proper job with a decent salary, and it was a challenge. (. . .) Did I encounter any difficulties? Huge difficulties. I had no knowledge of engineering production whatsoever. I knew nothing of production planning or engineering prioritising. Nothing.' She also had problems with managing the hourly paid non-staff employees who operated on a completely different basis from the permanent shop-floor staff, and there were difficulties for her in integrating the work of the two groups. Sally had had no university training relevant specifically to her new job; nothing to fall back on: 'my skills acquisition at this time was mainly on-the-job training; finding out as I went along.' The company did provide training opportunities over time to help her to cope with her new responsibilities. These included courses on interviewing skills, Health and Safety, disciplinary procedures, time management, IT, work study time and motion processes and procedures.

She found all this training very relevant and of good quality, and it helped her to build skills to tackle her job. It was as she began to 'get a handle' on her job that she decided to do a Master's degree so as to gain a greater understanding of the underpinning of the technical work of her department. On her own initiative, she had entered two courses at evening class level—one on the Japanese view of the auto industry. This was rather disappointing, but the other course was on leadership and self-management, and this was reasonably interesting and useful. The Master's in Engineering Business Management, however, offered the technical underpinning Sally was seeking. It was scheduled over a three-year period, organised in 12 units incorporating a week-long residential study block plus associated work assignments for each unit for the first two years, and a dissertation in year 3. She chose to do postgraduate study in engineering because she was by then in a management role in engineering whilst knowing little about the theory of the field of work. 'I wanted to understand what lay beneath what I was seeing on the shop floor, and what I was controlling in my job.' She chose this course because it was the one which had been researched by her bosses; which they had attended, and which they were now recommending and paying for. She had no independent choice in this, but was happy with the situation. Sally feels she has progressed satisfactorily through the course without too much trouble. In particular she valued the modules on 'leadership' and 'industrial engineering quality management'. The skills she has been learning have been intrinsic to her field of work, and she finds she has learned much on all three levels of the course—business, technical and operational. Her salary as production manager is over four times the salary at which she started less than ten years previously.

When reflecting upon her career development, Sally states that her 'career has gone every which way. It has gone differently to what might have been expected. I think there was a lot of luck involved in finding myself as a temp at my present company—being in the right place at the right time.' Sally considers she has come a long way in the last ten years. She is very satisfied with her salary now, and enjoys her job, but there are frustrations and these are to do with being a woman working in what is still very much a man's world. 'It's not so much a glass ceiling as a huge steel ceiling.' She has often felt that she could have done more, got further, but found she was not given the opportunities, and this she attributes to gender prejudice, 'although I am sure they would deny this'. She feels that the prevailing environment constrains her to behave in ways she does not like and which she believes others do not understand. 'I suppose I could have done more about this situation, but it is difficult, and I find myself coping with it by taking on some of the male attitudes, and this makes me feel guilty. I think I confront it with aggressive behaviour, and people don't always understand why this is happening.'

Sally had never expected to enter the engineering world. 'The last place I wanted to work was a factory. (. . .) I suppose because I saw factories as being mundane places with repetitive work; I would have thought of [the matchstick men of] Lowry, and terms like "factory fodder"'. She feels she has changed her view quite a lot since those days. 'I think I have changed. What I have come to realise is that it doesn't much matter what the workplace is, or where it is, or what it makes, most of the processes for getting something resourced and produced and delivered are the same.'

She considers that the learning she has undergone on her course has helped her considerably at all levels of her job, but especially in understanding the technical and operational aspects of her work with planning for the production process. The company-provided training down the years has always been of a high standard and has given her the skills she needed early on in her current job. Earlier, in her career with the company, this training was absolutely minimal, and what training she got was only because she pushed for it. It was all mainly 'on-the-job' learning. In the same way, her decision to do the Master's was her own idea, and she had had to negotiate her own entry onto the course. However, once she had indicated her wish to take further study, there had been no resistance from her bosses. As yet, she has no membership of any professional engineering associations.

The principal skills gaps she can identify are in the area of assertiveness to deal with the gender problem. 'Some influencing skills training is probably what I need to do.' She also wants to follow-up on work she has already done on her course on the personal performance module, and around issues in leadership and dealing with frustration. 'I need to learn how to deal with getting shouted down if I confront issues around gender discrimination. (. . .) But the gaps go right back, really. I went to an all-girls' school. Engineering was never, ever even mentioned. We were to be teachers or nurses, or librarians. Those who couldn't would have to marry and have babies. But never engineering; it was just not a subject for girls. (. . .) What would I change? I would have planned things differently from age 16; at that age, I would have got myself some career advice. I wouldn't have had to have re-planned and started again at age thirty then'. But even with all this, she is doubtful that she would want to have missed some of the good times she has had. Sally enjoyed her Sports Science course; enjoyed being at university at that time, and quite enjoyed some of her work in the leisure industry. She feels she has learned a lot through her various experiences, and whilst things have gone differently than she might have expected, she is fairly happy with where she is now.

Sally has been successful undertaking very different types of work, but feels that after mastering the work she needs to take on fresh challenges in relation to work and this is also reflected in a willingness to commit to further education and training. In her current organisational context it has proved possible to move both vertically and horizontally to take on new challenges. That she was able to do so without initial technical training demonstrates her flexibility, the extent of her organisational and communication skills and the value of these in the co-ordination that is at the heart of modern management manufacturing processes.

8.4.3   Richard from England Switching Sectors, Roles and Functions and Ending up in General Management

Richard is an engineering graduate, in his mid-forties, who first worked in engineering, then moved into the expanding IT industry in the 1980s working in contract electronics, before switching back to supply chain development with his job being underpinned by his IT expertise, and then deciding to move out of IT and into the commercial area. His career also involved changing employers several times. His case is included here, because it demonstrates that certain traditional pathways have always put a premium upon flexibility and have been underpinned by an expectation that some individuals will pass through organisations and occupations in active pursuit of individual development and a 'strategic career'.

Richard did an engineering degree and was sponsored while at university by a large engineering company for whom he then worked for seven years. Initially he undertook a range of project work within one division of the company. Part way through his time with the company he undertook a manufacturing management conversion programme for engineers at a university that specialised in technological subjects. Richard then returned to another division of the company in a management role concerned with logistics and supply chain management. He had, however, become increasingly interested in electronics in the early 1980s and decided strategically that he wanted to work in the expanding electronics industry. He applied for a job in another part of the country working in contract electronics. Richard worked there for a couple of years, learning while working on different contracts. One of the contracts involved working with a global IT company and eventually he moved with the contract as the company took the work in-house. He worked with this company for two years and then switched to being a supply chain manager with a large company of drinks suppliers.

The job as supply chain manager in the group planning division, although nominally similar to that which he had previously before going into the electronics industry, is now transformed because of technological development, restructuring of work processes and the changed nature of supply chain relationships. The job is totally underpinned by IT and it was his experience in this area that was responsible for him getting the job. Richard has now worked for his current company for thirteen years although it has expanded considerably as the company has been involved in a number of high profile mergers. Initially in the late 1980s his IT expertise coupled with the ability to combine this with business development and to lead project teams had been rather rare. However, since then and partly as a consequence of rationalisations following mergers, the standards of the company have gone up: 'you are working with some very, very capable people, very motivated people, and you have to work hard to keep ahead or to keep up with them. So this is a competitive environment . . .'

Richard is highly committed to his work and regards the company as a 'very good employer, a good company to work for, I enjoy working here and they reward you well'. He transferred to London where his work now involves being part of specially formed project teams with an international remit, whether they are engaged in managing a change programme, supporting global customer development or brand building. He is increasing his experience in areas that are business-led rather than technically-led, although he recognises he has much less international market experience than others in the commercial field. The work has though represented a new challenge and has been exciting—he had the feeling he was getting 'in a bit of a rut' in his previous job. On the technical operations side he had gone as far as he was likely to go. This was partly because he had had a very good relationship with his previous boss, who had sponsored his career development, but who had left the company when his counterpart from the other company had got his job in the merged organisation. Politically, Richard was then 'badged as one of his men', so he felt he had to move on. This is a 'classic' example of a strategic career with, for example, Richard's decisions to get into and out of the IT industry, switch employers and change jobs all being taken for strategic reasons linked to his longer-term career development. Richard was aware that he needed to be geographically mobile and flexible in terms of a willingness to learn new skills and undertake new experiences if he was to continue on an upward path.

8.5   Stability and Flexibility in Work Identities

Looking at the overall research results (Kirpal, 2004a), the vast majority of the employees who were interviewed connected the issue of flexibility primarily to the ability to cope with, and adapt to, changes at work such as new work tasks, job situations and work organisation, generally involving the need to broaden and even re-direct vocational skills and career plans. There was, however, great variation in whether flexibility was personally perceived as creating opportunities, or conversely, rather viewed as putting new demands and pressure on employees. As a consequence the forms of 'strategic action' undertaken by employees in forming their work-related identities and commitment patterns also varied greatly.

Employees with an affiliation towards 'classical' types of occupational identities typically identified either with their occupational specialisation, the company they worked for, the company's 'products' or the daily work tasks they performed. These types of employees were particularly to be found in the traditional segments of metalwork/engineering, health care and telecommunications (see Kirpal et al. in this volume). To those employees changes at work presented a conflict, often because as individuals they did not have the means or personal resources to adjust to new demands, for example due to lack of motivation, qualifications or self-confidence. Changes at work were typically perceived as being beyond their control and unpredictable. While the project identified this form of 'strategic action' as a 'retreat strategy', by which employees were largely resisting pressures for change and further learning, employees with a 'classical' type of identification with work could also respond in a more pro-active way in adjusting to the way their occupation or their employer was changing. If employees were able to move with, or were in the vanguard of changes and new requirements, they would develop what the project identified as a 'classical progressive' occupational identity. They would, for example, follow a classical career progression most likely by pursuing a higher level qualification (e.g. the *Meister* qualification) to move to supervisory or more specialist positions. They would still strongly identify with the classical elements of their occupation, but were at the same time able to make use of opportunities in the course of changing work situations to develop their professional career. Moving into more specialist or supervisory positions can also be considered a well-trodden path and they may retain their allegiance to their initial occupational specialisation. However, by assuming additional responsibilities and tasks they are also challenged to comply with new professional roles and adjust or even re-define their work identity.

The three narratives presented here illustrate how employees can perceive changes and new work demands as creating opportunities and what this can involve in terms of adjusting their work orientations and career strategies. They exemplify employees, who in the course of their employment trajectory have developed a highly 'flexible' identification with work with a much more individualist basis than any occupational and organisational commitment. One typical characteristic of these 'flexible' employees is the willingness and ability to use flexibility, mobility and learning as tools to achieve their broader professional (and personal) goals and in doing so our interviewees were ready to change organisations and/or their occupation if necessary.

Interestingly, from the overall project sample a flexible and individualised work identity could be found among the highly qualified, for example the IT specialist who combines a good mix of hybrid technical and social skills, but also among the less skilled workers with an unstable employment situation, for example in tourism. Typically, the 'flexible' employee is able to anticipate and internalise requirements for continuous adjustments and changes in the workplace, leading to a transitory work attachment and identity for the less qualified, and a highly individualised work identity based on professional skills and competences for the higher qualified. The key feature here is that the individual is active in pursuit of her or his own goals, professional development and self-realisation. Their work identity is highly individualised, primarily based on personal skills, a capacity for continuous learning and a rather project-oriented work attitude. A variation of this flexible type of identification with work would be the 'strategic careerists' who see their current occupational position and/or organisational attachment as one phase of a career that involves relatively frequent changes in the nature of work they do. They are committed to 'moving on' and see their careers as something that they actively construct. Their attachment to their current role is partly influenced by the knowledge that they are only 'passing through'.

The three narratives we introduced carry relevant features of such a 'flexible' type of work identity, although only one of the three cases, Richard, can be considered a 'strategic careerist'. While for 'strategic careerists' flexibility is used as an instrument to pursue a particular career plan, the other employees, Martina and Sally, had long periods when they were not acting strategically but rather can be characterised as being open towards how their work interests and career opportunities might develop. In this sense, flexibility can be regarded either as a strategic tool, or as a characteristic of the individuals themselves that is closely linked to their pursuit of self-realisation. In either case, in support of flexibility as a strategic tool or as an aspect of self-realisation learning can play a critical role. That learning can be used as a strategic tool for individual development can readily be seen in the biographies of the three employees presented here—each put in a lot of effort and investment in training and skills enhancement, mostly on their own account. Then, learning allied to flexibility becomes a major aspect of professional development and self-realisation. With Martina we also have a case where aspects of creativity, innovation and being in a position to 'move things' are valued more highly than performance of a particular role in a work context. She even stated that work stress for her is not related to the amount of work or work pressure (deadlines), but colleagues and organisational structures that inhibit progression is what causes stress for her.

This chapter aimed at illustrating and presenting a more in-depth analysis of the 'flexible' employee as one possible form of identification with work. From the sample of the research project, the three narratives presented here were exceptional cases we came across when interviewing over 500 employees. Apart from a considerable number of employees who were identified as holding on to 'classical' forms of work identities, the largest group of interviewees developed different forms of adaptation that resulted in various, very complex forms of responses along the continuum from 'classical' to 'flexible'. The changing nature of their attachment to work could be more or less intense and transitional. For example, adaptation and adjustment to work may be long-term or short-term oriented; be passive (accepting) or involve the individual in an active search for resolution of problems or conflicts. These results are presented in more detail elsewhere (see Kirpal, 2004a).

Interesting in the light of the issues presented here, however, is the aspect that among the different forms of 'adjustments' a considerable number of employees identified with their work, but were at the same time much more active in re-defining, rather than passively accepting, work-related roles. Actually, in all groups, from 'classical' to 'flexible' work identities, we found employees who were actively re-defining and challenging traditional professional roles and concepts of identification with work. We had examples of employees who used re-defining strategies operating at the cutting edge of norms and expectations, thus pushing at the boundaries of expectations of employers, colleagues and others. In certain aspects they could be considered change agents, typically negotiating, challenging and leading their peers in some respect. From the cases we presented we can see that while for Sally the conflicts that arise from this situation persist, but are at the same time a strong motor for learning and skills enhancement, Martina decided to 'move on' and look for an employment situation where she would feel less discriminated against and accepted.

What kind of work identity an individual develops over time depends on a variety of factors leading to a complex process of negotiation between personal resources, dispositions and constraints on the one hand, and structural conditions, on the other hand. What is important and could be illustrated is that work identities are subject to change as they are being adjusted over an individual's lifetime employment trajectory. These changes can also mean an individual can shift back and forth between developing forms of attachments and highly flexible forms of identification with work. What seems to be decisive in this context is the individual's response or 'strategy': whether he or she takes on a passive or active role; the level of risk affinity, the openness and ability to use flexibility, mobility and learning as tools to pursue their own interests; and general attachment to work. Some of those variables are clearly determined by an individual's personality such as the level of risk affinity or taking a passive or active role in negotiation processes that concern work and employment. Other variables, however, have to be interpreted in the light of work-related socialisation and learning. How individuals develop forms of attachment to work is highly influenced by work-related socialisation and work experiences in combination with personal interests. On the other hand, the extent to which employees are willing and able to use flexibility and mobility, and have developed an active learner's attitude, are closely linked to learning processes. At this point the project could identify a clear distinction between employees who had been socialised and trained to be more flexible and active in developing their professional orientation and identity, and employees who had not been socialised in this way.

Many employers increasingly expect that employees develop a proactive and 'entrepreneurial' work attitude based on multi-skilling and flexibility (FAME consortium, 2003). This implies for the individual the need to develop complex, flexible and multi-dimensional work attachments that can be continuously adjusted to the requirements of change. It also means that stability and continuity that former work arrangements promoted increasingly have to be actively constructed by the employees themselves, who are sometimes also expected to assume the responsibility to manage employment instabilities and to continuously up-date their vocational skills. The three individual cases we presented illustrate that complying with such demands requires personal efforts and a whole range of individual resources. From the research undertaken it is obvious that this cannot be taken for granted and it cannot be the individual alone who carries the burden for making these adjustments.

A highly flexible form of identification with work was rather exceptional among European employees in our sample and where employer support is insufficient or virtually lacking, employees were largely over-challenged to respond to changes at work in a way whereby their own professional development and employment could be progressing or even stabilise. Particularly employees at the intermediate skills level tend to develop their work identity in the complex discourse of adjustment and/or conserved more 'classical' forms of identification with work, and for some employees this meant largely resisting demands for flexibility and mobility. In segments of the economy that are characterised by fast changing technology and work organisation this could for the unprepared worker lead to stress, lack of control over work performance and lack of work commitment. Such a situation can also be risky and costly for the organisation as it may induce high levels of staff turnover, for example. In this context it is important to acknowledge that the majority of employees in Europe have undergone a work-related socialisation that did not yet anticipate the requirements for increased flexibility, mobility and lifelong learning. This strengthens the role of socialisation into the work context, one of the major functions of initial and continuing vocational training. In addition, preparing employees to meet future challenges at work also requires major organisational support. Only if employees are equipped with the right set of skills and sufficient self-confidence, will they be willing and able to deal with new flexibility and learning demands at work.

References

Abhaya, D. (1997). *Leaving home: E.M. Forster and the pursuit of higher values.* Western Buddhist Review Volume two. Birmingham: Windhorse Publications.
Baruch, Y. (1998). The rise and fall or organizational commitment. *Human Systems Management,* 17(2), 135–143.

Baruch, Y. and A. Winkelmann-Gleed (2002). Multiple commitments: A conceptual framework and empirical investigation in a community health service trust. *British Journal of Management*, 13(4), 337–357.

Beck, U. (1986). *Risikogesellschaft. Auf dem Weg in eine andere Moderne*. Frankfurt/M.: Suhrkamp.

Beck, U. (1994). The debate on the 'Individualization Theory'. *Today's Sociology in Germany*, 3 (Soziologie special edition), 191–200.

Beck, U. and P. Felixberger (1999). *Schöne neue Arbeitswelt. Vision: Weltbürgergesellschaft*. Frankfurt/M.: Campus.

Brown, A. (1997). A dynamic model of occupational identity formation. In A. Brown (Ed.), *Promoting vocational education and training: European perspectives* (pp. 59–67). Tampere: Universtity of Tampere.

Brown, A. (2004). Engineering identities. *Career Development International*, 9(3), 245–273.

Carruthers, B. and B. Uzzi (2000). Economic sociology in the new millenium. *Contemporary Sociology*, 29(3), 486–494.

Cohen, A. (1993). Organizational Commitment and turnover: A meta-analysis. *Academy of Management Journal*, 36(5), 1140–1157.

Dewey, J. (1916). *Democracy and education. An introduction to the philosophy of education* (1966 ed.). New York: Free Press.

Dif, M. (2004). Vocational identities in change in the telecommunications sector. *Career Development International*, 9(3), 305–322.

FAME Consortium (2003). *Work-related Identities in Europe: How Personnel Management and HR Policies Shape Workers' Identities*. ITB Working Paper Series no. 46. Bremen: Institute Technology and Education/University of Bremen.

Finegold, D. and K. Wagner (1999). The German Skill-Creation System and Team-Based Production: Competitive Asset or Liability. In P. Culpepper and D. Finegold (Eds.), *The German skills machine: Sustaining comparative advantage in a global economy* (pp. 115–155). Oxford: Berghahn Books.

Giddens, A. (1984). *The constitution of society*. Berkeley: University of California Press.

Giddens, A. (1991). *Modernity and self-identity: Self and society in the late modern age*. Stanford: Stanford University Press.

Gottlieb, B.H., E.K. Kelloway and E. Barham (1998). *Flexible Work Arrangements*. Chichester: Wiley.

Greinert, W.-D. (1997). *Das duale System der Berufsausbildung in der Bundesrepublik Deutschland*. Struktur und Funktion. Stuttgart: Holland & Josenhans.

Heinz, W.R. (1988). Selbstsozialisation und Arbeitsmarkt: Jugendliche zwischen Modernisierungsversprechen und Beschäftigungsrisiken. *Das Argument*, 168, 198–207.

Heinz, W.R. (1995). *Arbeit, Beruf und Lebenslauf. Eine Einführung in die berufliche Sozialisation*. München: Juventa.

Heinz, W.R. (2002a). Self-socialisation and post-traditional society. In R.A. Settersten and T.J. Owens (Eds.). *Advances in life course research: New frontiers in socialisation* (pp. 41–64). New York: Elsevier.

Heinz, W.R. (2002b). Transition discontinuities and the biographical shaping of early work careers. *Journal of Vocational Behavior*, 60(2), 220–240.

Heinz, W.R. (2003). From work trajectories to negotiated careers. The contingent work life course. In T.M. Jeylan and M.J. Shanahan (Eds.), *Handbook of the life course* (pp. 185–204). New York: Springer.

Heinz W.R. and A. Witzel, (1995). Das Verantwortungsdilemma in der berufliche Sozialisation. In E.H. Hoff and L. Lappe (Eds.), *Verantwortung im Arbeitsleben* (pp. 99–113). Heidelberg: Asanger.

Herrigel, G. and C. Sabel (1999). Craft Production in Crisis. Industrial Restructuring in Germany during the 1990s. In P. Culpepper and D. Finegold (Eds), *The German skills machine: Sustaining comparative advantage in a global economy* (pp. 77–114). Oxford: Berghahn Books.

Hoff, E.-H., L. Lappe and W. Lempert (1985) (Eds.). *Arbeitsbiographie und Persönlichkeitsentwicklung*. Schriften zur Arbeitspsychologie, Nr. 40, Stuttgart: Huber.

Holman, D., T. Wall, C. Clegg, P. Sparrow and A. Howard (Eds.) (2005). *The essentials of the new workplace: A guide to the human impact of modern working practices*. Wiley: Chichester.

Ibarra, H. (2003). *Working identity: Unconventional strategies for reinventing your career*. Boston: Harvard Business School Press.

Kirpal, S. (2004a). *Work identities in Europe: Continuity and change. Final Report of the 5th EU Framework Project 'FAME'*. ITB Working Paper Series no. 49. Bremen: Institute Technology and Education/University of Bremen.

Kirpal, S. (2004b). Introduction: Researching work identities in a European context. *Career Development International*, 9(3), 199–221.

Kirpal, S., A. Brown and M. Dif, (2006). The Individualisation of Identification with Work in a European Perspective. In A. Brown, S. Kirpal and F. Rauner (Eds.), *Identities at Work* (pp. 285–313). Dordrecht: Springer.

Kutscha, G. (2002). Regulation and deregulation: The development and modernisation of the German dual system. In P. Kamarainen, G. Attwell and A. Brown (Eds.), *Transformation of learning in education and training: key qualifications revisited* (pp. 53–69). Thessaloniki: European Centre for the Development of Vocational Training (CEDEFOP).

Loogma, K. (2003). *Workplace learning and competences: different contexts and different meanings in the case of a transition economy*. Paper presented at the 4th conference on human resource development research and practice across Europe: Lifelong learning for a knowledge based society. Toulouse 23–24 May 2003.

Marhuenda, F., I. Martínez Morales and A. Navas (2004). Conflicting vocational Identities and careers in the sector of tourism. *Career Development International*, 9(3), 222–244.

Moynagh, M. and R. Worsley (2005). *Working in the Twenty-first Century*. Leeds: ESRC Future of Work Programme and King's Lynn: The Tomorrow Project.

Pongratz, H.J. and G.G. Voß (2003). *Arbeitskraftunternehmer. Erwerbsorientierungen in entgrenzten Arbeitsformen*. Berlin: Edition sigma.

Reuling, J. (1996). The German Berufsprinzip as a model for regulating training Content and qualification standards. In W.J. Nijhof and J.N. Streumer (Eds.), *Key qualifications in work and education*. Dordrecht: Springer.

Sennett, R. (1998). *The corrosion of character: The personal consequences of work in the new capitalism*. New York: Norton.

Steers, R.M. (1977). Antecedents and outcomes of Organizational Commitment. *Administrative Science Quaterly*, 22(1), 46–56.

Tomassini, M. and A. Brown (2005). Technical workers learning while working in Rome. In A. Brown (Ed.) (2005), *Learning while working in small companies: comparative analysis of experiences drawn from England, Germany, Greece, Italy,*

Portugal and Spain, SKOPE Monograph No. 7. ESRC funded Centre on Skills, Knowledge and Organisational Performance, Oxford and Warwick Universities.

Voß, G.G. and H.J. Pongratz (1998). Der Arbeitskraftunternehmer. Eine neue Grundform der Ware Arbeitskraft? *Kölner Zeitschrift für Soziologie und Sozialpsychologie*, 50(1), 131–158.

Whetten, D.A. and P.C. Godfrey (1998). *Identity in organizations. Building theory through conversations*. Thousand Oaks: Sage Publications.

Wahler, P. and A. Witzel (1985). Arbeit und Persönlichkeit—jenseits von Determinantion und Wchselwirkung. Anmerkungen zur Rekonstruktion der Handlungslogik einer werdenden Arbeitskraft. In E.-H. Hoff, L. Lappe and W. Lempert (Eds.), *Arbeitsbiographie und Persönlichkeitsentwicklung* (pp. 224–236). Schriften zur Arbeitspsychologie, Nr. 40, Stuttgart: Huber.

Witzel, A. (1996). Auswertung problemzentrierter Interviews: Grundlagen und Erfahrungen. In R. Strobl, Rainer and A. Böttger (Eds.), *Wahre Geschichten? Zu Theorie und Praxis qualitativer Interviews. Beiträge zum Workshop Paraphrasieren, Kodieren, Interpretieren . . . im Kriminologischen Forschungsinstitut Niedersachsen am 29 und 30, Juni 1995 in Hannover*. Interdisziplinäre Beiträge zur kriminologischen Forschung Band 2. Baden-Baden: Nomos.

Part Three

Work and Commitment

9

The Dynamics Between Organisational Commitment and Professional Identity Formation at Work

Yehuda Baruch* and Aaron Cohen†
*School of Management, University of East Anglia, UK;
†Department of Political Science, University of Haifa, Israel

In our new age of boundaryless organisations (Ashkenas, et al., 1995) and boundaryless careers (DeFillippi and Arthur, 1994; Hall, 1996; Sullivan, 1999), the role of the organisation as identity creator and the major recipient of commitment would appear to be less prominent than it was in the past. Within the post-corporate career realm (Peiperl and Baruch, 1997), professional identity is one of the possible substitutes for organisational identity. Indeed as Rafaeli (1997) describes, traditional perspectives on organisations tend to view membership as a simple dichotomy and deny membership status to individuals with non-traditional work relationships.

Given that the major portion of an individual's life often revolves around organisations and work, investigations of forms of commitment in the workplace are vital for understanding the psychology of human behaviour. The need to explore more than one commitment form is timely given the changes in the workplace (Cohen, 2003; Cooper-Hakim and Viswesvaran, 2005). The typical working life of individuals is no longer tied to an individual organisation. In fact, individuals can anticipate changing jobs several times in their career. The rapid globalisation of business also suggests that individuals have multiple forms and bases of commitments (Cooper-Hakim and Viswesvaran, 2005).

In this chapter, we present and discuss a conceptual framework of two major constructs in the study of organisational behaviour and

A. Brown, S. Kirpal and F. Rauner (eds.), Identities at Work, 241–260.
© 2007 *Springer.*

management, Organisational Commitment (OC) and Professional Identity (PI). Both are highly relevant to people's working life. The two are inter-related and associated, and have major implications on both work-related outcomes and the wider life of a person. Our understanding of both OC and PI benefited from subjecting these constructs to intense study.

9.1   Organisational Commitment

The concept of organisational commitment (OC) has grown in popularity in the literature of industrial/organisational psychology and organisational behaviour (Mathieu and Zajac, 1990). Of all the forms of commitment, the organisational form still receives most attention (Griffin and Bateman, 1986, p. 166). This interest is apparent from the numerous studies that have examined the relationships between OC and its antecedents and outcomes (e.g. Mathieu and Zajac, 1990; Mowday et al., 1982). This high degree of attention, it is argued, stems from the fact that OC 'is theory based, broad in focus, holds significant integrative potential, and may be more manageable than other forms' (Griffin and Bateman, 1986, p. 166). Another reason is the perception that OC can predict labour turnover better than other work attitudes, especially job satisfaction (Williams and Hazer, 1986; Clugston, 2000). Moreover, it has been argued that organisations whose members have higher levels of commitment will show higher performance and productivity, and lower levels of absenteeism and lateness (Bateman and Strasser, 1984; Morris and Sherman, 1981).

Organisational commitment (OC) is defined in terms of attitude as well as a set of intentions. Attitudinal commitment exists when 'the identity of the person is linked to the organization' (Sheldon, 1971, p. 143), a definition that re-emphasises the association between OC and identity. A different definition is 'when the goals of the organization and those of the individual become increasingly integrated or congruent' (Hall et al., 1970, p. 177). Of all the individual characteristics and attitudes within the organisation, OC is a major focus for academic study. Much of it is due to the role it plays as an antecedent to other attitudes and behaviours. A large number of studies address OC and its effects in employment relationship. The growing interest in OC has probably contributed to the conceptual richness of its definition. This has correspondingly led to diverse approaches to measuring this construct (Griffin and Bateman, 1986; Morrow, 1983; Mowday et al.,

1982; Reichers, 1985). The differences among measures of OC have generally paralleled the distinction between two theoretical approaches to the construct: the side-bet or calculative approach, and the moral or attitudinal approach (Cohen and Lowenberg, 1990; Cohen and Gattiker, 1992; Ferris and Aranya, 1983; Griffin and Bateman, 1986; McGee and Ford, 1987).

The calculative approach rested on the 'side-bet' theory of Howard Becker (1960), who used the term to refer to the accumulation of investments valued by the individual that would be lost or deemed worthless if he/she were to leave the organisation. Becker argued that over a period of time certain costs accrue which make it more difficult for the person to disengage from a consistent line of activity, such as membership of an organisation. The threat of losing these investments, along with a perceived lack of alternatives to replace or make up for them, commits the person to the organisation. According to this view, the individual is bound to the organisation by extraneous factors, such as income and hierarchical position, and internal factors, such as 'knowing the ropes' and interpersonal relationships (Cohen, 1993; Cohen and Gattiker, 1992; Cohen and Lowenberg, 1990; Meyer and Allen, 1984; Wallace, 1997). The loss of friendships and seniority rights also can be a factor when employers are changed. Becker himself phrased his argument as follows:

> The man who hesitates to take a new job may be deterred by a complex of side-bets: the financial costs connected with a pension fund he would lose if he moved; the loss of seniority and 'connections' in his present firm, which promise quick advance if he stays; the loss of ease in doing his work because of his success in adjusting to the particular conditions of his present job; the loss of ease in domestic living consequent on having to move his household, and so on . . . (Becker, 1960, pp. 38–39).

The measure based on this theory attempted to reflect the basic arguments of this approach. Those were first developed by Ritzer and Trice (1969), with some methodological modifications added later by Hrebiniak and Alutto (1972) and Alutto et al. (1973). These measures question the respondents on the likelihood of their leaving the organisation, given various levels of inducement in pay, status, responsibility, job freedom and opportunity for promotion. The revised measure is used often, especially in research on the side-bet theory (e.g. Fukami and Larson, 1984; Hunt et al., 1985; Parasuraman and Nachman, 1987; Wittig-Berman and Lang, 1990).

The second approach sees commitment as affective or attitudinal, and has been called the 'organisational behaviour' (Staw, 1977) or 'psychology' (Near, 1989) approach. It regards the individual as identifying with the organisation, hence being committed to retaining membership in order to pursue his or her goals. The origins of this treatment of commitment perhaps lie principally in the work of Porter and his associates (e.g. Porter et al., 1974; Mowday et al., 1982); it has also been termed affective commitment (Meyer and Allen, 1984) and value commitment (Angle and Perry, 1981). This approach developed the most commonly used measure of OC, the attitudinal Organizational Commitment Questionnaire (OCQ) introduced by Porter and Smith (1970).

This scale, also known as the Porter et al. measure (1974), is 'the most visible measure of affective commitment [and] has enjoyed widespread acceptance and use' (Griffin and Bateman, 1986, p. 170). It consists of fifteen items (a shortened version has nine positively phrased items) reflecting the three dimensions of the definition of commitment suggested by Porter *et al.* (1974). These are: a desire to maintain membership in the organisation, belief in and acceptance of the values and goals of the organisation, and willingness to exert effort on behalf of the organisation. While Mowday *et al.* (1982) and Mowday *et al.* (1979) demonstrated the well-proven psychometric properties of this measure, they also noted that the relationships between their measure and some attitudinal variables such as job satisfaction and job involvement were too high for an acceptable level of discriminant validity. Later, in separate examinations of the OCQ characteristics, Morrow (1983), Blau (1985, 1987) and Commeiras and Fournier (2001) supported the general conclusion that it contains good psychometric properties.

Despite the existence of alternative conceptualisations and measures of OC such as the side-bet approach (Becker, 1960), the OCQ dominated the literature from the early 1970s to the mid-1980s. Most of the findings, conclusions and proposals for a future research agenda on OC are based on this measure. Furthermore, the many studies of OC and its relationships with antecedents and work outcomes have meanwhile been subjected to several meta-analyses (Mathieu and Zajac, 1990; Cohen, 1991, 1993; Cohen and Gattiker, 1992; Randall, 1990; Gaertner, 1999) that quantitatively summarised the findings on the concept. But recently some criticism has arisen regarding Porter *et al.*'s (1974) measure, the OCQ. The basic difficulty is that two of the dimensions of commitment of the OCQ, a strong desire to maintain membership in the organisation and a willingness to exert considerable effort on behalf of the organisation, overlap with intentions of outcome behaviours such as withdrawal and performance (Reichers, 1985; O'Reilly and Chatman, 1986; Bozeman and Perrewe, 2001). The response to that criticism has taken two directions. First, researchers have tended to use the nine-item version of the OCQ more frequently than the full fifteen items to avoid the six problematic negatively phrased items of the measure that dealt with withdrawal and performance (Beck and Wilson, 2001; Iverson, 1999). Second and possibly of equal importance, a new trend has started to evolve in the definition and measurement of OC (Baruch, 1998).

On the argument that OC can be better understood as a multi-dimensional concept, Meyer and Allen (1984) proposed a two-dimensional measure of OC. Conceptually their distinction between the two dimensions paralleled that between the side-bet calculative approach of Becker (1960) and the attitudinal approach of Porter and his colleagues (1974). The first dimension was termed *affective commitment* and was defined as 'positive feelings of identification with, attachment to, and involvement in the work organization' (Meyer and Allen, 1984, p. 375). The second was termed *continuance commitment* and was defined as 'the extent to which employees feel committed to their organizations by virtue of the costs that they feel are associated with leaving (e.g., investments or lack of attractive alternatives)' (Meyer and Allen, 1984, p. 375).

McGee and Ford (1987) in their factor analysis found that the continuance commitment scale is itself a two-dimensional construct. One sub-dimension represented the sacrifices made by an employee in staying with the organisation, and was termed high sacrifice, and the other represented available employment alternatives, and was termed low alternatives. Meyer et al. (1990) replicated this finding. In a subsequent paper Allen and Meyer (1990) added a third dimension termed *normative commitment*, which was defined as the employee's feelings of obligation to remain with the organisation.

The factor analysis of Allen and Meyer (1990) supported the proposed three-dimensional scales. In their assessment of the scales Hackett et al. (1994) generally supported the existence of three dimensions. However, based on a 'Confirmatory Factor Analysis' model, a better fit with the data was found for a four-component model with the continuance commitment being divided into two dimensions along the lines suggested by McGee and Ford (1987). However, certain studies (Jaros, 1997; Ko et al., 1997) indicated problems with the dimensionality of commitment based on Meyer and Allen's (1997) scales. In a later study Ko et al. (1997) found that reliabilities of the affective commitment and the normative scales were acceptable, whereas the reliability of the

Table 9.1　Table overview of approaches to measure organisational commitment

Characteristics	Conceptual Approach		
	Calculative	Affective	Multidimensional
Term	Side-bet theory approach	Organizational Commitment Questionnaire (OCQ)	Affective, normative, continuance
Definition	Refers to the accumulation of investments valued by the individual that would be lost or deemed worthless if he/she were to leave the organization	(1) A desire to maintain membership in the organization; (2) Belief in and acceptance of the values and goals of the organization; (3) Willingness to exert effort on behalf of the organization.	*Affective commitment*: positive feelings of identification with, attachment to, and involvement in the work organization; *Continuance commitment*: the extent to which employees feel committed to their organizations by virtue of the costs that they feel are associated with leaving (e.g., investments of lack of attractive alternatives); *Normative commitment*: the employees' feelings of obligation to remain with the organisation
Measurement	The measures question the respondents on the likelihood of their leaving the organization, given various levels of inducement in pay, status, responsibility, job freedom, and opportunity for promotion (Ritzer & Trice, 1969; Hrebiniak & Alutto, 1972: Alutto et al., 1973)	The scale consists of fifteen items (a shortened version has nine positively phrased items) reflecting the three dimensions of the definition of commitment as suggested by Porter et al. (1974).	Three eight-item scales for each of the commitment dimensions: affective, normative and continuance. Meyer and Allen (1997) suggested later on a longer nine-item version for continuance commitment, and a shorter six-item version for normative commitment

continuance commitment scale was low. The three scales had acceptable convergent validity, but the affective and the normative scales lacked discriminant validity. The construct validity of the affective commitment was supported, whereas the construct validities of the continuance commitment and the normative commitment scales were questionable. These authors concluded that a new measure should be devised for continuance and normative commitment (Table 9.1).

9.2 Identity and Identification

An individual's self-concept is made up from their personal identity, which derives in part from the combination of social groupings they belong to (in addition, of course, to their personality, intelligence and other personal traits). A person has a specific identity, which is 'the state of having unique identifying characteristics held by no other person (or thing); the individual characteristics by which a person (or thing) is recognized' (Oxford Dictionary, 2000). Certain basic identity constructs are *personal identity* and *social identity*. *Personal identity* represents individual aspects of how we see ourselves relative to others in the same social group, whereas *social identity* comprises those aspects of our self concept we believe we have in common with others in the same social group (Arnold, 2005, p. 333). Social identity theory was introduced to the behavioural sciences by Turner (1975) and Tajfel (1981), and continues to be relevant to management and behavioural studies (see Jenkins, 1996), as identity influences much of our approach to work and behaviour at work, including commitment.

Each person has a number of social identities, many of them concerned with their working life. Foreman and Whetten (2002) explored how members identify with multiple-identity organisations. They argued that the operationalisation of organisational identification can be expressed in terms of multiple and competing identities. Van Dick et al. (2004b) proposed different foci of identification (e.g. with own career, team, organisation, occupation). Indeed, like OC, identity is also multi-dimensional: People have self-identity, group/sub-group identity, organisational identity, National identity, and professional identity.

As indicated, in addition to commitment, identification is another major construct associated with employees' attachment to organisations. The more people identify with a certain group or organisation, the more they will be ready to devote their efforts for and be involved in the group or organisation. Of course, there are other work attitudes that shape the way people approach their careers and working life, for example work role centrality (Mannheim et al., 1997). Other types of attachments exist, for example, to the trade union (Cohen, 2003; Kelly and Kelly, 1994). These might account for a decline in the commitment to and in the identification with the organisation, and reduced levels of employees' attachment to organisations. Furthermore, there is a growing tendency for self-focused and individualisation of work-related attitudes and practices, clearly manifested in growing focus of individual career planning and management, compared with that conducted by organisations (Baruch, 2004).

9.3   Organisational and Professional Identification

Two of the most prominent social groups that working people belong to are their organisation and their professional group or community of practice. Hence organisational and professional identity are major social identities, and are of major importance within the realm of work and career. Jenkins (1996, p. 142) emphasises how both organisational identity and professional identity are 'achieved' identities, i.e. identities acquired or assumed through life development (as opposed to 'ascribed' identities, which are identities socially constructed on the basis of birth—see later for elaboration).

Organisational identification consists of the members' shared beliefs about the central, enduring and distinctive characteristics of the organisation (Golden-Biddle and Hayagreeva, 1997). It is one of the important forms of employees' attachment to organisations (Brown, 1969; Rotondi, 1975). Mael and Ashforth (1995) argue that organisational identification is a specific form of social identification by which individuals define themselves in terms of their membership of a particular organisation. Research establishes organisational identification as a perceptual cognitive construct that is different, both conceptually and empirically, from organisational commitment as well as from other related work and job attitudes (Mael and Tetrick, 1992). Mael and Ashforth (1995) distinguish organisational identification from organisational commitment as follows:

> Although identification is necessarily organization-specific, commitment may not be. The focal organization's goals and values may be shared by other organizations, such that one could score high on commitment without perceiving a shared destiny

with that particular organization. With proper incentives, the individual could readily transfer his or her commitment to a different, even competing, organization with similar goals and values. However, if one identified with the organization, then he or she would necessarily experience some psychic loss upon leaving the organization (Mael and Ashforth, 1995, p. 312).

As is the case for OC, different dimensions of organisational identification may exist, such as cognitive, affective, evaluative and behavioural (van Dick et al., 2004b).

Researchers have applied organisational identification in a variety of settings, not only to employees of work organisations (e.g. Wan-Huggins et al., 1998), but also to different types of psychological group members, such as soldiers (Mael and Ashforth, 1995), college alumni (Mael and Ashforth, 1992) and accounting firm alumni (Iyer et al., 1997). These studies find that organisational identification reflects the individual's psychological attachment to a specific organisation, and that organisational identification is associated with desirable outcomes for the individual and the organisation, including job involvement and intent to remain.

9.4   Professional Identity and Identification

Under social identity theory, individuals classify themselves into various social groups, both ascribed (e.g. gender, race) and achieved (e.g. organisational and professional memberships) (Tajfel and Turner, 1985; Dutton et al., 1994). Interestingly, religious affiliation is one identity that starts as ascribed, but later in life can be changed, thus achieved. Professionals are likely to identify with both their profession and their firm (in a similar way that 'cosmopolitans' share high commitment to their profession and organisation, as Gouldner (1957, 1958) argues). Of course, we can find other deviations, such as an engineer who highly identifies with his or her discipline, but not with the organisation, thus easily moving between employers, and an engineer who identifies with the employing firm, moves across projects, and possibly takes a managerial position, leaving his or her professional affiliation low on the agenda.

An individual typically decides to become a member of a profession (e.g. medical doctor, accountant or psychologist) long before he or she joins a particular employer. Thus, professional identification would normally be expected to develop before organisational identification. This is in line with Aranya et al. (1981), who argue that a professional affiliation is both separate from and precedes the development of an affiliation to a particular organisation. Furthermore, even when a professional leaves her or his organisation for another employer, they keep their professional affiliation and qualification.

One challenge for organisations is to get employees to associate, combine or connect their professional and organisational identities. Such is the case when companies like Intel or Digital build their image as leading in technology, enabling their employees to feel that being a member of, say, Intel, also means being a member of the electronics Research and Development (R&D) community. It can be easily assumed that the ability of the organisation to facilitate the individual's professional expectations and to strengthen a professional identity will also increase the individual's organisational identification (Aranya et al., 1981; Norris and Niebuhr, 1984; Meixner and Bline, 1989). In support of the cosmopolitan view, Kalbers and Fogarty (1995) find that internal auditors with higher levels of professionalism were more committed to their organisation. Along the same lines, Russo (1998) studied the organisational and professional identifications of a group of newspaper journalists and found that professional identification strengthens organisational identification. This may be because organisations provide the means necessary for an employee to work as a professional and share a professional identity.

Ibarra (2003, p. 18) suggest three approaches for managing transformation of identity within the professional identity context. These depend on three different aspects of working identity:

- When the working identity is defined by *What we do*, such as professional activities we are engaged with;
- When the working identity is defined by *Whom we do it with*, i.e. working relationships and membership in professional groups (e.g. associations);
- When the working identity is defined by *formative events in our lives*, events that change us and put us in different paths.

Corresponding to these three aspects with strategies for renewal and revival of working identity, Ibarra suggests:

- When the working identity is defined by *What we do*, the suggested route is *crafting experiments*, trying out, on a minor scale, new activities, roles, and according to the success and feeling of doing that, to embark on higher commitment to the change.
- When the working identity is defined by *Whom we do it with*, the suggested route is *shifting connections*, apply different networks, new role models, peers, and to benchmark our progress.

- When the working identity is defined by *formative events in our lives*, the suggested route is *making sense*—creating or identifying catalysts and triggers for change. These can be utilised to rework our 'story'.

9.5 Developing Professional Identity—A Social Learning Perspective

Social learning (Mitchell et al., 1979) is concerned with feedback from the environment, in particular in relation to career counselling and the development of self-efficacy (Bandura, 1977, 1997) as a result of reinforcement cycles. External intervention can help to facilitate high self-efficacy via learning that affect people's attitudes and behaviours. Self-efficacy has repeatedly been shown to be an antecedent of performance in organisational settings (Bandura 1977, 1997). Both feedback from the wider environment (i.e. not just from parents) and reinforcement of successful performance help people in choosing professions and careers that would fit them best (Baruch, 2004). Hogg and Terry (2000) argued that members' perceptions of an organisation (e.g. prototypical beliefs, attitudes, feelings and behaviours) are constructed, maintained and modified by features of both transitory and more enduring social contexts.

To make a 'proper' choice, i.e. to optimise their career prospects, people first need to realise their own type of vocational inclination, and second get acquainted with the occupational environment associated with their professional options (Baruch, 2004). Identification of this type depends on the motivation, knowledge, personality and competence of a person. Occupation is much more than a collection of activities and functions. It is the culture, the reputation, status and associated life style that go together. Cooper (2004) suggested that the lack of a strong professional identity means, from the organisational view point, leaving employees thinking only of their employment role rather than understanding with clarity the difference between the obligations of employment to an organisation and those associated with being a member of a profession.

Ibarra's (1999, 2003) study of novice investment bankers and consultants helps us to understand how individuals initially define their membership status or 'provisional selves' by seeking out role models, experimenting with behaviours and soliciting feedback. Bartel and Dutton (2001) describe the crucial role of social interaction tactics that novice and veteran members may exhibit within organisational contexts. Their idea is applicable and can be echoed or replicated within professional membership contexts, too. Bartel (2001) investigated how experiences in a particular boundary-spanning context (community outreach) affected members' organisational identity and identification. Inter-group comparisons with clients (emphasising differences) and intra-group comparisons with other organisation members (emphasising similarities) changed according to how members construed their organisation's defining qualities. Inter-group comparisons also enhanced the esteem members derived from their organisational membership, which in turn strengthened their organisational identification.

Becoming an organisational member is concerned not merely with acquiring certain technical information, but also with adopting or accepting its culture, which means shared ideologies, specialised language, customs and rituals, and appropriate member etiquette and demeanour (Van Maanen and Schein, 1979). We argue that the same applies to professional membership. Membership claiming is accomplished through more ways than talk. Individuals can equip themselves with the material and symbolic resources that help to legitimate the assertions to which they lay claim and that do, indeed, belong to them. Claiming by equipping can take the form of behavioural and artifactual displays that help to communicate the validity of an organisational self (Kunda, 1992). For example, individuals can use dress to claim organisational membership. Dressing appropriately for organisational membership can be an effortful activity involving physical, emotional and cognitive work (Rafaeli and Pratt, 1993). Similarly, certain groups will use dress to reinforce professional identity, be they medical doctors (or nurses), bakers, or army officers.

The boundaryless organisations (Ashkenas et al., 1995) generated boundaryless careers (DeFillippi and Arthur, 1994; Hall, 1996; Sullivan, 1999). As a result, the role of the organisation as identity creator has declined, compared with what we have known in the past. Within the post-corporate career realm (Peiperl and Baruch, 1997), professional identity is one of the possible substitutes for organisational identity.

Perceptions of organisational membership are context dependent (Bartel and Dutton, 2001). Identification is a perception of belonging (for example, to an organisation or to a profession) that is triggered when situational cues highlight common interests or shared outcomes between an individual and the organisation (Ashforth and Mael, 1989). The existing literature seems to contain some overlap between OC and identification, to which Ashforth and Mael (1989) draw attention. However, one can be committed to stay with an organisation for a number of reasons (Meyer and Allen, 1997) without necessarily identifying with what that organisation symbolises. Finally, organisational identity is a major factor influencing intentions to quit, and subsequently actual turnover. The intentions stem from the strength of the bond created with the organisation (van Dick et al., 2004a).

9.6   Integrated Model

Figure 9.1 presents a general model, which depicts what we believe to be an integrative framework embracing both, identity and commitment, their antecedents and outcomes.

Relating to the two major constructs, identity and commitment, we believe that while there is a reciprocal association between the two, it is mostly that identity influences, even formulates, commitment. Once a

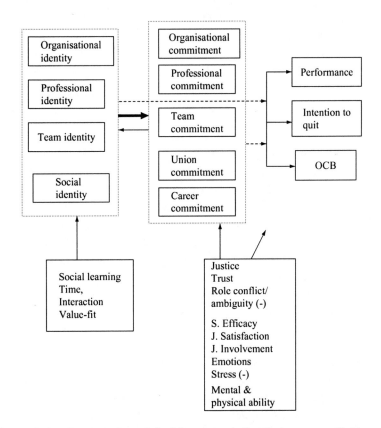

Figure 9.1   A general model of the association between multiple commitments, multiple identities, their antecedents and their work outcomes

person comes to identify with an organisation, he/she starts to become committed to it. Of course, being committed reinforces the identity in a cyclical manner. Within working life, both organisational identity and professional identity are powerful in influencing organisational and professional commitment. People have multiple identities, thus they also posses multiple commitments. Each person has several domains of life comprising multiple constituencies. The level of commitment to each constituency is different, and depends on a variety of antecedents. Carson and Bedeian (1994) acknowledged the existence of multiple commitments, and further studies manifested the relevance of distinguishing among these (Baruch and Winkelmann-Gleed, 2002; Cohen, 1999, 2003; Gregersen, 1993). Foreman and Whetten (2002) show that organisational identity congruence has a significant effect on member commitment, and form-level identity congruence has significant effects on both cognitive and pragmatic legitimacy, lending support for the use of identity as a multi-level construct.

A growing body of research seeks to establish theoretical parameters for organisational identity management (Ashforth and Mael, 1989; Elsbach and Kramer, 1996). Self-identification is closely linked to the identification with a group, be it the organisation, profession, or any other group to which the person belongs. Individuals seek a positive social identity through belonging to an in-group, which subsequently enhances personal worth and self-belief (Tajfel and Turner, 1985; Ashforth and Mael, 1989). Members of an organisation tend to apply the sociological categorisation of the group or organisation to define or transform their individual selves. Thus membership is linked to a deeper psychological process (Tajfel and Turner, 1985).

The model relates to sets of prospective antecedents that feed into identity constituencies (organisational, professional, team and social). Social interactions such as social learning can transform ambiguous memberships, providing the impetus for both organisational and professional identification. Individual identity is both internal (how I perceive myself) and external (professional as well as organisational) and identification depends also on whether or not other people affirm or validate this social claim of organisational and professional membership through different forms of identity granting. Other issues influencing identity development and sustainability are the time invested in the interaction, the type and depth of interaction and, of course, the match or fit between the value system of the person and the organisation, profession, team and social class to which they belong (Rokeach, 1973). Indeed, Ostroff (1993) found a positive relationship between person-environment congruence and organisational effectiveness (see also Osipow, 1987). A meta-analysis by Assouline and Meir (1987) found a close relationship between congruence and well-being measures, e.g. satisfaction and stability.

Similarly, a vast literature on organisational commitment lists a number of prospective antecedents to commitment (see in particular Cohen, 2003). At the organisational level, these include, but are not restricted to, issues such as justice, trust and the negative impact of role conflict and ambiguity. At the individual level, within working life aspects such as self-efficacy, satisfaction, involvement and a variety of emotions that would influence commitments, we can find both psychological and physical well-being. Most, if not all, of these constructs influence outputs such as performance and work-related behaviours, both directly and via the creation and maintenance of commitment.

9.7   Outcomes and Managerial Implications

Both identity and commitment are responsible, to a large extent, for people's work-related behaviour. While identity influences commitment, the outcomes of both are of crucial importance to organisations—and can be tangible or intangible. The most practical one is performance, but other outcomes exist, such as intention to quit, absenteeism (to represent possible negative outcomes) or organisational citizenship behaviour and life satisfaction and well-being (to represent positive outcomes). Organisational identity influences the construction and enactment of executive roles and relationships (Golden-Biddle and Hayagreeva, 1997).

While not 'hard' issues, the creation, development and maintenance of strong identity and commitment would result in outcomes that are most desirable to any organisation. The aspect of people management, industrial relations, psychology and sociology of work, all lead to the simple conclusion that soft issues, sometimes intangible, have the potential to generate very strong, hard tangible benefits for organisations.

References

Allen, N.J. and J.P. Meyer (1990). The measurement and antecedents of affective, continuance and normative commitment to the organization. *Journal of Occupational Psychology*, 63, 1–18.

Alutto, J.A., L.G. Hrebiniak and R.C. Alonso (1973). On operationalizing the concept of commitment. *Social Forces*, 51, 448–454.

Angle, H.L. and J.L. Perry (1981). Organizational commitment and organizational effectiveness: An empirical assessment. *Administrative Science Quarterly*, 26, 1–14.

Aranya, N., J. Pollock and J. Amernic (1981). An examination of professional commitment in public accounting. *Accounting, Organizations and Society*, 6, 271–280.

Arnold, J. (2005). *Work Psychology* (5th ed.). Harlow: FT/Prentice-Hall/Pearson.

Ashforth, B.E. and F.A. Mael (1989). Social identity theory and the organization. *Academy of Management Review*, 14, 20–39.

Ashkenas, R., D. Ulrich, T. Jick and S. Kerr (1995). *The boundaryless organization.* San Francisco: Jossey-Bass.

Assouline, M. and E.I. Meir (1987). Meta-analysis of the relationships between congruence and well-being measures. *Journal of Vocational Behavior*, 31, 333–336.

Bandura, A. (1977). *Social learning theory.* Englewood Cliffs, NJ: Prentice-Hall.

Bandura, A. (1997). *Self efficacy.* New York: WH Freeman.

Bartel, C.A. (2001). Social comparisons in boundary-spanning work: Effects of community outreach on members' organizational identity and identification. *Administrative Science Quarterly*, 46, 379–413.

Bartel, C.A. and J.E. Dutton (2001). Ambiguous organizational memberships: Constructing organizational identities in interactions with others. In M.A. Hogg and D. Terry (Eds.), *Social identity processes in organizational contexts* (pp. 115–130). Philadelphia, PA: Psychology Press.

Baruch, Y. (1998). The rise and fall of organizational commitment. *Human System Management*, 17, 135–143.

Baruch, Y. (2004). *Managing careers: Theory and practice.* Harlow: FT-Prentice Hall/ Pearson Education.

Baruch, Y. and A. Winkelmann-Gleed (2002). Multiple commitments: A conceptual framework and empirical investigation in a community health service trust. *British Journal of Management*, 13, 337–357.

Bateman, S.T. and S. Strasser (1984). A longitudinal analysis of the antecedents of organizational commitment. *Academy of Management Journal*, 27, 95–112.

Beck, K. and C. Wilson (2001). Have we studied, should we study, and can we study the development of commitment? Methodological issues and the developmental study of work-related commitment. *Human Resource Management Review*, 11, 257–278.

Becker, H.S. (1960). Notes on the concept of commitment. *American Journal of Sociology*, 66, 32–40.

Blau, G.J. (1985). The measurement and prediction of career commitment. *Journal of Occupational Psychology*, 58, 277–288.

Blau, G.J. (1987). Using a person environment fit model to predict job involvement and organizational commitment. *Journal of Vocational Behavior*, 30, 240–257.

Bozeman, D.P. and P.L. Perrewe (2001). The effect of item content overlap on organizational commitment questionnaire—turnover cognitions relationships. *Journal of Applied Psychology*, 86, 161–173.

Brown, M. (1969). Identification and some conditions of organizational involvement. *Administrative Science Quarterly*, 14, 346–355.

Carson, K.D. and A.G. Bedeian (1994). Career commitment: Construction of a measure and examination of its psychometric properties. *Journal of Vocational Behavior*, 44, 237–262.

Clugston, M. (2000). The mediating effects of multidimensional commitment on job satisfaction and intent to leave. *Journal of Organizational Behavior*, 21, 477–486.

Cohen, A. (1991). Career stage as a moderator of the relationships between organizational commitment and its outcomes: A meta-analysis. *Journal of Occupational Psychology*, 64, 253–268.

Cohen, A. (1993). Organizational commitment and turnover: A meta-analysis. *Academy of Management Journal*, 36, 1140–1157.

Cohen, A. (1999). Relationship among five forms of commitment: An empirical assessment. *Journal of Organizational Behavior*, 30, 285–308.

Cohen, A. (2003). *Multiple commitments in the workplace: An integrative approach.* Mahwah, NJ: Lawrence Erlbaum Associates.

Cohen, A. and E.U. Gattiker (1992). An empirical assessment of organizational commitment using the side-bet theory approach. *Relations Industrielles/Industrial Relations*, 47, 439–461.

Cohen, A. and G. Lowenberg (1990). A re-examination of the side-bet theory as applied to organizational commitment: A meta-analysis. *Human Relations*, 43, 1015–1050.

Commeiras, N. and C. Fournier (2001). Critical evaluation of Porter *et al.*'s organizational commitment questionnaire: Implications for researchers. *Journal of Personal Selling & Sale Management*, 21, 239–245.

Cooper-Hakim, A. and C. Viswesvaran (2005). The construct of work commitment: Testing an integrative framework. *Psychological Bulletin*, 131, 241–259.

Cooper, T.L. (2004). Big questions in administrative ethics: A need for focused, collaborative effort. *Public Administration Review*, 64, 395–407.

DeFillippi, R.J. and M.B. Arthur (1994). The boundaryless career: A competency-based career perspective. *Journal of Organizational Behavior*, 15, 307–324.

Dutton J.E., J.M. Dukerich and C.V. Harquail (1994). Organizational images and member identification. *Administrative Science Quarterly*, 39, 239–263.

Elsbach, K. and R.M. Kramer (1996). Members' responses to organizational identity threats: Encountering and countering the Business Week rankings. *Administrative Science Quarterly*, 41, 442–476.

Ferris, K.R. and N. Aranya (1983). A comparison of two organizational commitment scales. *Personnel Psychology*, 36, 87–98.

Foreman, P. and D.A. Whetten (2002). Members' identification with multiple-identity organizations. *Organization Science*, 13, 618–635.

Fukami, V.C. and W.E. Larson (1984). Commitment to company and union: Parallel models. *Journal of Applied Psychology*, 69, 367–371.

Gaertner, S. (1999). Structural determinants of job satisfaction and organizational commitment in turnover models. *Human Resource Management Review*, 9, 479–493.

Golden-Biddle, K. and R. Hayagreeva (1997). Breaches in the boardroom: Organizational identity and conflicts of commitment in a nonprofit organization. *Organization Science*, 8, 593–412.

Gouldner, A.W. (1957). Cosmopolitans and locals: Toward an analysis of latent social roles. *Administrative Science Quarterly*, 2, 281–306.

Gouldner, A.W. (1958). Cosmopolitans and locals: Toward an analysis of latent social identity. *Administrative Science Quarterly*, 3, 444–480.

Gregersen, H.B. (1993). Multiple commitment at work and extra-role behavior during three stages of organizational tenure. *Journal of business Research*, 26, 31–47.

Griffin, R.W. and T.S. Bateman (1986). Job satisfaction and organizational commit-ment. In C.L. Cooper and I. Robertson (Eds.), *International review of industrial and organizational psychology* (pp. 157–188). New York: John Wiley & Sons Ltd.

Hackett, D.R., P. Bycio and P. Hausdorf (1994). Further assessment of Meyer's and Allen's (1991) three-component model of organizational commitment. *Journal of Applied Psychology*, 79, 15–23.

Hall, D.T. (1996). *The career is dead–long live the career. A relational approach to careers*. San Francisco, CA: Jossey-Bass.

Hall, D.T., B. Schneider and H.T. Nygran (1970). Personal factors in organizational identification. *Administrative Science Quarterly*, 15, 176–189.

Hogg, M.A. and D.T. Terry (2000). Social identity and self-categorization processes in organizational contexts. *Academy of Management Review*, 25, 121–140.

Hrebiniak, L.G. and J.A. Alutto (1972). Personal and role related factors in the develop-ment of organizational commitment. *Administrative Science Quarterly*, 17, 555–573.

Hunt, S.D., L.B. Chonko and V.R. Wood (1985). Organizational commitment and mar-keting. *Journal of Marketing*, 46, 112–126.

Ibarra, H. (1999). Provisional selves: Experimenting with image and identity in pro-fessional adaptation. *Administrative Science Quarterly*, 44, 764–791.

Ibarra, H. (2003). *Working identity*. Boston, MA: Harvard Business School Press.

Iverson, S. (1999). An event history analysis of employee turnover: The case of hospital employees in Australia. *Human Resource Management Review*, 9, 397–418.

Iyer, V.M., E.M. Bamber and R.M. Barefield (1997). Identification of accounting firm alumni with their former firm: Antecedents and outcomes. *Accounting Organizations and Society*, 22, 315–336.

Jaros, S.J. (1997). An assessment of Meyer and Allen's (1991) three-component model of organizational commitment and turnover intentions. *Journal of Vocational Behavior*, 51, 319–337.

Jenkins, R. (1996). *Social identity*. London: Routledge.

Kalbers, L.P. and T.J. Fogarty (1995). Professionalism and its consequences—a study of internal auditors. *Auditingm—A Journal of Practice & Theory*, 14, 64–86.

Kelly, C. and J. Kelly (1994). Who gets involved in collective action? Social psychological determinants of individual participation in trade unions. *Human Relations*, 47, 63–87.

Ko, J.W., J.L. Price and C.W. Mueller (1997). Assessment of Meyer and Allen's three-component model of organizational commitment in South Korea. *Journal of Applied Psychology*, 82, 961–973.

Kunda, G. (1992). *Engineering culture: Control and commitment in a high-tech cor-poration*. Philadelphia, PA: Temple University Press.

Mael, F.A. and B.E. Ashforth (1995). Loyal from day one—biodata, organizational iden-tification, and turnover among newcomers. *Personnel Psychology*, 48(2), 309–334.

Mael, F.A. and L.E. Tetrick (1992). Identifying organizational identification. *Educational and Psychological Measurement*, 52, 813–824.

Mannheim, B., Y. Baruch and J. Tal (1997). Testing alternative models for antecedents and outcomes of work centrality and job satisfaction. *Human Relations*, 50, 1537–1562.

Mathieu, J.E. and D.M. Zajac (1990). A review and meta-analysis of the antecedents, correlates and consequences of organizational commitment. *Psychological Bulletin*, 108, 171–194.

McGee, G.W. and R.C. Ford (1987). Two (or more) dimensions of organizational com-mitment: Reexamination of the affective and continuance commitment scales. *Journal of Applied Psychology*, 72, 638–642.

Meixner, W. and D. Bline (1989). Professional and job-related attitudes and the behaviors they influence among governmental accountants. *Accounting, Auditing and Accountability*, 2, 8–20.

Meyer, P.J. and J.N. Allen (1984). Testing the side bet theory of organizational commitment: Some methodological considerations. *Journal of Applied Psychology*, 69, 372–378.

Meyer, P.J. and J.N. Allen (1997). *Commitment in the workplace: Theory, research, and application*. Thousand Oaks, CA: Sage.

Meyer, J.P., N.J. Allen and I.R. Gellatly (1990). Affective and continuance commitment to the organization: Evaluation of measures and analysis of concurrent and time-lagged relations. *Journal of Applied Psychology*, 75, 710–720.

Mitchell, A.M., G.B. Jones and J.D. Krumboltz (Eds.) (1979). *Social learning theory and career decision making*. Cranston, RI: Carroll.

Morris, J.H. and D.J. Sherman (1981). Generalizability of organizational commitment model. *Academy of Management Journal*, 24, 512–526.

Morrow, P.C. (1983). Concept redundancy in organizational research: The case of work commitment. *Academy of Management Review*, 8, 486–500.

Mowday, R.T., R.M. Steers and L.M. Porter (1979). The measurement of organizational commitment. *Journal of Vocational Behavior*, 14, 224–247.

Mowday, R.T., L.M. Porter and R.M. Steers (1982). *Employee-organizational linkage*. New York: Academic Press.

Near, J.P. (1989). Organizational commitment among Japanese and U.S. workers. *Organization Studies*, 10, 281–300.

Norris, D.R. and R.H. Niebuhr (1984). Professionalism, organizational commitment and job satisfaction in an accounting organization. *Accounting, Organization and Society*, 9, 49–59.

O'Reilly, C.A. and J. Chatman (1986). Organizational commitment and psychological attachment: The effects of compliance, identification and internalization on prosocial behavior. *Journal of Applied Psychology*, 71, 492–499.

Osipow, S.H. (1987). Applying person-environment theory to vocational behavior. *Journal of Vocational Behavior*, 31, 333–336.

Ostroff, C. (1993). Relationship between Person-Environment congruence and organizational effectiveness. *Group and Organization Management*, 18, 103–122.

Oxford Dictionary (2000). Oxford: Oxford University Press.

Parasuraman, S. and S.A. Nachman (1987). Correlates of organizational and professional commitment: The case of musicians in symphony orchestras. *Group and Organization Studies*, 12, 287–303.

Peiperl, M.A. and Y. Baruch (1997). Back to square zero: The post-corporate career. *Organization Dynamics*, 25(4), 7–22.

Porter, L.W. and F.J. Smith (1970). The Etiology of Organizational Commitment. Unpublished paper, University of California, Irvine.

Porter, L.W., R.M. Steers, R.T. Mowday and P.V. Boulian (1974). Organizational commitment, job satisfaction and turnover among psychiatric technicians. *Journal of Applied Psychology*, 59, 603–609.

Rafaeli, A. (1997). What is an organization? Who are the members? In C.L. Cooper and S.E. Jackson (Eds.), *Creating tomorrow's organizations. A handbook for future research in organizational behavior* (pp. 121–138). Chichester: John Wiley & Sons.

Rafaeli, A. and M.G. Pratt (1993). Tailored meanings: On the meaning and impact of organizational dress. *Academy of Management Review*, 18, 32–55.

Randall, D.M. (1990). The consequences of organizational commitment: Methodological investigation. *Journal of Organizational Behavior*, 11, 361–378.

Reichers, A.E. (1985). A review and reconceptualization of organizational commitment. *Academy of Management Review*, 10, 465–476.

Ritzer, G. and H.M. Trice (1969). An empirical study of Howard Becker's side-bet theory. *Social Forces*, 47, 475–479.

Rokeach, M. (1973). *The nature of human values*. New York: Free Press.

Rotondi, T. (1975). Organizational identification and group involvement. *Academy of Management Journal*, 18, 892–896.

Russo, T.C. (1998). Organizational and professional identification: A case of newspaper journalists. *Management Communication Quarterly*, 12, 77–111.

Sheldon, M.E. (1971). Investment and involvement as mechanisms producing commitment to the organization. *Administrative Science Quarterly*, 16, 143–150.

Staw, B.M. (1977). *Two sides of commitment*. Paper presented at the meeting of Academy of Management, Orlando, FL.

Sullivan, S.E. (1999). The changing nature of careers: A review and research Agenda. *Journal of Management*, 25, 457–484.

Tajfel, H. (1981). *Human groups and social categories*. Cambridge: Cambridge University Press.

Tajfel, H. and J. Turner (1985). The social identity theory of intergroup behavior. In S. Worchel and W. Austin (Eds.), *Psychology of intergroup relations* (pp. 7–24). Chicago: Nelson-Hall.

Turner J.C. (1975). Social comparisons and social identity: Some prospects for intergroup behavior. *European Journal of Social Psychology*, 5, 5–34.

Van Dick, R., O. Christ, J. Stellmacher, U. Wagner, O. Ahlswede, C. Grubba, M. Hauptmeier, C. Hohfeld, K. Moltzen and P.A. Tissington (2004a). Should I stay or should I go? Explaining turnover intentions with organizational identification and job satisfaction. *British Journal of Management*, 15, 351–360.

Van Dick, R., U. Wagner, J. Stellmacher and O. Christ (2004b). The utility of a broader conceptualization of organizational identification: Which aspects really matter? *Journal of Occupational and Organizational Psychology*, 77, 171–191.

Van Maanen, J. and E.H. Schein (1979). Toward a Theory of Organizational Socialization. *Research in Organizational Behavior*, 1, 209–264.

Wallace, J.E. (1997). Becker's side-bet theory of commitment revisited: Is it time for moratorium or a resurrection? *Human Relations*, 50, 727–749.

Wan-Huggins, V.N., C.M. Riordan and R.W. Griffeth (1998). The development and longitudinal test of a model of organizational identification. *Journal of Applied Social Psychology*, 28, 724–749.

Williams, L.J. and J.T. Hazer (1986). Antecedents and consequences of satisfaction and commitment in turnover models: A re-analysis using latent variables equation methods. *Journal of Applied Psychology*, 71, 219–231.

Wittig-Berman, U. and D. Lang (1990). Organizational commitment and its outcomes: Differing effects of value commitment and continuance commitment on stress reactions, alienation and organization-serving behaviors. *Work & Stress*, 4, 167–177.

10

Apprentices' Experiences of Occupational and Organisational Commitment: An Empirical Investigation in a German Automobile Company

Bernd Haasler
University of Bremen, Germany

10.1 Introduction

In respect of their professional development and future career path, withdrawal from schools of general education and transition into dual vocational training in Germany characterises young people starting out in working life for the long term. Even before this first hurdle is reached, choosing a particular vocational training route and company are crucial steps for setting the course for subsequent identity-forming processes through gainful employment. Such identity-forming processes at the first hurdle of transition into working life are the subject of research from various perspectives (cf. Broeder, 1995; Heinz, 1999; Müller and Gangl, 2003; Ryan, 2000; Schober and Gaworek, 1996; Stern and Wagner, 1999). One characteristic feature of the German initial vocational training system, which is respected worldwide, is that those completing their apprenticeship develop strong vocational ties, and form an identity associated with these. Those ties typically overlie company-specific loyalties to the employer (cf. Rauner in this volume). The vocational self-awareness of skilled workers is valued as an important factor in relation to human resources distinguishing the workforce of German companies in processes of global competition.

A. Brown, S. Kirpal and F. Rauner (eds.), Identities at Work, 261–284.
© 2007 *Springer.*

This chapter reports on the results of a research project, which examined vocational skills and competence development among young people, who started out their working life in the German automotive industry with Volkswagen (VW) automobile company.[1] Empirical data collected during the first year of their apprenticeship shall be used to discuss decisive factors that significantly influence learning and work performance as well as apprentices' attitudes towards their vocational specialisation and the company they work for during this first phase of transition from school to work. The contextual background is characterised by highly automated production processes of an automobile company that belongs to German large-scale industry.

Although the instrument of evaluation tasks was developed primarily to assess facets of vocational competence that should foster work-based practice and performance (Haasler and Beelmann, 2005), the interpretation of the results in this context takes a different direction in order to understand better the identity formation processes that take place through learning a particular trade or vocational specialisation. The task solutions that the apprentices developed after their first year with the company are taken as an indicator of whether and to what extent the subjects are developing an understanding of the occupation to be learned. This is derived from the manner in which they tackle, cope with or fail to complete routine work tasks. While the results of the written survey served primarily to record motivations behind the young people's choice of occupation and different dimensions of identification (e.g. identification with the company, the occupation, progressive career options), the two sub-investigations in combination (written survey and vocational evaluation tasks) help to draw conclusions on the development of a vocational self-awareness among young apprentices.

The presentation of the methodological structure and the results of the investigation obtained with each instrument are set out below in the order in which they were positioned in the design of the research project. Within the framework of the project, studies were carried out with trainees learning five different occupational specialisations. This chapter confines itself to present the results of only one occupational group—taking those training as industrial toolmakers as an example. In industrialised countries, the toolmaker is a key occupation in the mass production of items (e.g. automobiles, household appliances, toys, furniture, packaging). In Germany,

[1] The research project was conducted in Germany between 1999 and 2003 and funded by the Federal Ministry of Education and Research (BMBF) and the Bund-Länder Commission for Educational Planning and Research Promotion (BLK).

there are currently around 18,000 young people in trade and industry undergoing vocational training to become toolmakers (cf. Bundesinstitut für Berufsbildung (BIBB), 2000).

10.2   Results of the Written Survey

Initially, the research project surveyed the beginner status of the trainees, the status at which they entered the company, concentrating on the following dimensions: the motivation behind the choice of occupation to be learned; if the young people had any previous experience that could be related to their vocational training; the expectations they had of their vocational training; their overall perception of the occupation they were learning; and the image they had of the company. The apprentices' attitudes to these dimensions can provide important information about their motivation, learning strategies and orientations on the basis of which they will be able to meet future work demands typical of their occupational field. In order to gain insight into skill-developing and identity-forming processes in a longitudinal perspective, the young people's attitudes and expectations were assessed four times over a 3½ -years apprenticeship period. The first point of intervention that is subject to this analysis took place in the very initial phase of the training programme, just a few weeks after joining the company.

To generate the quantitative data, the apprentices were asked to fill out the first written survey three months after joining the company. All beginning apprentices from one year at five of the company's branches in Germany were surveyed. The written survey comprised around 70 questions and statements on which the participants were to give answers and opinions. The response categories were presented as a unified concept and those surveyed were able to select from multiple choices. The survey was carried out on a time-scale of one hour and on the basis of voluntary participation at the vocational training school.

At the time of the survey the 194 trainees were on average 17.7 years old, the proportion of young males participating was 77 per cent. The overwhelming majority of trainees (78 per cent) entered the company with the educational background of a general school-leaving certificate above average. This means that young people taken on by the company as toolmaker apprentices have a significantly higher level of general school education than the toolmaker apprentices in German industry on average, who enter into the occupation with an attested lower level of certificates (Bundesinstitut für Berufsbildung (BIBB), 2000). This is partly due to the large number of applicants for apprenticeships at Volkswagen from which trainees can be selected each year (even though these are primarily for business/administrative jobs). Although quite typical for big companies, it was striking that in the case of Volkswagen 74 per cent of all those surveyed affirmed that they had relatives who worked at the company (at the company's headquarters in Wolfsburg this figure even reached 86 per cent).

10.2.1　Motivation Behind Choice of Occupation

The first question of the survey dealt with motivations for choosing to train as toolmaker. Only 15 per cent of the participants chose 'I always wanted to be a toolmaker' as their primary motivation (see Figure 10.1). This means that only a rather small proportion of the young people consider their chosen occupational specialisation also to be their dream job. 42 per cent admitted that they actually wanted to learn a different trade, but Volkswagen only offered them to train as toolmaker. In the choice of occupational specialisation, the trend of preference for business/administrative over industrial/technical jobs is demonstrated here too: for 17 per cent of those who actually wanted to learn a different specialisation, training in a commercial field at Volkswagen was their first

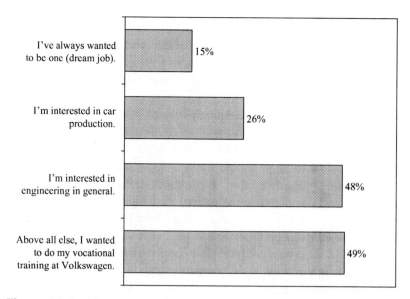

Figure 10.1　Motivation behind choice of occupation

choice. Overall, a large number of the applications for the approximately 30 different vocational training courses that the company offers are directed towards 'white-collar jobs'. After a general selection process that is identical for all applicants and occupational areas, many applicants who do not seem suitable for making a commercial career are advised to 'lower their sights' in that—against their original choice—the company offers them to follow an industrial/technical training path.

Taking into account the company's strategy to direct applicants to follow a technical instead of a commercial training route, it may not be surprising that the new apprentices are characterised by an evident distance from engineering. While about half of the young people confirm a general interest in engineering as their primary motivation, 26 per cent rather have a general interest in the production of cars. However, the primary motivation behind choosing the dual training programme to become a toolmaker is not the occupational field itself, but to work for Volkswagen: for 49 per cent of the participating apprentices being part of the company is the main reason behind their choice of occupation. Notably, the car manufacturer is the dominant employer over broad sections of particular regions in Germany, such as at the headquarters in Wolfsburg, where the company employs approximately 55,000 staff. This study, however, also included trainees from locations where Volkswagen does not hold the leading position in the labour market (e.g. in Brunswick and Hanover), but is just one employer among others where one can learn and practise the trade of toolmaker.

10.2.2 Previous Experience

The question about previous experiences may be another way to bring out the motivation behind occupational choices. It relates to experiences that the young people may have gained from the general education system or leisure through, for example, their hobbies, and that are considered useful for their vocational training. 44 per cent of the apprentices stated that while in general education prior to their vocational training they were interested in lessons relating to engineering (e.g. physics lessons). Nearly half of those surveyed had previous experience with technical equipment that they have dismantled and repaired (e.g. washing machine, moped, computer). Within the framework of practical work experience acquired during general education, 34 per cent of those surveyed had previously been to production works and gathered their first impressions of industrial/technical work there (see Figure 10.2).

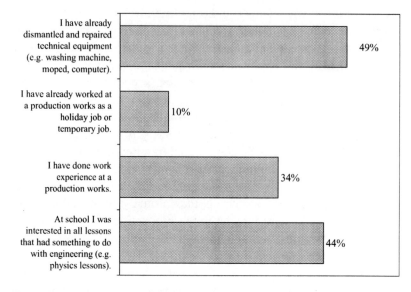

Figure 10.2   Previous experience

That about half of the young people have gained previous practical experience through dabbling with technical equipment (repairs to household appliances, vehicles, computers) corresponds with an interest in engineering as the main reason behind their occupational choice. However, the fact that fewer than half of the apprentices state interest in engineering or previous technical experience as their motivation is surprising, considering they are choosing to train in a rather demanding occupational area in the high-technology sector following a 3½-year apprenticeship programme.

10.2.3   Ideas and Expectations of the Vocational Training

In order to draw conclusions about the trainees' learning and work motivation, they were also asked about their ideas and expectations of the vocational training they were undergoing (see Figure 10.3). 8 per cent of the young people have no expectations of the 42-month vocational training, as what is more important to them is to make fast progress in their career development at the company afterwards. 13 percent of those surveyed showed a rather passive approach and displayed disinterest: they stated that they had not thought about the vocational training assuming that it is already mapped out anyway.

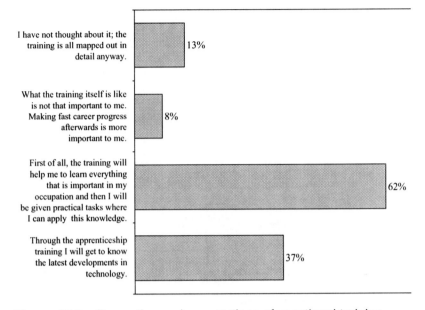

Figure 10.3   Perception and expectations of vocational training

The expectation of getting to know the latest developments in technology through training is shared by 37 per cent, a figure that appears rather surprising, considering that these are young apprentices, who start out their working life with Europe's biggest car manufacturer. In terms of technology, tool and mould design in the leading companies in the automobile industry are regarded as the 'cutting edge' in the sector of tool making. The young apprentices' expectations of their training and future vocational specialisation seem to be dissociated from this.

10.2.4   Image of the Company

For this question, the range of response categories in the survey was of a four-level gradation. The scale ranged from complete agreement ('correct'), via a toning down ('more correct than incorrect') through to the opposite pole of rejection ('more incorrect than correct' and 'incorrect'). For clearer presentation purposes, the following illustrations bring together both positive assessments and both negative assessments respectively. This section revealed the following: most of the young people (the overwhelming majority of those who did not yet have a driver's licence at the time the survey was performed) agreed that the car

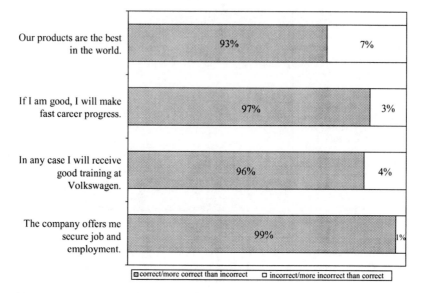

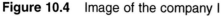

Figure 10.4   Image of the company I

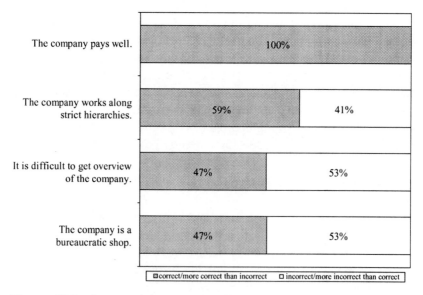

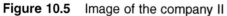

Figure 10.5   Image of the company II

manufacturer's product range is the 'best in the world'. One important reason for the extraordinarily positive image the employees have of the products they manufacture is probably the attractive offers that the car manufacturer makes to its employees for buying vehicles from the group's own range. Sales to its own employees—without costly sales channels—represent an important share of the group's turnover in Germany. The young people's expectations of the company include primarily receiving good training and, if one performs accordingly, to progress quickly in their careers (see Figure 10.4).

The trainees' belief that the employer pays well for its employees' work is prominent as is the impression that the company offers secure jobs and employment to its employees (99 per cent agreement). Rather ambivalent are the young people's feelings about the organisational structure of such a large company (see Figure 10.5): more than half of those surveyed attested that they experience rather fixed hierarchical structures at the company. Accompanying this assessment the apprentices find it difficult to get an overview of the company, which they regard as being highly bureaucratic.

10.2.5 Initial Experiences of Vocational Training

After three months at the company, the participants were asked about their experiences of learning and working at the company up to that point. Figure 10.6 shows in what way initial expectations of the vocational training at Volkswagen have been confirmed or rather disappointed and how learning and work practice reality differ from what the trainees initially expected. 94 per cent of the participating apprentices document the noted change of learning from general education to vocational training by affirming that 'you can knuckle down to work here'. At the same time, 41 per cent of the young people stated that what they experienced in the first three months of vocational training is that they have to learn a lot of theory before they are introduced to interesting job tasks. Accordingly, many trainees understand the way the week is arranged in the first year of the dual training programme (two days a week at the vocational school and three days learning and working at the company) as a predominantly theoretical way of accumulating knowledge. The provocative statement 'In principle, it is just like school, only with a bit more practical work involved' is affirmed by 18 per cent. In contrast to this, however, 82 per cent of all participating apprentices expect that they will be given challenging tasks very soon after starting training so that they can 'show their stuff'.

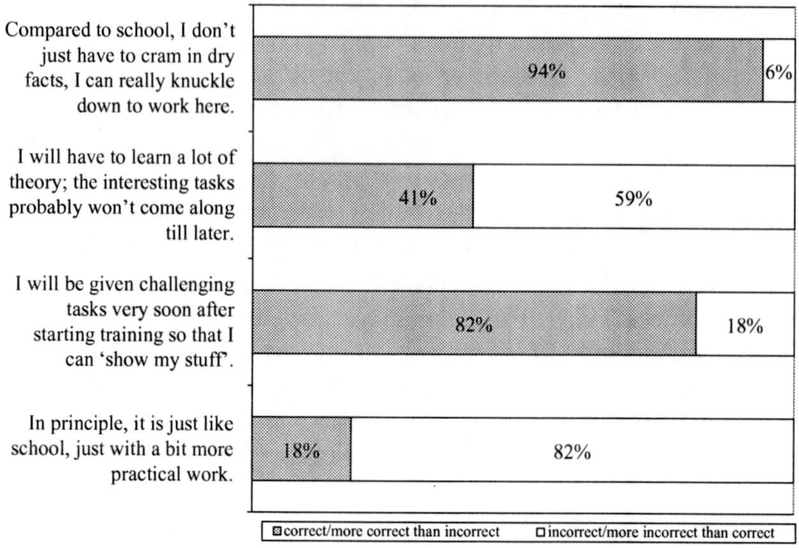

Compared to school, I don't just have to cram in dry facts, I can really knuckle down to work here.	94%	6%
I will have to learn a lot of theory; the interesting tasks probably won't come along till later.	41%	59%
I will be given challenging tasks very soon after starting training so that I can 'show my stuff'.	82%	18%
In principle, it is just like school, just with a bit more practical work.	18%	82%

☒ correct/more correct than incorrect   ☐ incorrect/more incorrect than correct

Figure 10.6   Initial experiences of vocational training I

What we produce here has hardly featured yet.	27%	73%
I have been given meaningful tasks.	57%	43%
I have mainly produced practice pieces.	43%	57%
I feel as though I am among friends and acquaintances here.	95%	5%

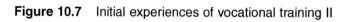
☒ correct/more correct than incorrect   ☐ incorrect/more incorrect than correct

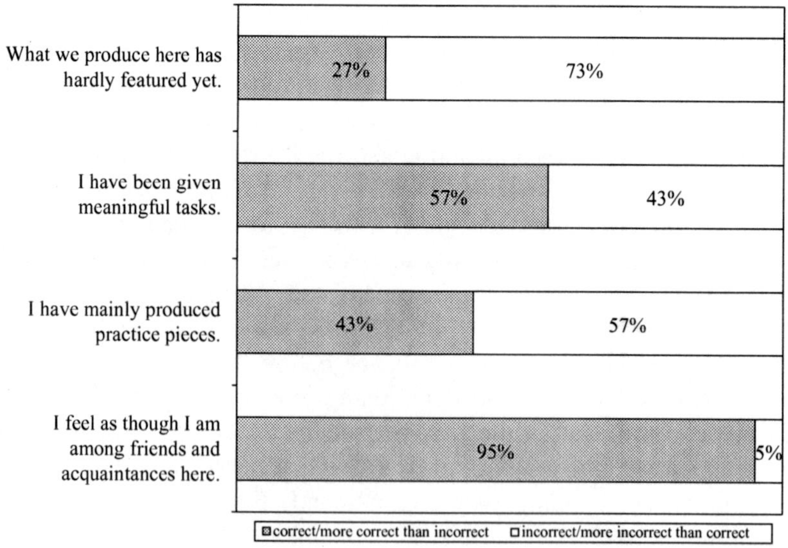

Figure 10.7   Initial experiences of vocational training II

As acquiring basic knowledge and skills during the first year mainly takes place in the company's training workshops, training centres and laboratories, 27 per cent of the young people agree with the statement that elements related to automobile production hardly appear in the first three months of their vocational training. Instead, the young apprentices mainly produce practice pieces and, according to the results of the survey, many of them are not sure of the connection between those workshop tasks and the occupational specialisation they are training for. The mainly context-free basic technical skills training in metal engineering led half of the trainees to believe that they have not been given meaningful tasks in the first three months at the company (see Figure 10.7).

The trainees' feeling of being integrated in the social milieu at the company scored the highest level of agreement. Due to their positive social experiences, 95 per cent of the new apprentices feel 'as though they are among friends and acquaintances' after just three months at the company.

10.2.6   Career Plans

The final section of the survey addressed forms of medium-term career planning that the apprentices are pursuing shortly after joining the company (see Figure 10.8).

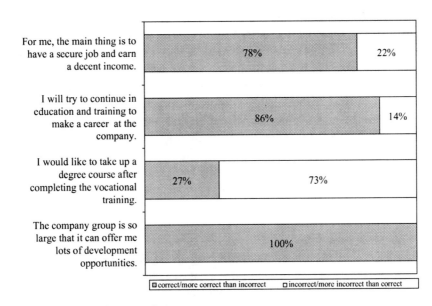

Figure 10.8   Career plans

The rather unambitious statement that the main concern would be a secure job and a decent income does not rule out the option of pursuing further continuing training. What stands out is the apprentices' willingness to offer long-term loyalty to the company, evidenced by 80 per cent of those surveyed in their statement that they wish to continue in education and make a career at the company. All participants consider there to be lots of professional development opportunities at the company, due to the company's size, employing approximately 340,000 staff worldwide. 27 per cent of the young people would like to take up a degree course after finishing their training.

In summary, the survey results lead to the conclusion that the primary motivation behind the young people's choice to enter into vocational training to become a toolmaker is not an interest in engineering or mass production, but to join the Volkswagen company and become a member of staff there. The toolmaker had only been the dream job of a very small number of participating apprentices. Instead, almost half the trainees wanted to learn a different trade, most of them wanting to enter into a business/administrative occupation rather than a technical one. Previous experience with, or a marked interest in, engineering among the young people, which could be useful in specialising as a toolmaker, is not present in any prominent form.

The young apprentices have an extremely positive image of the Volkswagen company in terms of working conditions, job security and product range, and are expecting to receive good training. Their initial experiences after having been training with the company for three months stand out for the extremely positive social climate among colleagues, supervisors and trainees. Desired career options for approximately one quarter of those surveyed involve a degree course after having completed the 3½-year apprenticeship programme. A large number of the new apprentices, however, also aim at making a career at the company, which is documented by their high level of willingness to pursue continuing company-based training.

10.3   Evaluation Tasks

In the research design, the written survey was supplemented by a second investigation applying an instrument of qualitative research. In combination with the written survey as presented above, vocational evaluation tasks were realised during the course of the apprenticeship training to evaluate stages of trainees' skills and competence development.

Evaluation tasks confront the apprentice with practical work challenges in the form of concrete work tasks that need to be mastered in a particular realistic work situation. These tasks are designed in a way so as to be considered prototypical of the domain-specific challenges, and therefore their solution characteristics can be abstracted and applied to similar tasks within the same domain. Based on the concept of development tasks (Havighurst, 1948), Gruschka (1985) developed domain-specific evaluation tasks, which were initially used in the area of vocational education as an instrument for evaluating in-school training of prospective teachers (Gruschka, 1985). An attempt to formulate such tasks for the area of industrial/technical vocational training has been presented by a German working group led by Rainer Bremer (Bremer, 2003; Bremer and Haasler, 2004).

In principle, vocational evaluation tasks present the subjects with a problem of a type that they have never before tackled (these tasks are expressly not an input-output measurement in the form of monitoring the ability to learn). The way in which the participants solve (or fail to solve) these problems demonstrates and reveals their work practice-oriented problem solving strategies. The formulation of the task should avoid any kind of help or guidance: from a professional point of view a concise and matter-of-fact formulation of the task must disclose a clear order, which implies and determines the route towards a solution by way of performance requirements, but without favouring one particular solution.

The identification and formulation of domain-specific evaluation tasks (which essentially represent core tasks of an occupation) require an intensive knowledge of the requirements of skilled work and the practical expertise of those who perform the daily work tasks typical of the particular occupational field. In order to be able to interpret the participants' various solutions in an adequate manner, it is also necessary to have a sound knowledge of the conditions under which vocational skills and competences are acquired (e.g. curricula, work environment, organisational forms of training).

Extensive empirical investigations of research into vocational training has led to the supposition that successful skilled workers have internalised three distinctive strategies that enable them to use new work experiences to enhance and update their professionalism (Bremer, 2003, p. 112f). Typically, they have adopted (i) a vocational learning strategy, (ii) a particular working strategy, and (iii) a strategy for professional cooperation. These strategies are embodied and 'interconnected' in the concrete work outcomes, methods, procedures and organisational forms of skilled work. The data collected by using and implementing evaluation tasks—in the form of the various problem-solving solutions that the subjects are presented with—are interpreted with the help of development hermeneutics and then structured and categorised according to the three strategies. The way in which a vocational evaluation task is tackled and the inherent problem resolved does not only give insight into trainees' competence development and the effectiveness of their vocational training, it also provides valuable information on the occupational understanding and self-awareness that the trainees develop in the course of their apprenticeship.

10.3.1   Tackling the Presented Evaluation Task

Out of the 194 toolmaker trainees, 90 were presented with a vocational development task at the end of the first year of training (46 per cent of the total number). The task consisted of the following exercise: to incorporate into existing blank dice made from light metal (length of edge: 30 millimetre) the 'number of spots' found on a dice (to mark the correct number of depressions for each of the six sides). In addition, a production proposal should be put forward to one customer who requires a lot size of 1,000 units, as well as to another customer who wants 50,000 dice. In the run-up to the investigation, several experts of skilled work generally accepted this task as a standard problem arising in the domain of tool making; one which, on the one hand, can be tackled successfully by trainees and, on the other, still possesses challenging problem characteristics for an advanced worker or an expert. Given a time limit of four hours, the trainees were asked to penetrate the problem theoretically and demonstrate various solutions by means of descriptions and sketches. The task was carried out in the company's training rooms; the aids the young people were allowed to use included textbooks, tables, calculators and drawing materials.

The main result of the investigation shall be explained below by taking two different types of solution generated by the subject groups as an example. While the trainees who suggest producing the depressions on the blank dice by following manual production processes (see Figure 10.9) prove that after a training period of 12 months they still have no concept of the work processes the toolmaker typically deals with, the second example illustrates a realistic professional solution.

The first example illustrates a solution type that is conceptualised along manual work processes. The trainees suggest processing the item 'directly', the 'indirect' production of items using tools characteristic of

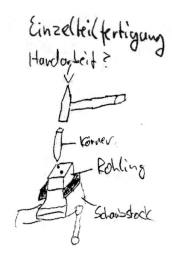

Figure 10.9 Solution type of a manual unit production—'the craftsperson'

the occupation is not present in the solutions offered. Here, the presented solution reflects the experiences the trainees gained at the training workshop. They provide a workable model of how the depressions can be made. They fail, however, to understand that the toolmaker does not manufacture the final product, but that the occupational profile essentially consists of making the tools to produce parts. Thus, the trainees present a solution that does not correspond with the occupational profile, because the solution may only work if the task was to consist of producing one single dice, but not for mass production.

The most obvious result is that a large number of trainees fail to realise that essentially the tool making occupation is an 'implementer of mass production'. This gross misunderstanding may be explained by the nature of the vocational training during the first year. Basic training in all aspects of the metal engineering trade in the first year—which in the field under investigation is mainly organised in training workshops and laboratories and taking forms of general instead of domain-specific teaching—does not seem to contribute to an understanding of the domain-specific problem solving processes at the level of skilled work. The learning and working strategies of the training workshop (embodied here by the manual production of units) are for the most part transferred directly by the trainees to practice-based professional problems and challenges. This is revealed clearly in the young people's obvious lack of general knowledge about the tool making sector. Knowledge from context-free basic training in the area of metal engineering is applied and characterises the various solutions presented for this evaluation task, which take completely insufficient account of the utility value aspect. With this kind of implemented working strategy only very few solutions satisfy the utility value aspect of mass production. Making thousands of punch marks 'by hand' without any aids would, without thinking, transfer learning and working strategies from the training workshop to realistic work problems in a way that is completely unsuitable for the task.

Trainees, whose various solutions could be designated to the type 'toolmaker', generated proposals for solutions ranging from simple aids through to complex tools (such as the impressing tool in Figure 10.10).

The illustrated proposal enables the 21 depressions on the dice to be manufactured in one stage of production. Although this production approach was generated by a trainee after just one year of training, it can be rated as a professional solution on the level of skilled work. The technical faithfulness to detail of the sketch or trouble-free implementation in practice is not a deciding factor in the interpretation of this solution type. Essentially, it is recognisable that the applied working and learning strategies are adequately geared towards the current problem situation. Trainees, who presented a solution of the type 'toolmaker',

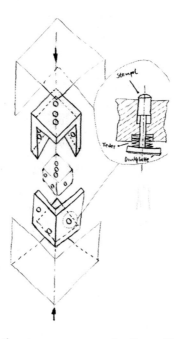

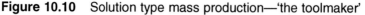

Figure 10.10 Solution type mass production—'the toolmaker'

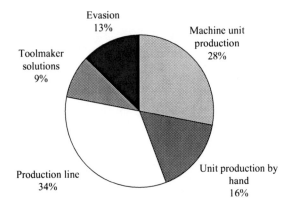

Figure 10.11 Overall categorisation and allocation of the presented solutions

demonstrate that they have developed both specialist skills as well as an understanding of the occupational field they are training for. Their proposed solution proves that they are able to approach realistic work tasks from a professional perspective.

Although all 90 apprentices chosen randomly were trained under very similar conditions in their first year of training, it is the 'range' of various solutions generated that stands out most of all (see Figure 10.11). The various solutions to the problem that the participants produced were allocated to five solution types developed from the material. In addition to the two solution types described above (the 'craftsperson' and the 'toolmaker'), the evasive solution type, which was chosen by 13 per cent of subjects, remains to be discussed. This group rejected the task by passing it on to others ('give the task to the milling shop in the form of an order') or by drawing a 'black box' sketch, in which the production step to be implemented is deliberately ignored. These examples show that a considerable number of participants evade the task, either because they are completely over-challenged or because they do not consider the task to be within their area of responsibility. In terms of directing the question under investigation towards assessing the young apprentices' vocational understanding and self-awareness as prospective toolmakers, we can conclude that evading the evaluation task means that the trainee has not developed an occupational identity as toolmaker in her or his approach to problems. The fist step would imply to try to develop a solution and to recognise that it is professional to be able to provide an answer to this type of problem.

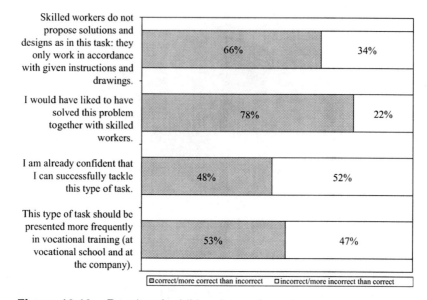

Figure 10.12   Results of additional questionnaire

At the end of the exercise, the evaluation task was complemented by a short questionnaire that the participants were asked to fill in directly after completing the task. The aim was to assess the participants' view on four pre-determined statements. The first statement presented the subjects with a deliberately polarising expression about the requirements of skilled work (see Figure 10.12). Here, 66 per cent confirmed that tasks such as the presented evaluation task typically do not or do not tend to form part of the duties of a skilled worker. The majority of the trainees pictured the skilled worker as somebody who mainly performs tasks under supervision and according to clear instructions with little scope for individual design. The second statement presented a collective dimension asking whether the trainees would have liked to solve this problem together with more experienced colleagues. A very significant majority (78 per cent) agreed with this item, while by contrast, 22 per cent expressed that they would not like to cooperate with other skilled workers to solve the problem. These responses allow for a preview of the trainees' concept of professional collaboration, which they need to develop in order to position themselves in their future community of practice. This group of participants, who prefer to work individually, reflects the training practice of the first year of industrial vocational training in the German large-scale industry, during which encounters or cooperation between the young apprentices and experienced workers do not occur. During the first year of training apprentices typically spend most of their time in training rooms, training workshops and laboratories away from the practical work environment. In-company operations, where apprentices learn to deal with and process real work orders under realistic working conditions, do not tend to start until the second year of training.

The third statement concerns issues of self-confidence and whether the trainees feel confident to be able to successfully tackle this type of task. Despite the large number of rather unsuitable and unprofessional proposals for task solutions (only 9 per cent can be considered a 'toolmaker' type of solution), almost half the young people confirm this item largely trusting in their vocational abilities and skills, while 52 per cent disagree professing that they cannot yet successfully tackle this type of task. The last statement assesses whether the apprentices think that such kinds of evaluation tasks should be presented more frequently in the vocational training. Just as in the previous question, one half of the trainees is polarised in the negative section, while the other half take a more positive view. The problems the young trainees experienced in grasping and tackling tasks that appeared to be highly unusual and open to interpretation were evident during the performance of the evaluation task. With abundant queries the participants aimed at obtaining more concrete guidelines to channel through to a correct result and rule out any incorrect possibilities. The much observed, expectant and intensive leafing through of textbooks with the hope of discovering a sample solution that could be adapted was a clear indication of helplessness, in many respects admitting the unsuitability of the learning strategies pursued until then.

10.3.2 Interpretation of the Results

The rather high percentage of solution types 'machine unit production' and 'unit production by hand' is clearly attributable to the training practice. One can favourably describe the still crafts-oriented basic training in metal engineering as a complete success. This training approach, however, has formed the trainees to such an extent that they tend to apply those basic metal working skills they have acquired during their first year of training to all kinds of work-related tasks and challenges. Those who had little previous contact with the field of the toolmaker occupation, and within the scope of training have only manufactured components manually and by unit production, cannot develop a comprehensible perception of industrial mass production. Up to this point, of course, the apprentices' contact with tools used in production was limited to the phase of 'exploring the company and the occupational field' during the first weeks at the company. This excursion, which tended to focus on the organisation of the company and less so on the occupation, provided even the most interested trainees with little insight into what is involved in mass production. The primarily context-free basic training in metal engineering has marked generations of electrical and metal engineering trainees in Germany—not just in large-scale industry—in the first phase of their training. Even though today they take a different shape and are full of melodious terminology specific to vocational education, the training courses are still strongly tied to their 1930s origins (following the motto 'Eisen erzieht' ('iron forms')).

From the investigation, it remains to be stressed that most of the trainees believe that skilled toolmakers act as 'executors' in accordance with the directions and instructions of others, and that they do not take a problem-solving approach independently. The idea the trainees have of the tasks of skilled work related to the occupational field they are training for after one year of training can well be explained by their formative working and learning environment, which is far away from the actual community of practice they will themselves become a part of at a later stage. In their perception of the occupation, the young people spectacularly underestimate the demanding tasks that the skilled toolmakers are required to tackle and the important role that the intermediate skills level in engineering plays at the interface between mass production and design.

The method of assessing vocational learning by way of evaluation tasks, as presented here, requires some final appreciation and also critical examination. This methodological approach to recording relevant domain-specific facets of competence presents the subjects with practically relevant, but not trivial, tasks, whereby it is assumed that these are prototypical of the requirements of the occupation and therefore their solution characteristics can be assessed to provide an indication of the vocational skills acquired to date. This encumbers the method with hermeneutically not unproblematic implications that are not accessible to any basic solution. Therefore, in principle, the objection cannot be refuted that ultimately it remains to be seen whether reliable conclusions can be drawn from the subjects' ability to penetrate and resolve problems theoretically, and their ability to act and deal with challenges and problems in a realistic work situation. It is possible and likely that skilled workers, who demonstrate their expertise every day in their work practice, are not necessarily experts on verbalisation or drawing.

As, in this sense, we cannot take for granted that they are 'experts on communication', there remains the suspicion that their ability to reveal their own learning and work strategies may be less developed than their actual ability to apply those strategies in a real work setting (cf. Hacker, 1996, p. 9). In this respect, it is worth taking this view into account when interpreting the presented solutions of the evaluation tasks. An appropriately sensitised investigation design and intelligently developed items for the accompanying written surveys can, however, limit the risk of misinterpretations.

10.4 Reflections

In conclusion for the two sub-investigations, it can be stated that the German apprentices at Volkswagen in the first phase of their vocational training identify with the company to a considerably stronger extent than they do with their chosen occupational specialisation. They are well informed about the products, working conditions and services offered by their employer. In contrast, after one year of training at the company most of the trainees are still unclear about the training content, the occupational profile they are training for and, above all, about the work demands that they are likely to encounter later on as fully skilled workers. Motivations behind their choice of occupational specialisation are not really connected to the occupational profile. Other elements prevail such as becoming a member of the company and job security. What is rather surprising for industrial/technical apprentices in the high technology driven automobile industry is the young people's apparent distance to engineering and mass production. The young apprentices do not display any distinct interest in engineering, neither in terms of motivation behind their choice of occupation, nor in respect of previous practical experience, which could be useful for the chosen domain.

From the perspective of the company, the trainees' first phase at the company can be regarded as very successful. For Volkswagen the vocational training programmes form part of a broader staff development strategy that works towards developing the young people's loyalty to the company, including already at a very early stage socialising them to become committed staff members. After just a few months, the young people have detached themselves from their status as students, now fully identifying themselves as Volkswagen employees. In the sense of a corporate strategy and aligning corporate and individual values this is highly desirable. The overall goal, however, of the German vocational education and training system, that an apprenticeship training should be the basis of young people's future autonomy in working life enabling the individual to actively use opportunities for professional mobility for enhancing the acquired knowledge and skills, does not become evident from this investigation.

Most of the young people, who participated in the investigation, feel at the company 'as though they are among friends and acquaintances'. This finding reflects, on the one hand, the high proportion of inter-generational connections among employees working for the company (nearly 80 per cent of the participants confirmed having relatives who work at the factory), and also, on the other hand, the positive social atmosphere that the trainees perceive while undergoing the vocational training. The 'soft transition' from school to the labour market, a distinct feature of the German Dual System, certainly contributes greatly towards the trainees' surprisingly smooth integration as employees of the company (cf. Rauner, 2000). In addition, the major company involved in this study shapes the young people's process of transition into learning and working arrangements in a very 'school-like' manner. The practical work environment does not appear during the first phase of the voca-tional training, and similarly, the domain-specific work challenges are not addressed and can largely be ignored. The first year of training at the company is distinguished by its protective character organised largely along school lines and dissociated from the day-to-day work of the skilled workers in the factory, and can be described as a toned down continuation of learning strategies used during general school education.

Based on the results of the investigation it can be stated that the level of development of vocational skills achieved by the trainees is markedly inferior to the level of integration as employees of the company. The young people's identification with the occupation and aptitude for fitting into the practical environment of a toolmaker are hardly noticeable after one year at the company. According to this investigation in a large-scale industry, it seems that the first phase of transition from pupil to employee is mainly shaped by the young people's identification with the company, the occupational specialisation is significantly less important. However, investigations into later stages of training show that as apprentices are being increasingly confronted with the day-to-day company-based work practice and demands, they also necessarily tend to focus on their occu-pational area. Whether the tradition of German employees' strong iden-tification with their occupational specialisation is actually showing signs of disintegration and which loyalties are moving to the fore instead (Haasler and Kirpal, 2004) addresses issues of wider research interest. The results could contribute to an elaboration on and evaluation of skilled workers' facets of identification with gainful employment.

References

Bremer, R. (2003). Zur Konzeption von Untersuchungen beruflicher Identität und fachlicher Kompetenz—ein empirisch-methodologischer Beitrag zu einer berufspädagogischen Entwicklungstheorie. In K. Jenewein, P. Knauth, P. Röben and G. Zülch (Eds.), *Kompetenzentwicklung in Arbeitsprozessen—Beiträge zur Konferenz der Arbeitsgemeinschaft gewerblich technische Wissenschaften und ihre Didaktiken in der Gesellschaft für Arbeitswissenschaft am 23/24, September 2002 in Karlsruhe* (pp. 107–121). Baden-Baden: Nomos.

Bremer, R. and B. Haasler (2004). Analyse der Entwicklung fachlicher Kompetenz und beruflicher Identität in der beruflichen Erstausbildung. *Zeitschrift für Pädagogik*, 2, 162–181.

Bundesinstitut für Berufsbildung (BIBB) (2000). *Statistische Datenblätter 'Werkzeugmechaniker'*. Retrieved 20 May 2002 from the World Wide Web: http://www.bibb.de/indexber.htm

den Broeder, C. (1995). *The match between education and work: what can we learn from the German apprenticeship system?* The Hague: Central Planning Bureau.

Gruschka, A. (1985). *Wie Schüler Erzieher werden*. Wetzlar: Verlag Büchse der Pandora.

Haasler, B. and G. Beelmann (2005). Kompetenzen erfassen—Berufliche Entwicklungsaufgaben. In F. Rauner (Ed.), *Handbuch Berufsbildungsforschung* (pp. 622–628). Bielefeld: Bertelsmann.

Haasler, B. and S. Kirpal (2004). Berufs- und Arbeitsidentitäten von Experten in Praxisgemeinschaften—Ergebnisse aus europäischen Forschungsvorhaben. In J. Pangalos, S. Knutzen and F. Howe (Eds.), *Informatisierung von Arbeit, Technik und Bildung—Kurzfassung der Konferenzbeiträge* (pp. 48–51). Hamburg: Technische Universität Hamburg-Harburg.

Hacker, W. (1996). Diagnose von Expertenwissen: von Abzapf- (broaching-) zu Aufbau- ([re-] construction-) Konzepten. Berlin: Akademie-Verlag.

Havighurst, R.J. (1948). *Development tasks and education*. New York: Longmans Green and Co.

Heinz, W.R. (Ed.) (1999). *From education to work: Cross-national perspectives*. Cambridge: Cambridge University Press.

Müller, W. and M. Gangl (2003). *Transitions from education to work in Europe: The integration of youth into EU labour markets*. Oxford: Oxford University Press.

Rauner, F. (2000). Offene dynamische Beruflichkeit. Zur Überwindung einer fragmentierten industriellen Berufstradition. In G. Kutscha (Ed.), *Deregulierung der Arbeit—Pluralisierung der Bildung?* (pp. 183–203). Opladen: Leske + Budrich.

Ryan, P. (2000). *The school-to-work transition: A cross-national perspective*. Cambridge: University of Cambridge/Department of Applied Economics.

Schober, K. and M. Gaworek (Eds.) (1996). *Berufswahl: Sozialisations- und Selektionsprozesse an der ersten Schwelle*. Nürnberg: Institut für Arbeitsmarkt- und Berufsforschung der Bundesanstalt für Arbeit (IAB).

Stern, D. and D.A. Wagner (1999). *International perspectives on the school-to-work transition*. Cresskill, NJ: Hampton Press.

11

The Individualisation
of Identification with Work in
a European Perspective

Simone Kirpal*, Alan Brown† and M'Hamed Dif‡

*University of Bremen, Germany;
†University of Warwick, UK;
‡University Louis Pasteur, France

Individuals are actors in society who shape their own occupational trajectories and careers. Through the process of individualisation (Beck, 1992) individuals take on a new role as coordinators of their personal work biographies: they become actors who actively shape their individualised work orientations and commitment patterns, which a few decades ago used to be shaped much more on a collective basis. While companies frequently respond to market competition in a global economy by increasing external and internal flexibility of work and employment (Müller and Scherer, 2003; Reilly, 1998), new skills demands and more flexible employment patterns have major implications for employees affecting their learning and skills development as well as employees' work and career orientations.

While inter-firm mobility increases (DeFillippi and Arthur, 1994; Kanter, 1989) and new forms of flexible work arrangements emerge (Gottlieb et al., 1998) job security and long-term company attachment are becoming less prevalent in many contexts. For many individuals this means that developing a vocational orientation and planning a progressive career become more complex and difficult processes (Beck and Beck-Gernsheim, 1994; Keupp et al., 1999). Today, employees in some contexts are challenged to plan and organise their individualised careers away from long-term company attachment and pre-structured

A. Brown, S. Kirpal and F. Rauner (eds.), Identities at Work, 285–314.

career patterns under the condition of much higher possibilities for occupational mobility and transitions. The notion of the 'boundaryless' career (DeFillippi and Arthur, 1994; Hall, 1996; Mirvis and Hall, 1994; Sullivan, 1999) not only suggests that in future organisational commitment and socialisation may lose their significance for employees, but also that careers become much more individualised. Even though these ideas are far from being realised in many contexts, and counter trends are also evident, it is clear that for some individuals who previously could have expected relatively stable organisational careers these hopes are being dashed. For such individuals, this means they need to integrate their changing work agenda and divergent work experiences into a coherent self-picture. Sennett (1998) has illustrated that this process can present quite a challenge to the individual, if unexpectedly made redundant, as it creates internal and external conflicts that need to be resolved in order to secure successful integration, not only into work, but also into society as a whole.

This chapter presents results of a qualitative study looking at how employees at the intermediate skills level working in manufacturing and service sectors respond to changes at work, high levels of work flexibility and changing skills requirements in particular. The objective is to illustrate and better understand how employees respond to changes in their working environment and working lives through identifying strategies that individuals develop in dealing with such changes and delineating patterns of individuals' reactions, adjustments and forms of adaptation.

11.1   Methods

The results we are presenting are based on interviews conducted in 2001 and 2002 with employees working in engineering, nursing and telecommunications in France, Germany and the UK. These data were generated in the context of the research project 'Vocational Identity, Flexibility and Mobility in the European Labour Market—FAME' funded under the 5th EU Framework Programme (for details see FAME Consortium, 2003; Kirpal, 2004a).

The three sectors were selected, because they represent different occupational traditions and work settings on the one hand, and different dynamics and challenges with regards to flexibility and mobility on the other hand. The metal working industry represents a traditional production sector that has gradually declined during the last two decades under the pressure of rationalisation. The strong industrial tradition in many areas attributes a significant weight to the national and cultural embedding of the industry, and findings for metal work and engineering differed considerably between the three countries of investigation. The tradition of strong collective identities can be attributed to the historical role of professional associations and unions, but changes in the structural context have led to changes in employees' identification with work, particularly in response to increased competition and changing patterns of work organisation. In health care, a traditional service sector, the focus was placed on nursing. Nursing represents a highly formalised profession showing many similarities in terms of nurses' identification with work across the three countries of investigation. Apart from being linked to a strong work ethic and moral commitment, the rather homogeneous professional profile across countries can be explained by a more or less standardised set of work tasks organised around direct patient care. Finally, telecommunications is characterised by dynamism and high pressures for flexibility and mobility of employees combined with fast changing job profiles, skills requirements and organisational structures. Here, we can observe the strong influence that flexibility, as well as internationalisation and globalisation, can have on the development of skills and work identities. More highly qualified young employees, in particular, use flexibility, mobility and learning as a means to develop transversality, shape their professional careers and improve their working conditions. In the modern segments of the sector the trend towards patterns of self-employment and individualised work identities was most obvious.

Overall, the project was structured into three research phases, each supporting the previous one both methodologically and with contextual information. After a literature review that investigated key topic-related concepts (see FAME Consortium in this volume), the empirical investigation aimed at assessing organisational as well as individual perspectives. Interviews with managers and representatives of human resources departments helped to assess the issue from the management or organisational perspective. The focus here was to explore structural conditions including changes in work organisation, work profiles and skilling needs, and identify employers' expectations in terms of employees' levels of identification with work or with the company. Interview questions related to how managers experience and value employees' capacity to deal with changes at work (in terms of flexibility, mobility, work organisation, working conditions and learning demands) and how this might affect employees' work and learning attitudes (for details see FAME Consortium, 2003). The interview results addressed company data and products, work profiles of skilled workers, skills requirements and recruitment principles, learning, initial and further education and training, career options, work organisation and demands for flexibility and mobility of employees.

As the emphasis of the project was placed on individuals' orientations and strategies of making adjustments at work over time, the major qualitative research focused on interviews with employees (see Table 11.1). This second part of the empirical investigation aimed at deciphering how employees perceive and cope with changes at work, and how these changes might affect their work identity, commitment patterns, work and learning attitude and career orientations. Interview questions included, for example, with what employees identify at work; how they respond to new skill requirements; how they perceive formal and informal learning; how they cope with changing work settings; and how they think all this affects their motivation and work performance. The project focused on employees at the intermediate skills level, mainly skilled workers, representing a wide range of qualifications, work experiences and job profiles. Based on common selection criteria (different levels of initial education and training; varying job profiles and occupational backgrounds; work experiences ranging from newly qualified to those having a work experience of 20 years or more; gender balance) the project partners attempted to sample a diversity of employees' backgrounds and work experiences. The results presented here are based on interviews with 345 individuals.

The project adopted a qualitative research approach applying semi-structured, problem-centred interviews (Witzel, 1996), which, depending on the situational appropriateness, were either individual, in-depth interviews or focus group discussions with 2 to 6 employees usually not exceeding 90 minutes. Typically interviews were tape-recorded and transcribed verbatim. The project partners reached a common

Table 11.1 Sample composition

	Sector of Investigation						
	Engineering		Health Care/Nursing		Telecommunications		N
Country	Managers	Employees	Managers	Employees	Managers	Employees	
France	8	30	7	25	6	30	106
Germany	10	33	8	35	7	31	124
UK	10	38	10	24	8	25	115
N	28	101	25	84	21	86	345

understanding on a set of interview guidelines that were slightly adapted according to the particularities of the respective national contexts. All partners carried out initial pilot interviews for each empirical research phase to pre-test the interview guidelines and the feasibility of comparing the results later on.

Data analysis followed an inductive, grounded theory development approach (Glaser, 1978; Strauss and Corbin, 1990) that was complemented by developing collective case studies (Stake, 2000). This material was synthesised according to evaluation categories that the partners commonly identified and that were adjusted and refined in the course of categorising and interpreting the empirical data. Evaluation categories included learning (the role of initial and continuing training); organisational features (such as work organisation, job profiles, hierarchical structures, demands for flexibility and mobility) and the individual (i.e. skills profile, employees' autonomy and types of responsibility, forms of identification with work and commitment). These categories were further refined and interpreted from two perspectives according to the two phases of the empirical investigation: the company and the individual. Finally, the categories were related to flexibility and mobility (for details see Kirpal 2004a).

In times of severe economic constraints, flexibility and mobility were initially regarded as demands that put pressure on companies and employees. However, both flexibility and mobility also create opportunities in terms of the learning environment at work, job profiles, professional development and career options of employees, autonomy and self-realisation. Companies' organisational strategies may open up new opportunities for employees, or they can create pressure, for example, through work intensification—a prevalent feature that was mentioned throughout all three sectors of investigation. The study revealed that flexibility and mobility are experienced and valued quite differently in the different occupational groups.

11.2 Changes in Work Organisation and their Implication for Skills, Identification with Work and Employee Commitment

11.2.1 Engineering

The extent of changes in the structural context means that patterns of identification with work in engineering are undergoing significant change, particularly in response to increased competition and changing patterns of work organisation. This is particularly the case for employees working in multi-functional teams, people working as company change agents, team leaders, supervisory staff whose influence has been reduced and skilled workers in companies where there is a shift from direct manufacturing to providing engineering services. In all these cases the type of work undertaken and the mix of skills required were changing, in some cases dramatically (Brown, 2004a).

The drivers of introducing greater flexibility in work in some cases were because of a switch to team working, while in others it was due to an attempt to improve manufacturing practice through a focus upon continuous improvement (on quality, costs and delivery). In the UK, there was an explicit attempt to follow Japanese 'best practice' with an emphasis upon machine turn-round times, 'right first time' and so on (Brown et al., 2004). All these changes are driven by a desire to improve competitiveness, and major manufacturers themselves have been pressurising their own suppliers, sometimes through the use of very aggressive year on year cost-downs. For the employees this has meant that employers have been changing roles and responsibilities and experimenting with different patterns of work organisation such as team working, manufacturing cells and varying skill mixes. In the UK in particular, organisational commitment rather than occupational specialisation drives much of the organisation of work, with particular emphasis being given to flexibility and possession of a wider set of competences than those usually associated with a single occupation (Davis et al., 2000; Mason and Wagner, 2002).

However, there are also enormous variations in the degree of skills required of workers in different workplaces and companies across the three countries. While many companies seek to move further towards knowledge intensive high value added strategies (through high skills levels and high performance standards), as in aerospace, others may still rely upon low technical specification and low levels of specialist knowledge intensive work (Doyle et al., 1992). The UK, for example, has in the past made more use of low skilled labour than France or Germany, particularly in small or medium size companies. Here, we can distinguish between companies where skilled workers are a very small minority and production is largely routine and those where more highly skilled workers play more of a role in production, support and related activities. In the latter case companies are in a position to make different choices about the appropriate skill mix, particularly in relation to the employment of graduates or those with craft or other intermediate skills (Mason, 1996; Drexel et al., 2003).

A clear distinction could be drawn between those cases where most workers are being given more autonomy and responsibility and those where the manufacturing process is being even more tightly controlled, with an emphasis upon cost reduction (Wood, 2005). While with major changes to flexible working human resources staff are trying to reshape the focus of commitment more towards the team and away from individual commitment to a particular occupational specialisation, identification with the company may also be encouraged, but not to the extent of in the past where workers were more likely to be expected to work with the same employer for a lifetime. This process is evident in all countries, but probably has gone furthest in the UK where employers are trying to achieve balances between autonomy, control and identification with the company without over-identification (and dependence) (Brown, 2004a). In addition, there is a greater emphasis upon mutual support by employees, whether or not this is part of a shift to team working. Also in Germany the greater commitment being demonstrated to the company is thereby mediated by a desire not to let colleagues down. This means that although organisational attachment (in the sense of an expectation of a long relationship with the particular employer) may be less than it was in the past, de facto commitment in terms of task completion and role fulfilment may be higher.

In terms of learning and skills development, companies vary greatly in the extent to which they facilitate an expansive or restrictive learning environment (Fuller and Unwin, 2004), depending upon how work is organised, the nature of production and the size of the company (Bull et al., 1995; Scott and Cockrill, 1997). General competitive pressures and actions across supply chains, however, seem to be driving some learning in the workplace, with greater attention being given to work-based learning, in relation to team working, continuous improvement programmes and supervisory training (Brown, 2004a). In France employers' hiring decisions act as a strong incentive for prospective employees to obtain relevant initial technical qualifications, while the German 'dual system' confine employers to support initial craft and technician education and training. Craft qualifications are valued by employers in the UK too, but there is a much greater variety of ways of becoming skilled, with the initial skills formation system being relatively under-developed (Brown, 2004a).

Employers increasingly demand skilled workers with 'modern' skill sets, including abilities to work in teams and communicate effectively (Davis et al., 2000). This means that employees who currently rely simply upon their technical skills may struggle to get similar status work if they lose their jobs. Particularly promotion opportunities for skilled workers through to supervisory or specialist positions are dependent upon having 'modern' skill sets and/or undertaking further training. Overall, there are far fewer promoted positions because of organisational restructuring, particularly at supervisory and junior managerial levels, and there is increased competition for such posts particularly from graduates (Drexel et al., 2003).

The increasing use of graduates in the engineering and metal working sector is a widespread trend (Drexel et al., 2003). In France, the principal driver for some large companies is the desire to get young, more highly qualified workers who are expected to be more flexible in their approach to work, easier to retrain as required, and willing to undertake a wide range of work. They are expected generally to display attitudes more in tune with 'modern workplaces' (Holman et al., 2005). These trends are typically reinforced where companies are making more complex sub-assemblies and/or are selling their expertise in collaboration over design and manufacture, not just selling components. Such changes, evident across Europe, though not in all companies, have resulted in the need for a more extended knowledge base, and this presents a significant challenge not only in terms of initial qualifications, but also in relation to a continuing commitment to learning and development. These changes favour the employment of graduates. However, such graduates need not necessarily have entered higher education straight from school. In all three countries employers also encourage progression routes that build upon work experience and work-based qualifications and lead through to degree qualifications (Brown, 2004a).

Whereas the employment of more graduates seems relatively unproblematic in France and the UK, potentially such developments are more disruptive in Germany as this has major implications for the work activities and learning and development of those skilled workers who seek to build a career within the company by becoming 'Meisters'. The whole structure of a progressive work-based route could be undermined in companies where work previously undertaken by experienced Meisters is now performed by graduate design and process engineers (Drexel et al., 2003). Overall, the German engineering sector gives the impression of a system in flux. While the sector has traditionally been based upon strong institutional support, employer interdependence and complexity of (high value-added) products (Rubery and Grimshaw, 2003), the dual system and Meister training are currently under strain (Kutscha, 1996; Culpepper and Finegold, 1999). Also companies are finding that strong attachments to a particular occupational field are under pressure in relation to the need for new forms of interaction with customers and working teams, and this has consequences for learning and development in relation to communication skills and multi-disciplinary cooperation.

In France, the attempts of employers to make greater use of more highly qualified labour, including graduates, seem to align with the efforts of the national training system. This includes the development of the vocational baccalaureate, the strengthening of technical education and training and giving more attention to both employer-directed continuing vocational training and employee self-directed continuing learning and development (including through the process of skills review contained within 'bilán de competences'). The UK shows a somewhat different picture. As apprenticeship and other intermediate skills development routes remain under-developed compared with most other countries, employers need to develop different strategies than their German and French counterparts in terms of product market and work organisation. Even where they are trying to follow a 'high value added strategy' or upgrade their skill base they have been making use of the expanded pool of graduates and/or using work-based development strategies, sometimes based around formulaic approaches to continuous improvement derived from Japanese manufacturing practices (Brown, 2004a).

A question of wider interest and significance arising from the research undertaken in engineering deals with the issue of congruence or divergence of different expectations, for example between employers and employees. One issue is whether employers' expectations in terms of levels of identification and commitment of their employees align with societal 'offers' and individual perspectives in a sustainable way. For example, should employees' identification with work in Germany be based around a more fully developed (graduate) knowledge base rather than building on the traditional strengths of 'incremental' innovation, built around specialised knowledge of work processes and practices based upon advanced craft skills up to Meister level? The model of incremental innovation is itself linked to powerful societal and institutional support, including employer networks, related to the use of medium-level technology and the production of high quality products in established industries. The old skill formation system, however, was also highly gendered and slow to respond to the increasing cultural diversity of the workforce (Krüger, 1999). In this sense patterns of identification and commitment have to be linked to related systemic and institutionalised mechanisms in the wider society. Some of the employee interviews though indicated the extent of resistance encountered in their everyday work practice by those who challenge stereotyped occupational roles even when they were offered a job by employers looking for talent beyond the ranks of young German males.

In summary, employers are seeking to actively shape employees patterns of identification and commitment through different strategies. The first concerns the level of engagement with work activities, work challenges in particular, and high levels of employee autonomy in the performance of work tasks and taking responsibility for the outcomes. A second strategy concerns the interaction with supervisors and developing a key relationship with the employer in the sense that high trust and high levels of commitment were expected. Third, learning through working presents the major form of development supported by training and the company's support for key roles, such as project leaders and system engineers. These at least the study identified as the classic forms of 'professional engagement' of highly skilled workers. These were, however, not unproblematic. The focus upon quality, personal performance and identification with a particular type of work could all in some circumstances cause problems, particularly where the employer was giving more emphasis upon balancing quality with cost and time considerations. Similarly where multi-disciplinary teamwork had been introduced and workers were expected to be willing to undertake a wide range of duties, then strong attachment to particular occupational perspectives could generate tensions.

11.2.2   Nursing

Changing work requirements, new skills profiles and a tendency towards professionalism in providing quality health care are major issues that have dominated debates around care provision during the past decade. Today, the provision of health care has become a growing sector due to demographic shifts. These shifts and an ageing European society demand greater work flexibility and mobility of nurses than in the past. Furthermore, health care needs and provision today require a broader perspective looking at staffing and skills demands across countries, but also shifting the focus from simply providing care to prevention, counselling and the support of a patient-oriented self-help approach (Kirpal, 2004b).

In the three countries of investigation the national health care systems have been challenged to deal with severe structural changes. This has affected health care professionals, particularly through adjustments in work organisation and human resources policies. In Germany, the factor pushing change is the financial burden of health care expenses that lead to the reform of the economic framework and financing conditions of the health care system since the mid 1990s. These interventions have affected the organisational structures of hospitals and other health care providers, work profiles, kinds of health care provision and the interaction with patients. The highly regulated French health care system seems to benefit from a strong potential for learning and openness for the implementation of technical innovations in the medical field by, at the same time, promoting rich learning environments and a strong ethical professional code of conduct for employees. More flexibility is introduced through the private sector, institutionalised inter-professional exchange and a more flexible allocation of nurses through the 'Service de Compensation et de Suppléance'. In the UK, the demand for high flexibility of staff has become less of an issue in the light of persistent problems in the recruitment and retention of nurses. Improved working conditions, interdependency of staff, team working, further training and promotion are major tools to combat the problem of staff shortages that occur throughout the UK health care sector.

There is an increasing demand for nurses to be flexible and mobile in terms of changing work positions, wards and tasks. In both private and public health care institutions nurses are expected to be universally appointed according to staffing needs. While in France and the UK nurses seem to be better prepared to adjust to these demands, nurses in Germany are more reluctant to accept changes in work organisation and taking over new task responsibilities. That German nurses commit very early in their career to a particular field of interest and may decide to stay with the same employer in the same position for their entire professional life is not unusual. Even under the circumstances of the current pressures, work structures in Germany still allow for those kinds of continuities and nurses rather perceive flexibility and mobility demands to meet staffing needs as an individual choice rather than a necessity. The French 'Service de Compensation et de Suppléance' (pool for supplementary labour) seems to provide a well-functioning model to deal with the increasing demand for flexibility due to staff shortages. Being a voluntary institution the pool recruits general, assistant and a few specialised nurses on the basis of permanent work contracts, who are functionally and horizontally mobile on demand between different departments of public hospitals. In the light of different departmental needs for temporary work or replacement nurses, the pool distributes the work between its members according to their profile and pre-planned time for shift work.

In terms of learning and skills development, the nursing profession in Europe relies upon a highly formalised education and training system with three to four years initial training in most European countries (León, 1995). In the light of establishing nursing as an independent profession, increasing its status and broadening the career perspectives for nurses all three countries have established the possibility to follow a higher education career path in nursing. This, however, is not unproblematic, because it also means an increase of theoretical knowledge while work practice during the initial training period is being reduced. Particularly in the UK this has resulted in young job entrants lacking a substantial amount of practical workplace knowledge and young nurses being over-challenged when they start working (Eraut, 2005). In addition, establishing nursing as a degree course results in a significant number of graduates not entering the profession, because with a science degree they may also be recruited into other kinds of jobs.

Continuing work-based learning and further training play a key formative role for nurses to develop levels of identification with work and the performance of their roles. While the professional profile is linked to a strong work ethos and moral commitment combined with high levels of responsibility and a certain degree of autonomy in the performance of tasks related to direct patient care, nurses typically develop a commitment towards the ethics of the profession (Benner, 1994; Seidl, 1991). These forms of commitment and identification with the professional ethics largely superimpose any kind of organisational commitment or attachment to a particular employer. In addition, nurses show a strong commitment towards their community of practice fostered through team working and mutual encouragement and recognition between colleagues. Apart from the field of specialisation, the immediate work group (the team) and the broader professional community (nurse association), it is the direct interaction with the patients that presents a key element with which nurses identify in their work.

In France, Germany and the UK, most hospitals and other health care providers offer a rich learning environment and a variety of training courses for skill enhancement and further qualification ranging from short courses to qualifying courses of one or more years generally leading to an additional qualification. Since implicit knowledge and competences are expected to grow with work experience, continuing development is important and instrumental for both employees and employers. For nurses continuing development through formal training predominantly plays a motivational role. Such training helps them to develop expertise, supports the process of becoming confident, facilitates the professional exchange with colleagues and balances the daily work routine with new options for learning and professional development. In addition, continuing training facilitates horizontal mobility and, to a much lesser degree and depending on the specific training, also vertical mobility. Since most training is not systematically linked to career progression, it is regarded as an individual choice rather than as a requirement for good work performance. Particularly in Germany and France, the predominant mode observed in nursing is internal horizontal mobility and not vertical mobility. Some hospital nurses may choose to change wards within the same hospital every couple of years, because it can be one way of gaining more expertise and fostering one's own professional development. This choice may sometimes be regarded as an alternative option or strategy for nurses who do not wish to assume a team leading position and who are keen not to lose responsibility for providing direct patient care.

Across all three countries nurses were expected to have highly developed interpersonal and communication skills, particularly with regards to working directly with patients. However, nurses stated that they often felt overwhelmed with performing a variety of caring tasks that, from a professional point of view, did not form part of their responsibilities. It was also perceived that this reality contributes towards lowering their professional status, particularly compared to other medical staff like doctors, who are not expected to perform such roles. Other conflicts arose between providing patient-oriented services and new forms of work organisation that increasingly allocate time and energy of nurses to more technical, instrumental, administrative or coordinating tasks. While major reasons for choosing the nursing profession relate to an almost intrinsic motivation of helping and caring for others, new pressures for cost control, time efficiency and documentation for quality assurance purposes lead to nurses finding themselves torn between caring and complying with efficiency demands (Kirpal, 2004b). Not being able to resolve those conflicts in a satisfactory way and having the feeling of not performing to the expected standards leads to the danger of a nurse becoming 'burned-out', loosening fundamental work motivation or even causing the individual to abandon the nursing profession after having been in the profession for a considerable length of time.

In summary, structural reforms, changes in work organisation and division of tasks, higher demands for flexibility and mobility and medical innovations considerably affect nurses' daily work routine, skills development and time allocation to different tasks, including direct patient care. Nurses experience increased pressure and time constraints leading to a conflict between providing patient-oriented care and rationalisation. The trend towards greater professionalism questions some of the core values of an idealised model of nursing which also includes full personal dedication. This may in some cases be regarded as a relief, particularly for those nurses who generally feel overwhelmed with a personally too demanding caring role. Whatever the personal perception may be, finding a balance between caring and efficiency demands will likely be entirely left to the individual nurse. The individualised character of this process seems to constitute a considerable burden for nurses, because typically they lack any kind of support from their employing institution. This is also true for dealing with psychological stress, as nurses expressed they do not feel sufficiently supported in their work environment. While newly qualified nurses tend to develop a more 'professional' work attitude and seem better prepared and trained to balance an idealised model of caring with a more functional caring approach, one reason for young nurses increasingly leaving the profession is that they are often over-challenged with managing the work practice, particularly in terms of work load and level of responsibility in the performance of their tasks. At the same time managers complained that they are lacking the dedicated attitude and commitment that were characteristic of the older generation of nurses and that are highly valued by patients and employers (Brown and Kirpal, 2004).

11.2.3   Telecommunications

The telecommunications industry has been undergoing rapid changes in terms of technological developments, product markets, job profiles and skills requirements. The principal drivers for change are technological innovation, privatisation, emerging markets and deregulation resulting in a high level of uncertainty that is affecting employees and the sector as a whole. Since the early 1990s work profiles and skills related to traditional telephony techniques have gradually become redundant in favour of the incorporation of new computer technology in all working areas. This development has largely transformed occupational structures and traditions and how employees relate to their work. Formerly, telecommunication technicians used to rely upon a highly formalised initial training scheme and a high level of employment security guaranteed by the formerly state-owned telecommunications companies. While this structure favoured stable and continuity-based identification and commitment patterns over a considerable length of time, telecommunication technicians had to re-define their work and learning attitudes in the course of coping with major organisational restructuring and new skill demands.

Today, both technical and hybrid skills are in great demand, as are 'soft skills' related to communication and team working and companies need to be very flexible in developing and deploying the skills of their workforce. Skill development strategies emphasise learning while working, training on-the-job and the acquisition of 'just-in-time' knowledge, particularly in responding to fast changing product cycles (Brown, 2004b). Companies in the sector can be differentiated according to two basic variations: well established large telecommunication firms on the one hand, and small companies including small and medium subsidiaries of multinational firms. Both kinds of companies are differentiated according to the nature of employees' identification with work, the characteristics of the implied model of flexibility and mobility and their implications for change, learning and professional development (Dif, 2004).

Large telecommunication firms in France are still anchored in their traditional organisational structure and mode of human resource management and development. However, they have been undergoing, during the last decade, important structural changes due to privatisation and technological development. In their patterns of work organisation they are introducing greater flexibility by increasingly loosening the link between job profiles and qualification requirements and more jobs require a combination of functional flexibility and mobility of employees and the use of transversal competences. Informal and experimental learning is gaining importance. Small firms show more flexible and simple organisational structures where individuals are highly autonomous and assigned greater responsibility. Employees also show higher levels of professional mobility and regard themselves as 'telecom professionals'. Work- and product-related learning and training is targeted towards responding to work demands in a prompt and functional manner, whereas continuing training opens up access to some sort of promotional mobility including higher professional status. Overall, the average size of telecom companies has been decreasing since the liberalisation of the telecommunication market in Europe resulted in both break-ups and the emergence of new firms. The decreased size of companies has been accompanied by a decreasing level of unionisation and bargaining coverage and individual negotiations to deal with tension and conflict situations is increasingly supplanting traditional forms of collective bargaining.

The German telecommunication sector underwent a similar process as in France, transforming from a state monopoly to a liberalised market. This caused considerable transformation processes through organisational restructuring and privatisation with the privileging of shareholder interests. However, given its overwhelming size and the historical domination of German 'Telekom' in the sector customers still adhere to the company's established products and services and small competitors and providers are only gradually gaining market share. The fast changing structural and technological environment generated great demands for new skills profiles and challenged the sector to come to terms with an unexpected lack of adequately qualified technicians. As a response the 'Telekom' launched major retraining programmes in order to promote employees' professional conversion to become telecom sales staff or acquire ICT-related technical knowledge, in particular. Under pressures of redundancies in the light of the company's rigorous rationalisation strategies, employees were required to adjust their skills profiles and develop advanced communication skills and competences in computer technology otherwise they were threatened with losing their jobs (Kirpal, 2006). Establishing new occupational routes as part of the German dual apprenticeship programme provided another strategy to meet changing skill demands and shortages. In 1996, four new IT-professions were created, two with a technical focus and two with a greater commercial component, generating more than 50,000 new IT jobs in Germany between 1997 and 2002. Today these training programmes provide the basis for skilled workers in the telecommunication and broader ICT sector.

Although the process of privatisation and restructuring of British Telecom started earlier than in France and Germany beginning in the early 1980s, the whole sector is still undergoing rapid change, especially in terms of its product markets. Like in the other two countries technological development, rapidly changing product markets and deregulation have been the principal drivers for change. Customers' demands for integrated technical solutions require telecom companies to recruit people with hybrid technical and soft skills. Communication-related ('soft') skills and team working are required as employees are expected to become increasingly flexible. One major skill development strategy lies in making greater use of graduates, work-based learning and on-the-job training. Transfer of skills and knowledge, including tacit knowledge, is facilitated by high levels of staff mobility. The increased utilisation and management of sub-contracting, including the use of staff from temporary employment agencies is another emerging feature. Work-related interactivity is high within the telecom industry not only due to deregulation and the need for standards, but also because people are moving around. In some cases large companies even encourage that technical staff are taken over by suppliers, thus facilitating better exchange of information, know-how and contacts. One implication of these high levels of flexibility and staff mobility is that employees' attachment to both organisations and particular occupational specialisations is decreasing (Brown, 2004b).

In all three countries, most of employees' learning and training is highly product oriented and to a large extent geared towards acquiring 'just-in-time' knowledge that is rapidly outdated. This kind of learning often needs to be complemented by self-directed learning based on employees' own initiative and time. Access to further continuing training generally favours employees with higher initial levels of qualifications. This tendency has effectively led to internal labour market segmentation into a 'core' segment of employees who are more able to cope with the requirements of change, flexibility and mobility thus having better career prospects; and on the other hand, the development of a 'peripheral' segment made up of socio-professionally disadvantaged employees who are unable to cope with changing work requirements and are more exposed to involuntary undervalued redeployment or redundancy schemes (Dif, 2004).

In terms of work organisation, companies are moving towards simpler and more flexible organisational structures, flat hierarchies and team working in particular. This tendency is reinforced by medium size and large firms increasingly concentrating on a few 'core' activities while outsourcing and externalising most of the rest. At the same time they follow a strategy of acquisition and merger to gain access to new skills, technologies and markets. Small to medium size companies tend to promote higher levels of flexibility not only in terms of work organisation, but also in relation to employees' identification with work. In the construction of their work identities employers expect them to intensify their work-related relational interactivity with customers (with high levels of autonomy and responsibility) and to identify highly with the products and services they are providing. This generates more individualised patterns of commitment and identification with work. Particularly newly qualified employees find it easier to develop those flexible and individualised forms of commitment combined with a proactive work attitude and multi-skilling abilities.

Overall in telecommunications, we can observe the decomposition of traditional occupational identities that used to be based upon a professional career-based mode of socialisation at work, and the emergence of more flexible, individualistic forms of identification with work. In between these two extremes we find cross-border redefinition strategies with varying levels of identification and commitment.

Traditional forms of occupational identities were largely constructed and reproduced through socialisation processes in the large national telecommunication companies in monopolistic positions. The socialisation into and training for occupations related to telephony lead to high levels of employees' identification with the company as well as their occupational field and the related technology. This was combined with adhering to their acquired secure work status within the organisation. A considerable number of telecommunication technicians, who continue to work for the ex-state monopoly companies, have been able to preserve their work status (generally as civil servants) and to some extent even their former job profiles. New structural requirements, however, are eroding these forms of identification and commitment and increasingly confront this group of employees with employment insecurity and discontinuities. While lower qualified and older employees are typically threatened by uncertain job-conversion, undervalued employment or redundancy and exclusion, higher qualified and managerial staff are faced not only with more employment insecurity, but also with fewer opportunities for internal promotional mobility and career development.

While both groups are being challenged to re-define their identification and commitment patterns, former telecommunication technicians, who felt disadvantaged by the process of rapid transformation and experienced a drastic devaluation of their former skills and competences, may be more likely to respond to new work demands with a kind of 'retreat' strategy largely resisting new challenges for learning and adjustment. The higher qualified, who were formerly recruited as executives on the basis of relatively high levels of specific technical knowledge, may be more likely to adopt a new work attitude with a more offensive response taking a proactive role in redefining professional roles and responsibilities. In this context continuing training, flexibility and mobility and developing transversal competences are regarded as important instruments in order to achieve these goals.

The more flexible and individualistic type of employee, typically qualified young telecom technicians or sales engineers, possess highly developed technical skills (increasingly incorporating ICT knowledge) as well as transversal competences. They consider themselves as 'telecom professionals' or 'experts' and are primarily committed to their current field of activity. They use either established telecom companies or small dynamic IT firms as a 'passing-through' stage for realising their career project that may involve frequent changes in the nature of work to be performed. Attachments to their current occupational position or employer are rather transitional. Work-related learning, relational interactivity, flexibility and mobility are used as tools to foster their professional development. These employees are committed to continuous adaptation and 'moving on' in order to actively enhance their skills and career prospects. They are confident in their skills and do not regard themselves as being threatened by unemployment. Given that flat hierarchies are steadily reducing opportunities for upward mobility, they seek to make a career through project-based personal strategies based on high levels of work-related interactivity, flexibility and mobility. Typically, they are more committed to their professional projects than to their employing organisation.

11.3   Employees' Patterns of Adjustment to Changing Work and Skill Demands

How individuals respond to structural changes and adjust their forms of identification and commitment depend to large extent on individual variables and dispositions ranging from socio-economic background, gender and age to skills, the capacity to learn and to cope with changing work requirements as well as personal interests. Overall, the research project identified different forms of identification, with 'classical' and 'flexible' as two poles of a continuum of possible responses. In addition, regardless of the level of identification, all employees, over time, adapt to their work environment and changing requirements in a variety of ways (see Table 11.2).

In all occupational groups across the sectors investigated, we found employees with an affiliation towards 'classical' forms of identification with work by which individuals highly identified either with their occupational specialisation they trained for, their daily work tasks, the company or the company's product. To the extent that some of these employees were trying to hold on to those rather traditional elements of identification we would argue that they were pursuing a 'retreat strategy' largely resisting pressures for change. To them changes in their work environment presented a conflict, often because they did not have the means or personal resources to adjust to new demands, for example due to lack of motivation, qualifications or self-confidence. They typically

Table 11.2 Patterns of employees' adjustment to changing work and skills demands

| | Patterns of Adjustments | | | | | |
| Individual Reactions | Classical forms of identification | | Long-term Adjustment | Short-term Adjustment | Flexible/individualised | Re-definition/negotiation |
	Retreat	Classical progressive				
Risk affinity	Low	Low	Low	High	Varies	Varies
Flexibility/ Mobility	Low	Low	Low	High	High	Varies
Motivation for Learning	Low	Gradual	Low	High	High	High
Occupational/ Organisational commitment	Strong	Strong	Conditional	Transitional	Conditional	Strong

experienced changes at work as not transparent, unpredictable and beyond their control, particularly in areas characterised by rapid and radical changes, as has been the case in telecommunications during the last decade. In order to establish some continuity these employees often tried to conserve as much as possible their current work status and work tasks with little or no inclination towards learning, professional development or changing working situations, including changing employers.

On the other hand, employees with a 'classical' type of identification could also be more or less open to change. Some individuals in this group developed a more proactive kind of response seeing themselves as comfortable with the way their occupation was developing and/or how their employer was changing. If employees were able to move with, or were in the vanguard of, changes and new requirements, they would develop 'classical progressive' forms of identification with work. Such employees would follow a classical career progression most likely by pursuing a higher level qualification (e.g. the German 'Meister' qualification) to move to supervisory or more specialist positions. They would still strongly identify with the classical elements of their occupation, but were at the same time able to make use of opportunities in the course of changing work situations to develop their professional career. Moving into more specialist or supervisory positions can also be considered a well-trodden path and they may retain their allegiance to their initial technical occupation. However, by assuming additional responsibilities and tasks they will most likely be challenged to adjust and even re-define their professional roles and forms of identification.

At the opposite end of the continuum were those employees who had developed a highly 'flexible' type of identification with work. This had a much more individualist basis than any occupational and organisational commitment. One typical characteristic of these employees was that they were willing and able to actively use flexibility, mobility and learning as tools to achieve their broader goals, and in doing so they were ready to change organisations and/or their occupation, if necessary. Flexible employees anticipate and internalise requirements for change, while making continuous adjustments in the workplace could lead to more transitory forms of work attachment for the less qualified, and highly individualised patterns of commitment and identification for the higher qualified. The key feature here is that the individual is active in pursuit of her or his own goals, professional development and self-realisation based on personal skills, the capacity for continuous learning and a rather project-oriented work attitude. A variation of this flexible type of identification with work would be the 'strategic careerists' who see their current occupational position and/or organisational attachment as one phase of a career that involves relatively frequent changes in the nature of work they do. They are committed to 'moving on' and see their careers as something that they actively construct. Their attachment to their current role is partly influenced by the knowledge that they are only 'passing through'.

The largest group of interviewees, however, developed different forms of adaptation that resulted in various, very complex forms of responses along this continuum. The changing nature of their attachment to work could be more or less intense and transitional and often depended on re-definition processes. For example, adaptation and adjustment to work may be long-term or short-term; be passive (accepting) or involve the individual in an active search for resolution of problems or conflicts. The pressures external to the individual to adapt may be high or low and they may be general (relating to all those involved in an organisation or occupation) or specific (relating to an individual or small group).

In any case, forms of those kinds of 're-definition strategies' generally represented a more conditional form of adaptation—the individual may remain in an occupation and/or with a particular employer, but he or she recognises that this represents a compromise rather than an ideal situation. Typically, factors from outside work (family commitments, personal networks, attachment to a particular location) may 'hold' an individual in place. The individual may still seek to satisfy expectations (of employer, colleagues and customers or clients) with regards to role performance, but she or he typically has some reservations about her or his work or employer. However, employees may remain in the same job for a considerable period of time, but may (internally or externally) move on, if the 'holding' circumstances or external conditions change. This means that patterns of identification with work and commitment may be adjusted, re-defined or stabilised. Depending on the level of flexibility involved and whether employees would take a rather passive or active role in the process of adaptation, the project distinguished between long-term and short-term adjustment. The first involves a rather passive approach leading to a certain continuity and stability, whereas the second presents a more proactive attitude of employees seeking to change their current situation by accepting a higher degree of flexibility and mobility, an approach that may also involve risk and insecurity.

'Long-term adjustment' represents a conditional form of adaptation by which employees somehow accept their current work situation as a compromise. In pursuit of job security and maintaining a certain level of stability, employees would remain in the same job for a considerable period of time despite the dissatisfaction they encounter at work. Many of them subordinated their own career and working life to other aspects of life, generally diminishing the overall meaning of work, at least for a certain period of time. Examples of reasons why interviewees felt 'locked into' their current work included accommodation to working patterns of a partner, attachment to a particular locality ('we have lived here all our lives') and attachment to their immediate work group. 'Short-term adjustment', by contrast, represents a fully conditional form of adaptation: the individual recognises that he or she only intends to remain in an occupation and/or with a particular employer for a relatively short period of time. Either because of individual circumstances, choice or long-term career plans, or because of dissatisfaction with the work, the individual is actively seeking or intending to seek alternative employment. Particularly in the UK sample, we had examples of interviewees who were in the process of changing employers or occupations.

However, also alongside people exhibiting these different forms of 'adjustment' a considerable number of employees identified with their work and were, at the same time, much more active in re-defining, rather than passively accepting, work-related roles. Actually, in all groups, from 'classical' to 'flexible' forms of identification with work, we found employees who were actively re-defining and challenging traditional occupational roles and work identities. We had examples of employees who used re-defining strategies operating at the cutting edge of norms and expectations, thus pushing at the boundaries of expectations of employers, colleagues and others. In certain aspects they could be considered change agents, typically negotiating, challenging and leading their peers in some respect. These were rare, but we did find some examples of these patterns of behaviour, as in the case of women taking leading roles in engineering or a dynamic young Turkish supervisor working in a German galvanising factory. Also German male nurses often challenged the traditional image of nurses, for example in terms of fulfilling expectations of being able to provide 'unconditional care' against gendered expectations.

The forms of identification with work that individuals develop over time depend on a variety of factors leading to a complex process of negotiation between personal resources and (internal and external) constraints on the one hand, and structural conditions, on the other. What seems to be decisive in this context is the individual's response or 'strategy': whether he or she takes a passive or active role, the level of risk affinity, the openness and ability to use flexibility, mobility and learning as tools to pursue their own interests and their general attachment to work. In addition, different forms of adaptation or responses must not be interpreted as 'exclusive categories'. They may be mutually exclusive at a given point in time, but may change and be adjusted in the course of the overall lifetime employment trajectory of an individual, shifting in either direction across a continuum of possible responses.

The approach (or approaches), which an individual adopts over a lifetime trajectory, combines a set of different individual variables. Taking a passive or active role, or the level of risk affinity with regards to employment and work, may to a large extent depend on an individual's personality, whereas attachment to work may be a combination of tertiary work-related socialisation, work experience and personal interest. On the other hand, the extent to which employees are willing and able to use flexibility and mobility, and have developed an active learner's attitude is closely linked to learning processes. At this point the project could identify a clear distinction between employees who had been socialised and trained to be more flexible and active in developing their professional orientation and identity, and employees who had not been socialised this way. This, in some cases, correlated with age in that skilled workers who trained during the last decade typically would be much better prepared to deal with changes and instabilities at work than a generation that had been trained during the 1970s in a sector that was then characterised by stability and progressive employment perspectives, but which was now encountering severe problems. However, age was not always the critical factor as we also interviewed highly dynamic 'older' and less flexible 'younger' employees across all occupational groups. In terms of learning, the national embedding and workplace specific conditions also played a decisive role. For example, UK and French employees generally seemed to be better prepared to anticipate and deal with changing work demands than German employees. The same was true for employees working in dynamic segments of engineering, for example, versus employees working in large institutions or companies.

11.4   Conclusions

The project identified a general trend towards the 'individualisation' of patterns of identification with work away from classical collective forms. Individuals are increasingly required and expected to develop a proactive and 'entrepreneurial' work attitude based on multi-skilling and flexibility. This also implies the need to develop complex, flexible and multi-dimensional levels of identification and commitment that can be continuously adjusted to the requirements for change. Stability and continuity that were formerly generated through, for example, permanent employment contracts and long-term company attachment, increasingly have to be actively constructed by the employees themselves. In addition, risk management of employment instabilities and responsibilities for relevant skills acquisition are being transferred from the company to the individual.

These developments have significant implications for employees' work orientations, forms of attachments and career plans. Whilst the 'entrepreneurial' model assumes highly dynamic and flexible levels of identification with work a potentially high number of employees at the intermediate skills level may rather wish to hold on to more 'classical' forms of identification with work, largely resisting high demands for flexibility, mobility and continuing learning. These employees often do not possess the personal resources to cope with the requirements of a fast changing work environment and this can lead to stress, lack of control over work performance, high levels of staff turnover, lack of commitment and, in some cases, poor work performance. This could be observed especially within occupations and organisations that demand high levels of flexibility and mobility due to a fast changing work organisation, such as in the telecommunication industry.

The model of the flexible 'entrepreneur' that is increasingly favoured and expected by managers and human resources departments (FAME Consortium, 2003) may exclude an increasing number of people who cannot or do not have the means to develop highly flexible work attachments. This may be because they either lack the right qualification or skills, come from a disadvantaged socio-economic background, may not be very flexible in general or may prefer to hold on to more classical forms of work attachment. Since the majority of employees in Europe have undergone a work-related socialisation that did not yet anticipate the requirements for increased flexibility, mobility and lifelong learning, the number of disadvantaged workers in Europe who are not of an 'entrepreneurial' type could be potentially huge.[1] The role of socialisation into the work context, one of the major functions of vocational and continuous education and training, plays a key role in this context.

If individuals are increasingly challenged to actively construct their own, mainly individualised, forms of identification and professional orientations, they need guidance on how to do this most effectively in order to meet changing demands. This may not be so much an issue of formal accreditation of prior learning, but rather a question of how to give individuals confidence in their own competences and to empower them to become agents of their own professional development. This means that employees need to be supported and guided to cope with changing work environments, including meeting new demands for being flexible and mobile. From the investigation it seems that to most employees this kind of support is insufficient or not given at all. However, such guidance, be it at institutional, employer or at a more individualised level, seems to be indispensable in order to avoid employees falling into a passive 'retreat' or 'long-term adjustment' strategy that may lead ultimately to their labour market exclusion.

Such forms of guidance could, for example, be integrated into formal and informal, initial and continuing vocational training schemes. Emphasising continuing training and informal learning against (formalised) vocational education would stress the importance of self-directed and work-based learning. If these forms of learning are also linked to the recognition of competences acquired through these

---

[1] Notably, the employee sample of this investigation represented a privileged segment of the workforce by only including individuals currently employed and with at least some level of basic vocational training. Individuals, who are already excluded like the large number of unemployed workers, were not represented in the study.

processes, then this trend may create new opportunities for employees. However, to the extent that this approach transfers the responsibility for skills acquisition from the company to the individual, it may also cause a high level of stress. Employees increasingly experienced a constant pressure for learning while working and self-study, in which they felt were not sufficiently supported by their employer and without such support they felt the pressure to continue learning was unsustainable over a longer period. Combined with lack of training support and high demands on flexibility, for many employees this also resulted in an imbalance and conflict between work and private or family life.

Employees who are equipped with the right set of skills and sufficient self-confidence are also usually willing and able to deal with new demands at their workplace. Some even actively use new concepts of flexibility and mobility at work as instruments to adjust their work to their personal needs. Given enough support they may also feel comfortable that in changing contexts earlier forms of identification and commitment are loosening their former role and significance and are being re-defined. This may be particularly the case where hybrid skills are in great demand involving a combination of business and technical skills, as well as 'soft' skills of communication and team working. In such environments employees could perform a wide variety of roles and there were examples of companies being very flexible in deploying the skills of such people. Indeed, that employers saw these individuals as capable of fulfilling a variety of roles was a key part of their attraction.

References

Beck, U. (1992). *Risk society: towards a new modernity*. London: Sage.

Beck, U. and E. Beck-Gernsheim (1994). *Riskante Freiheiten: Individualisierung in modernen Gesellschaften*. Frankfurt/M.: Suhrkamp.

Benner, P. (1994). *Stufen zur Pflegekompetenz: From novice to expert*. Bern: Huber.

Brown, A. (2004a). Engineering identities. *Career Development International*, 9(3), 245–273.

Brown, A. (2004b). *Learning, commitment and identities at work: Responses to change in the IT and telecommunications industries in the United Kingdom*. Learning Processes for Professional Development Symposium, European Conference on Educational Research (ECER 2004), Crete, Greece.

Brown, A. and S. Kirpal (2004). 'Old nurses with new qualifications are best': managers' attitudes towards the recruitment of health care professionals in Estonia, France, Germany, Spain and the United Kingdom. In C. Warhurst, E. Keep and I. Grugulis (Eds.), *The skills that matter* (pp. 225–241). New York: Palgrave.

Brown, A., E. Rhodes and R. Carter (2004). Supporting learning in advanced supply systems in the automotive and aerospace industries. In H. Rainbird, A. Fuller and A. Munro (Eds.) *Workplace learning in context* (pp. 166–182). London: Routledge.

Bull, A., M. Pitt and J. Szarka (1995). Commonalities and divergences in small-firm competitive strategies: textiles and clothing manufacture in Britain, France and Italy. In P. Cressey and B. Jones (Eds.), *Work and employment in Europe: A new convergence* (pp. 121–142). London: Routledge.

Culpepper, P.D. and D. Finegold (1999). *The German skills machine: Sustaining comparative advantage in a global economy*. New York/Oxford: Berghahn Books.

Davis, C., T. Buckley, T. Hogarth and R. Shackleton (2000). *Employers skills survey case study—engineering*. London: DfEE.

DeFillippi, R.J. and M.B. Arthur (1994). The boundaryless career: A competency-based career perspective. *Journal of Organizational Behavior*, 15(4), 307–324.

Dif, M. (2004). Vocational identities in change in the telecommunications sector. *Career Development International*, 9(3), 305–322.

Doyle, P., J. Saunders and V. Wong (1992). Competition in global markets—a case study of American and Japanese competition in the British market. *Journal of International Business*, 23(3), 419–442.

Drexel, I., M. Möbus, F. Gérardin, B. Grasser, H. Lhotel, A. Brown, M. Maguire and B. Baldauf (2003). *Cross-national Comparisons of New Career Pathways for Industrial Supervisors in France, Germany and the United Kingdom*. SKOPE Monograph No 6., ESRC funded Centre on Skills, Knowledge and Organisational Performance, Oxford and Warwick Universities.

Eraut, M. (2005). *Developing responsibility*. Symposium on Early Career Professional Learning, American Educational Research Association Conference, Montreal, Canada.

FAME Consortium (2003). *Work-related identities in Europe: How personnel management and HR policies shape workers' identities*. ITB Working Paper Series No 46. Bremen: Institute Technology and Education/University of Bremen.

FAME Consortium (2006). Decomposing and Recomposing Occupational Identities. A Survey of Theoretical Concepts. In A. Brown, S. Kirpal and F. Rauner (Eds.), *Identities at Work* (pp. 13–44). Dordrecht: Springer.

Fuller, A. and L. Unwin (2004). Expansive learning environments: integrating organizational and personal development. In H. Rainbird, A. Fuller and A. Munro (Eds.), *Workplace learning in context* (pp. 126–144). London: Routledge.

Glaser, B.G. (1978). *Theoretical sensitivity: Advances in the methodology of grounded theory*. Mill Valley, CA: Sociology Press.

Gottlieb, B.H., E.K. Kelloway and E. Barham (1998). *Flexible work arrangements*. Chichester: Wiley.

Hall, D.T. (1996). *The career is dead—Long live the career. A relational approach to careers*. San Francisco: Jossey-Bass.

Holman, D., S. Wood and T. Wall (2005). Introduction to the Essentials of the New Workplace. In D. Holman, T. Wall, C. Clegg, P. Sparrow and A. Howard (Eds.), *The essentials of the new workplace* (pp. 1–14). Chichester: Wiley.

Kanter, R.M. (1989). Careers and the wealth of nations: A macro-perspective on the structure and implications of career forms. In M.B. Arthur, D.T. Hall and B.S. Lawrence (Eds.), *Handbook of career theory* (pp. 506–522). Cambridge: Cambridge University Press.

Keupp, H., T. Ahbe, W. Gmür, R. Höfer, B. Mitzscherlich, W. Kraus and F. Straus (1999). *Identitätskonstruktionen. Das Patchwork der Identitäten in der Spätmoderne.* Reinbek: Rowohlt.

Kirpal, S. (2004a). Researching work identities in a European context. *Career Development International,* 9(3), 199–221.

Kirpal, S. (2004b). Work identities of nurses: between caring and efficiency demands. *Career Development International,* 9(3), 274–304.

Kirpal, S. (2006, in press). *Old and New Economies. Employees' Responses to Change in the German Telecommunications and IT Industries.* ITB Research Paper Series No 20/2006. Bremen: Institute Technology and Education/University of Bremen.

Krüger, H. (1999). Gender and Skills. Distributive ramifications of the German skill system. In P.D. Culpepper and D. Finegold (Eds.), *The German skills machine: Sustaining comparative advantage in a global economy* (pp. 189–227). New York/ Oxford: Berghan Books.

Kutscha, G. (1996). The dual system of education in the Federal Republic of Germany. An obsolescent model? *European Education,* 28(2), 49–62.

León, M.W. (1995). *Krankenpflegeausbildung in Europa.* Stuttgart/Berlin/Köln: Kohlhammer.

Mason, G. (1996). Graduate utilisation in British industry: The initial impact of mass higher education. *National Institute Economic Review,* 156, 93–103.

Mason, G. and K. Wagner (2002). *Skills, performance and new technologies in the British and German automotive components industries.* Research Report SPN1, London: Department for Education and Skills.

Mirvis, P.H. and D.T. Hall (1994). Psychological success and the boundaryless career. *Journal of Organizational Behavior,* 15(4), 365–380.

Müller, W. and S. Scherer (2003). Marktexpansion, Wohlfahrtsstaatsumbau und soziale Ungleichheit. In W. Müller and S. Scherer (Eds.), *Mehr Risiken—Mehr Ungleichheit? Abbau von Wohlfahrtsstaat, Flexibilisierung von Arbeit und die Folgen* (pp. 9–27). Frankfurt/M.: Suhrkamp.

Reilly, P.A. (1998). Balancing flexibility—meeting the interests of employer and employee. *European Journal of Work and Organizational Psychology,* 1(7), 7–22.

Rubery, J. and D. Grimshaw (2003). *The organization of employment: an international perspective.* Basingstoke, Hampshire: Palgrave Macmillan.

Scott, P. and A. Cockrill (1997). Multi-skilling in small- and medium-sized engineering firms: Evidence from Wales and Germany. *International Journal of Human Resource Management,* 8(6), 807–824.

Seidl, E. (1991). *Pflege im Wandel. Das soziale Umfeld der Pflege und seine historischen Wurzeln dargestellt anhand einer empirischen Untersuchung.* Wien/München/Bern: Maudrich.

Sennett, R. (1998). *The corrosion of character: the personal consequences of work in the new capitalism.* New York: Norton.

Stake, R.E. (2000). Case Studies. In N.K. Denzin and Y.S. Lincoln (Eds.), *Handbook of Qualitative Research* (pp. 453–454, 2nd Edition). Thousand Oaks/London/ New Delhi: Sage Publications.

Strauss, A. and J. Corbin (1990). *Basics of qualitative research: Grounded theory procedures and techniques.* Newbury Park: Sage Publications.

Sullivan, S.E. (1999). The changing nature of careers: A review and research agenda. *Journal of Management,* 25(3), 457–484.

Witzel, A. (1996). Auswertung problemzentrierter Interviews. Grundlagen und Erfahrungen. In R. Strobl and A. Böttger (Eds.), *Wahre Geschichten? Zu Theorie und Praxis qualitativer Interviews.* Beiträge zum Workshop 'Paraphrasieren, Kodieren, Interpretieren . . .' im Kriminologischen Forschungsinstitut Niedersachsen am 29. und 30. Juni 1995 in Hannover (pp. 49–75). Baden-Baden: Nomos.

Wood, S. (2005). Organisational performance and manufacturing practices. In D. Holman, T. Wall, C. Clegg, P. Sparrow and A. Howard (Eds.), *The Essentials of the New Workplace.* Chichester: Wiley.

12

Work Identity in the Japanese Context: Stereotype and Reality

Akihiro Ishikawa
Chuo University, Tokyo, Japan

12.1   Introduction

12.1.1   Background

Japanese companies are not just vehicles for economic performance; they also perform an important social function. Studies of Japanese human resource management have revealed that they attach much importance to providing their employees with job-security in the form of lifelong employment (Matsushima, 1962; Hazama, 1979). This stems from a human resource development practice which is founded upon a commitment to using the internal labour market for development and progression.

The classic stereotypical behaviour of large-scale Japanese companies, and to a certain extent medium-sized enterprises, was to recruit employees who have just graduated from school and do not have any occupational skills. It is after entering the company that the company trains them internally to become 'a company person'. This training endows the employees with both social and relevant occupational skills. It is also hoped that this training instills considerable organizational commitment. Indeed, most employees stay with the same company for a long time and experience both horizontal and upward mobility in the organization, in contrast to European workers, who largely remain in the same job (Ishikawa, 2004). Thus, the main decision new entrants to the Japanese labor market have to make is about which company they should join, not which occupation they should choose. Also, the range of work

A. Brown, S. Kirpal and F. Rauner (eds.), Identities at Work, 315–336.

undertaken by Japanese workers is wider than the work typically performed by European workers, and Japanese workers tend to adjust themselves more flexibly to reorganization at work than European workers. This is because they believe that however circumstances change they will share a common fate with their company.

It is understandable, therefore, that, when an employee is asked what their occupation is, they will almost always not relate their answer to a specific specialization or job profile, such as lathe operator or treasurer or designer, but will instead respond by focusing on the name of a company, for example: 'I am an employee of X Company', or if their company is unknown in the society they are in, they might reply, 'I am working in a company that is cooperating (or trading) with X Company'.

Japanese employees are not only trained occupationally in the company, but also socially. They are taught the social rules and norms with which they are expected to comply so as to behave as mature citizens. Furthermore, employees regard their company as their reference group from which they lead their social life (Ishikawa, 1992). Deviant behaviour by an employee inflicts 'shame' on the company for which they work. An employee's fear of shaming their company like this acts as a form of social control in their daily life. 'Disgracing the company in society' has fatal consequences for the prospects of an employee.

For the reasons mentioned above, Japanese employees' work identities are assumed to revolve around a 'company identity' rather than a 'job identity'. As a result, Japanese employees are stereotypically described as being 'group-oriented' and having 'collectivist' attitudes, and being prepared to devote themselves to the success of their company in the spirit of self-sacrifice. Consequently, Japanese workers are characterized as being 'workaholics' and having mind-sets that result in an over-commitment to work.

12.1.2 Aims and Methods

This conventional picture of Japanese workers has been outlined to provide a context for the rest of the chapter; this chapter aims to reveal some specific features about the work identities of Japanese employees based on relevant empirical data, and contrast these results with the stereotypical view outlined above. Three aspects of work identity are considered: normative, emotional and organizational. In this chapter, *Work Centrality* is used as an index for the normative aspect of work identity, *Work Satisfaction* for the emotional aspect, and *Company Commitment* for the organizational aspect.

Work Centrality (WC) describes the extent to which people regard work as important in their life. There is a research instrument in Japan that measures WC on a seven point scale. Although the following analysis uses this instrument respondents are classified into just three groups: those for whom work is regarded as 'very important' (points 6 and 7), 'more or less important' (points 3, 4 and 5), and 'not important' (points 1 and 2). *Work Satisfaction* (WS) refers to the degree to which people are satisfied with their present working life. For the following analysis, although the data is collected on a five point scale, it will again be reclassified such that respondents' answers are categorised into three groups: 'satisfied' (points 4 and 5), 'more or less satisfied' (point 3) and 'dissatisfied' (points 1 and 2). *Company Commitment* (CC) is an important index to consider when investigating Japanese work identities. It indicates the willingness of individuals to devote themselves to the company's success. The following analysis will order all responses into three categories of company commitment: 'self-devoting', 'calculative' and 'indifferent'. Responses similar to 'I would like to put my best efforts toward the company's success' will be classified as 'self-devoting'. Whilst 'calculative' describes responses similar to 'I would like to give as much effort to the company as the company gives to me in reward', responses such as 'I do not have much feeling toward the company' and 'I am indifferent to any matters concerning the company' will be categorized as 'indifferent'.

By using these indices, the work identities of Japanese employees will be illustrated within an international framework, and then the differences in these identities between the different strata of the Japanese employment structure will be considered.

12.2   International Comparison

12.2.1   Work Centrality

Data from two research studies which applied the same scale for measuring work centrality were available for this analysis. Some of the most important research on work centrality is provided by an international study on the 'Meaning of Work' (MOW research conducted between 1981–1983 which drew its data from samples which were nationally representative (Misumi, 1987). Therefore, this study provides an excellent illustration of the differences in WC between countries, as shown in Table 12.1.

Table 12.1   Work Centrality in percentages according to MOW
Research 1981–1983 (Misumi, 1987, p. 18)

	Very important	More or less	Not important
Japan	61	38	1
Israel	55	43	2
USA	54	44	2
Netherlands	40	57	3
Belgium	39	59	2
Germany (West)	38	56	6
UK	36	59	5

From the results presented in this table it is clear that, in terms of work centrality, Japan scores the highest among the presented countries. Over 60 per cent of respondents in Japan regarded work as 'very important' in their lives. This is significantly higher than in the other countries, but especially higher than in the West European countries, where it was 40 per cent or less. This research, however, was conducted at the beginning of the 1980s. Hence, it is rather out-dated and took place at a time when the idea of lifetime employment was unchallenged in Japan. Besides, the only countries surveyed were the USA, Israel, Japan and some from Western Europe. Nevertheless, the data is consistent with the stereotypical picture of Japanese workers as strongly committed to work.

The data shown in Table 12.2 (below) was obtained more recently, in the second half of the 1990s, and included countries from both Western and Eastern Europe, and East Asia. It was an international research study (Denki Rengo International Research:[1] Denki Rengo 1996, 2000; Ishikawa et al., 2000; Shikawa and Shiraishi (ed.) 2005) on the working life of employees from the electrical and electronic machine industry. Clearly, this research was carried out more recently than the MOW research and covered a broader range of countries, but the composition of its samples were also different. The MOW research was based on national

---

[1] Denki Rengo is the Japanese abridged name of the Japanese Electrical, Electronic and Information Union. Previously it was called Denki Roren, and its English name was 'Japanese Federation of Electric Machine Workers' Unions'. It is the largest trade union federation at branch level in Japan.

Table 12.2   Work Centrality presented in percentages from Denki Rengo Research 1994/1996 and 1999–2001 (Denki Rengo, 1996, 2000)

	Very important 1994/1996 1999/2001		More or less important 1994/1996 1999/2001		Not important 1994/1996 1999/2001	
Japan ($N = 981; 870$)[1]	24	30	72	64	2	4
France ($N = 105; 116$)	21	1	72	93	3	3
Italy ($N = 764; 246$)	64	–	30	–	–	4
Finland ($N = 363; 340$)	47	78	47	20	1	4
Sweden ($N = 570; –$)	50	–	42	–	–	7
Poland ($N = 640; 631$)	54	55	34	37	5	7
Czech R. ($N = 386; 308$)	35	42	56	54	3	7
Slovakia ($N = 411; 214$)	56	48	40	43	7	4
Hungary ($N = 411; 517$)	50	54	42	44	1	1
Slovenia ($N = 635; 339$)	52	47	37	46	3	4
China ($N = 549; 453$)	45	57	45	40	2	3

[1] The two figures are the numbers in the samples of 1994/1996 and 1999/2001 respectively.

representative samples in a given country, while the samples of the Denki Rengo research consisted only of employees of large-scale electrical or electronic machine producing plants in each country. More specifically, a research partner from each participating country selected two plants (except in Japan where four plants were selected), one that produced electronic communication equipment and one that produced household electrical appliances, both of which had more than 500 employees each. From these plants, participants were selected randomly from all the employees that existed below the managerial level.

The research from the 1990's suggests WC in Japan decreased after the MOW research was conducted in 1981–1983. There are two possibilities of explanations for this decline. First, it is possible that between the two periods there may have been a fundamental change in the work values of Japanese workers. This explanation is supported by longitudinal research conducted by the Japan Broadcasting Corporation (NHK,

2000). Second, it is possible that the different sampling strategies used by the two studies generated the contrasting results. For example, the degree of WC among the employees working for large-scale enterprises might be lower than among Japanese workers in general. These two explanations will be further examined later in the text.

When considering Table 12.1, it was noted that the data suggested the WC of Japanese employees was higher than that of all their counterparts. However, the data from Table 12.2, which is only concerned with the WC of employees of large-scale electrical and electronic machine producing companies, implied that while this was still true when Japan and some Western-European countries (France) were compared, it was no longer true when Central- (former East-) and North-European countries, as well as Italy and China were compared to Japan; these countries had higher ratings of WC than Japan. Therefore, it seems that if the number of countries for comparison is extended and more recent data is included, then Japan defies its stereotypes and demonstrates a level of WC which is not particularly high.

12.2.2 Work Satisfaction

The Denki Rengo International Research (Denki Rengo 1996, 2000; Ishikawa et al., 2000) also considered the working life of employees from the electrical and electronic machine industry in terms of work satisfaction (WS). This data is presented below in Table 12.3.

This data reveals that in the international context Japan does not have a markedly high level of WS. The number of employees in Japan who rated themselves as 'satisfied' was below 50 per cent, which is lower than the majority of the other surveyed countries. The data from both 1994/1996 and 1999/2001 indicate that the WS of Japanese employees was lower than that of their counterparts from most of the European countries. Poland and Slovenia are the only two countries where the WS of their employees was significantly lower than in Japan in 1994/1996, but even then their WS figures improved to either an almost equivalent or higher level than Japan by the end of the 1990s. In 1994/1996, the levels of WS for employees from the other former communist countries in Central Europe were similar to those in Japan, but by 2000, when their socio-economic transitions had been in the most part completed, these WS levels were significantly higher than in Japan. Whilst in China in 1994/1996, their employees' WS was conspicuously higher than to that of their Japanese counterparts; by 2000 it had declined to a level that

Table 12.3 Work Satisfaction presented in percentages from Denki Rengo Research 1994/1996 and 1999–2001 (Denki Rengo, 1996, 2000)

Country	Satisfied 1994/1996 1999/2001		More or less satisfied 1994/1996 1999/2001		Dissatisfied 1994/1996 1999/2001	
Japan	44	47	30	28	26	22
France	62	53	17	27	11	17
Italy	65	72	11	12	25	13
Finland	67	78	27	16	6	6
Sweden	57	–	28	–	15	–
Poland	17	41	53	49	29	8
Czech Republic	45	64	30	21	25	14
Slovakia	47	65	35	31	18	4
Hungary	41	58	47	36	11	6
Slovenia	35	65	38	30	24	4
China	63	36	20	35	16	27

was significantly lower than that in Japan; this is attributed to Chinese state-owned enterprises being thrown into the stormy situation of privatization and restructuring in the intervening period.

12.2.3 Company Commitment

The stereotypical view of Japanese employees supports the image that they are deeply involved in company life with a strong commitment toward the organization. The data from the research both in 1994/1996 and in 1999/2001, however, provide another picture.

As seen in Table 12.4, the proportion of 'self-devoting' attitudes in Japan is the lowest among the surveyed countries, and the proportion of those holding 'indifferent' attitudes is greatest in Japan together with France. Roughly speaking, around 20 per cent of Japanese employees are very positive, while another 20 per cent are negative, and 60 per cent are in between. In this respect, Japanese employees no longer seem to be such 'company persons as pictured stereotypically. The reasons for this

Table 12.4   Company Commitment in Denki Rengo Research
1994/1996 and 1999–2001 in percentage (Denki Rengo, 1996, 2000)

Country	Self-devoting[1] 1994/1996 1999/2001		Calculative[2] 1994/1996 1999/2001		Indifferent[3] 1994/1996 1999/2001	
Japan	19	26	54	49	24	20
France	24	34	49	42	26	20
Italy	33	39	44	42	19	15
Finland	62	69	32	22	4	2
Sweden	41	–	49	–	8	–
Poland	40	30	42	48	16	9
Czech Republic	36	44	55	51	8	4
Slovakia	44	49	46	47	11	4
Hungary	28	35	57	51	14	13
Slovenia	44	51	50	44	4	2
China	49	70	24	17	9	7

[1] Self-devoting: 'I would like to put my best efforts toward the company's success'.
[2] Calculative: 'I would like to give as much effort to the company as the company gives to me in reward'.
[3] Indifferent: 'I do not have much feeling toward the company' and 'I am indifferent to any matters concerning the company'.

have been hypothesized from two viewpoints. One points to the particular Japanese mentality of preferring a moderate reaction like 'in between', and therefore the responses gather somewhere in the medium, but not at the extreme poles. This trait of Japanese respondents is revealed by Hayashi and his research group in the study of the methodology of international comparison (Hayashi et al., 1991: Part III). The other explanation considers that the figures in the table represent a reality, referring to managerial experiences that 20 per cent of 'self-devoting' employees would be enough for a company. These 20 per cent would promote the activities of business and production and others would follow their example. From this viewpoint, what should be stressed is not the proportion of active employees, but the managerial and organizational skill with which their self-devoting spirit is connected organically with the others who do not necessarily pursue as active a company commitment[2].

In practice, although the stability of permanent full-time employees is objectively quite high in Japanese firms, particularly in large-scale ones, a considerable number the employees have a latent desire for quitting from their present employer. According to Denki Rengo research in 1999/2001, the proportion of employees who have never moved between companies are rated 89 per cent in Japan, while 12 per cent in Finland, 25–40 per cent in France, Poland, Czech Republic, Slovakia and Hungary, and 45–64 per cent in Slovenia, France and China. On the other hand, those who consider leaving their present company 'very frequently' or 'frequently' (on a five point scale) are rated 20 per cent, which is larger than in other surveyed countries except for France.

In the Japanese context, these findings imply that the high level of staff stability in companies does not necessarily mean a strong commitment of employees to company life. In the system of conventional seniority-based wage increase and career promotion inside the firm, it is disadvantageous for an employee to move from one company to another. If an employee moves to another firm, his/her length of service in the new firm would be surely shorter than that of his/her colleagues. This means that he/she would receive a smaller allowance at retirement age, experience stagnancy in relation to promotion prospects, and be regarded as 'an outsider'. Therefore, even when suffering from an unpleasant treatment at work, an employee would rather prefer to stay patiently in his/her current workplace, sometimes dreaming to move somewhere else and hoping for something better.

Such situations where there are expectations of internal progression after initial recruitment have changed to some extent, due initially to a shortage of workers in the labour market around 1990 caused by 'bubble economy', and then to pressures to reduce labour costs in the face of global competition after the collapse of the domestic economy. This spread a preference of human resource management to hiring 'ready-made skilled workers', above all in the newly developing industries like IT-related businesses. But the permanent full-time employees of large-scale firms in established industries still kept the conventional attitudes about the value of staying for a long time in a given firm.

---

[2] This viewpoint was presented by audiences at a conference for Japanese managers, where the author gave a speech on employees' corporate identity.

12.3   Patterns of Work Identity of Japanese Employees

Looking at patterns of work identities, the focus will be kept on the permanent employees of Japanese large-scale enterprises. The data are an outcome of a research study in four plants of electrical and electronic machine industry in 1999. For reference, a statistically significant correlation exists between WC, WS and CC, which means there is a possibility that one indicator can substitute for the others in measuring aspects of work identity.

12.3.1   Differentiation of Work Centrality by Different Employee Groups

Initially WC will be analyzed from two perspectives. One concerns the differentiation of the extent of WC between different Japanese employee groups sorted by job profile, gender, age and educational background. The other aspect will be devoted to figuring out the nature of work identity by analyzing the meaning of WC. Table 12.5 displays the degree of WC among different employee groups by showing the average point score, and standard deviation, of each group on a seven-point scale.

This analysis points to the following features:

- The degree of WC is highest among supervisors, while it is lowest for technical staff such as engineers and technicians. Manual workers and administrative staff are located in between. It is noteworthy that *t*echnical staffs' WC is not higher than the WC of manual workers.
- There is no great difference between men and women in the degree of WC. This implies that permanently employed women are mostly as work oriented as men, in spite of the fact that, according to a prevailing view, women are usually allocated to subordinate jobs.
- The degree of WC rises with age. This might be understandable from the fact that older employees would involve themselves in work and the company and benefit from the practice of long-time employment and age-linked wage stratification. This might also partly reflect a generational shift away from more traditional attitudes towards work commitment.

Table 12.5   Work Centrality by different employee groups

	Average point score	Standard deviation
(1) Job Strata		
Manual workers (*N* = 155)	5.03	1.231
Administrative staff (*N* = 240)	5.01	1.032
Technical staff (*N* = 403)	4.86	1.077
Supervisors (*N* = 38)	5.20	0.994
(2) Gender		
Male (*N* = 625)	4.94	1.111
Female (*N* = 194)	5.03	0.978
(3) Age Group		
Below 30 (*N* = 231)	4.79	1.120
30–39 (*N* = 400)	4.92	1.021
40–49 (*N* = 139)	5.21	1.054
50–59 (*N* = 54)	5.53	1.182
(4) Educational Level		
Low[1] (*N* = 40)	5.33	1.137
Middle (*N* = 397)	5.09	1.086
Upper Middle (*N* = 89)	4.86	0.930
High (*N* = 300)	4.78	1.095

[1] The low educational group consisted largely of older employees.

- Interestingly, educational level shows a negative correlation with WC, with the most highly educated exhibiting lower degrees of WC.

In Japan, like other advanced economies, industrial and technological changes have resulted in reduced demand for manual workers with a lower educational background, while the number of technical staff with a higher level of education has increased, and this trend is continuing. The findings above might imply a gradual decline of WC of Japanese employees is in part due to the structural change in the workforce as a whole.

12.3.2   The Meaning of Work Centrality

Now, let us shift the concern from the degree of WC to what it means. In the research of 1999/2001 six items were available for the analysis of the meaning of WC. These were: 'Working gives you status and prestige', 'Working provides you with an income that is needed', 'Working keeps you occupied', 'Working permits you to have interesting contacts with other people', 'Working is a useful way for you to serve society', and 'Working itself is basically interesting and satisfying for you'. The answer for each item was chosen from a five-point scale. A regression analysis, putting WC as the dependent valuable, reveals the figures in Table 12 6.

The data in Table 12.6 indicate that the most meaningful factors connected with WC are 'status and prestige' and 'keeping occupied' and then 'work in itself', while 'income' is not correlated to work centrality at all. In other words, those who attach an importance to work (WC) perceive 'working' as a source of social recognition and belonging, giving you something to do and insofar as it is interesting and satisfying then as a place for self-actualization, rather than the centrality of work being related to income. More generally, attitudes to WC appear to be related more to moral and self-realizing values of work than to materialistic ones. However, the meaning of 'working' is significantly differentiated between job strata, as shown in Table 12.7.

In the case of manual workers in particular, the factor most related to WC is 'income'. It means that the most work-centred manual workers

Table 12.6   Correlation of 'work centrality' with 'meaning of working' (regression analysis)

	Standardized B	T	Significant Probability
Status and prestige	0.121	3.656	0.000[1]
Income	0.001	0.023	0.981
Keeping occupied	0.129	3.034	0.002[1]
Contact with others	0.075	1.984	0.048
Serving society	0.088	2.327	0.020
Work in itself	0.115	2.563	0.011[1]

[1] Significant correlation.

Table 12.7   Meaning of 'working' by job strata (correlation coefficient)

	Manual worker	Administrative staff	Technical staff	Supervisor
Status and prestige	0.083	0.373	0.026	**0.088**[1]
Income	**0.071**[1]	0.415	0.187	0.712
Keeping employed	0.079	**0.024**[1]	0.066	*0.814*
Contact with others	0.366	0.276	*0.635*	0.471
Serving for society	0.281	0.137	0.195	0.549
Work in itself	*0.937*	*0.514*	**0.002**[1]	*0.917*

[1] The most significant factor for each group.

tend to regard 'working' as a means to generate an 'income'. Their work orientation seems to be based largely on materialistic values, with 'work in itself' not being regarded as interesting and satisfying and therefore not related to WC for this group. WC for manual workers is not so much concerned with the self-actualizing value of work.

By contrast, WC for technical staff is most strongly connected with 'work in itself' being seen as interesting and satisfying, but not with 'income'. Their WC is presumably bound up with the value of self-actualization, and not with the materialistic value of work. The next most important factor for technical staff after 'work in itself' is 'status and prestige'. For technical staff social recognition and reputation at work seem to be important as well. WC for administrative staff is mainly related to 'keeping employed' and neither 'work in itself' nor 'income' show a significant influence. Their WC might be characterized as neither materialistic, like manual workers, nor self-actualizing, like technical staff, but it seems influenced more by a need for a sense of belonging. For supervisors, WC is most positively related to 'status and prestige', and neither 'work in itself', nor 'income', nor 'keeping occupied' are significant influences for this group. Their WC seems to be rooted in a strong concern with social recognition and their reputation at work.

These findings recall Maslow's (1954) hypotheses of the five phases of need: physiological, safety, belonging, social recognition and self-realization. If this scheme would be adapted to the findings above, it might be said that WC for manual workers is related mostly to concerns about what is needed to make a living, that is focusing on the elementary phases; for administrative staffs the focus is on a need for belonging; for supervisors the primary need is social recognition; and for technical staffs the goal is self-realization, that is the highest phase of the needs hierarchy. If the ratio of manual workers further decreases and of technical staff increases in the employment structure of post-industrial society, the meaning of self-realization would be enhanced all the more in Japan.

12.3.3 Traits of Employees in Small- and Medium-sized Enterprises

The data outlined and analyzed above are concerned only with permanent full-time employees of large-scale enterprises. Now, let us look into the traits of workers in small- and medium-sized enterprises (SME) compared to large-scale enterprises (LE). There is, however, a lack of data available to be able to make a direct comparison between enterprises of different sizes. Therefore, at first, some traits of SME employees will be drawn in an indirect way.

Denki Roren research in 1984 (Denki Roren, 1986), close in time to the MOW research considered earlier, did not use the tool of a seven-point scale for measuring WC that was used in their research in the 1990s, but another tool was applied which makes a comparison with the data of MOW more meaningful. This tool considered five areas of life, namely 'work', 'leisure', 'community', 'religion' and the 'family'. The MOW respondents were asked to give points to each of these categories in order for the total number of points to be 100, while the Denki Roren respondents were asked to rate two fields as most important. From both sets of answers in aggregate it was then possible to calculate the average relative importance of each area in percentage terms. The average point score (from a possible total of 100) for each of the five fields for the two sets of data is illustrated in Table 12.8.

As seen in Table 12.8, MOW data that included working people from SMEs show a comparatively higher percentage defining 'work' as more important than those of Denki Roren drawn exclusively from LEs. From this we can assume that WC would be a little higher among SME employees than LE ones, though the difference between the two groups is not great. In contrast, a stronger 'leisure' orientation of employees can be surmised to exist among LE employees than SME ones. This

Table 12.8 Importance of different fields of life

	Work	Leisure	Community	Religion	Family	Total
MOW Data (1981/83)	36	20	5	4	35	100
Denki Roren Data (1984)	28	33	3	1	34	100

The number in the sample in the Denki Roren data is 3,077.

could be understood from the fact that income and living conditions among SME workers are not so favorable than for LE employees, whose wage level on average is higher and employment situation more secure, thus giving them a stronger base from which to enjoy their leisure.

The preceding part of this chapter pointed out that the degree of WC of Japanese employees in the Denki Rengo research of the 1990s was recorded as lower than for those employees involved in the MOW research in 1981–1983. Two reasons may account for this. First, changes of the work value structure might have occurred accompanying the decline of WC; and second, the different sample structure of the two research studies may account for the difference, since WC is generally lower for permanent employees of LEs than for all other categories of employees, including those of SMEs. The first assumption will be examined later, but the second one can be considered to be more or less valid.

Another comparison between LEs and SMEs employees is possible by looking at data obtained from two research studies that applied common variables of Work Satisfaction (WS) and Company Commitment (CC). One is the study on SMEs conducted by the Tokyo Metropolitan Labor Research Institute in 1999 (Okunishi, et al., 2000), and the other is the Denki Rengo research conducted in the same year (Denki Rengo, 2000). For reference, as mentioned earlier, there is incidentally a positive correlation between WC, WS and CC. Therefore, the trait of WC can be presumed from findings on the situation or condition of WS and CC. The outcomes of both researches are outlined in Table 12.9.

The figures in this table point to a higher degree of work satisfaction of employees in LEs compared to those working in SMEs. This trait was found also in the research on employees working in the chemical industry (Ishikawa, 2002, p. 147). This research revealed a larger satisfaction

Table 12.9   Work satisfaction by size of enterprise

	Satisfied	More or less	Dissatisfied
SME (Tokyo)	42	8	32
LE (Denki Rengo)	47	28	22

Table 12.10   Company commitment by the size of enterprises

	Self-devoting	Calculative	Indifferent
SME (Tokyo)	29	42	18
LE (Denki Rengo)	26	49	20

by LE employees not only with their work, but also with their companies. It is noteworthy, however, that 'satisfied' employees outnumber 'dissatisfied' ones not only in LEs but also in SMEs. In summary, one could conclude that SME employees are more work oriented, but less satisfied with work than employees working for LE, though the difference between those two groups is not large in these respects.

Additional data is also available that allows us to make a comparison of work satisfaction between full-time permanent and part-time temporary employees. According to this data, 'satisfied' people among the permanent employees are rated at 61 per cent (male) and 66 per cent (female), while satisfaction among temporary employees scores 51 per cent (male) and 59 per cent (female) respectively (Iwai and Sato, 2002, p. 85). This indicates a higher satisfaction with work for permanent employees than temporary ones, but the difference between them in this respect is not great. In both groups the 'satisfied' account for more than half of those surveyed. With respect to company commitment, as seen Table 12.10, there is comparatively little difference between employees in SMEs and LEs. This means that CC in SME is not necessarily weak.

However, a component of CC does vary between the two groups. According to the research in the chemical industry (Ishikawa, 2002), a wish for a security of employment up to the retirement age is larger in SMEs, while a wish for actualizing one's own professional potentiality is greater in LEs. This in part reflects the greater prevalence for security of employment in large companies compared to smaller enterprises, such that employees in the latter case are more likely to aspire to greater security. For reference, manual workers are more prevalent in SMEs, while specialists in different jobs are mainly in LEs.

12.4 Trends and Perspectives

Two pieces of research conducted in the first half of the 1980s, mentioned before (cf. Table 12.8), indicated LE employees were rather more leisure-oriented than work-oriented, while SME employees were rather more work-oriented. According to longitudinal researches on Japanese people's perception of their life, leisure-oriented people exceeded those who were primarily work-oriented from the second half of the 1980s according to trends (NHK 2000), as shown in Table 12.11. Presumably, the mid 1980s was a turning point from a predominant work-orientation to a predominant leisure-orientation in the mind of Japanese people.

These figures, however, do not necessarily mean that there is a general trend for work commitment to be declining, as having seen in the Denki Rengo research data (cf. Table 12.2 and 12.3), between 1994/1996 and 1999/2001 WC increased and WS kept at almost the same level (Denki Rengo, 1996, 2000). Therefore, the data could be interpreted as follows: life orientation has been visibly diversified and the concern for leisure has been increasing, but attachment to the importance of work has not collapsed and is maintaining a certain level, though this is fluctuating.

Japanese employees are still devoting much of their time to work. According to government statistics, the total working time of Japanese employees is 140.5 hours a month (January 2005), of which overtime work is 10.1 hours (Ministry of Welfare and Labor, 2005). This is an average figure including part-time workers, who occupy 25 per cent of the whole workforce (but excluding casual workers). Lengthy overtime work is particularly conspicuous for specialists in technical or administrative jobs, and for employees working in sales and marketing. Specialists work an

Table 12.11 Trend of orientation in life

	1978	1983	1988	1993	1996
Work-oriented	43	39	31	26	26
Both-oriented	25	28	32	35	35
Leisure-oriented	29	31	34	36	37

average amount of 39.2 overtime hours, while the figure for marketing and sales employees is 36.4 hours a month (Fujimoto, 2005). In spite of such overtime work, their WS is significantly high (Ishikawa, 2002). This is supposedly because their main concern is focused on 'work itself' related to a desire for self-actualization at work, and this concern is often realized. On the other hand, dissatisfaction with their working time and workload is high as well, as revealed by technical staff in the Denki Rengo research (Denki Rengo, 2000). In their case, presumably, dissatisfaction with working time does not always damage the satsifaction at work as a whole.

As has been shown, work centrality (WC) is rated higher by manual workers and employees with lower levels of education, whose main concern is 'income' and 'employment security'. These groups of workers, however, are decreasing in both proportion and number. Instead, the ratio of technical staff and sales workers with a higher educational level has increased, and this trend is continuing. They are bound to devote a considerable amount of their time to work leaving little spare time for other activities in life, although their concerns and values are largely diversified today. Unsurprisingly, they are mostly dissatisfied with the extent of their working time and workload, but they still keep a certain degree of WC as the interesting and satisfying nature of 'work itself' is often their main concern in work. Their attachment to the company could be maintained and developed, as long as they are provided with work they consider interesting and that gives them the possibility for self-actualization at work, while seeking a balance between work and other spheres of life such as family and leisure.

Apart from those employee groups considered above, we can observe an increase of irregular workers such as part-time, casual or remote workers, due to the diversification in the structure of employment. Workers with a working time of less than 35 hours a week were rated 13 per cent of the total number of the workforce in 1990, and this figure increased to 23 per cent in 2003 (Ministry of Welfare and Labor, 2003), though the real figure might be much higher if illegal foreign workers were included in the count.

Those irregular employees receive much lower wages than regular employees. Reasons why people have the status of an irregular employee vary (Ishima, 2003). On the one hand, there are those workers, who do not have any other choice because they have difficulties in finding regular employment in the labour market. This, however, is not always the major reason. On the other hand, many workers also choose irregular positions willingly, because they are combining their work with other obligations they have at home (mainly women) or at school (mainly students), or because they prefer not to be bound to an organization as a regular staff member. Just because their priority is focused on family, school or some other area of life, however, does not mean they exhibit less attachment to the importance of their work. As outlined previously, 50 per cent or more of all irregular employees are satisfied with their work, while the proportion of dissatisfied workers is rather small.

It is clear that both regular and irregular employees are integrated in the framework of working life. A problem today is the increase of those workers who are floating outside this framework. They are drifting from one place to another without any intention of finding a stable job and have no concern for the formation and accumulation of their occupational skills, and, subsequently, do not develop any specific kind of work identity. These (mostly young) people are called 'fleeters'[3]. Their number was estimated to be 2,090,000 in 2003, a figure ten times higher than only ten years before (Ministry of Welfare and Labor, 2003). Another type of 'floating' person, again mostly to be found among the young, has also been increasing recently: the so-called 'NIET', who are not in education, employment or any kind of training. The number of these people was roughly estimated to be 520,000 in 2004 (Ministry of Welfare and Labor, 2004). They are individually isolated from society and refuse to be integrated in mainstream society at all.

The increase of this type of semi- or fully-jobless people during the past 10 years is, on the one hand, presumably due to the tight labor market after the collapse of the 'bubble economy' in the 1990s. On the other hand, we can observe a cultural change accompanied by weakening social bonds in an 'affluent society'. This is the area where there now appears to be a new crisis of work identity in Japan, and the young people concerned show attitudes to work very different from those stereotypically attributed to earlier generations.

Empirical data in this chapter portrays another picture of Japanese workers than their stereotype that characterizes them as believing in the centrality of work to their lives and strongly identifying with the companies for whom they work. Attitudes of workers with permanent full-time jobs in the core industries of the Japanese economy reflect lower levels of work centrality, work satisfaction and company dependence than those of workers in many other countries. These traits are found more frequently among highly-educated groups such as engineers.

---

[3] 'Fleeter' comes from the English word 'fleet' which means 'swift'. The Japanese government defines 'fleeters' as people of the age between 15 and 34 (except students and housewives) who are engaged with part-time or casual jobs or are jobless in spite of a will to work (Cabinet Office, 2003).

Technical workers as a proportion of all employees in Japanese industry have been growing and their values and attitudes may be influencing the representation of work identities of Japanese workers as unchanging. However, as discussed in this chapter, groups in other segments of the labour market, whether belonging to the periphery of the labour market workforce like 'fleeters' or those who form part of the non-technical employment structure in large-scale enterprises, do certainly undermine the traditional stereotype of the 'company employee' strongly committed to his/her work. The work identities of Japanese employees have become increasingly multi-faceted and the differences in attitudes to work between different groups are marked even among those who are part of the mainstream employment structures.

References

Cabinet Office (2003). *White paper on the national life-style*. Tokyo: Gyosei (in Japanese).

Denki Rengo (1996). *Research report of electrical machine workers' consciousness in 14 countries* (Chosa Jiho No. 287). Tokyo: Denki Rengo (in Japanese).

Denki Rengo (2000). *Research report of electrical machine workers' consciousness in 14 countries* (Chosa Jiho No. 315). Tokyo: Denki Rengo (in Japanese).

Denki Roren (1986). *Research report of electrical machine workers' consciousness in 10 countries* (Chosa Jiho No. 212). Tokyo: Denki Roren (in Japanese).

Fujimoto, T. (2005). Overtime work by white-collar employees. *Business Labor Trend*, 6, 2–6 (in Japanese).

Hayashi, Ch. et al. (1991). *Cultural link analysis for comparative social research*. Tokyo: Institute of Statistical Mathematics (in Japanese).

Hazama, H. (1979). *Toward managerial welfarism*. Toyokeizaishinpo-sha (in Japanese).

Ishikawa, A. (1992). Labour relations and Japan's social structure: Focusing on the social function of the company. *International Revue of Sociology*, 2, 105–118.

Ishikawa, A. (Ed.) (2002). *Work and union in chemical industry*. Tokyo: Nihon-hyoron-sha (in Japanese).

Ishikawa, A. (2004). Human resource management of Japanese firms in the Czech industry. In A. Ishikawa (Ed.), *Employment and work in the transitory period of the Czech Republic* (pp. 129–149). Tokyo: Chuo University Press (in Japanese).

Ishikawa, A. and T. Shiraishi (Eds.) (2005). *Japanese workplace and working life: An international comparative perspective*. Tokyo: Gakub un-sha (in Japanese).

Ishikawa, A., R. Martin, W. Morawski and V. Rus (Eds.) (2000). *Workers, firms and unions Part 2: The Development of dual commitment*. Frankfurt: Peter Lang.

Ishima, T. (2003). The view of irregular worker on employment. *Business Labor Trend*, 12, 19–21 (in Japanese).

Iwai, N. and H. Sato (Eds.) (2002). *Japanese values and behavioral patterns seen in the Japanese general social survey*. Tokyo: Yuhikaku (in Japanese).

Maslow, A.H. (1954). *Motivation and personality*. New York: Harper and Row.

Matsushima, S. (1962). *Japanese characteristics of personnel management and their change*. Tokyo: Diamond-sha (in Japanese).

Ministry of Welfare and Labor (2003). *White paper of labor economy*. Tokyo: Gyosei (in Japanese).

Ministry of Welfare and Labor (2004). *White paper of labor economy*. Tokyo: Gyosei (in Japanese).

Ministry of Welfare and Labor (2003; 2005). *Monthly employment statistical survey report*. Tokyo: Japan Ministry of Welfare and Labor (in Japanese).

Misumi, J. (Ed.) (1987). *Meaning of working life*. Tokyo: Yuhikaku (in Japanese).

NHK Hoso Bunka Kenkyujo (Ed.) (2000). *Consciousness structure of Japanese people today* (5th ed.). Tokyo: Nippon Hoso Shuppan Kyokai (in Japanese).

Okunishi, Y., N. Tsuchiya, A. Ishikawa and H. Hatai (2000). *Human resource management and employees' consciousness in transition*. Tokyo Metropolitan Labor Research Institute (in Japanese).

Part Four

Modern Work and the Creation of New Professional Identities

13

The Construction of a New Professional Self: A Critical Reading of the Curricula for Nurses and Computer Engineers in Norway

Monika Nerland and Karen Jensen
University of Oslo, Norway

13.1 Introduction

The vision of what it means to be a professional has changed profoundly in the course of the last decades. In contrast to prior phases of history, where the professional was envisioned as a collective being whose main challenge was to appropriate the shared knowledge and values of the occupation and to act in accordance with these, we now face an era where the professional 'self' is cast as innovative and autonomous; as an 'overriding self' who is expected to bear the brunt of producing new knowledge as well as creating new relationships of commitment and trust in an ever-changing and increasingly complex society. The shifts entail what sociologists have described as 'insourcing' (Lash, 2003), that is, a reallocation of functions, activities and responsibilities onto the individual, that were traditionally understood to be a collective matter. In this chapter[1] we aim to draw attention to a

---

[1] This chapter is written as part of the project *Professional Learning in a Changing Society*, which is being carried out at the University of Oslo, Institute for Educational Research. For more information, see Jensen and Lahn (2003).

A. Brown, S. Kirpal and F. Rauner (eds.), Identities at Work, 339–360.

theme that has been less discussed, namely how new notions of the self are envisioned and realized within the framework of formal education. What is done to enhance the development of this new professional self, and how do these efforts play out in the current policy reform of the education and training of professionals?

Focusing on how qualities of the self are sought and inscribed in the curricula for initial professional education[2] in Norway, we approach these questions by way of several steps. First we provide a theoretical and methodological ground for exploring the role of policy documents in the construction of professional selves. Using concepts and ideas introduced by Foucault and his followers, we point to how curricular documents serve as governing technologies that seek to 'transform' the students and shape their subjectivity in accordance with dominant discourses in contemporary society. Then we use these insights to analyze notions of the self in recent policy documents, first within the field of Norwegian higher education in general, and thereafter delving into the particulars of two professional groups to point out ways in which the self is constructed in the new curricula for these groups. The groups on which we are focusing are nurses and computer engineers.

13.2   The Professional Self as Constituted within Curricular Games of Truth

From a Foucauldian point of view, the curriculum represents a system of knowledge and reason that regulates the students' (and teachers') possible ways of thinking, learning and knowing. Through the organization of knowledge, a curriculum expresses expectations to the students regarding how to reason about the world and about the self in the world. The curriculum could thus be understood as

> part of a discursive field through which the subjects of schooling are constructed as individuals [who ought] to self-regulate, discipline, and reflect upon themselves as members of a community/society (Popkewitz and Brennan, 1998, p. 13).

In this way, curriculum serves as a constitutive force in the construction of the learning professional self. It seeks to 'transform' the

---

[2] Throughout this chapter we restrict the concept of professional education to the three-year initial professional education qualifying for the bachelor's degree.

individual student by means of knowledge acquisition and participation in educational practices, and hence to provide the student with a new potential for (socially approved) agency.

The specific means of organizing knowledge are the products of negotiation and of dominant ways of thinking in the current period of time. One important feature of curricular documents is that they *take up crucial contemporary discourses about society and the individual*. For instance, a worldwide ideological trend in curriculum today is described as related to a notion of societies built on citizenship and of individuals imbued with choices and capacities in a rationalized, lawful world (McEneaney and Meyer, 2000). Such notions are powerful in the construction of aims and learning activities, although they are often taken for granted by those who participate in the educational practices. Another feature of curricula, at least where Norwegian professional education is concerned, is that they are the *products of negotiation* between professional associations and educational authorities. This holds especially true for the development of the nursing curriculum, in which the Norwegian Nurses' Association has played a crucial role. The general plans for professional education thus encompass tensions between diverse needs and interests, for example between dominant ways of thinking in the professions and in the system of education, respectively. As Popkewitz (2001) notes, the curriculum is a means of governing that is historically formed within the accepted systems of ideas, and that also has a productive effect on the individuals through its selection of knowledge and incorporated systems of reason. The processes of construing and deploying curricular documents could thus be conceptualized as participation in 'curricular games of truth'.[3]

Foucault (2001) uses the term *governmentality* to describe modes of governance in modern societies. In light of these perspectives the curriculum can be said to comprise three dimensions of governmentality that interrelate in the constitution of the self (Rose, 1996). First, it entails a *political dimension* in governmentality that concerns how political authorities seek to act upon institutions and individuals to achieve social wealth, welfare and so forth. In the curriculum this comes into play in the manner in which authorities seek to manage and control the underlying norms and values that guide education. Second,

---

[3] Popkewitz borrows the concept of 'truth games' from Foucault (1994a, b), who uses it to explore the way sciences and disciplines operate as social games in which the production of knowledge is regulated through certain rules, standards, and techniques that human beings use to understand themselves.

the curriculum involves an *institutional dimension* of governmentality that operates through the organizing of knowledge as well as in the learning goals and proposed methods for teaching and assessment. Third, a dimension of *self-technologies* is displayed in how the curriculum provides standards and rules that regulate the ways in which students are to understand and govern themselves. Such technologies of the self are about the individuals' ways of defining and regulating themselves by means of both subjugating and contesting the legitimate standards, norms and values embedded in the system of knowledge (Infinito, 2003). Alternatively, as Foucault describes them, they are technologies which 'permit individuals to effect by their own means, or with the help of others, a certain number of operations on their bodies and souls, thoughts, conduct, and way of being, so as to transform themselves in order to attain a certain state of happiness, purity, wisdom, perfection, or immortality' (Foucault, 1994a, p. 225)

According to Foucault (1994a, p. 225) the types of technologies hardly ever function separately. On the contrary, it is in the encounter between the political/institutional technologies and the technologies of the self that governmentality operates. The curriculum thus represents a site where powerful discourses merge and regulate the formation of identities and selves. Its constitutive force derives from the power of language and the provision of categories through which people understand both themselves and the world. In the case of Norway there is a strong tradition of regulating professional education by means of national curricula provided by the Ministry of Education. Although this method of regulation in advance of the actual pedagogical practice is increasingly being replaced with forms of output controls of educational results, the curriculum still has a crucial position in structuring professional education. Viewed in an overall perspective, this makes the curriculum, with its written statements, goals and designated learning activities etc., an interesting arena for exploring the construction of a new professional self.

13.3 A Curriculum Analysis of Two Core Groups

In our analysis we employ these understandings as a point of departure in exploring recent constructions in Norwegian curricular documents for two professional groups, namely nurses and computer engineers. Nursing is among the oldest professions in Norway, and the first nursing educational program was established in 1868. For the first 80 years, however, there was no state regulation of nurse education. The Norwegian Nurses' Association had—and still retains—a strong position in the development of educational standards, and state regulation in the form of government directives gradually emerged from the 1950s (Karseth, 2002). In 1977, nursing education gained status as a higher education program; in 1981 the education of nurses was incorporated into the programs offered by the regional colleges and placed under the authority of the Ministry of Education; and as from 1987, nursing education has been regulated by curriculum guidelines provided by the Ministry (Karseth, 2002).

Computer engineering first gained status as a three-year professional program in 1987. Together with other programs in engineering it is regulated today by a national curriculum. The program is, however, strongly influenced by international standards and trends and is thus less open for negotiations by local and national interest groups (Hatlevik, 2000). This is illustrated in the close link between the goals provided in the national curriculum and the standards listed in the FEANI index.[4]

During recent decades, the training programs for nurses as well as computer engineers in Norway have been the object of extensive reform and revision. The regional colleges have been granted status as university colleges, and both programs have thus now become integrated into the Norwegian system for higher education. Further, both groups have deep roots in practical work and have struggled to legitimize themselves as full-fledged professions. Today, however, both are enjoying increasing popularity and a high level of public trust and respect, indicating their ability to adapt to the needs of our time.[5] The two groups also differ in interesting ways. Where gender is concerned, the education in computer engineering is mainly (and increasingly) occupied by male workers. For the nurses, however, a Norwegian study shows that

---

[4] FEANI is an international federation for engineering organizations in Europe, 'Fédération Européenne d' Associations Nationales d'Ingénieurs'.

[5] A survey among leaders in the public community sector in Norway showed that between 75 and 90 per cent of the leaders regard the competence of recently educated nurses and engineers as satisfactory, and express trust in the educational programs when it comes to preparing students for working as a nurse or engineer (Folkenborg and Jordfald, 2003). However, they also point to needs for curricular changes at the time when the survey was conducted (2002). Among the competences they would like to be strengthened are practical skills for the nurses and knowledge about legislation and community organization for the engineers.

every 5th woman, who applied for higher education in 2003, listed the program in nursing as her first choice (Abrahamsen and Smeby, 2004; Christiansen et al., 2005). Further, the two professions have different traditions of knowledge. While nurses traditionally exhibit a strong commitment towards moral obligations and the concept of care, the engineering traditions are based on technological knowledge and procedures for problem solving. Although this division of knowledge is currently somewhat diffuse, as we will show later, the differences in knowledge cultures may produce different manifestations of the policy trends in the respective educational programs.

In our analysis of the curricular documents we employed a deconstructive approach inspired by Foucauldian perspectives (Popkewitz and Brennan, 1998; Burr, 1995). This approach entails a back and forth reading of central documents, focusing on specific statements as well as their interrelational context. The aim of the analysis was to explore how the organization of knowledge and learning activities, as well as the aims and goals of the program, contribute to the production of a new professional self, both implicitly and explicitly. In line with the three dimensions of governmentality described above, the documents we have examined represent diverse 'levels' of educational governance. At the level of political technologies we have looked into national policy documents related to reforms in higher education carried out in 2003 and 2004, which again are related to the Bologna process aiming at creating a common framework for higher education in Europe. At the level of institutional technologies we examined the national curricula for nurses and engineers as well as the local curricula within one university college. The main documents selected for analysis are thus as follows:

- A government white paper (Report no. 27 [2000–2001] to the Storting) initiating the latest reform in Norwegian higher education;
- Central documents from the Norwegian Ministry of Education that guided the reform;
- The national curriculum for the bachelor's degree in engineering (2003);
- The national curriculum for the bachelor's degree in nursing (2004);
- The local curricula for nurses and computer engineers within Oslo University College.

In the following we start by exploring notions of the self in the documents that guided the reform in higher education, since these provide an important basis for the emergence of the subject-specific curricula.

13.4   Constructions of the Self in Recent Reforms in Norwegian Higher Education

In 1994 the vocational programs, along with the rest of the non-university sector, were integrated into a unified system for higher education. The aim of the merger was to improve qualities related to management and governance and to make the programs more cost effective. Although these goals have to some degree been achieved, the merger has had dramatic side-effects. It has led to increased bureaucratization and, even more importantly, to what researchers describe as an academic drift and a weakening of the distinctiveness of the programs (Kyvik, 2002).

In 2001, a Government white paper (Report No. 27 [2000–2001] to the Storting) entitled 'Do your duty—demand your rights'[6] called for massive reforms within the field of higher education. Driven by a desire to partake in what the Bologna Declaration (1999) describes as 'a European area of higher education' (p. 1), Norway agreed to amend its degree and credit systems to conform to a common European framework. This implied implementing a more flexible study structure and, ultimately, also contributed to a fragmentation of the students' learning environment. Guided by the wish to promote an educational system that ensures 'mobility, flexibility and employability', a modularized system has been developed and a new pedagogy involving teaching methods aimed at ensuring a high level of student activity and more regular forms of feedback has been introduced.

In order to underline the responsibility the students themselves have for their own learning process, the Ministry of Education also stipulates that contracts be drawn up defining not only the rights but also the obligations entailed in participating in a European network of learning:

> In order to enhance learning . . . and progression, emphasis shall be placed on teaching methods involving a high level of student activity combined with assessments that promote learning by means of regular feedback. Educational institutions are to enter into agreements with students clearly outlining the rights and obligations of the institutions and students in relation to each other (Norwegian Ministry of Education and Research, 2002, p. 2).

---

[6] An English summary of the white paper was provided by the Ministry of Education in 2002. The quotations we have included are taken from this summary.

Thus, in Norwegian policy documents a notion of the 'self-driven student' appears to coalesce with educational discourses emphasizing the institutions' role in ensuring educational quality. In recent years, the mechanisms used to govern the institutions have changed relative to previous phases of history. The individual colleges are afforded greater freedom when it comes to the range of subjects, courses and disciplines they offer. At the same time they have been given greater responsibility for realizing national educational ambitions. As the Minister of Education stated in a recent speech (2004), 'Norwegian higher education institutions have been exposed to a more demanding environment, but also given the tools and the opportunity to foster their own growth' (p. 3). And the standards for growth are defined by what the Minister herself has described as a 'new quality assurance regime' focusing on outcomes, results and outputs (Ministry of Education, 2004). In a broader perspective, these policy documents represent strategies for responding to the new challenges raised in the 'knowledge society,' where—according to the Norwegian Ministry of Education and Research (2002)—universities and colleges are to function as 'spearheads for competence' (p. 1).

Viewed together the policy documents represent *governing technologies at the 'political' level* that contribute to a shift of responsibility from the institutions and collectives to the individual learner. Students in professional education are conceptualized as having autonomy, rights and responsibility regarding their learning processes and it seems to be a central notion that the continuous desire and ability to learn will emerge as a motivating force in the student, provided that the educational aims are explicit and the learning possibilities are good. Such technologies of individualization are the products of contemporary discourses operating both in Norway and in other European countries. As Edwards and Nicoll (2001) have shown, the idea of lifelong learning represents a generally embraced notion in post-industrial societies, and this is closely related to the development of a knowledge-based economy. It might be said to work as a powerful technology for 'human capital development', which aims at harnessing people's desires and values, and which prescribes to a notion of the individual as an active citizen who desires to learn and willingly adapts to changes (Edwards and Nicoll, 2001).

For the professional self, however, the current political technologies also serve to position the subject in a counter-discursive space. As pointed out above, the notion of the 'self-driven student' coalesces with discourses that emphasize the institutions' role of ensuring educational quality by means of establishing close ties to the student's work, e.g. by means of regular feedback and written agreements between the student and the institution. This trend towards 'intimization' also implies a governing of the student by means of technologies of surveillance (Foucault, 1984; Sennett, 1992; Krejsler, 2004). The motto 'Do your duty—demand your rights' thus points to a kind of double positioning of the learning self; a sense of freedom is offered to the student, while at the same time he/she is expected to adapt to certain values, interests and collective forms of agency, which are up to the educational institution to define and manage. It points towards what Beck *et al.* describe as 'quasi-subjectivity,' that is, 'a situation of *socially constructed autonomy* that is understood and experienced as such' (Beck et al., 2003, p. 26).

13.5 Constructions of the Self in the Curricula for Nursing and Computer Engineering

In this section we illustrate how these overall trends play out within the curriculum for nurses and computer engineers. The national curricula for nurses (2004) and engineers (2003) have similar structures, consisting of the descriptions of aims, goals, content, organization of subjects and learning activities, and assessment procedures. Further, both plans conclude by quoting the regulations for the programs in question, underlining the formal character of the documents. While the curriculum for nurses applies exclusively for nurses, the program for engineers comprises several specialties. At the local level, however, both programs are specific.[7]

For the sake of comparison we have chosen not to present the two groups separately, but rather to portray four common attributes of the self that emerge as implicitly stipulated qualities in our analysis of both curricula. The attributes relate in various ways to the above-described changes in higher education, and represent nuances of what it implies to be a 'self-driven student' within the new 'quality assurance regime'. New dimensions are, for instance, brought to the learning self as a result of the new ways of organizing knowledge and the individualization of responsibility for learning. A joint thematic organization of the discussion allows us to elucidate how these tendencies manifest themselves in the current curricula for nurses and computer engineers: How do contemporary

---

[7] Quotations from the national and local curricula have been translated by the authors.

notions of the professional self come into play in these documents? And which corresponding demands are raised for the students to master in order to regulate themselves as 'good professionals'?

13.5.1   The Binding Self

We will start out by pointing to how current ways of organizing knowledge and learning impose new demands upon the learning self. As mentioned earlier, higher education is characterized by an *increased fragmentation of learning arenas*. This also applies to the professional programs, where we find indications that the learning community, in which the students are supposed to participate, is broken up into diverse subjects, courses and locations. For the computer engineering students, this takes the form of a module-based curriculum consisting of five-to-ten-credit modules, which cover both theoretical and practical issues (Curriculum for computer engineering, Oslo University College, 2004). Although the curriculum for nurses consists of larger thematic components (30–72 credits) and still contains a substantial element of practical training,[8] this plan, too, is characterized by what Bernstein (1990) describes as strong classification of knowledge and a diversity of sites for learning.

Against this background it is interesting to note the emphasis both plans place on the capacity to link together knowledge provided through the different parts of the program into a coherent whole, expressed as goals that encourage the students to reflect over their experiences and develop learning strategies, which transcend disciplinary boundaries and the divide between knowledge forms. For instance, the national nursing curriculum states that 'transference and integration between theoretical and practical knowledge work' is required if good learning is to take place (p. 10). Correspondingly, the national engineering curriculum stresses the importance of getting the students involved in cross-disciplinary activities, that is, activities that demonstrate 'connections between diverse disciplines and domains of knowledge' (p. 7). Another example of the emphasis placed on the capacity to link together knowledge may be found in goals related to reflective qualities: the engineering students must be able to reflect on 'technological solutions from economical, organizational and environmental perspectives' (p. 4). For

---

[8] From the 180 credits which comprise a bachelor's degree in nursing, 90 credits are to be earned in practice and 90 in the school (General plan for bachelor's programme in nursing 2004).

the third-year students, this culminates in a request to carry out a 'main project' as part of their final exam. Here they are expected to draw insights and knowledge from different subjects and combine these in a 'methodological and problem-oriented project'. This 20-credit project is often carried out in groups, and preferably in cooperation with an engineering company or another work-life enterprise.

Another curricular characteristic that contributes to a fragmentation of knowledge and identities is what we will describe as a shift towards *more individualized learning trajectories*. With a weakening of the community as a provider of visible learning trajectories and professional identities, the task of constructing meaningful professional biographies is given to the student. Using nursing education as an example, portfolio assessment has emerged as a widespread means of organizing learning activities. As Wittek (2004) shows, the portfolio serves as an artefact in nursing education through which actions and knowledge are mediated, learning cultures are transformed and professional trajectories constructed. However, what generally distinguishes portfolio-organized learning is that the learner herself is responsible for constructing a portfolio that meets the appropriate educational requirements and, in this way, also for building a professional trajectory by drawing connections between the diverse learning experiences. Portfolio assessment is also deployed in engineering education. The curriculum for the two first years of this program is largely structured by mandatory modules. In the third year however, the students are requested to choose elective courses in addition to the mandatory subjects, in order to specialize their competence and distinguish themselves in relation to the general community. The learning self thus bears the responsibility for producing a biography that justifies his/her professional choices and provides him/her with the necessary distinctiveness to be perceived as attractive on the labor market.

In both cases the students are positioned as the site where the binding functions are expected to take place. The division of learning activities and knowledge and the module-based curriculum may result in an 'insourcing' of binding functions, where the processes of integrating knowledge and experiences earned at the diverse learning arenas are allocated to the individual student. It leaves to the individual student to make sense of and draw lines between different subjects, between theory and practice as well as the myriad of experiences that constitute a professional identity. The student is thus construed as a *binding self*, who is supposed to develop an understanding of professional work as a whole through partaking in diverse and fragmented arenas for learning.

13.5.2   The Boundary-setting Self

A second characteristic in the two curricula that brings new dimensions to the self is related to an *expansion of the domains of knowledge* in which the students are expected to gain competence. The range of topics and spheres in which the education is supposed to provide students with insights and skill is increasing, challenging the traditional demarcation of professional knowledge domains and communities. For instance, the computer engineers are expected to gain competence not only in technical issues but in moral and aesthetic issues as well. They are also requested to 'take on a responsibility for the environment, broadly defined, in both a local and a global sense' (p. 4), and to acquire an array of interpersonal as well as self-reflexive competencies and skills. For the nursing students, we find formulations of goals where the students are requested to deal with and respect the client's right to influence medical decisions, as well as to take responsibility for 'strengthening the healthiness and preventing illness among healthy and vulnerable groups' (p. 5). And parallel to these extensions of the knowledge domain, the students are also expected to specialize through enrolling in and profiling elective subjects. The curriculum for computer engineering at the Oslo University College (2004–2005) even encourages the students to take more exams and credits than the 180 required for the bachelor's degree.

The curricula thus introduce an unending range of complex relationships and themes for the students to deal with, generating a vision of knowledge acquisition as a never-ending process. Similar expansions are also found to be a general trend in curricula worldwide, and may be related to the emergence of what researchers describe as knowledge societies (e.g. Chisholm, 2000). This is discussed by for instance McEneaney and Meyer (2000), who identify three arenas in curricula that are currently expanding: rationalities of society, of the individual, and of the natural environment. It is thus not surprising that we also find an expansion of knowledge domains in the professional curricula. The important question for the discussion in this chapter, however, is how the expanding demands contribute to the formation of professional identities. In the face of seemingly over-ambitious aims and goals, impossible to fulfill for any individual, boundaries must be drawn and limits set. This task, too, appears to be left to the individual student. The learner is thus constituted as a *boundary-setting self,* responsible for developing appropriate self-technologies to deal with limitless goals and demands.

13.5.3   The Self-monitoring Self

A third characteristic in the general plans is the *conceptualization of professional ethics as a matter of individual responsibility*. This differs from earlier notions of professionalism, where collective regulation within the professional group was emphasized. As Karseth (2004) shows in a discussion of nursing education, a shift in conceptualizing moral and ethical issues seems to have taken place in the course of the past decades. The Norwegian nursing curriculum of 1987 emphasized the learning of disciplinary ethical concepts and modes of argumentation, while the curriculum of 2000 links the moral obligations to the single practitioner and his/her performative skills.

In the current curricula for both nurses and computer engineers this trend is continued in a focus on quality assurance and self-surveillance. In the general engineering curriculum plan this comes into view in objectives, which state that the candidates are 'required to manage to take care of the concept of quality in all situations,' and to 'understand and be able to function as morally responsible agents' (p. 4). The nursing curriculum contains comparable formulations, but this plan is at the same time more concrete, possibly due to this group's more extensive negotiations within the professional association regarding the formulation of goals. The students are here expected to 'document, to ensure the quality of, and to evaluate their own nursing practice' (p. 7). Further, they are expected to possess the capacity both to *define* standards for good work, and to *assess* their own practice in accordance with these. Also, in addition to maintaining high ethical standards in their relationship to clients, the nursing candidates are requested to 'act for the profession in an ethically distinctive manner,' to 'beware of their professional and ethical responsibility in society in general,' and to 'support colleagues in difficult professional or personal situations' (p. 7).

This strong emphasis on ethics combined with the absence of explicit standards or descriptions of good practice, implies a construction of the self as an *inventor, regulator and evaluator of his/her own ethical practice*. The shift in organizing ethical responsibility from the collective to the individual level implies mechanisms of insourcing that could be related to the increasing focus on managing risk in today's society. As Ericson and Doyle (2003) argue, the rise of risk discourse and risk management entails a rise in new moralities of responsibility and accountability at multiple levels of society, where the level of the individual is given emphasis in contemporary liberal regimes. For the professional self, however, meeting such demands requires trained skills in ethical reflexivity as well as self-monitoring and self-inventing skills.

13.5.4   The Knowledge-producing Self

In our introduction we claimed that thinking in terms of innovation and change are crucial aspects in today's general notion of the professional self. We find these ideas reflected in the two curricula in the form of a present '*ethos of innovation*,' that is, an emphasis on preparing the students to partake in research-like activities. At the bachelor's level this comes into view in aims and goals that encourage the students to develop an interest for and understanding of the importance of such activities as a basis for continuing education and lifelong learning.

The nursing general plan describes it as an aim to 'work systematically with the development of the discipline and quality assurance, to contribute to developing the role of the nurse, and to participate in clinical research and in disseminating results from such research' (p. 7). An emphasis on scientific thinking is also reflected in a described task where the students are requested to discuss observations from the hospital and to suggest improvements in the light of research literature.

The engineering plan (2003) reflects a similar take, in formulations such as the following:

> The educational programs should provide insights in the use of research in engineering, and in the importance of research where innovation is concerned. (p. 3)
>
> Engineering education should educate candidates who show a positive attitude towards innovation—engineers who acknowledge the usefulness of participating in such activities, in their work or in continuing education. (p. 4)
>
> The education should provide the candidates with the updated technological knowledge necessary for contributing to innovation. They should build up a basis for developing their innovative skills, and be prepared for entrepreneurial teamwork. (p. 4)

Such formulations incorporate a way of thinking that we conceptualize as an 'ethos of innovation'. The importance of questioning the existing truths and developing new insights is emphasized. Inherent in this is also a notion of continuous learning. The limited scope of initial education is recognized and the bachelor's programs in no way seek to provide the candidates with all the knowledge and skills needed in their forthcoming innovative work. Hence, an attempt is made to resolve the problem by allocating the task of further learning to the individual professional. It is not surprising, then, that we also find this discourse reflected in descriptions of working life. For instance, a Norwegian study describes how competence development and documentation among engineers appears to be allocated to the individual practitioner and left to personal initiative (Eldring and Skule, 1999). Nurses are also expected to carry a personal responsibility for further learning and knowledge development after having finished their formal education (Christiansen et al., 2005)—a responsibility that moreover is stated explicitly in the national code of ethics for nurses (Norwegian Nurses' Association, 2001).

For the learning professional self, the conveyed importance of innovation implies demands for developing the *right desire and motivation* for further education and research activities. The student is constructed as a *knowledge-producing self*—as a coming innovator and agent of change, who paradoxically is asked to appropriate the innovative way of thinking while at the same time postponing this kind of practice to a later stage in his/her professional career.

13.6   Discussion

Obviously, history is never clear-cut. Among the diverse trends and flows operating in today's professional education we have highlighted a story that concerns how the professional self is altered by means of new demands and stipulated qualities. One reservation to this narrative involves the fact that our analysis is limited to the written curriculum. It should thus not be read as a description of how students and teachers actually engage with the goals and demands of their everyday work practice. Further, we find aspects in the curricula that are counter-discursive to the description above. One example of this is the relatively structured curriculum for the first two years of the computer engineering program, in which the knowledge domains and learning activities are somewhat more fixed in time and space and where the idea is apparently that the students need to develop basic knowledge and skills before they are able to use these innovatively or to make choices to specialize their competence during their third year. The plans could thus be read as multi-signifying locating the learner in contested sites that will also inevitably be sites of resistance. Nevertheless, the notion of an overriding and self-regulating professional self is strongly exposed in the reform policies as well as in the national and local curricula. The curricular constructions at both levels forge a vision of the individual as self-motivated, self-regulated, and self-driven: able to bear the brunt of setting boundaries and constructing meanings in a fragmented and complex learning ecology.

In these ways the Norwegian curricula for nursing and computer engineering reflect general trends in curricular documents worldwide, often described in terms of increased organization around choice and expanded formulations of goals (McEneaney and Meyer, 2000). Although the curricula do not provide the students with fixed professional identities, their formulation of goals and ways of organizing knowledge implicitly *require a certain mentality* where the 'good student' is requested to show 'commitment to a particular view of self in environment' (McEneaney and Meyer, 2000 p. 200). Above all the curricula help to shape a self who is requested to understand himself/herself as an active member of a professional community, responsible for managing knowledge, making good choices, and for keeping involved in a process of continuous learning and self-improvement. This notion of the professional is part of a wider trend whereby government authorities seek to empower their populations to become more responsible for their own life courses (Edwards and Usher, 2001). It could be described as a variant of *the enterprising self*, who is responsible for carrying out best practice, for overriding existing structures and for producing new insights. Further, becoming such a self implies notions of a search for autonomy, freedom and personal fulfillment, where the self is to find meaning in existence by shaping its life through acts of choice' (Rose, 1996, p. 151).

Viewed together, the current movements imply a *shift in the governing mechanisms*, where the self emerges as the core object for regulation and change. Regulation has become 'transferred' in the way that practices at the micro-level have emerged as increasingly important sites for regulation (cf. also Martínez Lucio and MacKenzie, 2004). Governmentality in the mode of self-formation seems to be brought to the fore, apparently taking the place of previously powerful institutions. At this point our analysis of the two curricula corresponds to other findings in contemporary research on governmentality and education, which describe how the inner self becomes the core object for regulation, and how the individual is positioned as the central 'place' where societal paradoxes and complex relations are expected to be managed (Fendler, 1998; Krüger and Trippestad, 2003; Miller, 1993; Rose, 1989). As Fendler (1998, p. 55) puts it, 'Becoming educated, in the current sense, consists of teaching the soul—including fears, attitudes, will and desire.' This shift does not, however, necessarily imply a weakening of political and institutional forms of governmentality. Social theorists discuss whether these changes imply a deregulation or rather a change in, and perhaps a strengthening of, the disciplinary mechanisms. Such strengthening could take place through a 'governing at a distance' by way of articulating explicit standards that the individuals are supposed to realize (Amoore, 2004; Evetts, 2003; Fournier, 1999).

For the *professions* however, this is not merely a question of whether the regulation is in decline or in growth. More importantly, the shifts entail changes regarding the *instances and institutional levels where the regulatory mechanisms are located*. Traditionally, professions were recognized by a high degree of autonomy and dominance and by their abilities to exercise occupational control of work (Freidson, 2001). Professionalism was related to an exclusive ownership of an area of expertise, to the power to define the nature of problems in that area, to the control of access to potential solutions, and to the ability to motivate and control work from 'within', by way of collegial organizations, shared values and identities—all principles in what Freidson (2001) conceptualizes as a 'third logic' of organizing work, distinct from that of the market and that of the bureaucracy. Today the characteristics of society and the shifts in governing mechanisms imply that a number of functions, activities and responsibilities previously attributable to the professions have been otherwise located—changes that also come into view in professional education. On the one hand, we find what Lash (2003) describes as *insourcing*, that is, a reallocation of functions, activities and responsibility onto the individual which traditionally were understood to be a collective matter. The constructions of the self in the current curricula reflect insourcing mechanisms in the way that the individual practitioner is held responsible for professional ethics, innovation and the construction of a professional identity. On the other hand, there is a general trend in the professions towards an *outsourcing* of functions by way of managerial and bureaucratic control systems. In our discussion the emergence of a national 'regime for quality assurance' in higher education could be read as a process of outsourcing, in the way that the power to define educational standards and quality indicators is relocated from the professional communities to the national authorities.

The potential consequences of these shifts on the professions are open to question. The processes of detraditionalization and individualization in today's society are said to challenge the embeddedness of individuals in 'communities of practice' and to undermine the professions' abilities to motivate and control work from 'within'. In this regard the mechanisms of insourcing may represent a productive step in their response to the contingency, ambivalence and rapid shifts of today's society. The notion of the self-managing self offers a 'vision of mastery' that goes beyond the modernist attempt to overcome ambivalence and uncertainty. It paves the way for a reconfiguration of the notion of the profession in a direction that is more sensitive to the contingent and specific, but is not entirely left afloat. The new positioning of the professional self corresponds to Bauman's description of the postmodern demands, where the self is expected to be 'taking stocks of the dangers and opportunities inherent in the scene' (1995, p. 9). Assigning the responsibility for learning to the individual may be a constructive way to deal with challenges related to incredulity and doubt in a so-called 'postmodern condition of knowledge', where knowledge-creating practices are left in a state of permanent instability and change. As Edwards and Usher proclaim; 'learning is the condition of flexibility, and flexibility is seen as the condition of learning' (2001, p. 279). One possible impact of the current constructions of the self may thus be a *potential for renewal of confidence and affiliation.* Provided that the students embrace the positions they are offered, the standards and ideals conveyed in the curriculum may be transformed to desires, wants, and productive self-technologies. This may contribute to creating new collective identities based on a more 'post-modern attitude' that goes beyond the stable communities and knowledge hierarchies. Further, the new visions of the self provide a space for engaging with a fuller range of professional learning without bestowing privileges on certain predefined models and bodies of knowledge as inherently worthwhile. The opening of epistemological spaces and possible trajectories may bring new modes of practice into the professions that may also help to reshape and strengthen the communities.

However, there is no guarantee that such promises will be realized. A positive outcome requires individuals who are truly able to cope with the multiple demands. This again requires a learning environment that provides students with the tools necessary to do this. Competence in self-management could be understood in terms of skills, and where development of skills is concerned, extensive research on learning has highlighted the need for guided training within clearly defined boundaries. However, the insourcing of functions related to, for example, binding and boundary setting may undermine the scaffolded training of such capabilities. In the case of Norway, research also indicates that many students in higher education are not provided with the supervision needed to develop flexible and generic skills (e.g. Bråten et al. 2003). It is thus crucial for the educational institutions to avoid over-adapting in their response to the new needs and demands. If the educational institutions withdraw themselves as agents of knowledge, for instance by avoiding developing standards for ethical responsibility, this may create an opening for societal and neo-liberal forces to act directly upon the individual. At the next juncture, this could have a dramatic under-mining effect upon the professions as autonomous and self-regulating communities.

The current forms of regulation thus represent ambivalent and multi-signifying forces that could assume a myriad of forms, as is the case for constructions in the postmodern world in general. As we see it, they could take at least two imagined directions where the professions are concerned. They could have an emancipatory effect upon the individuals, laying the groundwork for the growth of revitalized and strong communities. At the same time however, there is a risk that they could have a paralysing effect upon the overloaded selves, thus resulting in an undermining of collective structures in the professions. Such scenarios need to be investigated empirically, a task that goes beyond the scope of this chapter.

References

Abrahamsen, B. and J.-C. Smeby (2004). *Sykepleierstudenten—rekruttering, studietil-fredshet og studieutbytte*. [The nursing student—recruitment, perception of learning environment and educational outcome]. (HIO Publication No. 7). Oslo: Oslo University College.

Amoore, L. (2004). Risk, reward and discipline at work. *Economy and Society*, 33(2), 174–196.

Baumann, Z. (1995). *Life in fragments. Essays in postmodern morality*. Oxford: Blackwell.

Beck, U., W. Bonss and C. Lau (2003). The theory of reflexive modernization. Problematic, hypotheses and research programme. *Theory, Culture and Society*, 20(2), 1–33.

Bernstein, B. (1990). *Class, codes and control: Vol. 4. The structuring of pedagogic discourse*. London: Routledge.

Bologna Declaration, 1999. (Joint declaration of the European Ministers of Education). Retrieved August 20, 2005, from http://www.bologna-bergen2005.no/Docs/00-Main_doc/990719BOLOGNA_DECLARATION.PDF.

Bråten, I., H.I. Strømsø and B.S. Olaussen (2003). Self-regulated learning and the use of information and communications technology in Norwegian teacher education. In *Research on sociocultural influences on motivation and learning: Vol. 3. Sociocultural influences and teacher education programs* (pp. 199–221). Greenwich, CT: Information Age Publishing.

Burr, V. (1995). *An introduction to social constructionism.* London: Routledge.

Chisholm, L. (2000). The educational and social implications of the transition to knowledge societies. In O. von der Gablenz, D. Mahnke, P.-C. Padoan and R. Picht (Eds.), *Europe 2020: Adapting to a changing world* (pp. 75–90). Baden-Baden/ Brussels: Nomos Verlag.

Christiansen, B., B. Abrahamsen, B. Karseth and K. Jensen (2005). *Utredning om motivasjon, yrkesutøvelse og kompetanse i pleie- og omsorgssektoren.* [Report on motivation, professional practice and competence in the nursing professions]. Oslo: University of Oslo, Institute for Educational Research.

Edwards, R. and K. Nicoll (2001). Researching the rhetoric of lifelong learning. *Journal of Educational Policy,* 16(2), 103–112.

Edwards, R. and R. Usher (2001). Lifelong learning: A postmodern condition of education? *Adult Education Quarterly,* 51(4), 273–287.

Eldring, L. and S. Skule (1999). *Kompetansedokumentasjon for ingeniører. Praksis, behov og utfordringer.* [Documentation of competence among engineers]. (Issue Brief No. 6). Oslo: Fafo Institute for Labour and Social Research.

Ericson, R.V. and A. Doyle (2003). *Risk and morality.* Toronto: University of Toronto Press.

Evetts, J. (2003). The sociological analysis of professionalism. Occupational change in the modern world. *International Sociology,* 18(2), 395–415.

Fagplan for bachelorstudium i ingeniørfag—datalinjen, 2004–2005. [Curriculum for the bachelor degree in computer engineering 2004–2005]. Oslo: Oslo University College.

Fagplan for bachelorstudium i sykepleie, 2004–2005. [Curriculum for the bachelor degree in nursing 2004–2005]. Oslo: Oslo University College.

Fendler, L. (1998). What is impossible to think? A genealogy of the educated subject. In T. Popkewitz and M. Brennan (Eds.), *Foucault's challenge. Discourse, knowledge, and power in education* (pp. 39–63). New York: Teachers College Press.

Folkenborg, K. and B. Jordfald (2003). *Kommunale lederes vurdering av sykepleier- og ingeniørutdanningen* [Community leaders' assessment of the educational programmes for nurses and engineers] (Issue Brief No. 11). Oslo: Fafo Institute for Labour and Social Research.

Foucault, M. (1984). The means of correct training. In P. Rabinow (Ed.), *The Foucault reader.* New York: Pantheon Books.

Foucault, M. (1994a). Technologies of the self. In P. Rabinow (Ed.), *Essential works of Foucault 1954–1984: Vol. 1. Ethics. Subjectivity and truth* (pp. 223–251). New York: The New Press.

Foucault, M. (1994b). The ethics of the concern of the self as a practice of freedom. In P. Rabinow (Ed.), *Essential works of Foucault 1954–1984: Vol. 1. Ethics. Subjectivity and truth* (pp. 281–301). New York: The New Press.

Foucault, M. (2001). Governmentality. In J.D. Faubion (Ed.), *Essential works of Foucault 1954–1984: Vol. 3. Power* (pp. 201–222). London: Penguin Books.

Fournier, V. (1999). The appeal to 'professionalism' as a disciplinary mechanism. *Social Review,* 47(2), 280–307.

Freidson, E. (2001). *Professionalism: The third logic.* London: Polity Press.

Hatlevik, I.K.R. (2000). Styring og regulering av sykepleier-, lærer- og ingeniørutdanningen i fire land. En sammenliknende studie av Norge, England, Finland og

Nederland [Steering and regulation of the educational programmes in nursing, teaching and engineering in four countries. A comparative study of Norway, England, Finland and the Netherlands]. (Report No. 4). Oslo: Norwegian Institute for Studies in Research and Higher Education.

Infinito, J. (2003). Ethical self-formation: A look at the later Foucault. *Educational Theory*, 53(2), 155–171.

Jensen, K. and L. Lahn (2003). *Professional learning in a changing society*. Project proposal for the national research programme Competence, Education and Learning (KUL). Retrieved March 30, 2005, from http://www.pfi.uio.no/prolearn/ index.html.

Karseth, B. (2002). The construction of curricula in a new educational context. Roles and responsibilities in nursing education in Norway. In A. Amaral, G.A. Jones and B. Karseth (Eds.), *Governing higher education: National perspectives on institutional governance* (pp. 121–140). Dordrecht: Springer.

Karseth, B. (2004). Curriculum changes and moral issues in nursing education. *Nurse Education Today*, 24, 638–643.

Krejsler, J. (Ed.). (2004). *Pædagogikken og kampen om individet*. [Pedagogy and the struggle for the individual]. Copenhagen: Hans Reizels Forlag.

Krüger, T. and T.A. Trippestad (2003). Regjering av utdanning: Kulturkapitalismen og det veltempererte selvet. [Governmentality in education: Cultural capitalism and the well tempered self]. In I.B. Neumann and O.J. Sending (Eds.), *Regjering i Norge* (pp. 176–193). Oslo: Pax forlag.

Kyvik, S. (2002). The merger of non-university colleges in Norway. *Higher Education*, 44, 53–72.

Lash, S. (2003). Reflexivity as non-linearity. *Theory, Culture & Society*, 20(2), 49–57.

Martínez Lucio, M. and R. MacKenzie (2004). 'Unstable boundaries?' Evaluating the 'new regulation' within employment relations. *Economy and Society*, 33(1), 77–97.

McEneaney, E.H. and J.W. Meyer (2000). The content of the curriculum. An institutionalist perspective. In M.T. Hallinan (Ed.), *Handbook of the Sociology of Education* (pp. 189–211). New York: Springer.

Miller, T. (1993). *The well-tempered self: Citizenship, culture, and the postmodern subject*. Baltimore/London: The John Hopkins University Press.

Norwegian Ministry of Education and Research (2002). *Do your duty—Demand your rights*. (Fact sheet, English version). Retrieved March 30, 2005, from http://www.odin.dep.no/ufd/engelsk/publ/stmeld/014071–120002/dok-bn.html.

Norwegian Ministry of Education and Research (2004, February). *The quality reform*. (Speech at the University of the Western Cape, by Minister Kristin Clemet). Retrieved March 30, 2005, from http://www.odin.dep.no/ufd/norsk/aktuelt/taler/ statsraad_a/045021–990039/dok-bn.html.

Norwegian Nurses' Association (2001). *Yrkesetiske retningslinjer for sykepleiere*. [Code of ethics for nurses]. Oslo: Norwegian Nurses' Association.

Popkewitz, T. and M. Brennan (1998). Restructuring of social and political theory in education: Foucault and a social epistemology of school practices. In T. Popkewitz and M. Brennan (Eds.), *Foucault's challenge: Discourse, knowledge, and power in education* (pp. 3–35). New York: Teachers College Press.

Popkewitz, T. (2001). The production of reason and power. Curriculum history and intellectual traditions. In T. Popkewitz, B.M. Franklin and M.A. Pereyra (Eds.), *Cultural history and education. Critical essays on knowledge and schooling* (pp. 151–183). New York: RoutledgeFalmer.

Rammeplan for ingeniørutdanning, 2003. [General plan: The bachelor's degree in engineering, 2003]. Oslo: Norwegian Ministry of Education and Research.

Rammeplan for sykepleieutdanning, 2004. [General plan: The bachelor's degree in nursing, 2004]. Oslo: Norwegian Ministry of Education and Research.

Report to the Storting No. 27 (2000–2001). *Gjør din plikt—Krev din rett. Kvalitetsreform av høyere utdanning*. [Do your duty—demand your rights. The quality reform of higher education]. (Government white paper). Oslo: Norwegian Ministry of Education and Research.

Rose, N. (1989). *Governing the soul: The shaping of the private self*. London: Routledge.

Rose, N. (1996). *Inventing our selves: Psychology, power, and personhood*. New York: Cambridge University Press.

Sennett, R. (1992). *The fall of public man*. New York: W.W. Norton & Company.

Wittek, L. (2004, June). *Portfolio as an artefact for learning and assessment*. Unpublished paper presented at the biennal conference of the European Association for Research on Learning and Instruction in Bergen, Norway.

14

US Efforts to Create a New Professional Identity for the Bioscience Industry

David Finegold and Robert Matousek
School of Management and Labor Relations, Rutgars University
New Brunswick, NJ, US

14.1   Introduction

Computers and related information technologies (IT) were the key drivers of the technological revolution of the latter half of the 20th Century, affecting most industries and the daily lives of individuals across the advanced industrial countries. The first half of the 21st Century has already been dubbed 'The Age of Biology', as break-throughs in biotechnology have given birth to an entirely new industry and are having major impacts on large existing sectors of the economy. Shahi (2004) estimates that new developments in the biosciences will have major effects on up to half of global GDP in the coming decades, with the largest impact being felt in the health and agricultural sectors.

These two revolutions—computers and biology—are closely inter-twined. The continuous improvements and sharply falling costs in com-puting power have been one of the key technologies that have enabled the historic transition in biology from a descriptive to a quantitative science. As Figure 14.1 illustrates, the advances in decoding of differ-ent organisms' DNA have been highly correlated with the advances in computing captured by Moore's Law—that the amount of information a chip can process will double every 18 months. At the same time, it is the growing computational demands of large scale quantitative biology—such as the Human Genome Project (HGP)—that have supplanted

A. Brown, S. Kirpal and F. Rauner (eds.), Identities at Work, 361–390.
© *2007 Springer.*

defense and entertainment applications as a key driver of cutting-edge computing technology, such as Blue Gene, IBM's record-setting super computer.

Although the decoding of the 3 billion base pairs in the human genome, along with deciphering of the genetic code for many other key crops and animal species, represents a tremendous scientific accomplishment, it is only the most recent in a series of research breakthroughs that have given birth to a new sector of the economy: the biotechnology industry. In the mid-1970s the twin breakthrough in genetic engineering by Stanley Cohen and Herbert Boyer in San Francisco and monoclonal antibodies by Cesar Milstein and Georges Kohler in Cambridge made possible the creation of the first biotechnology companies, like Genentech and Cetus. Within 20 years the US biotechnology industry

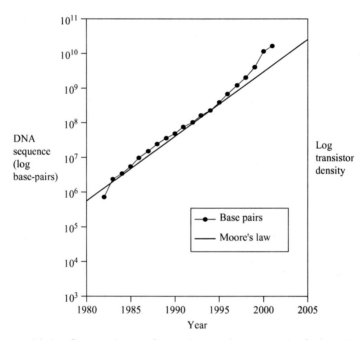

Figure 14.1 Comparison of the increasing speed of decoding of different organisms' DNA with the advances in computing captured Moore's Law—that the amount of information a chip can process will double every 18 months

had grown to approximately 1500 firms. Today the European Union also has approximately 1500 biotech companies, and Asia has another 1900 and is growing rapidly (although these newer firms tend to be much smaller than their US counterparts and have thus far brought fewer products to market) (Shahi, 2004). Virtually all of the industrialized countries and many industrializing nations are investing heavily to grow their own biotechnology industry (Cooke, 2003).

To fill the growing number of positions in the biotech industry and to turn the rich new genetic knowledge and other advances in biotechnological research into beneficial products and processes requires new types of professionals with new skill sets. Historically, the diverse knowledge and skills required were embodied in specialists trained in different disciplines (e.g. biology, chemistry, computer science, business), who spoke different technical languages, and had very different mindsets and approaches to solving problems. As the technology and biotech industry have continued to evolve, it became apparent that new types of professionals who could integrate these different disciplines were needed (Riggs, 1999). Specifically, this chapter will focus on US efforts to develop two new types of bioscience professionals: bioinformaticists or computational biologists who are able to integrate programming skills and biological knowledge to come up with new scientific discoveries or tools to enable them, and bioscience business professionals who can integrate science and business to help commercialize these new innovations.

Although our primary focus is on understanding the evolution of these new professional identities in the biosciences and the wider institutional context in which these new identities are developing in the US, the insights from this field may apply to the creation of new professional identities involved in other forms of complex knowledge work. As in the biosciences, many of the most challenging problems facing contemporary society—such as climate change, educational underachievement in the inner cities, and sustainable development—are systemic in nature, and hence beyond the scope of a single discipline. Likewise, many of the most important discoveries and innovations—ranging from the Manhattan Project and the discovery of the structure of DNA to the development of the IBM personal computer (PC)—were produced through cross-functional work.

The need for interdisciplinary work is at odds with the growing division of labor among academic disciplines brought about by the explosion in new knowledge creation and the accompanying need for individuals to specialize in order to develop and maintain an area of expertise. The different parts that make up complex systems require highly specialized inputs which in turn lead to social and cognitive boundaries between the professions that make it harder for people to work together effectively. Such barriers are thought to be especially problematic when professionals have well-defined roles, identities and traditional work practices (Ferlie et al., 2005). Our focus on efforts to overcome these difficulties in the biosciences by creating new professionals—or boundary spanners—may thus yield important insights for other areas of knowledge work that involve different functional specialists and where the different tasks to be carried out are highly interdependent.

The rest of this chapter is organized as follows. First, we provide a brief overview of the core elements of a professional identity and the historical evolution of professional identities in the biological sciences. Then we look at the US higher education (HE) system's recent efforts to create new identities in computational biology and professional science masters programs to prepare scientists for careers in the bioscience industry. We then turn to a case study of a new start-up within higher education—the Keck Graduate Institute of Applied Life Sciences (KGI)—and discuss the environment it is trying to provide for such an interdisciplinary degree and the outcomes of the program. The key factors affecting success with respect to the labor market, organizational and individual levels are discussed. Finally, some conclusions and comparisons are drawn about the ability of the US educational system to establish new professional identities in these two, related fields.

14.2   Creating New Professional Identities

A professional identity is defined as the relatively stable and enduring constellation of attributes, beliefs, values, motives, and experiences in terms of which people define their careers and work roles (Ibarra, 1999). Professional identities are embedded in communities of practice in which individuals interact with other members of their profession. Commitment to the values of this community is the outcome of a prolonged training and socialization process during which an individual is effectively shielded from competing vocational and intellectual interests, becoming dependent on others within the profession who strongly influence the fate and the self-conception of the individual (Hagstrom, 1965). This commitment is reinforced by selecting individuals for entry into the profession based on their commitment to its attitudes and values, by then conditioning them through routines (ways of working that evolve over time within the community of practice), and by distributing rewards in exchange for their contributions to the goals of the community (Hagstrom, 1965).

When a new professional identity starts to come into being, professionals inevitably must enter from related fields as there is no well-defined educational or career path yet devoted to the new profession. Eventually, however, for a professional identity to become established, new educational options and career paths will need to be developed to provide different points of entry into the profession depending on the skills and experience of an individual. Establishing a new professional identity thus requires a form of institutional change and innovation in order to provide subsequent stability, continuity and direction through coordination of the profession (Ibarra, 1999). When thinking about how professional identities come into being or change, we therefore need to take into account the different levels (individual and inter-personal, organizational, and the wider institutional and labor market environment) at which such change is occurring.

The professional identities that are the focus of this chapter provide a useful means to study both change in professions and change in the organizational settings in which such work is performed. Such occupations can be defined by the traits that are characteristic of the individuals in the profession, such as a particular knowledge base, the required training period and the tasks to be performed for example. The organizational settings in which such work is performed constitute a second-level of analysis. They determine in part the decisions made and procedures undertaken during the work process (content), the characteristics of employment or work contract (terms), and the settings in which such work is performed (context) (Leicht and Fennell, 2001). The final level of analysis needed to understand changes to a profession or a new profession coming into being, is that of the position of the profession as an institution within society. As such, professions represent 'identifiable structures of knowledge, expertise, work and labor markets, with distinctive norms, practices, ideologies, and organizational forms' (Leicht and Fennell, 2001, p. 90). Analysis of professional labor markets, for example, needs to consider both the demand for new skills coming from hiring organizations, and how the supply of new people entering the profession may be controlled by institutional actors who regulate the flow through qualification examinations, and peer review of funding and publications.

14.3   The Need for New Professional Identities in the Biosciences

The integration of computers into biology has fundamentally transformed how the science is conducted. With the advances in technology and the accompanying greater understanding of underlying biological processes, the focus is shifting from small-scale experiments focused on individual elements of organisms to analysis of complex systems. At the same time, the vast amounts of data being produced by large-scale genome projects and high throughput techniques for screening potential drug candidates are making the development of computer algorithms and data analysis skills essential components of life science research and development (R&D). The skills needed for this research, however, have traditionally not been strong within the biological community. Fortunately there are signs of increasing acceptance of quantitative methods in biology. The emerging fields of computational or systems biology are seeking to develop professionals who can organize and analyze this data and build models that can provide real insights into the basis for disease (Gatenby and Maini, 2003). While comprehensive models capable of describing even relatively simple examples of such systems are still in the early phases of development, the hope is that they could eventually help transform the drug development process, reducing the cost, time and very high failure rates associated with current methods (IBM, 2004).

Along with computational biologists, another requirement for society to obtain the full potential benefit from new biotechnologies is developing professionals who can bridge the gap between science and business. Although good quality scientific research provides the foundation for biotech innovation, it is only a starting point. Turning R&D into new drugs or devices requires the capabilities to raise finance and manage product development, manufacturing, the regulatory approval process and marketing of new products. The complementary assets needed to commercialize biotech products lie mainly in the private sector, whereas a substantial part of the capabilities needed for biotechnological research are located in public research organizations. Yet historically there was outright animosity between many of the scientific and medical professions and the bioscience industry in the US and Europe. The American Medical Association's (AMA) first code of ethics, written in 1847, considered the patenting or advertising of drugs to be unethical, while the American Society for Pharmacology and

Experimental Therapeutics, founded in 1908, stated in its bylaws that 'no one shall be admitted to membership who is in the permanent employ of industry' (Hilts, 2003, p. 97). These restrictions remained in force until 1941. Professor John Jacob Abel of Johns Hopkins University, the leading US pharmacologist prior to WW II, summed up academia's attitude to industry: 'I personally would not think of working on a problem suggested to me by any firm, anywhere' (Hilts, 2003, p. 97).

This situation began to change in the 1970s with the birth of the modern biotechnology revolution. University research produced the key breakthroughs that made possible the creation of the first biotechnology companies. Most of these new start-ups were located close to the university labs that spawned them, and the star scientists typically stayed closely connected to the firms (Zucker and Darby, 1996), sitting on the Scientific Advisory Boards and sending their graduates to work in them. The passage of the Bayh-Dole Act in 1980 further strengthened the growing ties between US HE institutions and industry, by giving universities both the right and obligation to commercialize the federally-funded research conducted by their faculty (Mowery et al., 2004). But as Leroy Hood, the inventor of some of the key technologies that made possible the HGP, observed, academia's skepticism regarding industry remained strong even when there were potentially large amounts of money to be made by the universities. He recalled his experience at Cal Tech where he developed the concept for the first automated DNA and protein sequencers:

> When I approached Murph Goldberger, the President of Cal Tech, about creating a company to commercialize the technology in the late 1970s, he said the University wanted nothing to do with it. I offered Cal Tech a 25 per cent stake in what became Applied Biosystems, but he turned me down. That stake was eventually worth about a billion dollars (Hood, 2003, Telephone and in-person interviews with author. May–June).

Hood's own subsequent career path, as both a pioneer in the field of systems biology and a co-founder of ABI and Amgen, suggests the need for individuals who can bridge the gap between academia and industry. People integrating science with business are thought to play a critical role in transferring technology from research to industry by acting as disseminators of new technology and translators of competencies to user sectors (Fontes, 2001).

Although the task of developing new professional identities that bridge the gaps between computing and biology and biology and business may appear daunting, a recent example from within the biosciences suggests it may be possible—the case of bioengineering. Bioengineering is the application of systematic, quantitative and integrative way of thinking about and approaching the solutions important to biology and medicine (NIH, 1997). The last two centuries have laid the groundwork in physics needed for understanding biology and medicine from an engineering perspective. Many of the early engineering concepts and instruments found applications in biomedical research, such as X-ray imaging. This prompted more and more investigators to start using the concepts of physics and engineering in biological and medical research, but it was due to a number of radical breakthroughs in medicine, such as the cardiac pacemaker and heart-lung machine, that engineering has been able to establish a prominent position in medicine.

> The 1950's saw the first steps towards bioengineering as a discipline, with professional societies, regular meetings and publications, and formalized training programs (Nebeker, 2002, p. 10).

Before assuming a distinct identity, bioengineering had been intertwined with biophysics and medical physics, but since then it has moved from being an inter- and multi-disciplinary activity to a discipline in its own right (Nebeker, 2002). This has required significant changes to the engineering profession as well as the professional educational curriculum of engineering students in universities. In the process, it has changed the context in which engineering is defined and put to use—what are the tasks of a bioengineer and what is her or his relationship with others. This change has been driven in part by the demand for innovative approaches to solve problems in biology and medicine as well as the numerous opportunities for the application of engineering to the biological sciences and for commercial development (Nerem, 1997).

14.4   Educating New Types of Professionals for the Bioscience Industry

The way in which different nations respond to the perceived need to educate a new type of professional will be strongly shaped by the structure of the higher education system and surrounding institutions (Finegold, 2006). In most countries, all or most HE institutions are public—that is, funded and governed by the state. The government typically regulates the content and quality of what is offered in these public institutions, and has to approve the development of new qualifications.

In contrast, the US has a variety of public and private colleges and universities, including for-profit HE institutions, operating in a market environment. The stiff competition and lack of regulatory barriers generates a high degree of responsiveness to student and company needs and to economic and technological changes. The free market for HE, however, also results in very uneven quality across institutions, making it difficult to know in many cases what completion of a degree signifies.

The US HE system benefits from a greater diversity of funding sources for new educational innovations, such as the development of courses for new professionals. While individuals and the government pay for basic tuition and student living costs, research universities rely heavily on their often substantial endowments, raised predominantly through alumni contributions, to invest in new programs. In addition, a very large and growing set of private foundations, each with a distinctive mission, provides a major, flexible source of funding for new program development that is largely absent in other advanced industrial countries. The Gates Foundation, for example, has been in existence less than a decade but, with an endowment of over $30 billion, is already providing more money to fund innovations in global health than most national governments. In addition, US universities are able to leverage their own endowment funds to invest in new courses that are seen to have promise for the future.

The US experience with creating new qualifications for bioscience professionals reveals both the advantages and some of the dangers of this very flexible HE system. Until very recently, the educational options for students interested in entering this sector in the US were very limited. They could enroll for a science PhD—which is designed to prepare people to conduct research in a narrow scientific discipline—or become a medical doctor or pharmacologist. These educational routes are very costly to deliver and time-consuming, with Biology PhDs averaging more than 7 years to completion and medical students typically completing an internship and three or four-year residency after their MD (Doctor of Medicine or Medical Doctor) if they want to enter a specialty. Unlike engineering, biology and chemistry have not had well-established and respected career paths for individuals to obtain a master's degree and then to put their new specialized skills to use in industry. Typically, a student only got a master's in biology if he or she decided to drop out of a PhD program.

Although the Bayh-Dole Act significantly altered the relationships between academia and industry, bringing universities and companies much closer together, traditional PhD programs still did little or nothing to prepare researchers for a career in industry. As Table 14.1 illustrates, however, the creation of the biotech industry in the late 1970s not only opened up new, private-sector career options for PhDs, but also spurred the growth of new technical masters programs. Although computer scientists are not recognized as a biology-related profession in these US Department of Labor occupational statistics, such skills are increasingly deemed essential for biologists as employers prefer job applicants who are able to apply computer skills to modeling and simulation tasks and to operate computerized laboratory equipment. So too are strong business and communication skills, familiarity with regulatory issues and marketing and management techniques for people who aspire to management or administrative positions.

To address these skill needs, universities began in the late 1990s to experiment with a new type of degree program: Professional Science Master's (PSM). With start-up support from the Sloan and Keck Foundations, colleges created new, more applied course offerings that combine science with some business skills intended to help graduates prepare for careers in commercializing biotechnology. 'Science faculty are realizing and beginning to enjoy the fact they can help educate people for important roles in society other than researchers and teachers,' said Jesse Ausubel, a program manager at the Sloan Foundation.

From virtually none a decade ago, there are now around 100 PSM programs spread across the US, with most located in established research universities. Although the number of programs has been growing rapidly, most are still quite small and seeking to establish themselves. They span a wide range of science subjects, but most are concentrated in the biological sciences, with a particular concentration in bioinformatics and computational biology. As more of the biological innovation process has moved from *in vivo* to *in silico*, HE institutions have sought to fill the perceived shortage of biologists with computational skills by creating new PSM programs, as well as adding computational biology options to traditional degrees, from undergraduate to doctoral studies. A recent survey by Black and Stephan (2004) demonstrated the extreme responsiveness of the US HE system to changes in industry demand. In just the four years between 1999 and 2003, number of bioinformatics programs grew from 21 to 74, with the largest growth taking place at the Masters level (see Figure 14.2).

Table 14.1 Biologists: work settings and job characteristics 1980–2005 (Leicht and Fennell, 2001; Bureau of Labor Statistics, 2005)

1980	1985	1990	1996–97	2004–05
WORK SETTINGS				
60% faculty in colleges/ universities	Same as 1980	Same as 1980, 1985	33% faculty in colleges/ universities	(Same as 1996–97)
40% in fed/state/local government, private sector, nonprofit research organizations			33% federal/state/local government	<50% in fed/state/local government
			33% drug industry— pharmaceutical and biotech establishments; hospitals, research and testing labs	<50% in scientific research and testing laboratories, pharmaceutical and manufacturing industry, or hospitals
				Rest faculty in colleges/universities
REQUIRED TRANING				
Ph.D. for college teaching, independent research, advancement to administrative positions	Same as 1980	Ph.D.—same as 1980, 1985	Same as 1990	Ph.D.—Same as 1980, 1985, 1990. 1996–97)
Masters for applied research		Masters for applied research and jobs in management, inspection, sales, service		Masters for some jobs in basic research, applied research or product development, management, or inspection
Bachelors sufficient for some non-research jobs		Bachelors—same as 1980, 1985	Bachelors—same	Bachelors—same as 1980, 1985, 1990, 1996–97)
JOB OUTLOOK				
Good for these with advanced degrees more competition with leser degrees increase faster than average for all	Expected to grow faster than the average for all	Expected to grow faster than the average for all occupations	Expected to grow faster than the average for all occupations through 2005, continued genetics and biotech research,	Expected to grow as fast as average for all occupations through 2012. continued biotech research and development

Continued

Table 14.1 Continued

1980	1985	1990	1996–97	2004–05
occupations through the 1980s because of increased attention to preserving the natural environment, medical research growth in industry and government	occupations through the mid-1990s due to recent advances in genetics research biological technology, efforts to clean and preserve environment Better for those with advanced degrees	through 2000 mostly in private industry, continued growth in genetics and biotech research growth due to efforts to clean and preserve environment Slow growth in federal government	growth due to efforts to clean and preserve environment, expected expansion in research related to health issues, such as AIDS, cancer and the Human Genome Project	Doctoral degree holders can expect to face considerable competition for independent research positions particularly in universities increase in number of newly trained scientists Applied research positions in private industry in private industry may become more difficult to obtain if increasing numbers of scientists seek jobs in private industry Holders of bachelor's or master's degrees in biological science can expect better opportunities in non-research positions, increase in number of science related jobs, in sales, marketing, and research management
RELATED PROFESSIONS Conservation occupations, agricultural scientists, biochemists, soil scientists, oceanographers, and life science technicians	Same as 1980	Conservation occupations, animal breeders, horticulturist, other agricultural scientists, medical scientists, medical doctors, dentists, vets	Same as 1990	Medical scientists, agricultural and food scientists, and conservation scientists and foresters, as well as health occupations such as physicians and surgeons, dentists, and veterinarians

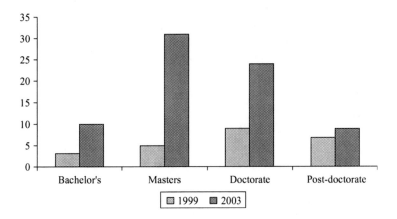

Figure 14.2 Number of US degree programs in bioinformatics

14.5   A Case Study: The Keck Graduate Institute

The Keck Graduate Institute of Applied Life Sciences (KGI) was the first new HE institution created specifically to offer a PSM. Launched in 1997 with a $50 million grant from the W.M. Keck Foundation, KGI is the newest of the Claremont Colleges, a collection of institutions that operate on a similar model to Oxford and Cambridge Universities in the UK. There are seven independent Claremont Colleges, each with its own faculty, endowment, and distinctive identity—e.g. Harvey Mudd College specializing in undergraduate science and engineering or all-women's Scripps College. The colleges are physically co-located, allow students to cross-register for free in each other's courses, and share some collective resources (such as a central library, payroll, benefits administration, etc.). KGI is the second graduate college in Claremont, joining Claremont Graduate University, which contains the Drucker School of Management.

KGI was created without traditional academic departments to foster interdisciplinary collaboration in research and teaching among its faculty. It offers a new two-year Masters of Bioscience (MBS) degree. The MBS combines computational biology, systems biology and bioengineering in project-based learning oriented around the key tasks facing bioscience companies in fields such as drug development, diagnostics, medical devices, bioprocessing and industrial biotechnology, along with a mini-MBA, pharmaceutical development, regulatory and ethics training all tailored to the life science industry. The MBS was designed as a professional degree, with the intent that graduates would be provided with a broad foundation of management and science skills that would help them eventually to advance into leadership roles in the life science industry. For students who elect to pursue a career in research, KGI has launched a small PhD program in Computational Biology in partnership with CGU. KGI is thus seeking to develop both types of professionals needed for the commercialization of the biosciences: developing applied researchers who have mastered computers and biology and professionals who bridge the gap between the business and science of biotechnology.

One of the central ways in which KGI has tried to foster new professional identities for the biosciences is by building close partnerships with industry, taking advantage of its proximity to Southern California's wealth of bioenterprises, from San Diego's dense biocluster (Casper, 2005) to the less concentrated, but growing number of medical device and biotech firms in Orange and Los Angeles Counties. Some elements of these industry partnerships are quite standard within HE—i.e. creating a strong industry advisory board to shape the initial curriculum, inviting industry experts to serve as guest lecturers and adjunct faculty, attracting company sponsorship for applied research, and requiring all students to undertake a paid internship in industry between their first and second years. Others are more unusual: under a National Science Foundation-funded 'Partners for Innovation' program, teams of KGI students partner with leading research institutes (e.g. Scripps, Salk, Burnham, Buck, Karolinska) or early-stage bioentrepreneurs to write market analyses or a full business plan for a promising technology. And in lieu of a master's thesis, all KGI students conduct a full-year Team Masters Project, which is a company-sponsored consulting project where groups of 3–5 students can perform a wide range of tasks, i.e. designing and building a prototype for a new piece of equipment or diagnostic assay and the marketing strategy and business plan for this product. Since admitting its first class in 2000, KGI has already spun out several companies. Students have been involved in all aspects of creating these businesses, from helping to develop the technology, to writing the business plan and negotiating the first supplier partnership. The first of these spinouts, Ionian Technologies (Upland, CA), is based on a dramatic advance in amplifying DNA, an essential step in virtually all drug development and diagnostics that represents a potential $7 billion/year market.[1] In essence, KGI has sought to create a learning laboratory for the commercialization of biotechnology, believing that the best way for students to learn and become socialized into a new professional identity is to work on real problems and novel technologies in cooperation with scientists and entrepreneurs.

For a brand new institution, KGI has had a high degree of success placing its graduates in jobs in the bioscience industry. Approximately 90 per cent of graduates from KGI's first three classes found jobs or pursued continuing education in the bioscience industry within six months of completing their degree, many staying in Southern California's large biotech cluster. Amgen, the world's largest biotech company, has been KGI's top employer and provided evidence of the breadth of the degree, hiring over 20 of the first 115 graduates to work in 11 different departments, ranging from competitive intelligence and business development to project management, process engineering and quality control. What these jobs have in common is that individuals need to be able to analyze both the science and business side of an opportunity, to work in teams, and to communicate effectively with the different functions within an organization.

14.6   Challenges to Creating a New Professional Identity

Our research on KGI and PSM programs more broadly suggests that there are a number of barriers that must be overcome to establish a new professional identity in the biological sciences. These challenges occur at three levels: labor market and technological trends, organizational, and individual and inter-personal.

14.6.1   Labor Market for Bioscience Professionals

A clear sign that a new professional identity has been established is when talented individuals compete to enter the profession and are then able to secure good jobs once they have become qualified. Although

---

[1] Ionian was recently awarded two of the first dozen contracts granted by the US Department of Homeland Security and a major contract from the Defense Advanced Research and Planning Agency (DARPA) to use its technology to develop detection devices to combat bioterrorism.

still very early in their development and after encouraging starts, both the Computational Biology and PSM programs have faced issues with attracting a supply of top students to enter the programs and with establishing clear career pathways for their graduates. On the supply side, the new PSMs are competing for the best applicants from a limited talent pool of science undergraduates whose alternative is a free education: the PhD. They must convince individuals who want to remain in the biosciences, but are not seeking a career in basic research, that the upfront costs of paying for a two-year professional degree offer substantial benefits compared to the substantial opportunity cost of many years of study required to complete a PhD and subsequent post docs.

A key to making this case is demonstrating that a high percentage of graduates in the new field area are able to secure well-paying jobs. A comparison of job advertisements for bioinformatics graduates that appeared in *Science* from 1996–2002 (Black and Stephan, 2004, pp. 21–24) indicates that at the time the new Masters and PhD courses in computational biology were being created the demand for their graduates was rising rapidly, from 209 positions in 1996 to 443 in 2000. By the time the flow of graduates from these new programs was beginning to enter the job market, however, demand had fallen substantially, with the number of positions declining to 254 by 2002. In addition, there was a shift in the type of employer—industry accounted for the majority of jobs in 1996–97, but by 2002 nearly 80 per cent of the openings were in academia. The job picture was even worse for Masters graduates, as the number of openings dropped from 42 to just 6.

This sharp decline in the labor market for bioinformatics graduates reflected a broader shift in the industry, as many of the leading companies created to capitalize on the decoding of the human genome—Incyte, Celera, Human Genome Sciences—ran into trouble in 2000–01. After the initial exuberance surrounding the HGP, it became clear that once this genomic information was placed in the public domain these firms did not have a sustainable business model to go with their exciting technological capabilities. Combined with the more general downturn in high-tech stocks following the dot-com collapse and 9/11, the failure of many bioinformatics companies created a double blow for the new programs: some of the firms that were fueling the demand not only stopped hiring, but also were laying off experienced personnel who were competing with new graduates for jobs. This suggests a broader difficulty with trying to prepare individuals for a still emerging, rapidly changing new professional field—because of the inevitable time lag in creating new professional qualifications, there is a risk that the demand may have shifted before the new supply of professionals can be generated.

In a slack job market, it can be particularly difficult for new graduates emerging with a new form of professional qualification to find jobs. As KGI Professor Bob Watson[2] observed:

> It's hard for young people trained as interdisciplinary scientists to find jobs. A computer science graduate is generally not going to find a good job in a biology department as an academic faculty member. It's very difficult. A biology graduate is never going to find a job in the computer science department. So people will be labeled and will have to demonstrate that they're very good at either computer science or biology. So these interdisciplinary post docs are somewhat of a liability. In the industry it's the same problem; you're either a very good programmer or a you're a very good experimental biologist or you could go to a bioinformatics software development company which requires both, but these days such companies are in a precarious state as there is little funding for pure bioinformatics companies. They're dying like flies. The job opportunity for purely interdisciplinary young scientists at companies is somewhat difficult these days. I'm only hoping that there will be more opportunities both in academia as well as companies, but it's going to be difficult.

For those seeking to pursue an academic career in the emerging fields of bioengineering, computational and systems biology, the prospects have been a bit more encouraging. The two essential elements for establishing a new professional identity in academia are the ability to secure funding to support research and to publish the results of this work in prestigious journals. These new, interdisciplinary researchers have benefited from significant new Federal and foundation funding initiatives in these emerging fields and the growth in university departments and faculty positions this has stimulated and the rapid growth of new journals in these areas, along with a growing acceptance among the most established journals of the value of this work. Despite this progress, overcoming the strength of traditional disciplinary approaches can still prove a barrier to academics in these new fields, as Harry

---

[2] The names of KGI professors, researchers and students have been changed to protect their confidentiality.

Brenner, a post doc in computational biology at KGI noted:

> At smaller universities, people are likely to follow the leaders within a certain field without questioning the approach used. When you mention that this approach is incorrect, they refer to the people from *Nature*—'the people from *Nature* said it's ok'—and their authority is not to be questioned.

Likewise, in today's highly competitive environment, these traditional attitudes can hurt the chances of obtaining research funding from the largest, more general sources not targeted specifically at interdisciplinary research. KGI Professor Tom Gilbert described his experience with seeking support for an innovative line of research creating artificial life within computers as an accelerated way of studying evolution:

> We've had a lot of trouble getting funding . . . The interdisciplinary nature doesn't help. The problem is if you write a proposal that has a theoretical and an experimental component then inevitably you get referees who don't understand both aspects and therefore never get really excited. In a proposal that can be the difference between getting the money or not. In a paper that would be fine, for example if one referee says, 'The experiments are fine. I don't understand the theory,' and the other referee says, 'The theory is fine, but I don't understand the experiments,' then that's fine and the paper will go through. For a proposal that might kill it because both reviewers might only give it a very good instead of an excellent, because they don't understand the other part.

Most PSM graduates, however, are not interested in academic jobs, but instead would like to find managerial positions in the bioscience industry. To secure these positions they must often compete with graduates of business schools who have a much more established MBA qualification and PhDs. The graduates of the new PSM programs are well aware of the relative advantages and disadvantages they face in the labor market. Hank Roberts, a member of KGI's first class, observed:

> I think it depends on the position I'm going for. If I'm going for a position, a clinical research type of position for example, somewhere where you interface between working with management and working with biologist, with doctors, this (degree) is pretty ideal for something like that. Anywhere you have to work with

multiple disciplines, work in a team of people with a lot of different backgrounds, the education at KGI pretty much taught me how to do that. I can talk to the engineers and understand what they're saying and then go talk to the biologists and understand what they're saying and find a way to relay that to my manager who might be just fresh out of an MBA program and might not have much of an engineering or a biology background. I feel like I can pick up such things really easy which gives me a head start. For doing laboratory work, I think someone would be better off doing a straight masters degree, like a person who did the masters in biology and focused on that for two years.

Joan Curie, a member of KGI class of 2005, added:

I feel that my degree is more competitive than an MSc in a more traditional discipline since I have a broader background. Obviously my degree is not as competitive as a PhD, since I don't have as much experience. I feel comfortable however discussing results and making suggestions on subjects that I'm familiar with, otherwise I need to dig in. Computational biology requires very specific skills such as familiarity with a specific programming language, whereas biology seems to require more general skills and competencies within the field of biology.

To better position themselves in the labor market, a few of KGI's graduates have also chosen to obtain an MBA despite the MBS's significant and more bioscience-specific business content. They have done this in two ways: by studying for an MBA part-time that is paid for by their employer's tuition reimbursement program, or by enrolling in a pilot MBS/MBA dual-degree program that KGI established with the nearby Drucker School of Management.[3] This 2-plus-1 program enabled them to accumulate just under half of the credits towards an MBA during their time at KGI, and then to complete their MBA in another 6–12 months of full-time study. Perhaps surprisingly, it was some of the KGI graduates who had the most work experience and best job prospects, who elected to pursue the MBA. For example Hannah McClintock (KGI, 2004), who had extensive project management and marketing experience in online science-content providers,

---

[3] KGI and Drucker subsequently decided not to continue the 2-plus-1 program despite its popularity with students. One of KGI's concerns was that it was competing with the objective of establishing the MBS as an alternative, standalone professional degree for the biosciences.

turned down a good job offer when she graduated from KGI in order to complete her MBA. She explained her rationale for staying on in the 2-plus-1 program:

> So much of my reason for doing it was credibility. When my boss introduces me, he mentions my MBA, which doesn't go unnoticed. The title is more important than the content . . . My hope is that in 10 years KGI grads won't require an MBA. But my decision was driven by the current circumstances in a very competitive market. I wanted the best job I could find. You're always going to find MBAs are in a higher salary bracket.

Ironically, McClintock notes that while the position she was able to secure as a Product Manager and her salary were heavily influenced by the MBA qualification,

> "my contributions are valued more for my science and what I learned at KGI than at Drucker." David Crick, one of Sawyer's classmates who elected not to pursue the MBA, echoes her sentiments: "The problem is the brand name. I feel we're very qualified for many jobs, but the firms don't know who we are. They might just want to go to a place they know like Harvard (Business School)."

His solution to secure a job as a Program Systems Analyst at Amgen was, like many KGI grads, to try to differentiate his skill set, rather than compete head-to-head with MBAs. Crick remarked that:

> You try to sell yourself as someone specialized, who can understand science and the business. You don't want to compete against MBAs for finance jobs, go for more integrator roles then move up from there.

Even one of KGI's top-earning graduates, Dr. Tom Salk, who leveraged his prior medical training in India to join Amgen's Medical Affairs Department, has elected to enroll part-time in UCLA's Anderson School of Management to obtain an MBA. He described his motivation:

> I would eventually like to move from my current department into a more general leadership position, and when I look around the company I see that the people being chosen for these roles all have an MBA.

14.6.2   Organizational

A second type of barrier to creating these new cross-functional professional identities is the way the work and accompanying hiring practices in many organizations are structured. Most universities are set up along traditional disciplinary lines with relatively limited interaction among the faculty in different departments. Hood, one of the pioneers of computational and systems biology, recalled how hard he had to struggle as a tenure-track professor at Cal Tech to pursue his chosen research strategy of dividing his time between doing cutting-edge biological experiments and building the tools that could enable quantitative biology:

> One of the interesting experiences came after three years there, when the chairman [of the Biology Department] came to see me and recommended in the strongest terms I give up working on technology. All the senior faculty felt it was *unseemly* for me to be doing technology development. They felt I should go to engineering if I wanted to do that kind of work. Cal Tech biologists still have that view to a certain extent today. There is a refusal by many to recognize a cross-disciplinary approach to biology.

Hood went on to explain some of the underlying personal reasons for this resistance (see next section):

> Biologists were very unsophisticated; most hadn't used much technology. They felt you could learn the whole sequence of life from studying phage in a test tube [an influential line of research that Cal Tech had pioneered]. It was a kind of arrogance on their part. Building new tools to push biology forward seemed like something an engineer should be doing rather than a *real* biologist. I was never sympathetic to that point of view.

Watson confirmed that the difficulties of conducting interdisciplinary research have persisted, describing his experience trying to build an early collaboration with a colleague in computational biology:

> I was in the biology department and he was in the computer science department. The two buildings were side by side, but until then there was absolutely zero communication between the two departments; nobody knew anybody.

When it was first established, the University of California San Diego (UCSD) made a series of design choices to try to foster interdisciplinary work that closely mirrored KGI—avoiding traditional departments, alternating the offices of biologists and chemists to maximize informal interactions, creating common core labs, and team-teaching core courses.

> 'It worked very well initially,' recalled Prof. Russell Doolittle, one of UCSD's initial biology faculty members. 'Until budget crises came, and then people began to fight over whose centrifuge it was.'

As UCSD grew dramatically, it was cheaper and easier to revert to traditional courses and disciplinary departments located in separate buildings.

The tenure process, and accompanying pressure to become an expert and publish in a narrow area within a particular discipline, can create strong disincentives for new scientists to pursue interdisciplinary work. As Watson noted:

> The reward structure within universities is extremely important. In fact it's one of the most important factors. I faced this problem . . . Some of the people in biology who were most closely connected to computing, the evolutionary biologists, came in and told me it was fantastic stuff I was doing, but where was the biology in it? When the tenure situation came up, I realized there was tremendous conflict going on among the senior faculty about what to do.

One way around the traditional departmental boundaries is to create new inter-disciplinary organizations, but as Watson observed, this can be difficult within traditional university structures:

> The older model of just getting interdisciplinary people in conventional departments is not going to work because there are very old ivory towers that do not like the pollution of their department by other kinds of people. So university administrators will probably have to side step this by producing interdisciplinary institutes or centers in their universities. Money for those is a big problem because no department wants to spare any of its hard-earned funds if they don't see how they're benefiting directly. So there has to be an external input of funds to create these institutes and there is a limitation to external funds. Foundation money may be the only way to go to develop these institutes.

Some leading universities—such as UCSF, Harvard and Purdue—
have recently adopted just this strategy for going around traditional
barriers in the biosciences, creating new interdisciplinary research
institutes outside the normal department structure. Purdue, for example, has raised $1 billion to endow 200 new professorships, all located
in new interdisciplinary centers.

Even where US foundations or wealthy individuals provide the support to create entirely new research institutes, such as San Diego's Salk,
Scripps and Burnham Institutes or KGI, there may be barriers to fostering interdisciplinary work and identities. One problem is that of
scale, as it is hard for a new institute to hire a sufficient number of
experts in different areas to get sufficient depth in individual professional areas and breadth to encourage cross-disciplinary research. As
KGI's Roberts observed:

> Most of my collaborations are external right now. With our current
> number of computational [biology] faculty, to have a good balance
> so that we could really collaborate internally, we would probably
> have to double or triple the research activities on the experimental
> side . . . . Essentially it's an obstacle of critical mass.

Several faculties cited the need for scientific leadership that can help
identify exciting problems that require close collaboration among
researchers from different disciplines and secure the resources needed
to enable them to work together.

The organizational environment within bioscience companies
appears to closely parallel higher education when it comes to impeding
new cross-disciplinary work and professional identities. The traditional functional departments within large pharmaceutical companies can
discourage these new approaches. As KGI Prof. Nancy Franklin noted
to work in this new way,

> especially in the bigger companies, people have to step outside
> their comfort zone. That is [a biologist might think] if it's a prob-
> lem in the chemistry department, it's not my problem.

To try to combat this and address the more general problem of
falling R&D productivity, many large pharmaceutical firms have
recently shifted from functional departments to cross-disciplinary
teams or small business units focused on particular therapeutic areas.
Along with internal reorganization of existing firms, a whole new tranche
of biotech start-ups has emerged that have pioneered the commercialization

of these new technologies by being more open to new identities and cross-disciplinary ways of working (Oliver and Montgomery, 2000). 'The smaller companies really do not have the kinds of attitudes or boundaries' that impede cross-disciplinary work, according to Franklin.

The close interaction between many biotech start-ups and the university labs or research institutes that have spawned them can help transfer these new organizational models back into academia.

> "Biotech companies commercialize the fundamental discoveries originating from research institutes," said Franklin. "The investigators or scientists get invited to the company to become the founder or sometimes work as consultants or scientific advisors and get exposed to a new way of working."

For research universities not located near a biotech cluster, however, this lack of two-way exchange can impede the transition to a new model, according to Franklin:

> They aren't exposed to interdisciplinary work. Even their director or chairman doesn't know what interdisciplinary research is about; they've never seen it happen. Places where biotech is housed have had many interactions, many examples or models right in front of them; their view of science and how the science is conducted is very different from someone in the Midwest, because they just don't get the exposure, experience or education about how it really can be conducted. You can read it from a book, but if you've never done that, it's totally different.

Although the informal organization and team environment of smaller firms may be more conducive to interdisciplinary work, even in these settings the lack of experts with sufficient knowledge of both computational and wet-lab biology can be a major stumbling block to integrating the two domains effectively. One senior leader within a start-up that was using a buddy system, pairing a biologist and programmer to build new computational tools for drug discovery commented:

> The difficulty for the employees developing these tools was that they didn't really understand what they were doing. They were trying to build a really complicated database with many functions. Because it's a complex product, the project needs to be well coordinated and it wasn't. Not many people had an overall view of what the product entails or what it needs to be composed of. I tried many times to convince the company to set aside time to

educate the employees, to make them communicate better. Even if they don't have an overall view, they will at least be able to talk to their colleagues about another component that the other person is building. Since they were all too busy with the individual elements, that didn't happen.

Another potential pitfall with this approach can be the difficulty of motivating programmers who aren't themselves deeply interested or expert in biology, as the same leader observed:

> Although they have the programming capability, they don't know what the purpose is of the piece that they are building. They're just told to do something. How can that be successful? If you build it right you don't know what has been accomplished. It's just work done, code, nothing more. It's very hard to get them motivated or make them feel gratified by their own work.

14.6.3   Individual and Interpersonal

A third challenge in forging new interdisciplinary professional identities in the biosciences is finding ways to integrate the very different individual approaches to framing and solving problems associated with the different disciplines from which people come to this new field. The differences in mindset between the more quantitative, theory-driven disciplines such as applied math, computer science and physics versus biology occur at each step in the research process. The differences begin with the way a problem is defined, according to KGI Professor Jim Baltimore, who was making the transition from physics to computational biology:

> There are differences in the way we approach problems, because they [biologists] come from the other end. They come from the results. Let me give you an example. I was working on protein-fold recognition. To me that was a very interesting problem because it involves a lot of very complex modeling. I was interested in the models, in learning how to treat the models to improve accuracy and things like that. From a biologist's point of view that's not interesting at all. The interesting thing is, if you figure out the fold accurately, what can you do with it? How would our improved models help in terms of elucidating cellular function? That's what a biologist is interested in.

A second difference occurs in establishing the best way to approach solving a problem, said Brenner:

> Every single step needs to be clearly defined in order to construct a model. However, when confronting biologists with this question, they don't seem to care about and understand why one would use such a model. They only think about how to do the experiment. They use a 'picture or schemata' for representing the natural world under investigation.

Baltimore agreed:

> The idea of a controlled experiment is very common in biology, but not too common in physics. Because physics experiments tend to be extremely precise, you don't need a control. But biologists are looking for qualitative results. They don't trust the numbers that come out of the experiments, so the numbers are extremely error prone. To physicists that would be a completely stupid experiment to do. It's a good experiment for biology. Again there are detailed theoretical models in physics, described by differential equations and mathematical equations, and they want to check if the data fits those models perfectly. So they need very precise measurements. Biologists don't need precise measurements, they just want to know if they were on one side of the control or on the other side of the control and that's it.

A third difference occurs in how to interpret the findings. Observed Baltimore:

> If I find for example a disagreement between my model and some data, I'm disappointed as a physicist, whereas a biologist considers that extremely interesting because that's an outlier and outliers are classically interesting in biology. Any gene that doesn't obey the normal rules is an interesting gene. Whereas to a physicist, it means that it's a failure of their model. To biologists it's not a failure of the model. It tells us that most genes behave according to the model, but then there are some really interesting genes. They can now go into the lab and work on these genes for a number of years.

And a final difference occurs in how to write up the results and where to publish them, as Watson observed:

> Computer scientists want to write a paper on the tool itself and there are a lot of good reasons for that because their professional

recognition is dependent on making those tools and those tools are very generalizable. The tools that they're making for me can be used for other things. These tools are of general use, but of course it's for a particular case, biological data . . . So they're interested in a publication on the tool itself in a computer science journal. That's not very exciting to me. I want this tool to perform some computation on a biological dataset that will give me some insights in biology. So there is this conflict for recognition and it's extremely important to satisfy them on their needs and also satisfy ourselves for our needs and to come to some sort of common ground given the limited resources.

Overcoming these issues of differences in problem definition, approach, and interpretation can be done in several ways. One approach is to attempt the difficult task of creating a shared mindset among individuals from different disciplines (Mohrman et al., 1997). An alternative is for an individual trained in one discipline to make a full transition to the other, which appears to have occurred more from quantitatively-trained physicists or computer scientists entering biology, than the reverse. Brenner contrasted those who have succeeded and failed in this transition, and his personal journey:

> I've looked at a lot of work done by physicists and the good ones tend to make a complete crossover—they almost exclusively read biological journals, cite biological journals and publish in biological journals. The ones that do bad work typically are the ones that ultimately don't want to go the whole way. I really want to evolve into the role of a computational biologist. What happens with a lot of physicists who try to just enter the field without having all the knowledge, they make models that you cannot test, because they use parameters that you cannot measure. They don't contribute to science, because although they might address the right questions, they don't do it in such a way that it is possible for people to verify the results. That could be a problem and I hope I'm not doing this anymore. That was certainly a problem of my early work.

14.7   Conclusions

Recent US experience with initiatives to develop new skill sets and qualifications for individuals in the biosciences suggests some of the potential and pitfalls of efforts to create new professional identities in today's rapidly changing global economy. The institutional flexibility of the US higher education system means that generating a supply of professionals with new qualifications is relatively unproblematic. Creating such a labor supply, however, is only half of what's needed to establish a new professional identity—there must also be a steady employer demand for individuals with the new competencies and qualifications.

We analyzed two very new and still evolving efforts in the US to prepare professionals to lead the biotechnology revolution of the 21st Century—training interdisciplinary PhDs in computational or systems biology to develop the next generation of biotechnology tools and breakthroughs, and developing a new type of professional masters degree that integrates business and technical skills for individuals who want to help turn research breakthroughs into commercial products. The preliminary results of this comparison suggest that it may be quicker and easier to create a new cadre of computational biology researchers within the established PhD track, rather than to create an entirely new type of degree that lacks recognition or established career paths in industry. One reason for this is that at the PhD level, the HE sector is capable of generating not just a supply of new graduates, but also the demand for them to fill its research and teaching positions. Most cutting-edge biotechnologies are developed first in universities and only gradually reach the stage where they have commercial applications, so the initial demand for these researchers is concentrated in academia. The private sector then began to hire them, but when demand for bioinformatics graduates dropped, most of the hiring that remained was in higher education.

This study also showed that the ability of US universities to generate quite rapidly a new professional identity for academics integrating biology with computational and engineering skills has been dependent on a number of institutional factors that have helped overcome the traditional barriers between departments and professional bodies. These include:

- Support from alumni and foundations (Sloan, Keck, Whittier) to fund the creation of new institutes or interdisciplinary departments.
- Encouragement from the main Federal funding bodies (NIH, NSF, DoD) to support interdisciplinary and translational research.
- The relative ease in today's global, Internet-connected economy with which it is possible to create new scientific journals and professional meetings to share information among members of a new professional field.

What remains to be determined is whether the members of this new academic field can firmly establish a new and distinct professional identity, like their predecessors in biochemistry and bioengineering, or whether computational skills will simply become part of the tool kit for all 21st Century biologists. If, as appears likely, a separate, more specialized discipline does succeed in carving out a distinctive niche or niches, alongside a more generally computer literate biologist population, then the competition that is now underway is over what this identify will be: bioinformatics, computational biology, and/or systems biology.

For those who've followed the PSM route, the more difficult challenge will be demonstrating that there is a legitimate third way—integrating science and business—between the twin, well-established peaks of the PhD and MBA. The ultimate success in meeting this challenge will be companies' willingness to hire these graduates and how quickly they are able to advance into leadership roles in the bioscience industry. Dennis Fenton, Amgen's Executive Vice President of Operations, has little doubt about the value of this interdisciplinary education:

> Success in biotechnology business depends on both an understanding of science and the practical business management techniques. KGI's MBS degree is superb preparation for an individual who wants to translate the promise of science into products.

References

Black, G.C. and P.E. Stephan (2004). *Bioinformatics: Recent trends in programs, placements and job opportunities*. Report to the Alfred P. Sloan Foundation Department of Economics, Andrew Young School of Policy Studies, Georgia State University.

Bureau of Labor Statistics, U.S. Department of Labor (2005). *Occupational Outlook Handbook, 2004–05 Edition, Biological Scientists*. Retrieved April 20, 2005 from http://www.bls.gov/oco/ocos047.htm

Casper, S. (2005). *How do technology clusters emerge and become sustainable? Social network formation and inter-firm mobility within the San Diego biotechnology cluster*. Paper presented for EGOS Annual Conference, Free University, Berlin, June 30–July 2.

Cooke, P. (2003). The evolution of biotechnology in three continents: Schumpeterian or Penrosian? *European Planning Studies*, 11, 757–763 (Special Issue on Biotechnology Clusters and Beyond).

Ferlie, E., L. Fitzgerald, C. Hawkins and M. Wood (2005). The nonspread of innovations: The mediating role of professionals. *The Academy of Management Journal*, 48(1), 117–134.

Finegold, D. (2006). The role of education and training systems and innovation. In G. Hage and M. Meeus (Eds.), *Institutions and innovation*. Oxford: OUP.

Fontes, M. (2001). Biotechnology entrepreneurs and technology transfer in an inter-mediate economy. *Technological Forecasting and Social Change*, 66(2), 59–74.

Gatenby, R.A. and P.K. Maini (2003). Mathematical oncology: Cancer summed up. *Nature*, 421, 321.

Hagstrom, W.O. (1965). Social control in science. In L. Beckman and B.T. Eiduson (Eds.), *Science as a career choice: Theoretical and empirical studies* (pp. 593–601). New York: Russell Sage Foundation.

Hilts, P. (2003). *Protecting America's health*. New York: Alfred A. Knopf.

Ibarra, H. (1999). Provisional selves: Experimenting with image and identity in pro-fessional adaptation. *Administrative Science Quarterly*, 44(4), 764–791.

IBM (2004). *Pharma 2010: Silicon reality*. Somers, NY: IBM Business Consulting Services.

Leicht, K.T. and M.L. Fennell (2001). *Professional work: A sociological approach*. Malden, MA: Blackwell Publishers, Inc. (Oxford: Blackwell Publishers Ltd).

Mohrman, S., S. Cohen and A. Mohrman (1997). *Designing knowledge work teams*. San Francisco: Jossey-Bass.

Mowery, D.C., R.R. Nelson, B.N. Sampat and A.A. Ziedonis (2004). *Ivory tower and industrial innovation: University-industry technology transfer before and after the Bayh-Dole Act*. Stanford: Stanford University Press.

National Institute of Health (1997). *Working definition of bioengineering*. Washington, DC: NIH Bioengineering definition committee. Retrieved from http://www.becon.nih.gov/bioengineering_definition.htm

Nebeker, F. (2002). Golden accomplishments in biomedical engineering. *IEEE Engineering in Medicine and Biology Magazine (IEEE Eng Med Biol Mag)*, 21(3), 17–47.

Nerem, R. (1997). The emergence of bioengineering. *The Bridge*, 27(4). Retrieved April 12, 2005 from http://www.nae.edu/nae/bridgecom.nsf/weblinks/NAEW-4NHMP9?OpenDocument.

Riggs, H. (1999). *Venturing*. Claremont: Keck Graduate Institute.

Oliver, A. and K. Montgomery (2000). Creating a Hybrid Organizational Form from Parental Bluprints: The Emergence and Evolution of Knowledge Firms," *Human Relations*, January, 53,1, 33–56.

Shahi, G. (2004). *Biobusiness in Asia*. Singapore: Pearson/Prentice Hall.

Zucker, L. and M. Darby (1996). Star scientists and institutional transformation: Pattern of invention and innovation in the formation of the biotechnology industry. *Proceedings of the National Academy of Sciences*, 93, 12709–12716.

Concluding Chapter

Alan Brown* and Simone Kirpal[†]
*University of Warwick, UK;
[†]University of Bremen, Germany

This edited volume on *Identities at Work* has brought together a range of perspectives on dealing with continuity and change in work-related identity formation processes at a time when in many contexts there has been considerable change in the organisation of work, the labour market and in the wider environment in which work is situated as well as in the expectations of employers. Such changes in work contexts, employment conditions and patterns of work organisation affect individuals' career orientations and in many contexts patterns of commitment and identification with work are themselves undergoing significant change. However, the extent to which these changes affect different groups of workers varies considerably and for many workers there are also significant continuities with how work was performed in the past.

Both the occupation and the organisation remain key elements in work-related identity development, which itself constitutes a significant element of a person's more general social identity. While vocation can still be a significant organising principle for the identity development this is mediated for many people by a much stronger sense of 'self' whereby the balance of the internal dimension of 'making' an identity as opposed to the externally-oriented 'taking' an identity is shifting towards the former. It is worthwhile reviewing what the various contributions to this book can contribute to such issues.

The contributions to Part One looked at the meaning of vocational identity for different occupational groups. The *FAME Consortium* contribution drew attention to how an individual's identity is made up of

A. Brown, S. Kirpal and F. Rauner (eds.), Identities at Work, 391–402.

'a basket of selves which come to the surface at different social moments as appropriate' (Cohen, 1994, p. 11). Thus the self-definition of a person's work-related identity may vary between contexts, as identities are flexible, conditional and subjectively modifiable. In this process the individual assumes a crucial role in actively shaping her or his work identity, as part of a dynamic interaction where work shapes the individual, while at the same time the individual shapes work processes and structures. The self is not an autonomous agent, but it is socially and culturally constructed and certain elements of a person's identity will always be collectively imposed. However, the individual possesses the ability of conscious, purposeful action, of choice of roles and performances even under a situation of constraints (Cohen, 1994).

While work remains a formative element of the overall identity of an individual, it has become just one component among a variety of factors influencing identity development. Still, being able to master a particular occupational specialisation often plays a strong role in developing a social identity. Skilled work can be a medium for personal realisation of meaning and interpretation of existence and the implementation of biographic intentions and interests. An occupation may prove to be a normative horizon for one's entire life, as well as representing one of the key sites for meaningful social relations. Thus, to be able to work in a chosen vocation occupies a special position between 'social structure' and action in the 'private sphere'. It remains important in social life as a defined passage for social and economic participation and can be regarded as a major source of the feeling of one's own value or one's view of oneself, and the means through which someone presents herself or himself to the outside world (Goffman, 1959).

In his chapter on being a Danish banker *Morten Smistrup* argued that while training is of fundamental importance for developing an initial vocational identity and becoming part of a community of practice, an individual's vocational identity is reproduced and transformed in the course of working and learning throughout life. This duality between continuity and development is an essential element of vocational identity, not least during times of change. Additionally, the work situation of bankers is characterised by conflicting interests and demands. This means that the individual banker continuously has to balance these demands in relation to each other and deal with these in relation to his or her self-understanding as a banker. This highlights how vocational identities are not necessarily internally consistent but may be a frame within which individuals have to create some kind of coherence or meaning in a work life characterised by conflicting interests. Vocational identities can establish shared ways of containing contradictions but these may typically be shared by more experienced practitioners, whereas those who have recently completed their initial training may feel that they are struggling to achieve such a resolution (Eraut, 2004).

The vocational identity of an individual is strongly situated in a particular context, but also has elements of biographical continuity, as any learning process is building upon previous knowledge, understanding and values. The biographical aspect, however, includes not only an image of what you are and were, but also a vision of what it is possible to become. In this sense a vocational identity is not just a construction of the present based on a reconstruction of the past but is also a forecast for the future. The contribution of *Gwendolyn Paul* and *Uta Zybell* on teenage mothers in Germany provides a powerful reminder of how entry into the world of work can have significant social and psychological benefits, helping young mothers overcome possible social isolation and a feeling that they were using only a limited set of their capabilities. Integration into and participation in work settings influences the overall identity of these mothers, underlining the interdependence between work and family life in identity formation processes and drawing attention to how for many people participation in a community is now based around work rather than the place where they live.

The contribution of *Nikitas Patiniotis* and *Gerassimos Prodromitis* also pointed to the interdependence between work and family life in identity formation processes in their investigation of the work-related identities of people working in small, often family-run, businesses in the Greek tourist industry. These people have to respond to the challenge of having multiple identities that have significance for how they perform their work. Not only are family identities often entwined with work, but individuals may also engage in a variety of other work on a seasonal or part-time basis; work which may be subject to precarious employment conditions. In such contexts, the challenge of being flexible and adaptable in the labour market appears to be spread across the family rather than simply being an individual concern—the work in the family business can be tailored to fit the shifting demands of other work on the family members.

The contribution by *Felix Rauner* provides an account of the extent to which countries with 'strong' initial vocational education and training (VET) systems, as in Germany, can provide socially recognised pathways to particular types of work and work-related identities and how this approach can have clear organisational benefits in terms of employees' performance orientation and quality awareness. The value of VET pathways leading to skilled work and 'strong' occupational identities is clear in systems with well defined occupational labour markets and Finegold and Wagner (1999) highlight how this works particularly well in areas of manufacturing built upon a system of diversified quality production, using the abilities of highly skilled workers and engineers. Finegold and Wagner (1999) also point out, however, that this system was essentially based around individual performance and how the shift towards the multi-functional team as the basic organisational unit for work performance in lean manufacturing, typical of US practice, posed particular challenges in a German context. Mason and Wagner (2000) take this line of argument a stage further, highlighting how the 'strong' occupational identities, formal structures and institutional support that have been so successful in supporting traditional manufacturing in Germany appear less suitable for high technology industries, whereas the reverse is true for the UK, where trade and innovation performance is much stronger in fast changing areas like electronics rather than in traditional manufacturing industries like chemicals and engineering. Mason and Wagner (2000) argue that the high degree of individual mobility of highly-qualified scientists and engineers helps to spread tacit knowledge and experience and to develop collaborative research links between enterprises. Overall then, the extent to which work-related identities are individual or collective, occupational or organisational at a systemic level can have differential effects for organisational performance in different sectors and work contexts.

Part Two brought together contributions that examined the dynamics between personal identity, work and employment and, particularly, how individuals deal with the demands for flexibility of some modern work settings and manage to integrate diverse work experiences into coherent self-images in order to generate continuities in their personal identities and career narratives. *Sabine Raeder* and *Gudela Grote* explored personal identity in the context of work flexibility in an investigation of Swiss workers who experienced career changes. They concluded that most of these workers had generally succeeded in integrating career changes in their identity through emphasising biographical continuity and a high overall ecological consistency. Where individuals had been able to construct a coherent career narrative this proved to be psychologically valuable, although Raeder and Grote argue that individuals may need support in making sense of their individual biographies in the light of changed circumstances and may need help in the construction of new work-related identities that can link to what had happened in the past and look towards the future.

Stephen Billett also looked at how individuals construct continuity in their lives when experiencing changes that included major redirections in their careers and employment. As with Raeder and Grote, a quest to create a coherent self-image was clearly evident and individuals were active agents in this process influenced by their own sense of self. The quest to create a coherent self-image included the negotiation of a new work-related identity and this in turn influenced how they engaged in their new work. This was important as these individuals were not passively accepting new roles, but rather they were engaged in processes of learning and remaking work practice. That is, the work itself became different—there was not a one way process whereby they adapted to the 'new' work, rather they were also active in adapting work processes. As a consequence their new work-related identities were actively shaped in ways that were important to the individuals concerned and this in turn gave a sense of the individual being able to construct a coherent career narrative where they were able to exercise a degree of control over the direction their careers were taking, even if the initial disjunction in their careers was involuntary. The importance of aligning policies and practices associated with lifelong learning with engagement with this individual sense of self needs acknowledging—support needs to be available to these individuals not just those who have not yet formulated a clear career direction. These individuals were eager to engage in learning to shape work in the direction they wanted in order to align with their sense of self and the type of work-related identity they saw as consonant with that sense of self.

Simone Kirpal and *Alan Brown* focused upon three case studies drawn from England and Germany of individuals who were 'flexible' in their attitudes towards work, actively using flexibility, mobility and learning to meet their broader vocational goals and develop their careers and who were ready to change aspects of organisations and/or their occupation if necessary. They exemplified employees who, in the course of their employment trajectory, had developed a highly 'flexible' identification with work with a much more individualist basis and this was more powerful for them than any occupational or organisational commitment. Their work identities were highly individualised, primarily based on personal skills, a capacity for continuous learning and a project-oriented attitude to work. A variation of this flexible type of identification with work was apparent in the 'strategic careerists' who saw their current occupational position and/or organisational attachment as one phase of a career that involved relatively frequent changes in the nature of work they do. They are committed to 'moving on' and see their careers as something they actively construct. Their attachment to their current role is partly influenced by the knowledge that they are only 'passing through'.

Flexibility can be regarded either as a strategic tool or as a characteristic of the individuals themselves that is closely linked to their pursuit of self-realisation, and Kirpal and Brown highlight cases, drawn from the wider sample of over 500 employees from seven countries across Europe, of how workers in a wide variety of contexts were active in re-defining, rather than passively accepting, work-related roles. They were actively re-defining and challenging traditional work roles and concepts of identification with work. Work identities, also, are subject to change as they are adjusted over individuals' lifetime employment trajectories. This can mean the identities shift back and forth between developing forms of attachment and highly flexible forms of identification with work. What seems to be decisive in this context is the individual's response or 'strategy': whether he or she takes on a passive or active role; the level of risk affinity, the openness and ability to use flexibility, mobility and learning as tools to pursue their own interests; and general attachment to work. There was a clear distinction between employees who had been socialised and trained to be more flexible and active in developing their occupational orientation and identity, and employees who had not been socialised in this way.

The contributions to Part Three examined the links between occupational identity formation and organisational commitment. *Yehuda Baruch* and *Aaron Cohen* discussed the relevance of commitment and identity for the working life of individuals, and suggested one focus for further studies could be into the combined effect of both constructs. Personal identity represents individual aspects of how we see ourselves relative to others in the same social group, whereas social identity comprises those aspects of our self concept we believe we have in common with others in the same social group (Arnold, 2005, p. 333). One challenge for organisations is to get employees to associate, combine or connect their occupational and organisational identities. Ibarra (2003, p. 18) suggests that when a working identity is defined by formative events in his or her life, the individual response is often an attempt at making sense—creating or identifying catalysts and triggers for change. These can be utilised in career narratives that involve a reworking of our 'story'. Relating the two major constructs, identity and commitment, Baruch and Cohen believe that while there is a reciprocal association between the two, it is mostly identity that influences, or even formulates, commitment. Once a person comes to identify with an organisation, he or she starts to become committed to it. Of course, being committed reinforces identity in a cyclical manner. Within working life, both organisational identity and occupational identity are powerful influences upon organisational and occupational commitment.

Bernd Haasler in his study of first year apprentice toolmakers in a major Volkswagen plant in Germany found that their identification with the company was very much stronger than their attachment to their chosen occupational specialisation. Indeed most engineering apprentices in the company would have preferred to have undertaken a commercial apprenticeship—they did not display any distinct interest in engineering, neither in terms of motivation behind their choice of occupation, nor in respect of their previous practical experience. They saw themselves, first and foremost, as company employees. Even if identification with their occupational specialisation builds later in their training or employment, it is interesting that occupational interest is no longer the common driver it was in the past (Haasler and Kirpal, 2004). Heinz (1995) had drawn attention to how the socialising function of apprenticeships worked in two directions: from the individual's point of view as a learner in order to become equipped and prepared to succeed in a given occupation; and from the occupational community's point of view to 'mould' a person to conform with the established norms and standards within a particular community.

One conclusion to be drawn from the evidence of Haasler's contribution could be that attention needs to be given to the development of organisational commitment, particularly if the roles to be performed within the organisation are liable to shift over time. This is particularly interesting in the light of Herrigel and Sabel's (1999) earlier argument that 'most German assemble-to-order and customized plants had made relatively little use of multi-functional teams, at least in part because the personal identity of German skilled workers appeared to conflict with the blurring of individual roles and narrowing of some technical skill requirements that can accompany the move toward a team-based organization' (pp. 152–153). It may be that this becomes less of an issue for more recently qualified skilled workers, if Haasler's findings are part of a wider trend for employees to have less strong occupational identities when compared to the influence of their organisational attachment and individual orientation to work.

The qualitative study with over 300 employees from France, Germany and the UK by *Simone Kirpal*, *Alan Brown* and *M'Hamed Dif* showed how individuals' attachments to classical forms of commitment and identification with work may conflict with increased demands for flexibility and learning at work. They observed a general trend towards the 'individualisation' of employee commitment and work identities which challenge the individual to develop a proactive and 'entrepreneurial' work attitude based on multi-skilling and flexibility. As with the cases outlined by Billett and Raeder and Grote some workers coped well with new challenges, engaged in learning and incorporated the changes into new career narratives. On the other hand, the challenges of change daunted some workers because they lacked the necessary resources, skills and capacities, and they were not sufficiently supported at work to meet changing work demands and this could potentially lead to their labour market exclusion.

In his contribution, *Akihiro Ishikawa* showed that some contemporary stereotypes of Japanese workers are far from the mark, in that even for many permanent full-time workers work is not seen as so central in their lives, satisfying or as company dependent as compared to workers in other countries. The meaning of work and working, however, differs considerably between different job strata (between manual workers, administrative staff, supervisors and technical staff). This is not to say that long hours and additional work-related commitments do not exist for many workers, but it does question the extent to which positive attitudes towards work are widely shared as part of a supposed exceptional organisational commitment. The negative attitudes towards a strong commitment towards work of those not in permanent employment, especially among Japanese youth, further undermines the traditional picture of a widespread dedicated work-oriented life style in Japan.

Individual agency can play a significant role in how work-related identities are adapted to changing conditions, but the contributions to Part Four show how work identities are also shaped by organisational and institutional mechanisms, as when changing job profiles or work demands facilitate the emergence of new forms of work identity. *Monika Nerland* and *Karen Jensen* show how changes in initial education can play a role in the construction of new professional identities that are more individualised than those created in the recent past when there was a stronger collective sense of the professional role. The curricular and policy documents associated with becoming a nurse or computer engineer in Norway outline, either implicitly or explicitly, expectations of students as creators of knowledge, boundary crossers and innovators of self and ethics. These studies showed how important it is to contextualise identity development—identities are strongly influenced by place and time—but increasingly identities at work are differentiated from each other too. This is due not only to the general trend towards individualisation, but also specifically because the task of constructing meaning within identity development processes is increasingly individualised. Lash (2003) describes this process as *insourcing*, that is, a reallocation of functions, activities and responsibility onto the individual which traditionally were understood to be a collective matter.

David Finegold and *Robert Matousek* in their contribution showed how changing skill requirements in the bioscience industry in the US have led to a desire for new curricular forms that could lead to the emergence of two new types of bioscience professionals. These new professionals would embody new skills mixes: computational biologists who are able to integrate programming skills and biological knowledge, and bioscience business professionals who can integrate science and business to help commercialise new products. However, even when such students emerge with new prototypical vocational identities from these newly designed programmes there are still key labour market and organisational challenges to surmount before these new professional profiles and identities are translated into new roles at work.

Overall then, the contributions to this volume highlight how individuals are actors who shape important aspects of their own occupational trajectories and careers. Many of the contributors identified that individuals have increasingly taken an active role as coordinators of their personal work biographies. They become actors who actively shape their individualised work orientations and commitment patterns, which a few decades ago were often more collectively shaped. However, employers too shape work-related identities, for example as in their demands for skilled workers with 'modern' skill sets, including abilities to work in teams and communicate effectively (Davis et al., 2000). Broader societal influences come into play too; for example, in France, the strengthening of technical education and training and giving more attention to employer-directed continuing vocational training has been complemented by an emphasis on self-directed continuing learning and development (including through the process of skills review contained within 'bilán de competences').

The contributors identify that while some work-related identities retain strong continuities with those of the past, in other cases there has been a decomposition of traditional occupational identities that were based on relatively strong work-related collective socialisation processes. Thus some traditional identification processes have been supplanted with the emergence of more flexible, individualistic forms of identification with work. It is important, however, to acknowledge both continuity and change within identity development processes: 'classical' forms of identification with work whereby individuals identified with the occupational specialisation for which they had trained, their daily work tasks, and/or the company or the company's products partly persist, while other employees are developing a more 'flexible' type of identification with work. The latter had a much more individualist basis that was more developed than any occupational and organisational commitment. One typical characteristic of these 'flexible' employees was that they were willing and able to actively use flexibility, mobility and learning as tools to achieve their broader goals, and in doing so they were ready to change organisations and/or their occupations, if necessary.

While in some contexts occupations and organisations remain key elements in shaping individual work-related identity development, several of the contributors illustrated how for many people the internal dimension of 'making' an identity has gained in significance, whereby self-definition processes and the individual's agency in actively shaping her or his work identity are emphasised. Where individuals were aware of their active role in this process this was often influenced by their own sense of self. The quest to create a coherent self-image included the negotiation of a new work-related identity and this in turn influenced how they engaged in their work. Instead of passively accepting new roles, these individuals were actively engaged in processes of learning, remaking work practice and shaping work in the direction they wanted in order to align their sense of self with dimensions of their work-related identity.

Several contributors highlighted how initial training could give a particular emphasis to the development of a work-related identity, but that this could be reproduced and transformed in the course of subsequent working and learning throughout life. Indeed one common theme across many contributions was how hard individuals worked to create some coherence or meaning even where a work life was characterised by conflicting interests, changes in direction or other discontinuities. The commentaries used to express that these self-defined biographical continuities often involved elements of growth, learning, recovery or development as individuals moved between images of what they were, had been in the past or thought they might become, thereby emphasising biographical continuity and ecological consistency. While major dislocations in individual careers could obviously be traumatic, where individuals had been able to construct coherent career narratives and 'move on' this proved to be psychologically valuable.

Individuals, who were able to adapt to change and to shape important aspects of their own occupational trajectories and careers, actively co-ordinated their personal work biographies, and sought to shape the patterns of their work orientation and commitment. Although occupations, organisations and broader societal influences all still influence the nature and set of work offers available to individuals, work-related identities are becoming less collectively shaped than they were a few decades ago. Thus, we can observe the emergence of more flexible, individualistic forms of identification with work. Evidence for continuity and change persist, but the number of people who strategically develop a flexible approach to their work-related identity and career development appears to have grown considerably.

The drivers of this more flexible approach appear two-fold. First, there are those individuals who have a strong strategic sense of the need to actively shape their own career development. Second, the desire for many individuals to make sense of their evolving work history and to construct career narratives that emphasised biographical continuity and ecological consistency meant that a common response to an externally induced change in their work situation was to take action whereby they regained a certain degree of control. This latter point appears particularly significant, psychologically robust work-related identity development has a strong sense-making component. This means there could be real value in helping individuals disoriented by change in their work situations to make sense of their evolving careers in order to produce a career narrative that is forward-looking and could generate the drive necessary for active work-related identity development.

Although individual agency plays a significant role in how work-related identities are adapted to changing conditions, work identities are also shaped by organisational and institutional mechanisms that may be used in realising employers' expectations or policy goals. These institutional mechanisms can also play a role in helping individuals respond to changing job profiles and work demands. One major challenge for institutions and organisations, then, is to get employees to associate, combine or connect their occupational, organisational or individualised identities to foster their engagement with work. A significant number of individuals certainly need support in making sense of their individual biographies in the light of changed circumstances and in constructing a work-related identity that can link to what had happened in the past and look towards the future. This means that some employees need to be supported to cope with changing work environments, including in some environments meeting demands for being more flexible and mobile, and making sense of their evolving careers under changing and sometimes apparently contradictory directions. One key challenge therefore is to give those individuals confidence in their own competences and to empower them to become agents of their own career development.

References

Arnold, J. (2005). *Work psychology* (5th edition). Harlow: FT/Prentice-Hall/Pearson.

Cohen, A.P. (1994). *Self consciousness: An alternative anthropology of identity.* London: Routledge.

Davis, C., T. Buckley, T. Hogarth and R. Shackleton (2000). *Employers skills survey case study—engineering.* London: DfEE.

Eraut, M. (2004). Informal learning in the Workplace. *Studies in Continuing Education,* 26(2), 247–274.

Finegold, D. and K. Wagner (1999). The German skill-creation system and team-based production: Competitive asset or liability? In P. Culpepper and D. Finegold (Eds.), *The German skills machine: Sustaining comparative advantage in a global economy* (pp. 115–155). New York and Oxford: Berghahn Books.

Goffman, E. (1959). *The Presentation of Self in Everyday Life.* New York: Doubleday.

Haasler, B. and S. Kirpal (2004). Berufs- und Arbeitsidentitäten von Experten in Praxisgemeinschaften—Ergebnisse aus europäischen Forschungsvorhaben. In J. Pangalos, S. Knutzen and F. Howe (Eds.), *Informatisierung von Arbeit, Technik und Bildung—Kurzfassung der Konferenzbeiträge* (pp. 48–51). Hamburg: Technische Universität Hamburg-Harburg.

Heinz, W.R. (1995). *Arbeit, Beruf und Lebenslauf: Eine Einführung in die berufliche Sozialisation.* Weinheim: Juventa.

Herrigel G. and Sabel, Ch. (1999). Craft production in crisis: Industrial restructuring in Germany during the 1990s. In P. Culpepper and D. Finegold (Eds.), *The German skills machine: Sustaining comparative advantage in a global economy* (pp. 77–114). New York and Oxford: Berghahn Books.

Ibarra, H. (2003). *Working identity.* Boston, MA: Harvard Business School Press.

Lash, S. (2003). Reflexivity as non-linearity. *Theory, Culture & Society,* 20(2), 49–57.

Mason, G. and Wagner, K. (2000). *High-level skills, knowledge transfer and industrial performance: Electronics in Britain and Germany.* York: Anglo-German Foundation.

Index

UNESCO-UNEVOC Book Series
Technical and Vocational Education and Training:
Issues, Concerns and Prospects

1. J. Lauglo and R. Maclean (eds.): *Vocationalisation of Secondary Education Revisited.* 2005 ISBN 1-4020-3031-2
2. M. Singh (ed.): *Meeting Basic Learning Needs in the Informal Sector.* Integrating Education and Training for Decent Work, Empowerment and Citizenship. 2005 ISBN 1-4020-3426-1
3. H. C. Haan: *Training for Work in the Informal Micro-Enterprise Sector.* Fresh Evidence from Sub-Sahara Africa. 2006 ISBN 1-4020-3827-5
4. F. Bünning: *The Transformation of Vocational Education and Training (VET) in the Baltic States – Survey of Reforms and Developments.* 2006 ISBN 1-4020-4340-6
5. Brown, Alan, Kirpal, Simone, Rauner, Felix (eds.): *Identities at Work.* 2006 ISBN 1-4020-4988-9
6. S. Billett, T. Fenwick and M . Somerville (eds.): *Work, Subjectivity and Learning.* Understanding Learning Through Working Life. 2006 ISBN 1-4020-5359-2

springer.com

Printed in the United States
73015LV00001B/112-147